Rumiko Takahashi

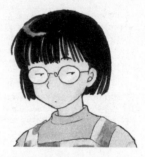

The spotlight on Rumiko Takahashi's career began in 1978 when she won an honorable mention in Shogakukan's annual New Comic Artist Contest for *Those Selfish Aliens*. Later that same year, her boy-meets-alien comedy series, *Urusei Yatsura*, was serialized in *Weekly Shonen Sunday*. This phenomenally successful manga series was adapted into anime format and spawned a TV series and half a dozen theatrical-release movies, all incredibly popular in their own right. Takahashi followed up the success of her debut series with one blockbuster hit after another—*Maison Ikkoku* ran from 1980 to 1987, *Ranma ½* from 1987 to 1996, and *Inuyasha* from 1996 to 2008. Other notable works include *Mermaid Saga*, *Rumic Theater*, and *One-Pound Gospel*.

Takahashi won the prestigious Shogakukan Manga Award twice in her career, once for *Urusei Yatsura* in 1981 and the second time for *Inuyasha* in 2002. A majority of the Takahashi canon has been adapted into other media such as anime, live-action TV series, and film. Takahashi's manga, as well as the other formats her work has been adapted into, have continued to delight generations of fans around the world. Distinguished by her wonderfully endearing characters, Takahashi's work adeptly incorporates a wide variety of elements such as comedy, romance, fantasy, and martial arts. While her series are difficult to pin down into one simple genre, the signature style she has created has come to be known as the "Rumic World." Rumiko Takahashi is an artist who truly represents the very best from the world of manga.

RIN-NE

VOLUME 14
Shonen Sunday Edition

STORY AND ART BY
RUMIKO TAKAHASHI

KYOKAI NO RINNE Vol. 14
by Rumiko TAKAHASHI
© 2009 Rumiko TAKAHASHI
All rights reserved.
Original Japanese edition published by SHOGAKUKAN.
English translation rights in the United States of America,
Canada, the United Kingdom and Ireland arranged with
SHOGAKUKAN.

Translation/Christine Dashiell
Touch-up Art & Lettering/Evan Waldinger
Design/Yukiko Whitley
Editor/Mike Montesa

Printed in the U.S.A.

Published by VIZ Media, LLC
P.O. Box 77010
San Francisco, CA 94107

10 9 8 7 6 5 4 3 2 1
First printing, March 2014

www.viz.com   WWW.SHONENSUNDAY.COM

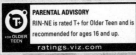

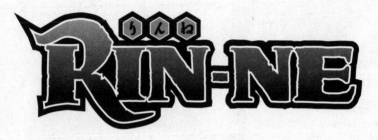

Story and Art by
Rumiko Takahashi

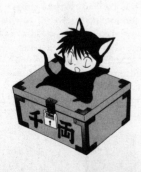

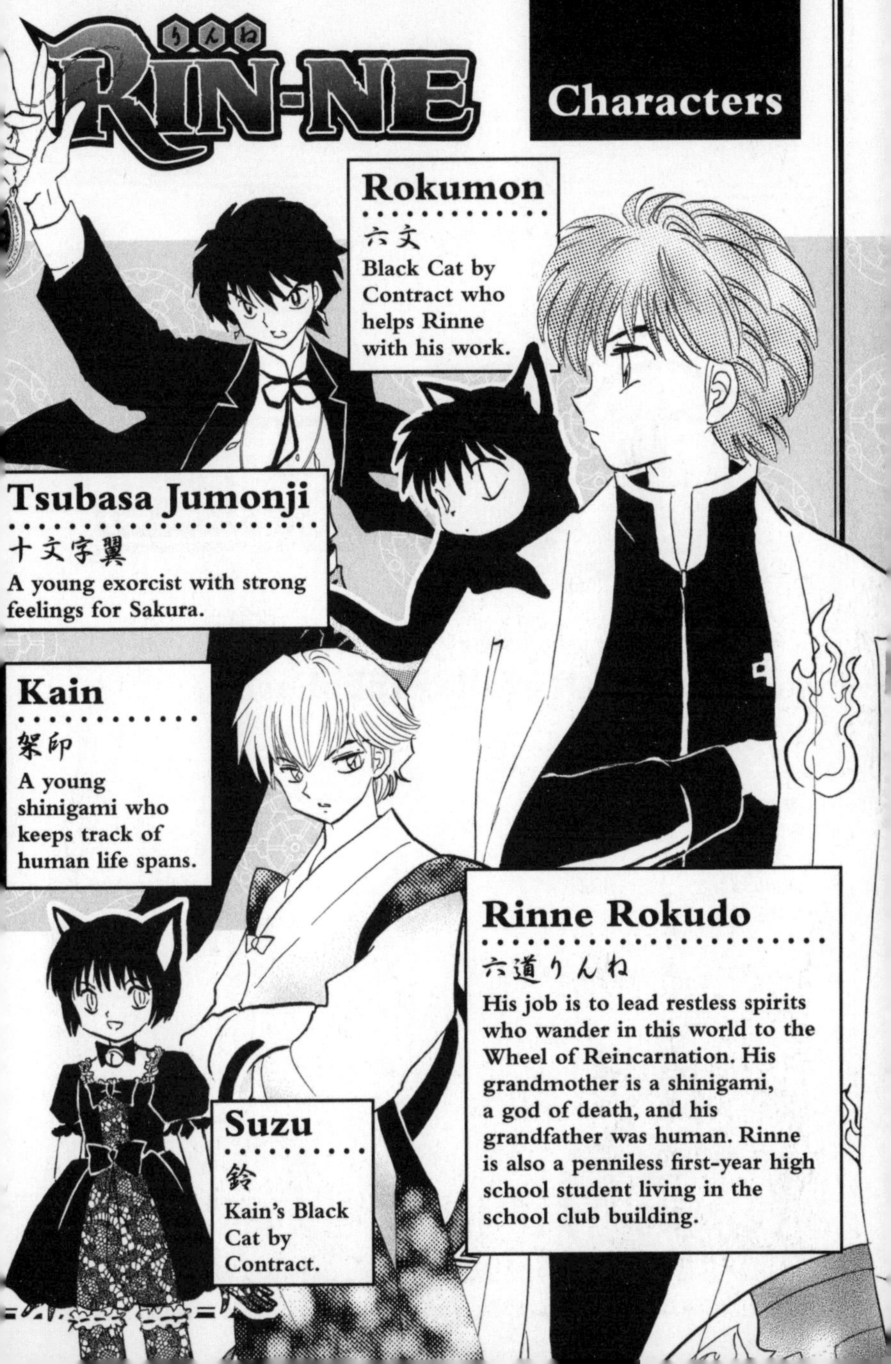

RIN-NE

りんね

Characters

Rokumon

六文

Black Cat by Contract who helps Rinne with his work.

Tsubasa Jumonji

十文字翼

A young exorcist with strong feelings for Sakura.

Kain

架印

A young shinigami who keeps track of human life spans.

Rinne Rokudo

六道りんね

His job is to lead restless spirits who wander in this world to the Wheel of Reincarnation. His grandmother is a shinigami, a god of death, and his grandfather was human. Rinne is also a penniless first-year high school student living in the school club building.

Suzu

鈴

Kain's Black Cat by Contract.

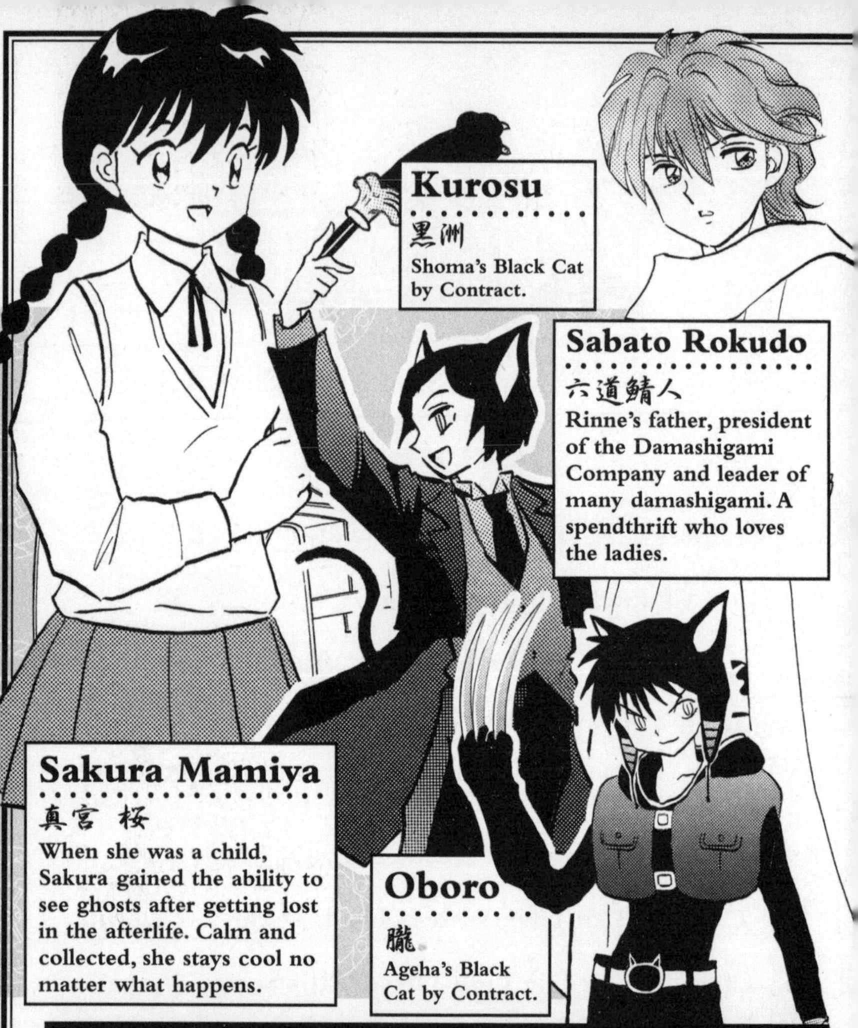

Kurosu

黒洲

Shoma's Black Cat by Contract.

Sabato Rokudo

六道鯖人

Rinne's father, president of the Damashigami Company and leader of many damashigami. A spendthrift who loves the ladies.

Sakura Mamiya

真宮 桜

When she was a child, Sakura gained the ability to see ghosts after getting lost in the afterlife. Calm and collected, she stays cool no matter what happens.

Oboro

朧

Ageha's Black Cat by Contract.

The Story So Far

Together, Sakura, the girl who can see ghosts, and Rinne the shinigami (sort of) spend their days helping spirits that can't pass on reach the afterlife, and deal with all kinds of strange phenomena at their school.

One day Rinne meets the rabbit-eared twins, Right and Left, in the afterlife. They turn out to be the proprietors of a scythe shop. Rinne is happy to have his broken scythe repaired for free, but something's not quite right. Then Rinne's deadbeat dad causes all kinds of problems when he's suspected of making off with some cash to pay his debts!!

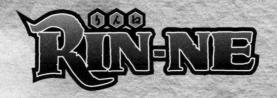

Contents

CHAPTER 129: THE SPIRIT ON DEAD-TIRED HILL

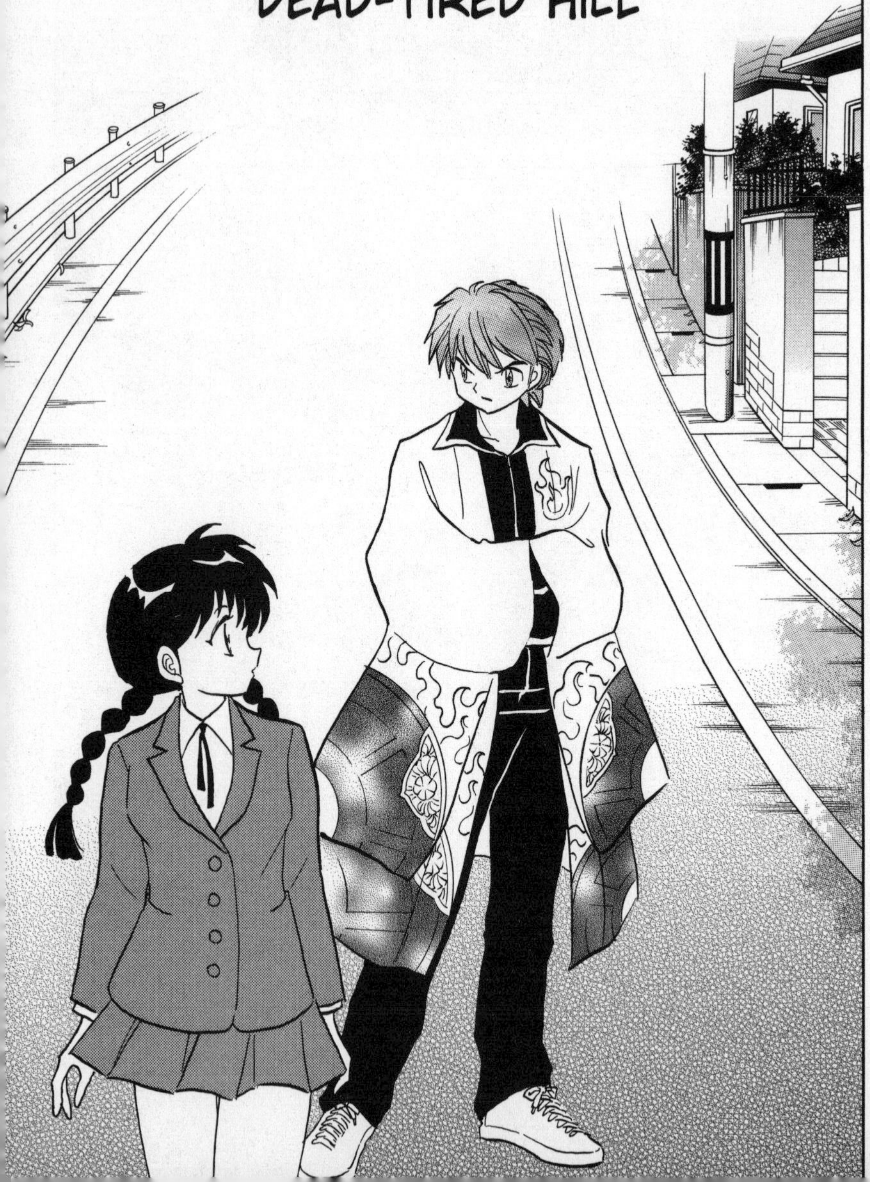

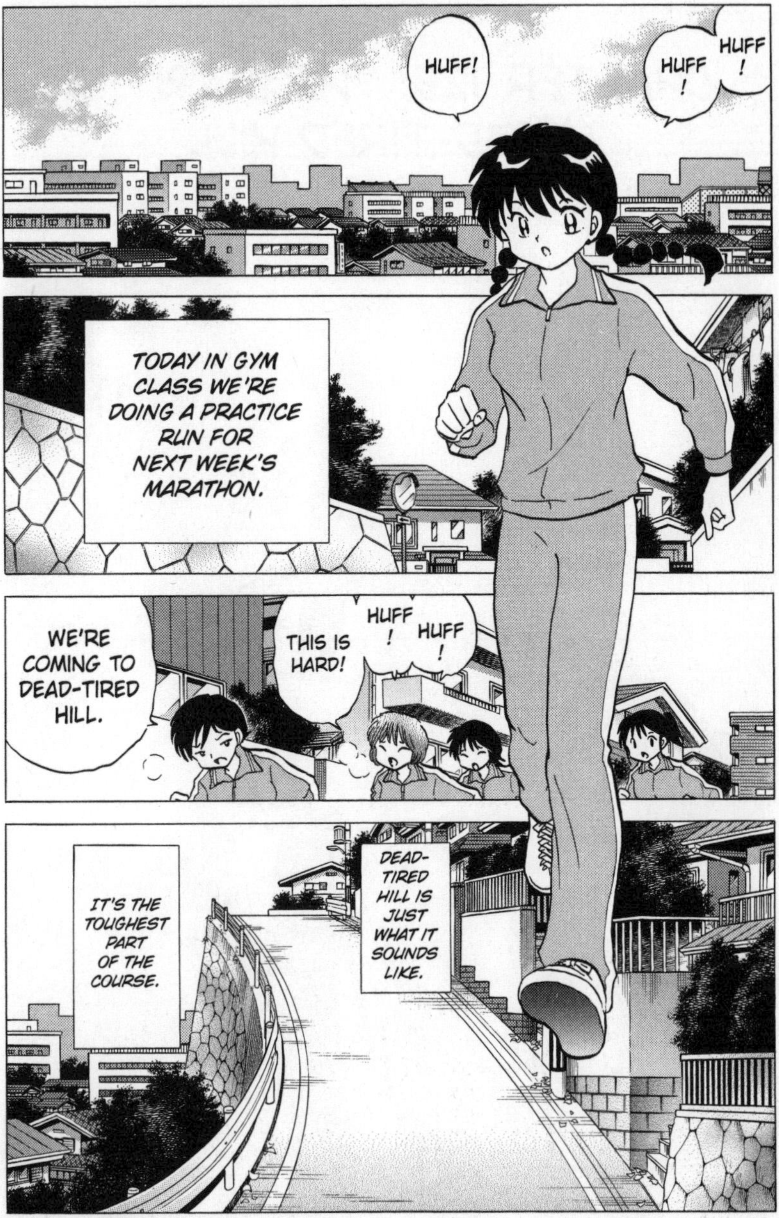
HUFF! HUFF!
HUFF!
TODAY IN GYM CLASS WE'RE DOING A PRACTICE RUN FOR NEXT WEEK'S MARATHON.
HUFF! HUFF!
THIS IS HARD!
WE'RE COMING TO DEAD-TIRED HILL.
DEAD-TIRED HILL IS JUST WHAT IT SOUNDS LIKE.
IT'S THE TOUGHEST PART OF THE COURSE.

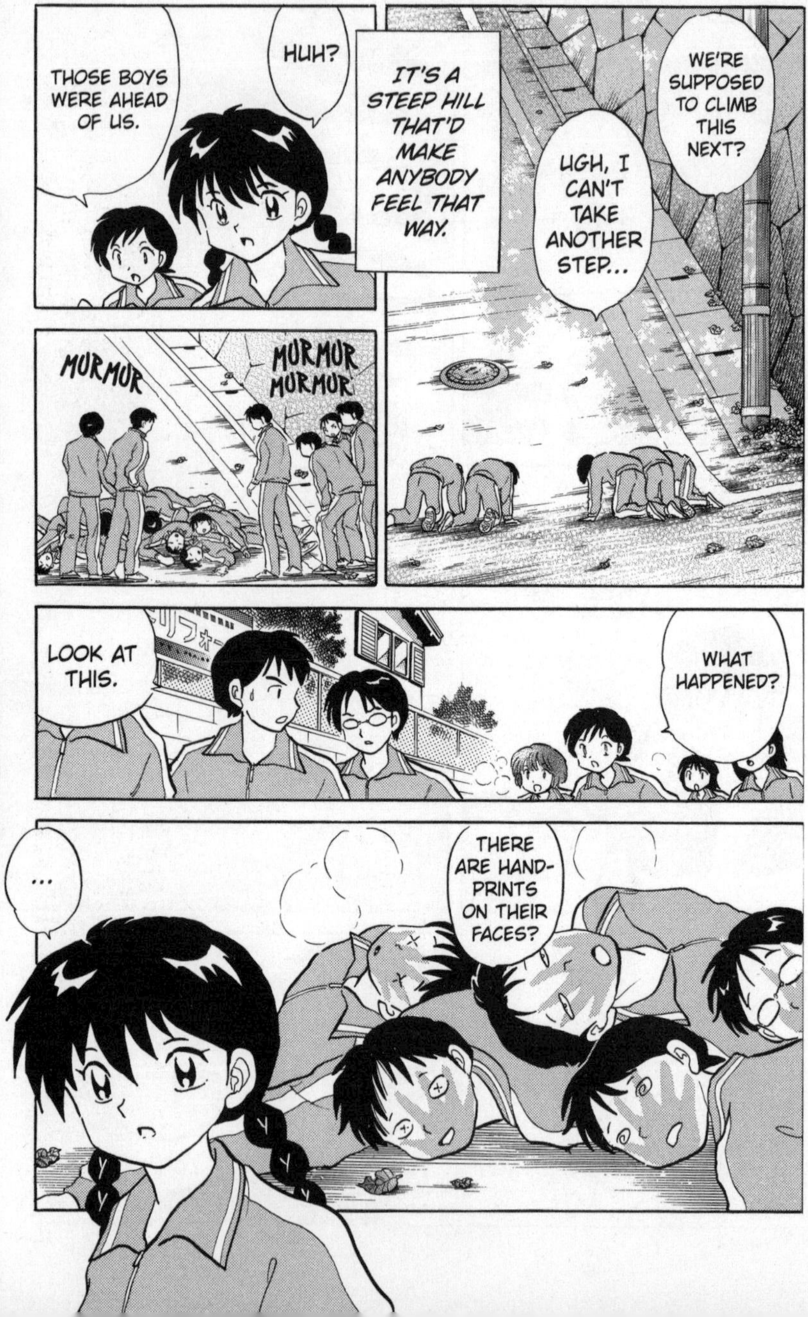
WE'RE SUPPOSED TO CLIMB THIS NEXT?
UGH, I CAN'T TAKE ANOTHER STEP...
IT'S A STEEP HILL THAT'D MAKE ANYBODY FEEL THAT WAY.
HUH?
THOSE BOYS WERE AHEAD OF US.
MURMUR MURMUR
MURMUR
WHAT HAPPENED?
LOOK AT THIS.
THERE ARE HAND-PRINTS ON THEIR FACES?
...

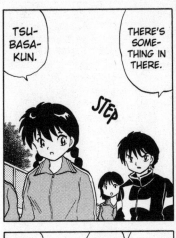

TSU-BASA-KUN.

THERE'S SOMETHING IN THERE.

STEP

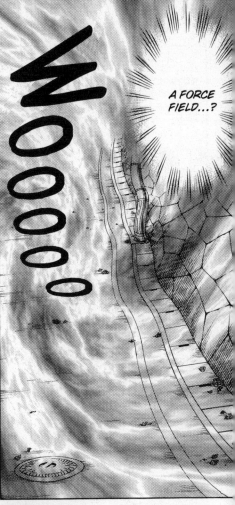

A FORCE FIELD...?

WOOOOOO

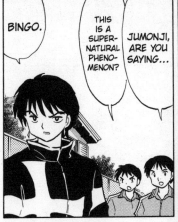

JUMONJI, ARE YOU SAYING...

THIS IS A SUPERNATURAL PHENOMENON?

BINGO.

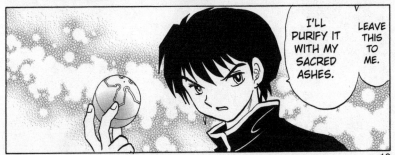

LEAVE THIS TO ME.

I'LL PURIFY IT WITH MY SACRED ASHES.

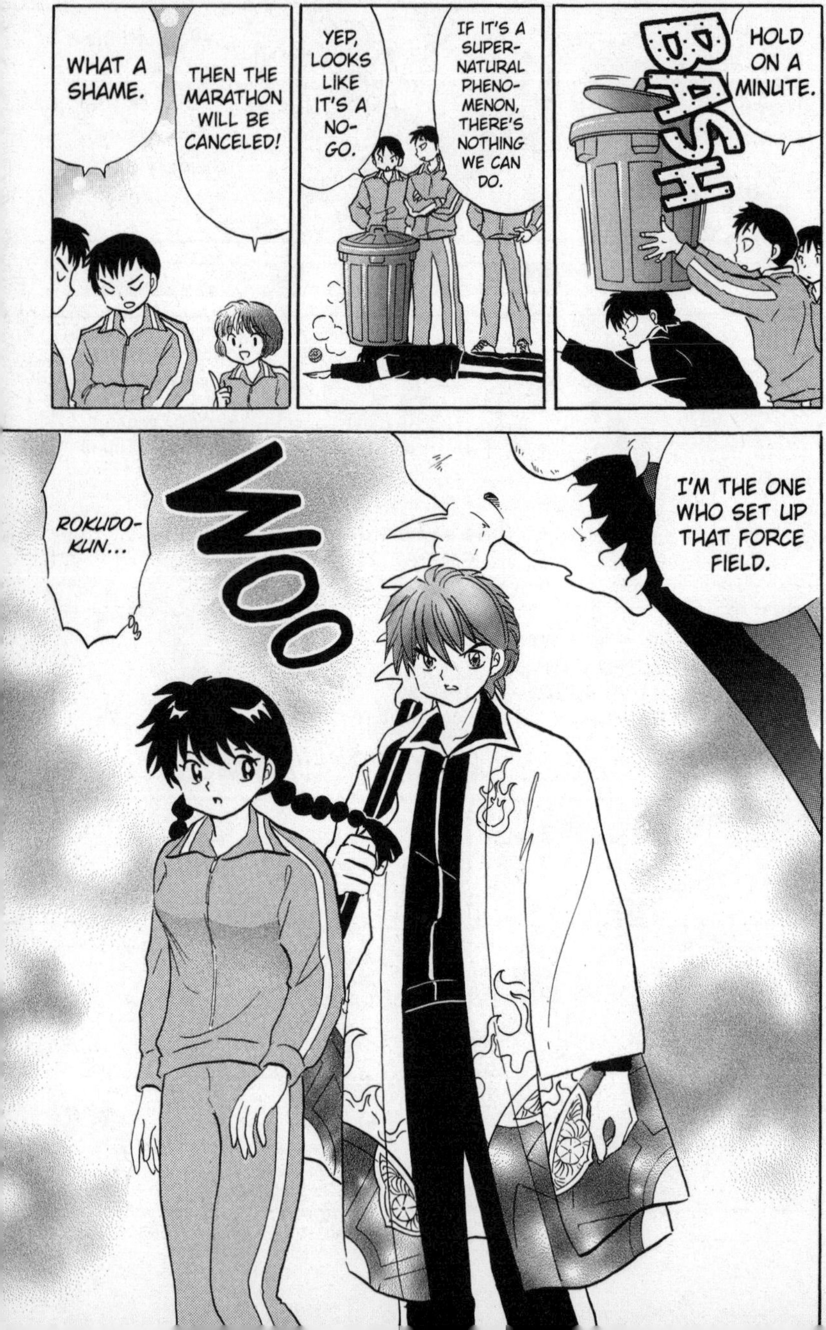
BASH
HOLD ON A MINUTE.
IF IT'S A SUPER-NATURAL PHENO-MENON, THERE'S NOTHING WE CAN DO.
YEP, LOOKS LIKE IT'S A NO-GO.
THEN THE MARATHON WILL BE CANCELED!
WHAT A SHAME.
I'M THE ONE WHO SET UP THAT FORCE FIELD.
WOO
ROKUDO-KUN...

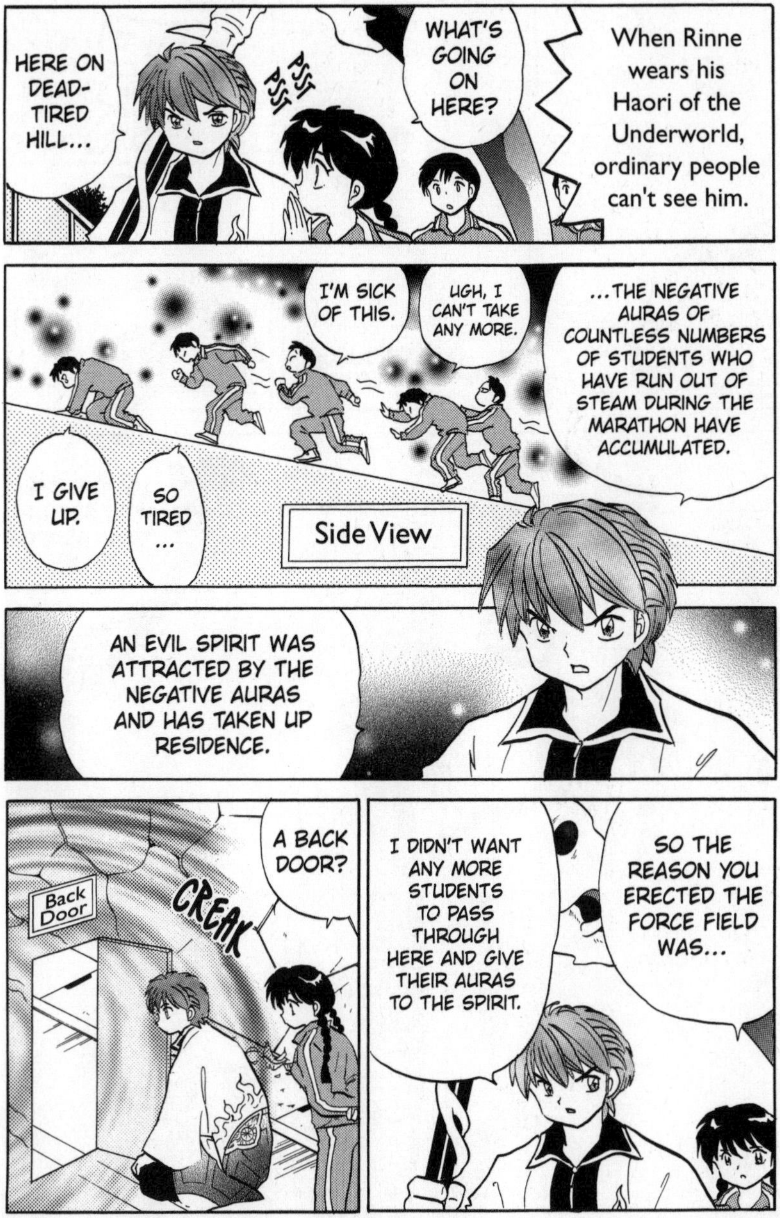
When Rinne wears his Haori of the Underworld, ordinary people can't see him.
WHAT'S GOING ON HERE?
PSST PSST
HERE ON DEAD-TIRED HILL...
...THE NEGATIVE AURAS OF COUNTLESS NUMBERS OF STUDENTS WHO HAVE RUN OUT OF STEAM DURING THE MARATHON HAVE ACCUMULATED.
UGH, I CAN'T TAKE ANY MORE.
I'M SICK OF THIS.
Side View
SO TIRED ...
I GIVE UP.
AN EVIL SPIRIT WAS ATTRACTED BY THE NEGATIVE AURAS AND HAS TAKEN UP RESIDENCE.
SO THE REASON YOU ERECTED THE FORCE FIELD WAS...
I DIDN'T WANT ANY MORE STUDENTS TO PASS THROUGH HERE AND GIVE THEIR AURAS TO THE SPIRIT.
A BACK DOOR?
CREAK
Back Door

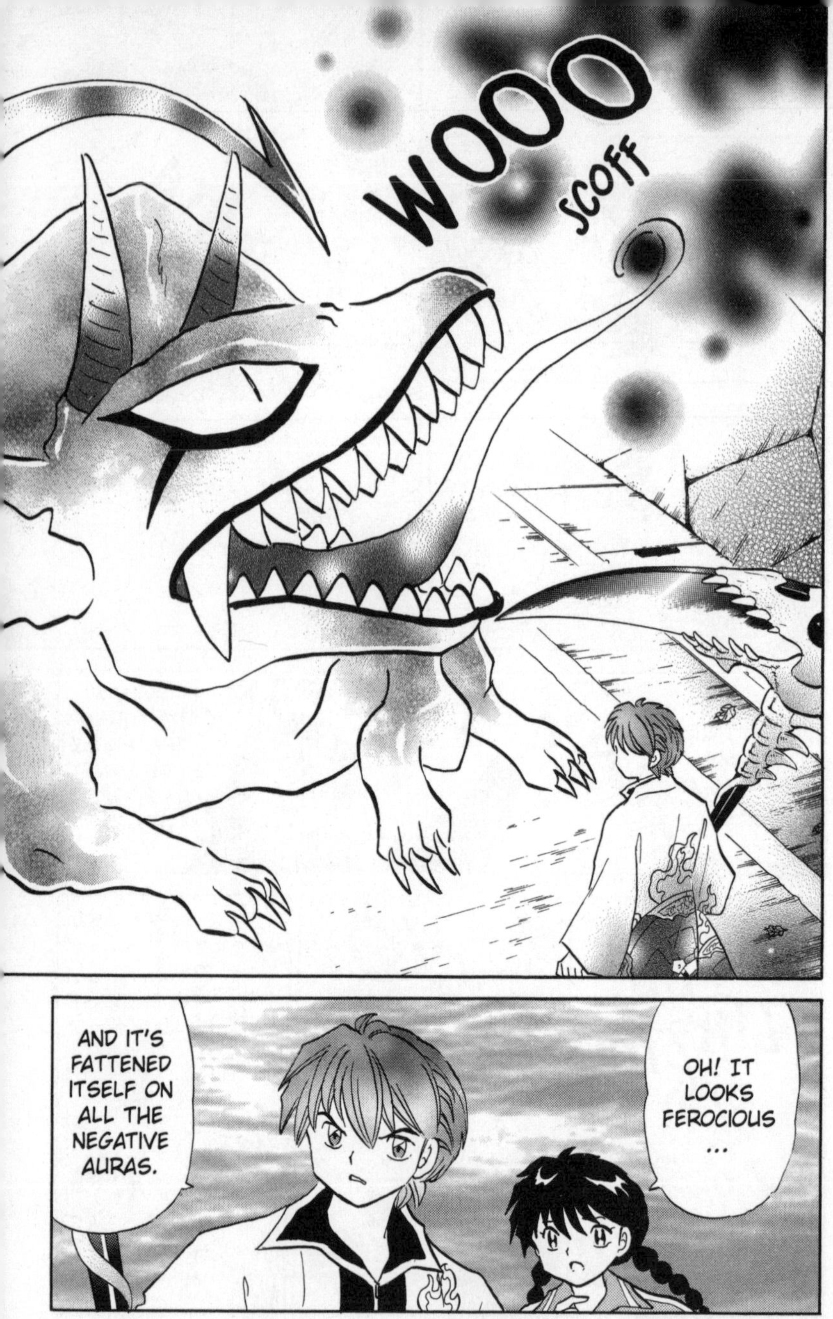
WOOO
SCOFF
OH! IT LOOKS FEROCIOUS ...
AND IT'S FATTENED ITSELF ON ALL THE NEGATIVE AURAS.

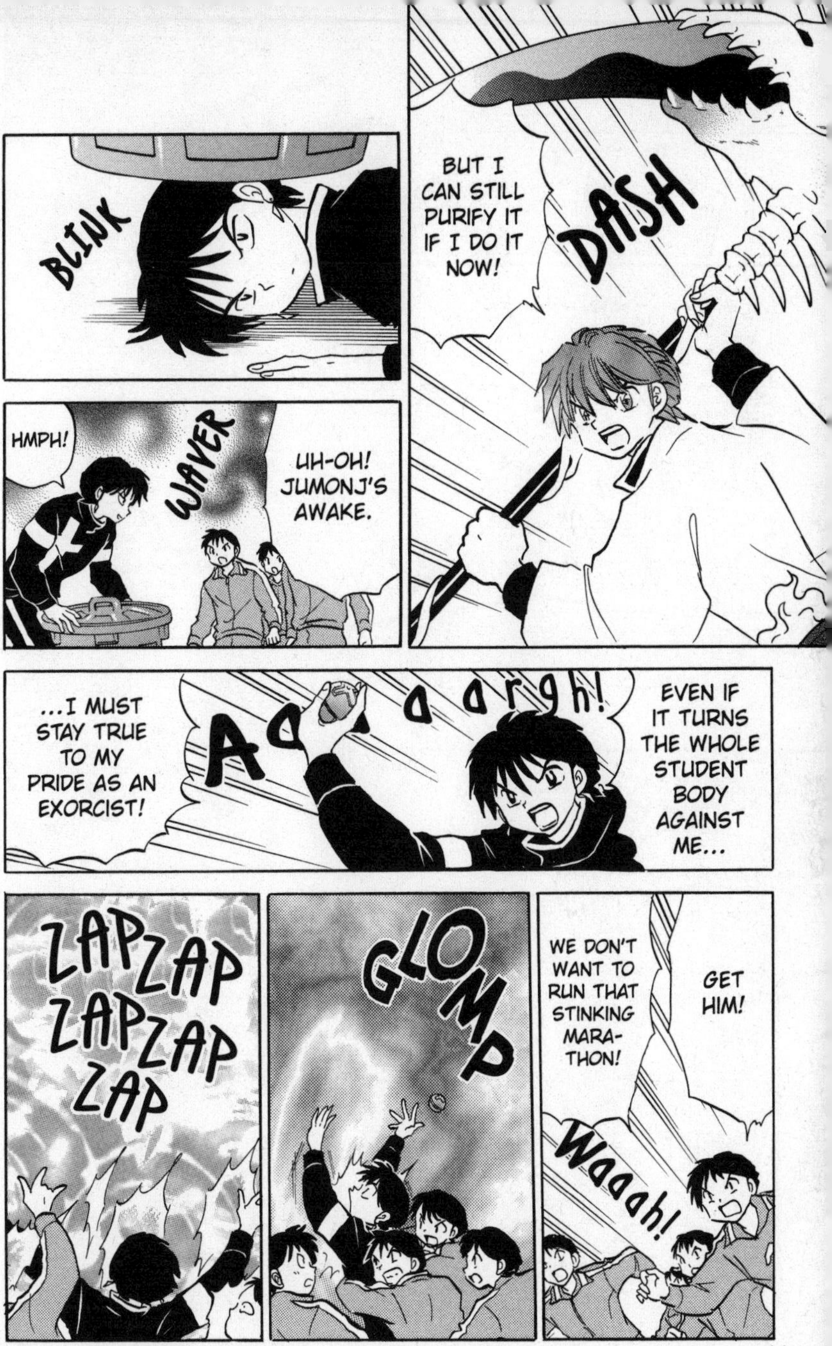
BUT I CAN STILL PURIFY IT IF I DO IT NOW!
DASH
BLINK
UH-OH! JUMONJ'S AWAKE.
WAVER
HMPH!
EVEN IF IT TURNS THE WHOLE STUDENT BODY AGAINST ME...
Aaaargh!
...I MUST STAY TRUE TO MY PRIDE AS AN EXORCIST!
GET HIM!
WE DON'T WANT TO RUN THAT STINKING MARA-THON!
Waaah!
GLOMP
ZAPZAP ZAPZAP ZAP

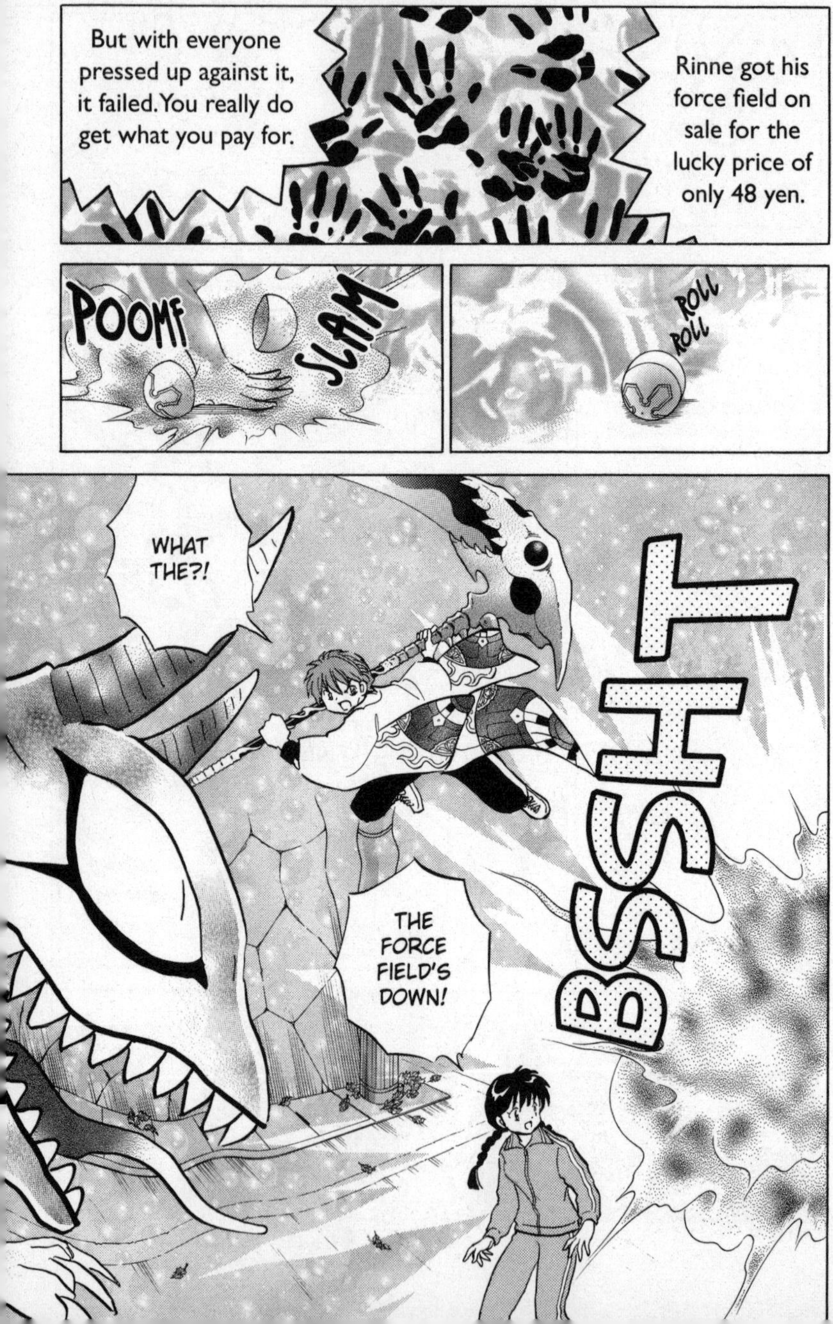
Rinne got his force field on sale for the lucky price of only 48 yen.
But with everyone pressed up against it, it failed. You really do get what you pay for.
ROLL ROLL
POOMF
SLAM
BSSHT
WHAT THE?!
THE FORCE FIELD'S DOWN!

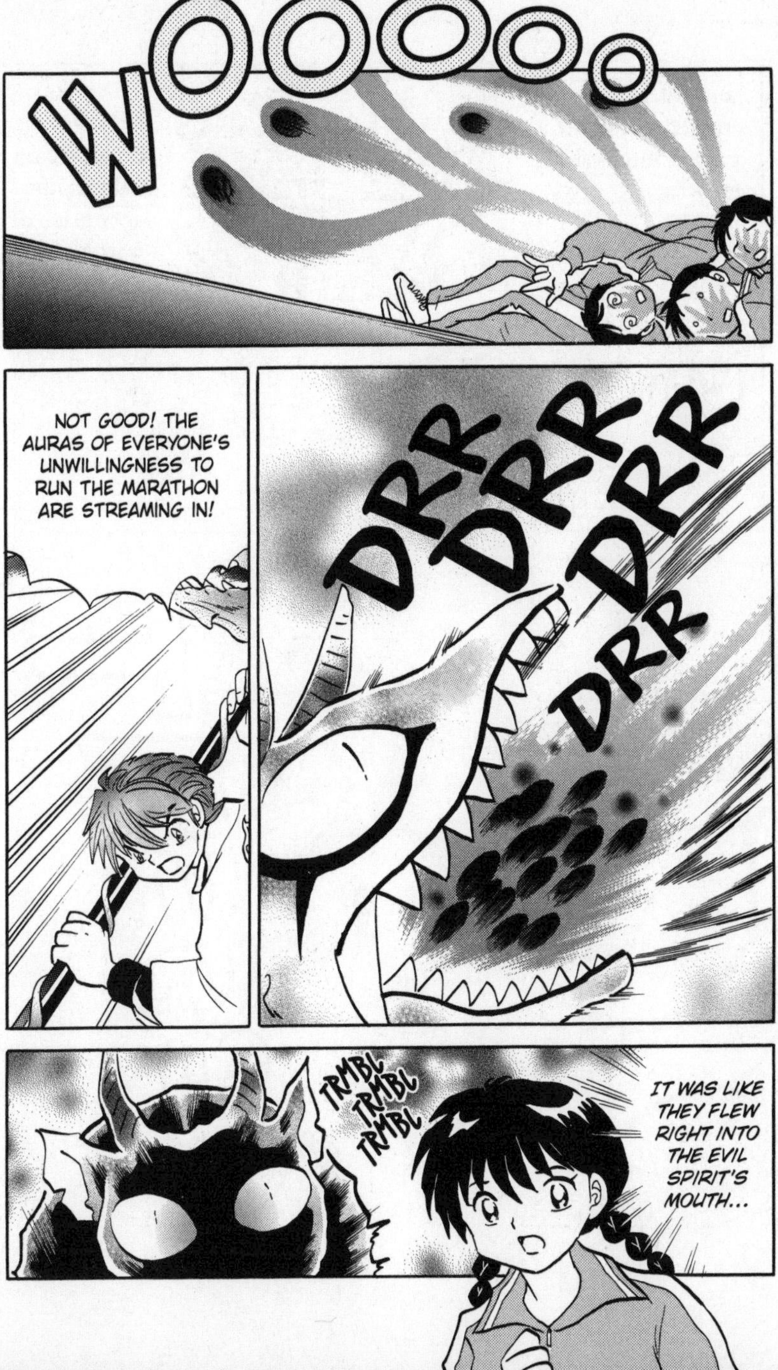
WOOOOOO
DRR DRR DRR DRR DRR
NOT GOOD! THE AURAS OF EVERYONE'S UNWILLINGNESS TO RUN THE MARATHON ARE STREAMING IN!
IT WAS LIKE THEY FLEW RIGHT INTO THE EVIL SPIRIT'S MOUTH...
TRMBL TRMBL TRMBL

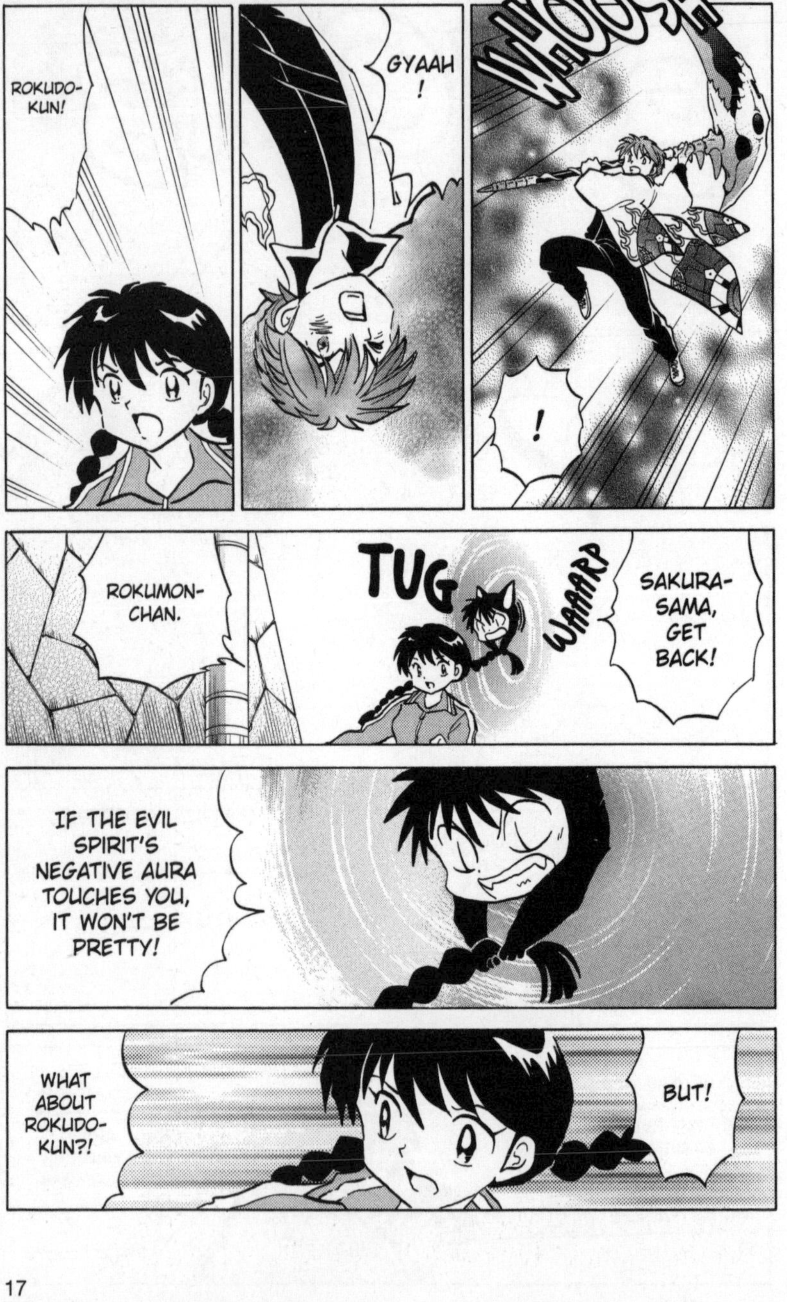
WHOOSH!
!
GYAAH!
ROKUDO-KUN!
SAKURA-SAMA, GET BACK!
WAAARP
TUG
ROKUMON-CHAN.
IF THE EVIL SPIRIT'S NEGATIVE AURA TOUCHES YOU, IT WON'T BE PRETTY!
BUT!
WHAT ABOUT ROKUDO-KUN?!

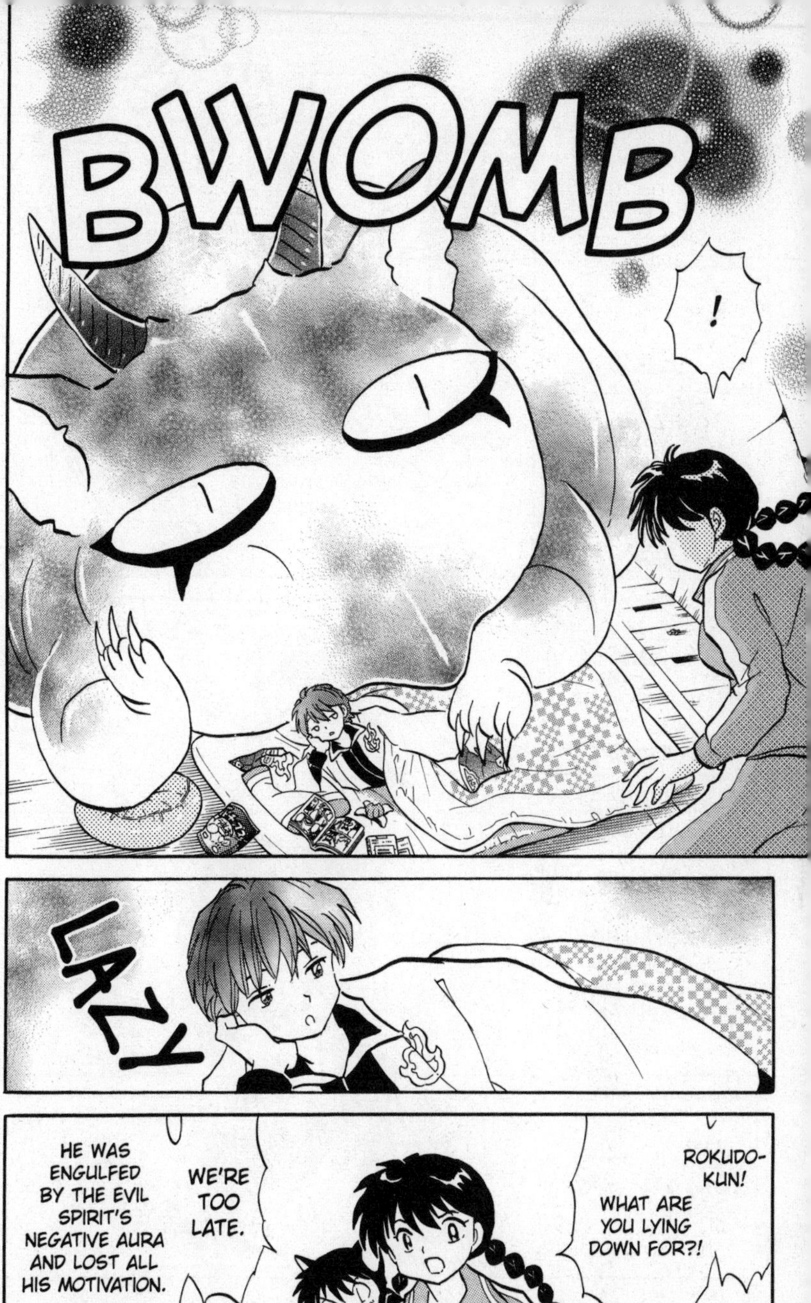
BWOMB
!
LAZY
ROKUDO-KUN!
WHAT ARE YOU LYING DOWN FOR?!
WE'RE TOO LATE.
HE WAS ENGULFED BY THE EVIL SPIRIT'S NEGATIVE AURA AND LOST ALL HIS MOTIVATION.

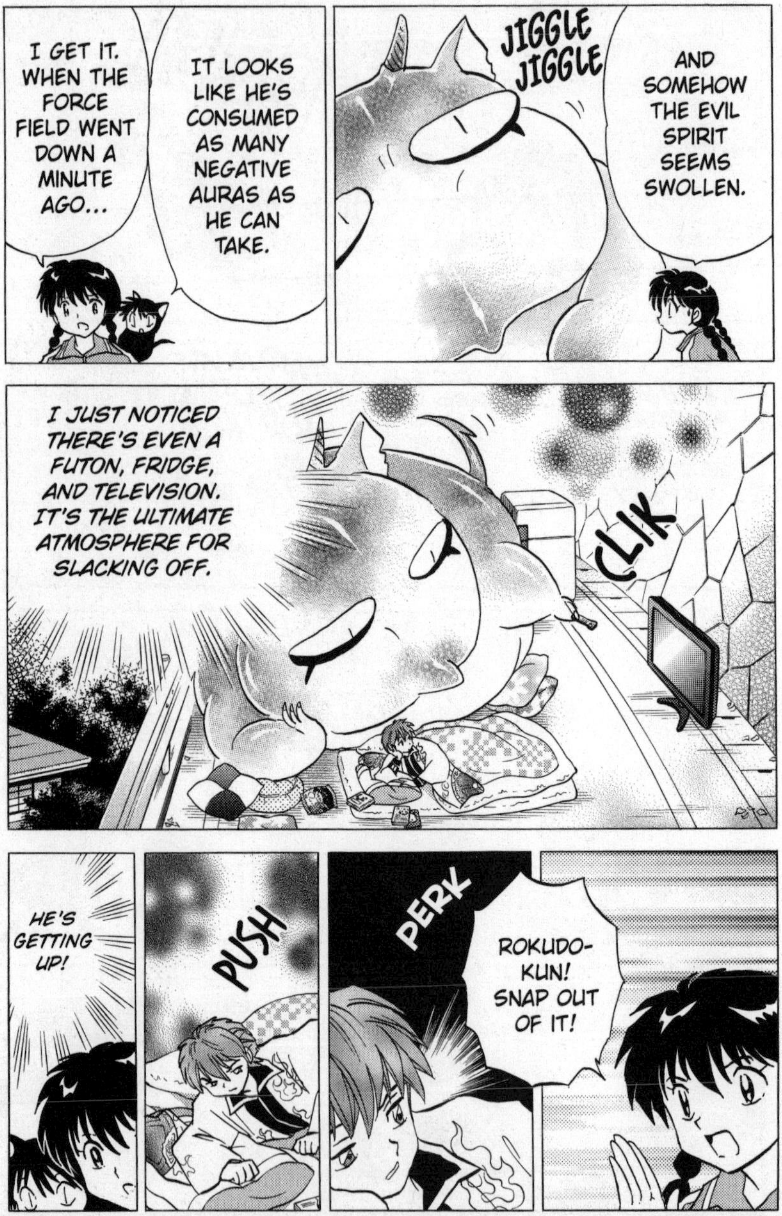
JIGGLE JIGGLE
AND SOMEHOW THE EVIL SPIRIT SEEMS SWOLLEN.
IT LOOKS LIKE HE'S CONSUMED AS MANY NEGATIVE AURAS AS HE CAN TAKE.
I GET IT. WHEN THE FORCE FIELD WENT DOWN A MINUTE AGO...
CLIK
I JUST NOTICED THERE'S EVEN A FUTON, FRIDGE, AND TELEVISION. IT'S THE ULTIMATE ATMOSPHERE FOR SLACKING OFF.
ROKUDO-KUN! SNAP OUT OF IT!
PERK
PUSH
HE'S GETTING UP!

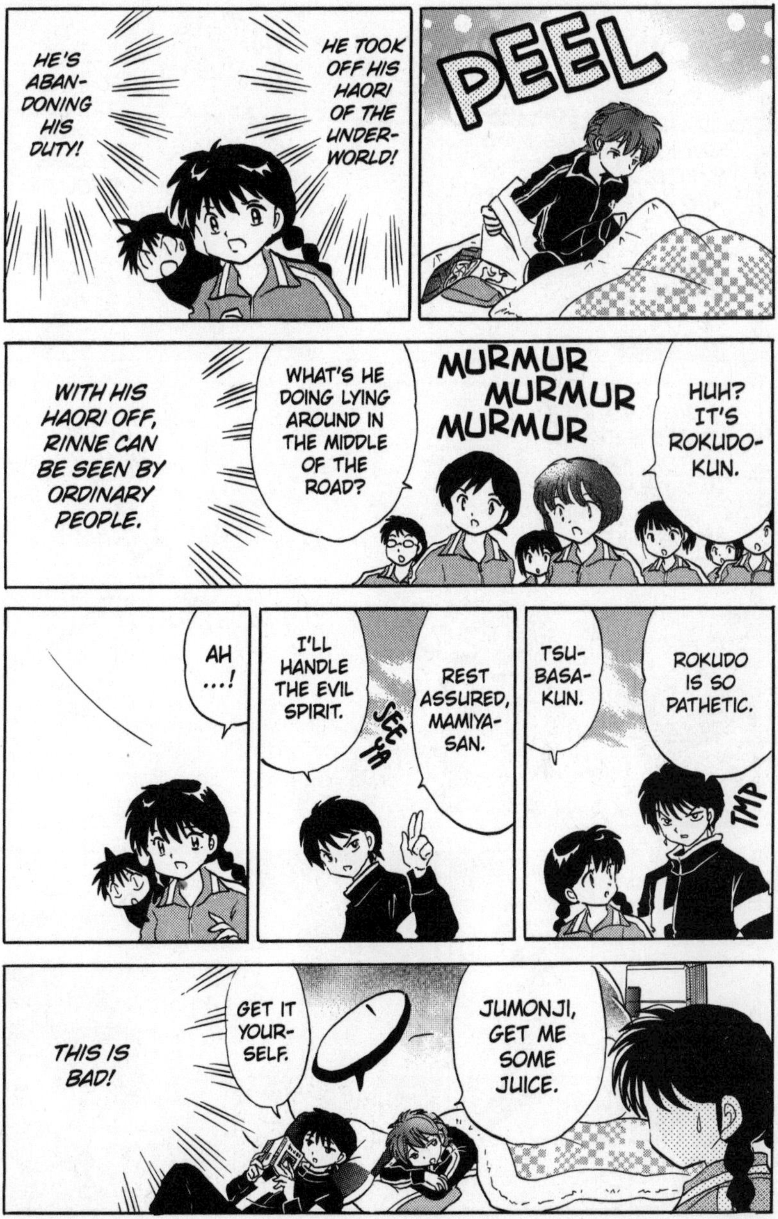
PEEL
HE TOOK OFF HIS HAORI OF THE UNDER-WORLD!
HE'S ABAN-DONING HIS DUTY!
HUH? IT'S ROKUDO-KUN.
MURMUR MURMUR MURMUR
WHAT'S HE DOING LYING AROUND IN THE MIDDLE OF THE ROAD?
WITH HIS HAORI OFF, RINNE CAN BE SEEN BY ORDINARY PEOPLE.
ROKUDO IS SO PATHETIC.
TSU-BASA-KUN.
TMP
REST ASSURED, MAMIYA-SAN.
I'LL HANDLE THE EVIL SPIRIT.
SEE YA
AH ...!
JUMONJI, GET ME SOME JUICE.
GET IT YOURSELF.
THIS IS BAD!

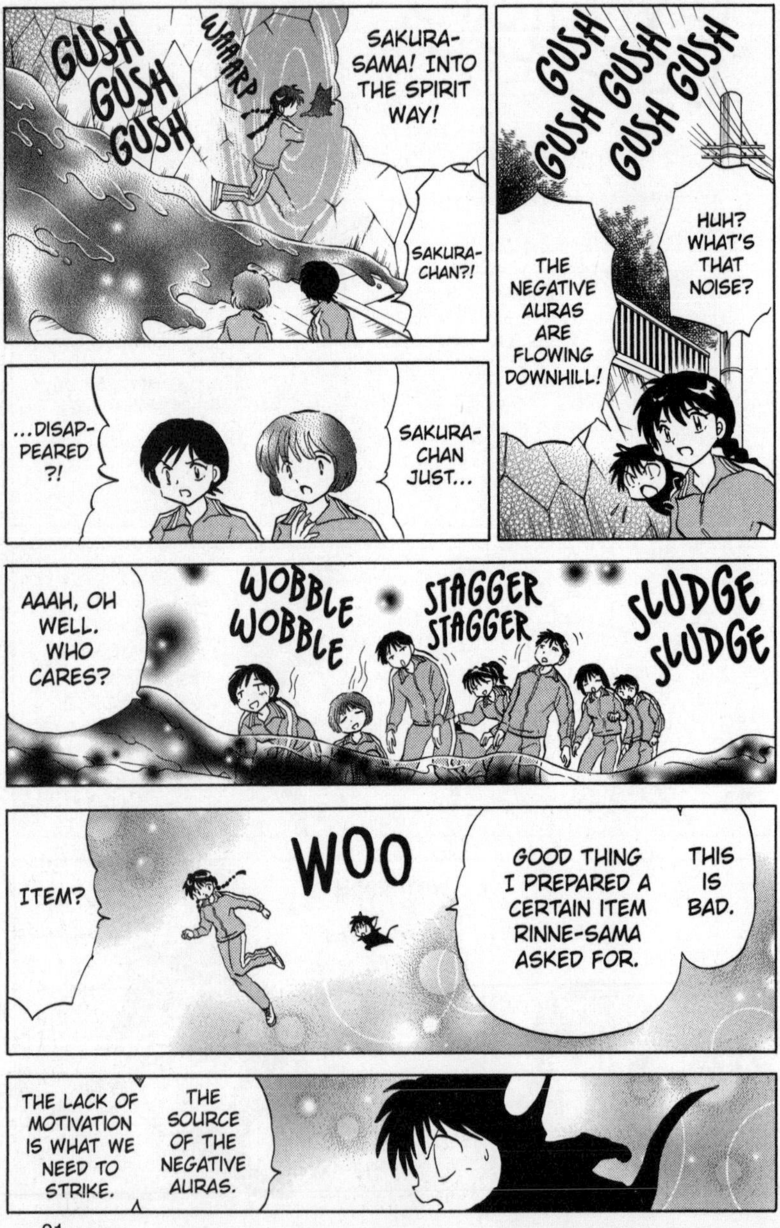
GUSH GUSH GUSH
GUSH GUSH GUSH
HUH? WHAT'S THAT NOISE?
THE NEGATIVE AURAS ARE FLOWING DOWNHILL!
SAKURA-SAMA! INTO THE SPIRIT WAY!
WHAAR?
GUSH GUSH GUSH
SAKURA-CHAN?!
SAKURA-CHAN JUST...
...DISAPPEARED?!
SLUDGE SLUDGE
STAGGER STAGGER
WOBBLE WOBBLE
AAAH, OH WELL. WHO CARES?
THIS IS BAD.
GOOD THING I PREPARED A CERTAIN ITEM RINNE-SAMA ASKED FOR.
WOO
ITEM?
THE SOURCE OF THE NEGATIVE AURAS.
THE LACK OF MOTIVATION IS WHAT WE NEED TO STRIKE.

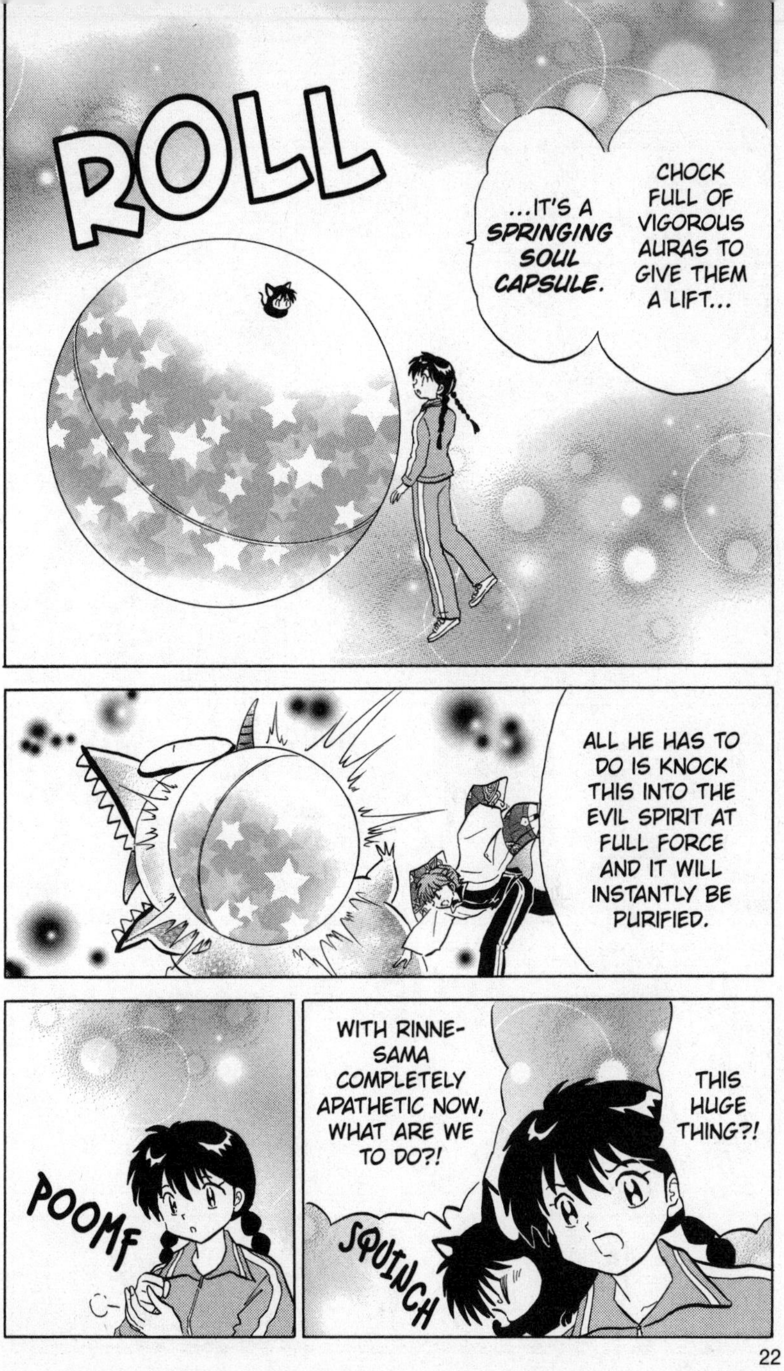
CHOCK FULL OF VIGOROUS AURAS TO GIVE THEM A LIFT...
...IT'S A SPRINGING SOUL CAPSULE.
ROLL
ALL HE HAS TO DO IS KNOCK THIS INTO THE EVIL SPIRIT AT FULL FORCE AND IT WILL INSTANTLY BE PURIFIED.
THIS HUGE THING?!
WITH RINNE-SAMA COMPLETELY APATHETIC NOW, WHAT ARE WE TO DO?!
SQUINCH
POOMF

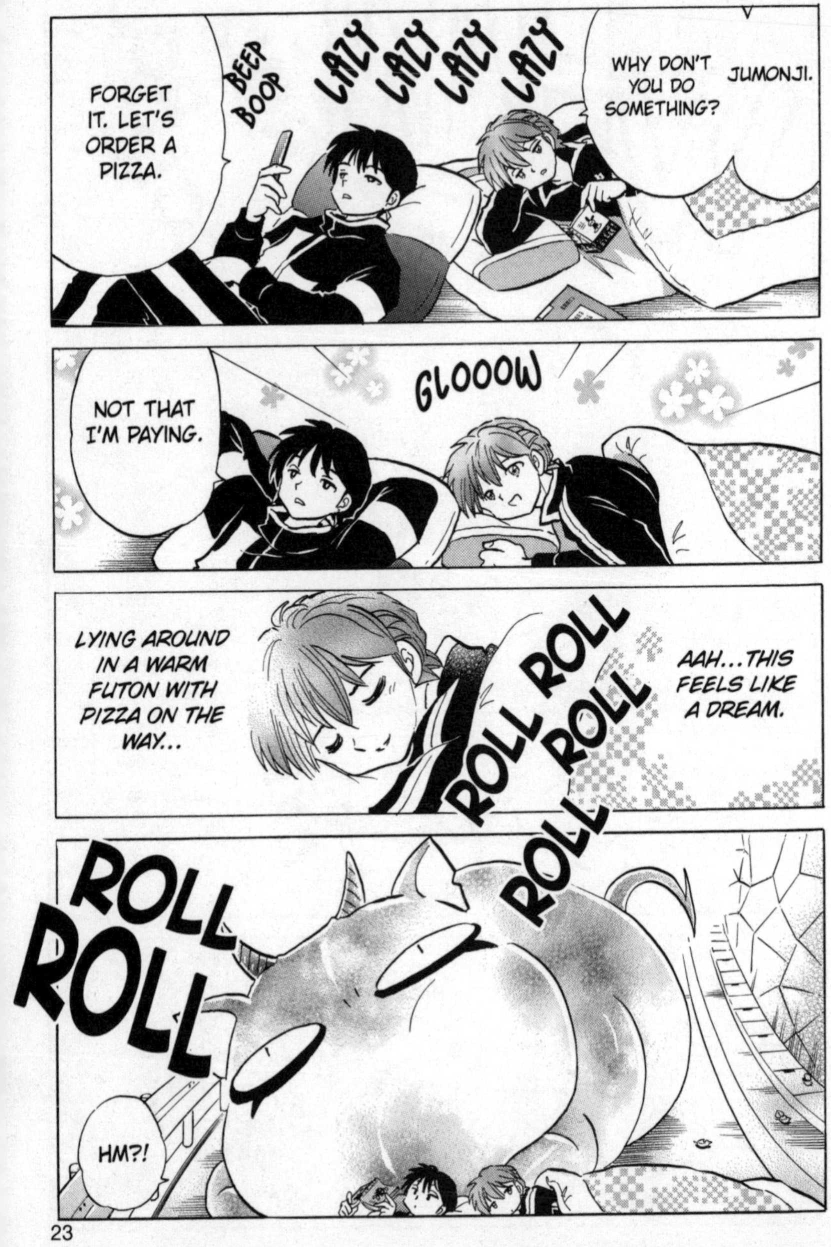
JUMONJI.
WHY DON'T YOU DO SOMETHING?
LAZY LAZY LAZY LAZY
BEEP BOOP
FORGET IT. LET'S ORDER A PIZZA.
GLOOOW
NOT THAT I'M PAYING.
AAH...THIS FEELS LIKE A DREAM.
ROLL ROLL ROLL ROLL ROLL
LYING AROUND IN A WARM FUTON WITH PIZZA ON THE WAY...
ROLL ROLL
HM?!

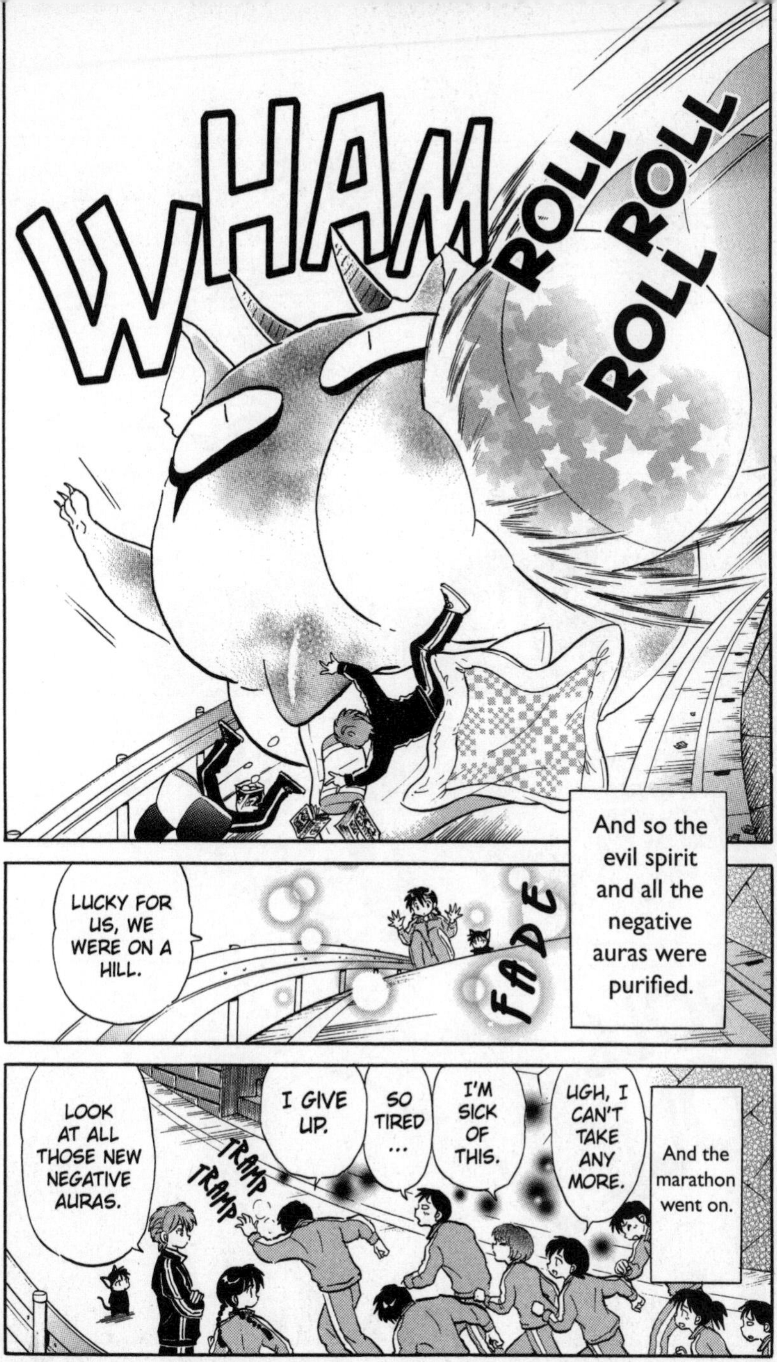
WHAM
ROLL ROLL ROLL
And so the evil spirit and all the negative auras were purified.
FADE
LUCKY FOR US, WE WERE ON A HILL.
And the marathon went on.
UGH, I CAN'T TAKE ANY MORE.
I'M SICK OF THIS.
SO TIRED...
I GIVE UP.
TRAMP TRAMP
LOOK AT ALL THOSE NEW NEGATIVE AURAS.

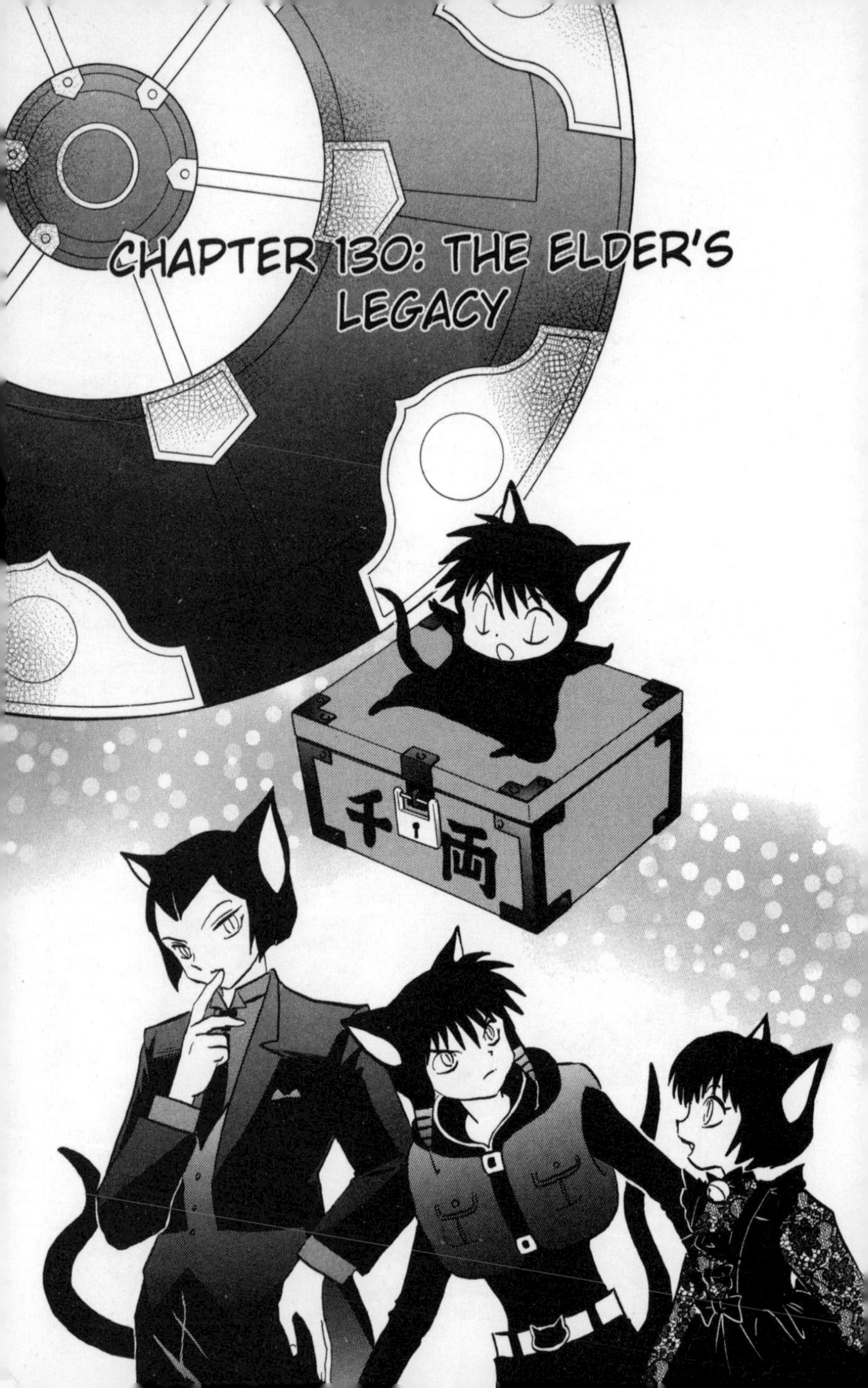
CHAPTER 130: THE ELDER'S LEGACY
千両

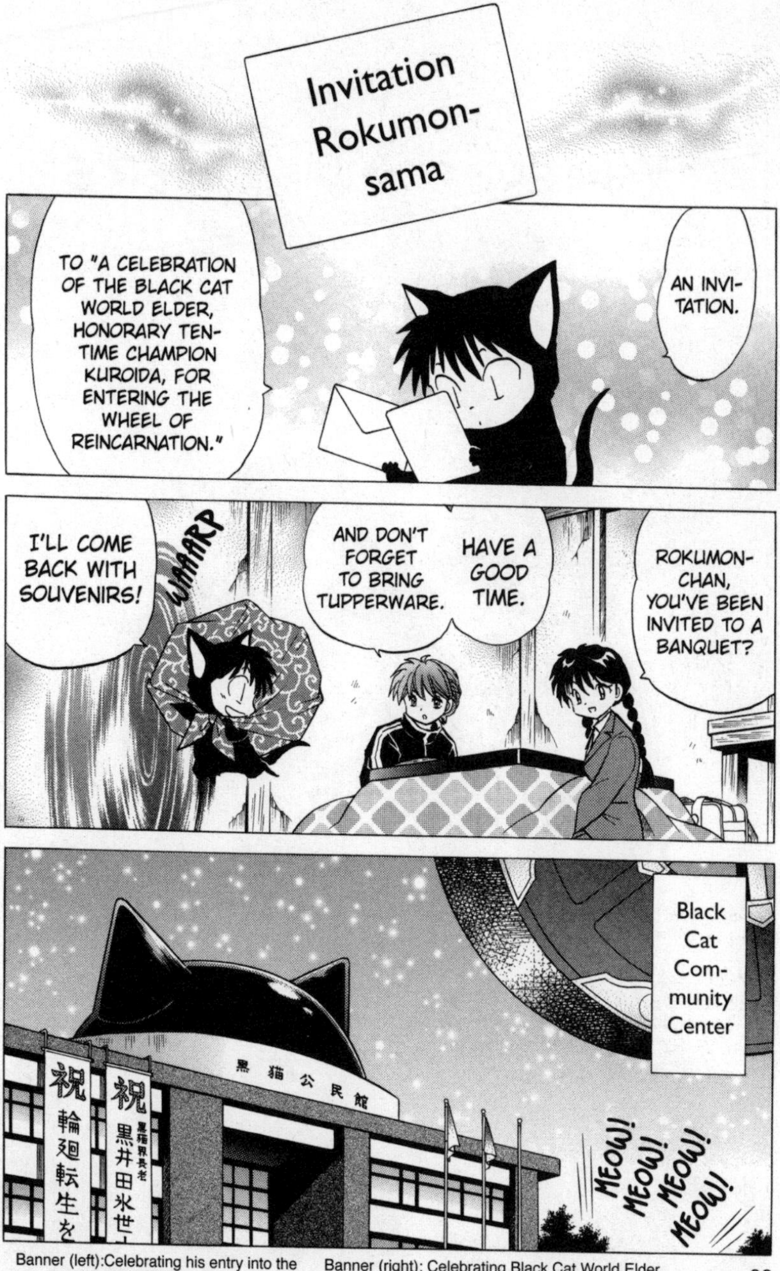
Invitation Rokumon-sama
AN INVITATION.
TO "A CELEBRATION OF THE BLACK CAT WORLD ELDER, HONORARY TEN-TIME CHAMPION KUROIDA, FOR ENTERING THE WHEEL OF REINCARNATION."
ROKUMON-CHAN, YOU'VE BEEN INVITED TO A BANQUET?
HAVE A GOOD TIME.
AND DON'T FORGET TO BRING TUPPERWARE.
WAAARP
I'LL COME BACK WITH SOUVENIRS!
Black Cat Community Center
MEOW! MEOW! MEOW! MEOW!
黒猫公民館
祝 黒猫界長老 黒井田氷世
祝 輪廻転生を

Banner (left):Celebrating his entry into the Wheel of Reincarnation

Banner (right): Celebrating Black Cat World Elder, Honorary Ten-Time Champion, Kuroida

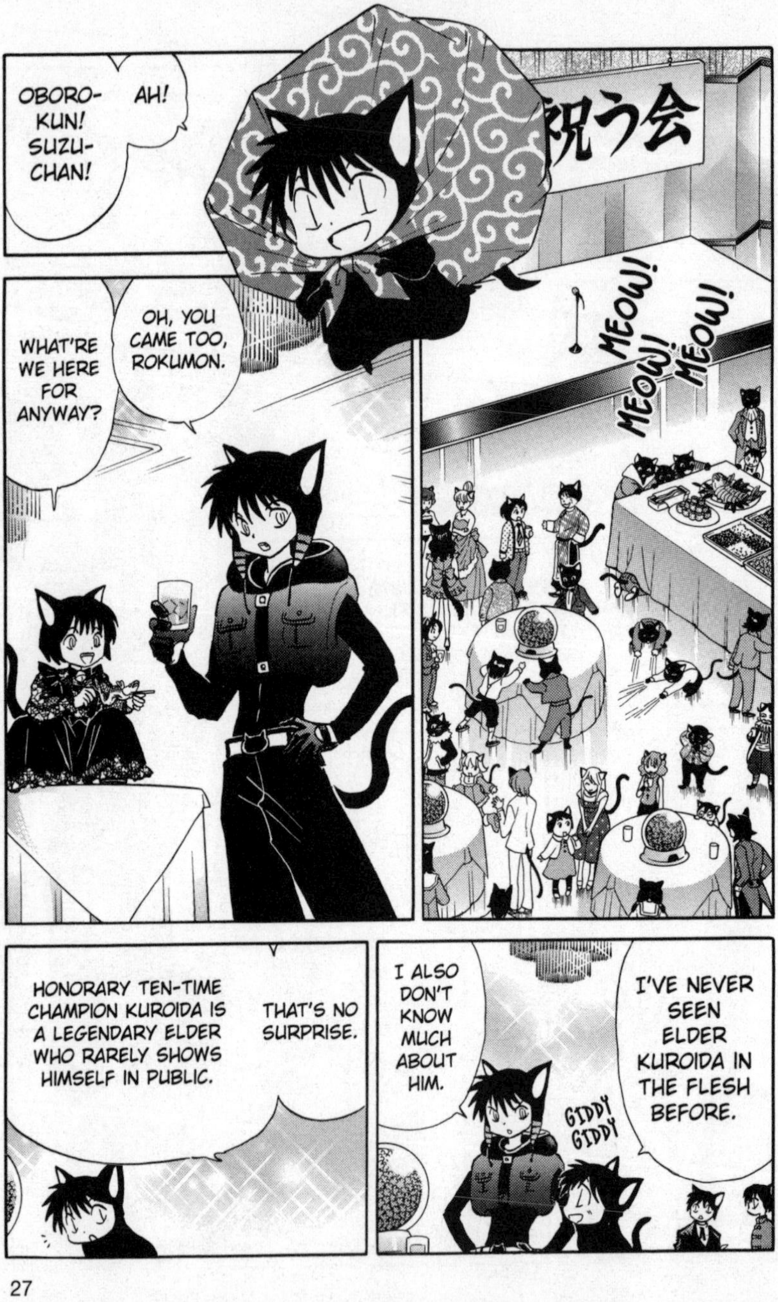
祝う会
MEOW! MEOW! MEOW!
AH!
OBORO-KUN! SUZU-CHAN!
OH, YOU CAME TOO, ROKUMON.
WHAT'RE WE HERE FOR ANYWAY?
I'VE NEVER SEEN ELDER KUROIDA IN THE FLESH BEFORE.
GIDDY GIDDY
I ALSO DON'T KNOW MUCH ABOUT HIM.
THAT'S NO SURPRISE.
HONORARY TEN-TIME CHAMPION KUROIDA IS A LEGENDARY ELDER WHO RARELY SHOWS HIMSELF IN PUBLIC.

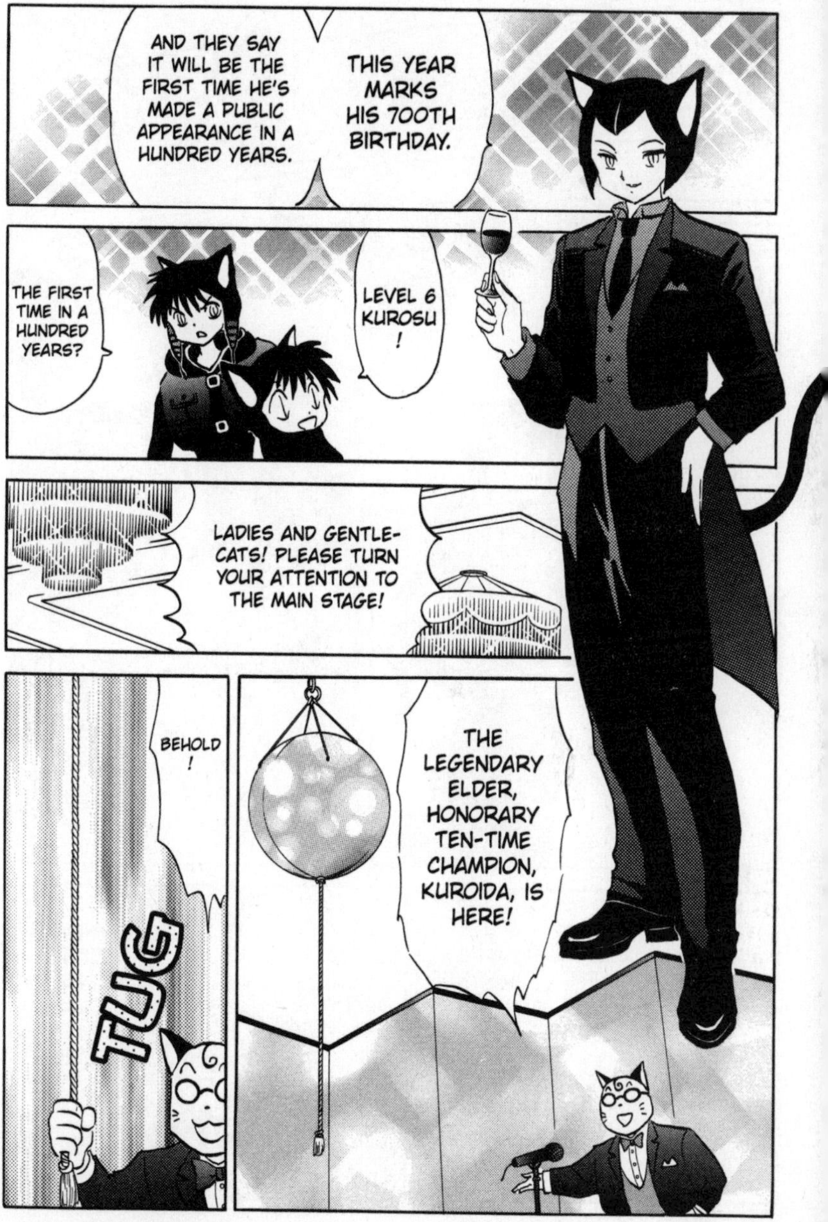
THIS YEAR MARKS HIS 700TH BIRTHDAY.
AND THEY SAY IT WILL BE THE FIRST TIME HE'S MADE A PUBLIC APPEARANCE IN A HUNDRED YEARS.
LEVEL 6 KUROSU!
THE FIRST TIME IN A HUNDRED YEARS?
LADIES AND GENTLE-CATS! PLEASE TURN YOUR ATTENTION TO THE MAIN STAGE!
THE LEGENDARY ELDER, HONORARY TEN-TIME CHAMPION, KUROIDA, IS HERE!
BEHOLD!
TUG

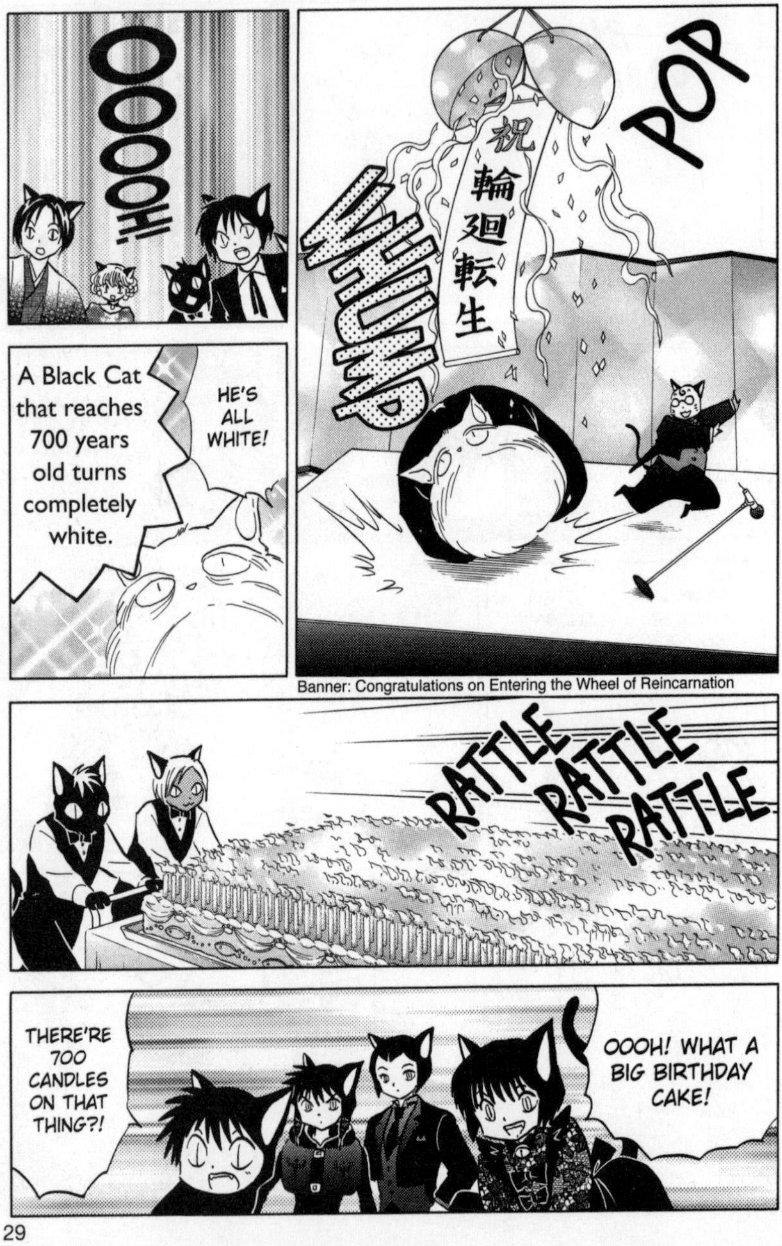
POP
祝輪廻転生
WHUMP
Banner: Congratulations on Entering the Wheel of Reincarnation
OOOOH!
A Black Cat that reaches 700 years old turns completely white.
HE'S ALL WHITE!
RATTLE RATTLE RATTLE
OOOH! WHAT A BIG BIRTHDAY CAKE!
THERE'RE 700 CANDLES ON THAT THING?!

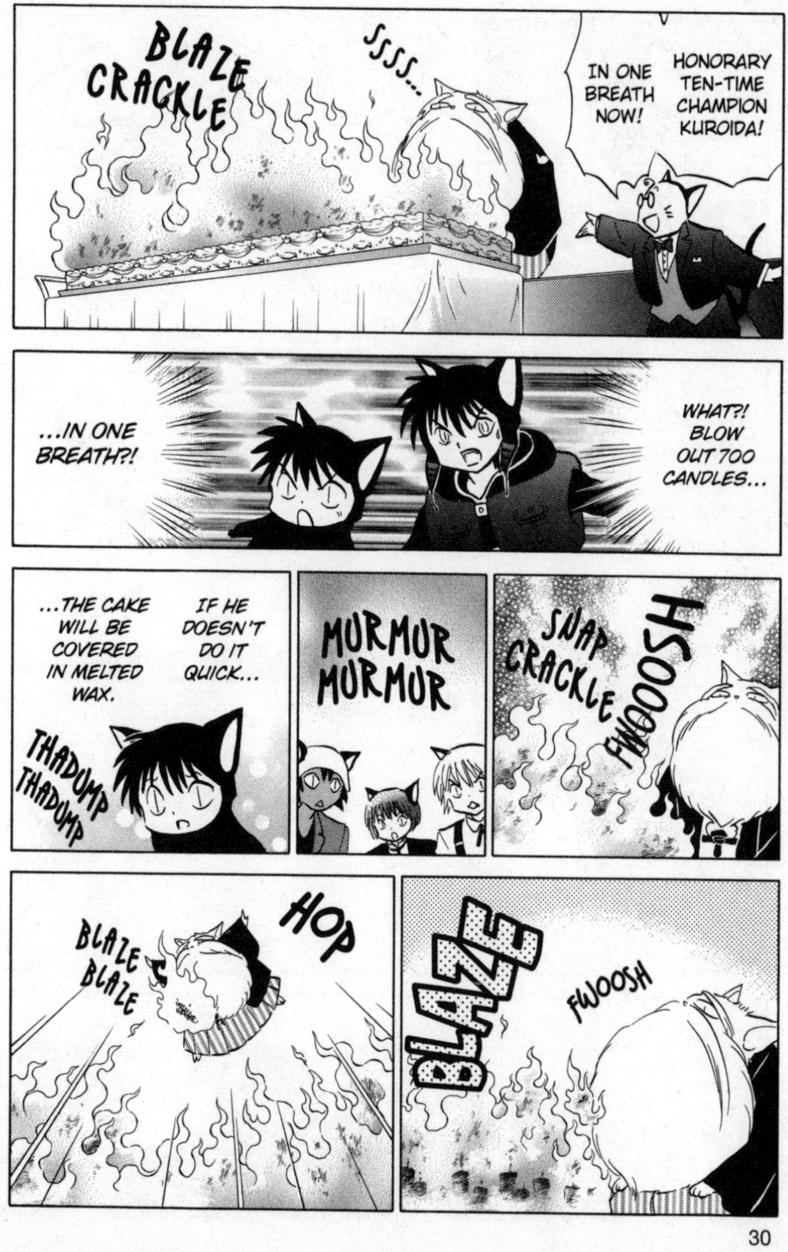
HONORARY TEN-TIME CHAMPION KUROIDA!
IN ONE BREATH NOW!
SSSS...
BLAZE CRACKLE
WHAT?! BLOW OUT 700 CANDLES...
...IN ONE BREATH?!
SNAP CRACKLE
FWOOOSH
MURMUR MURMUR
IF HE DOESN'T DO IT QUICK...
...THE CAKE WILL BE COVERED IN MELTED WAX.
THADUMP THADUMP
BLAZE
FWOOSH
HOP
BLAZE BLAZE

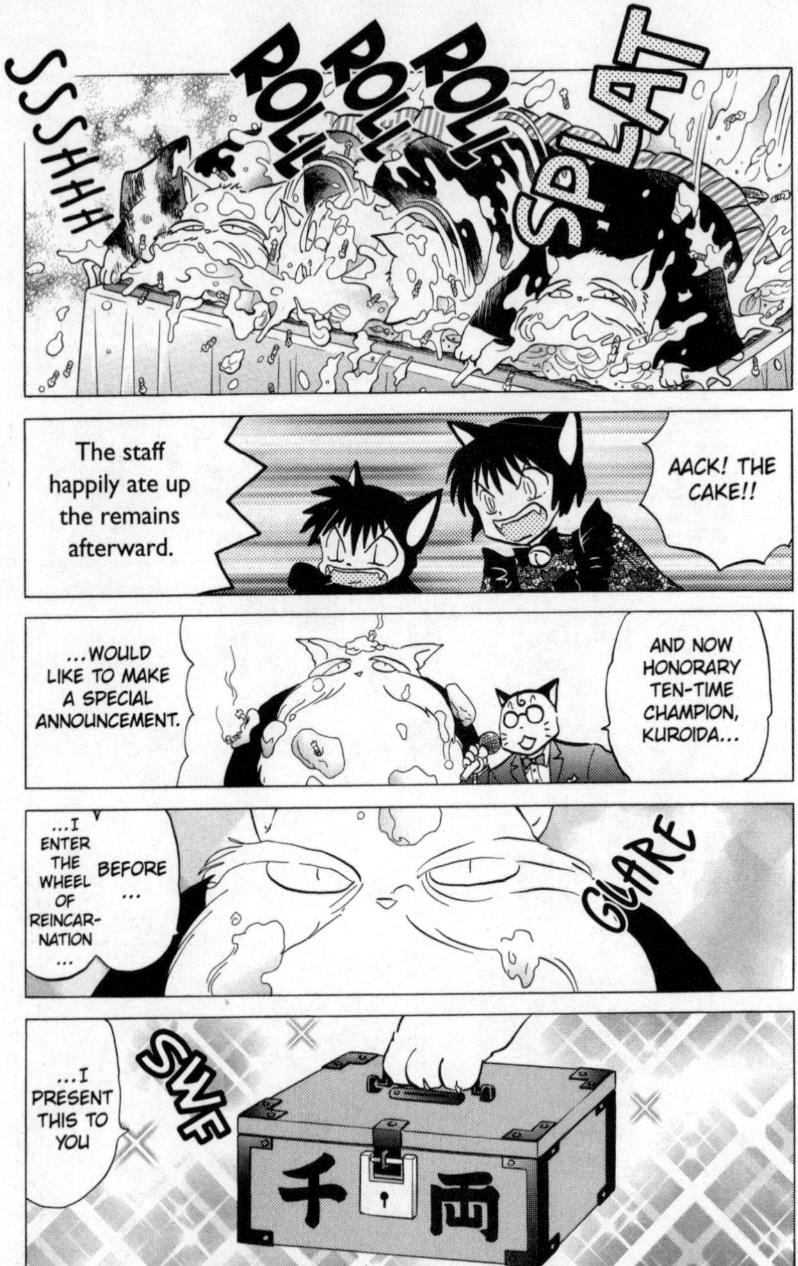
SPLAT
ROLL ROLL ROLL
SSSHHH
AACK! THE CAKE!!
The staff happily ate up the remains afterward.
AND NOW HONORARY TEN-TIME CHAMPION, KUROIDA...
...WOULD LIKE TO MAKE A SPECIAL ANNOUNCEMENT.
GLARE
BEFORE ...
...I ENTER THE WHEEL OF REINCARNATION ...
SWF
...I PRESENT THIS TO YOU
千両

Sign: Money Box

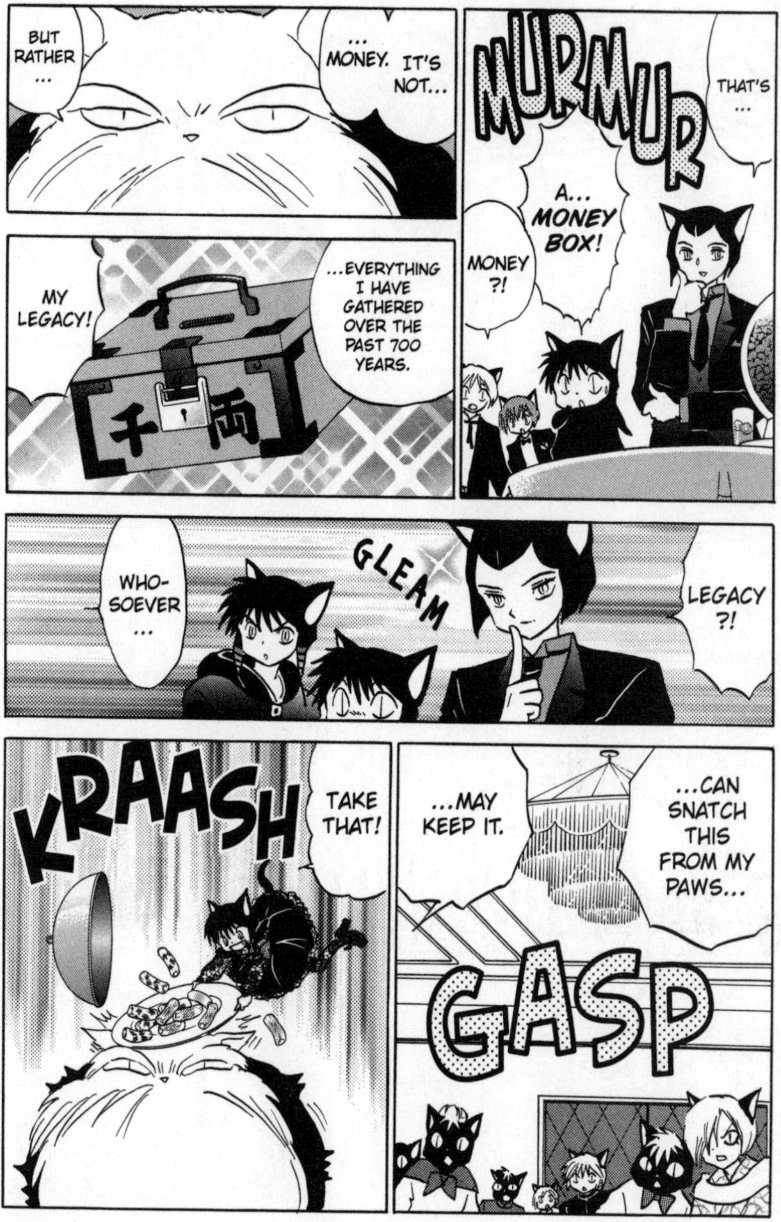
THAT'S ...
MURMUR
A... MONEY BOX!
MONEY ?!
IT'S NOT... ... MONEY.
BUT RATHER ...
...EVERYTHING I HAVE GATHERED OVER THE PAST 700 YEARS.
MY LEGACY!
千両
LEGACY ?!
GLEAM
WHO-SOEVER ...
...CAN SNATCH THIS FROM MY PAWS...
...MAY KEEP IT.
GASP
TAKE THAT!
KRAASH

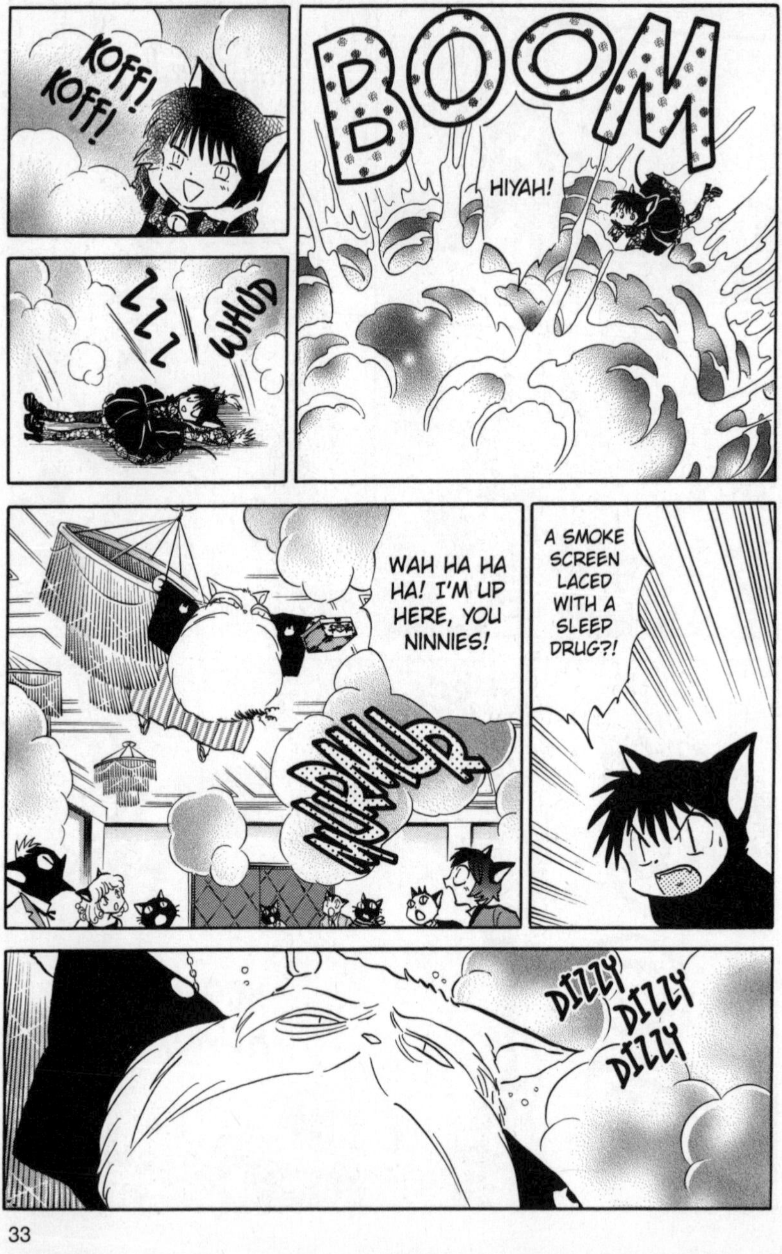
BOOM
HIYAH!
KOFF! KOFF!
ZZZ
WHUD
A SMOKE SCREEN LACED WITH A SLEEP DRUG?!
WAH HA HA HA! I'M UP HERE, YOU NINNIES!
DIZZY DIZZY DIZZY

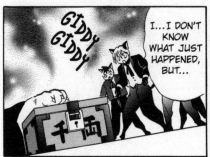

GIDDY GIDDY

I...I DON'T KNOW WHAT JUST HAPPENED, BUT...

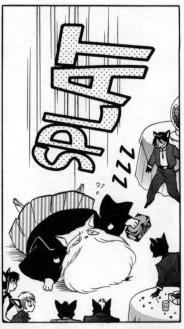

SPLAT

ZZZ

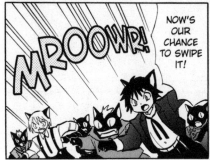

MROOWR!

NOW'S OUR CHANCE TO SWIPE IT!

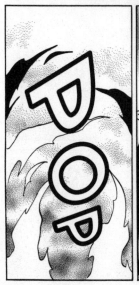

POP

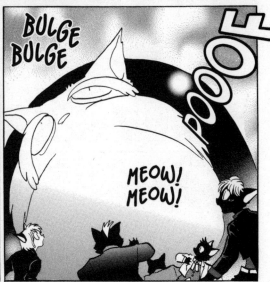

BULGE BULGE

POOOF

MEOW! MEOW!

34

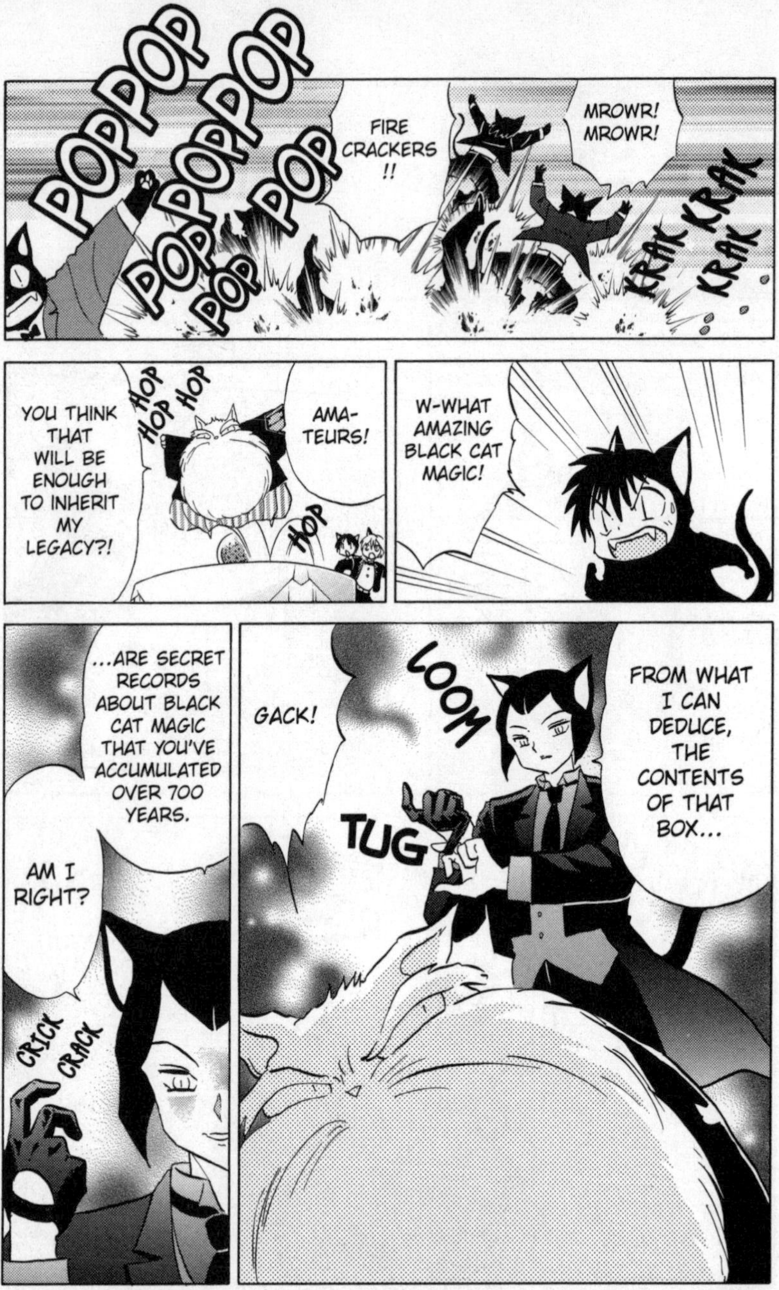
MROWR! MROWR!
KRAK KRAK KRAK
FIRE CRACKERS !!
POPPOP
POPPOPPOP
POP POP POP
W-WHAT AMAZING BLACK CAT MAGIC!
AMA-TEURS!
HOP HOP HOP
HOP
YOU THINK THAT WILL BE ENOUGH TO INHERIT MY LEGACY?!
FROM WHAT I CAN DEDUCE, THE CONTENTS OF THAT BOX...
LOOM
GACK!
TUG
...ARE SECRET RECORDS ABOUT BLACK CAT MAGIC THAT YOU'VE ACCUMULATED OVER 700 YEARS.
AM I RIGHT?
CRICK CRACK

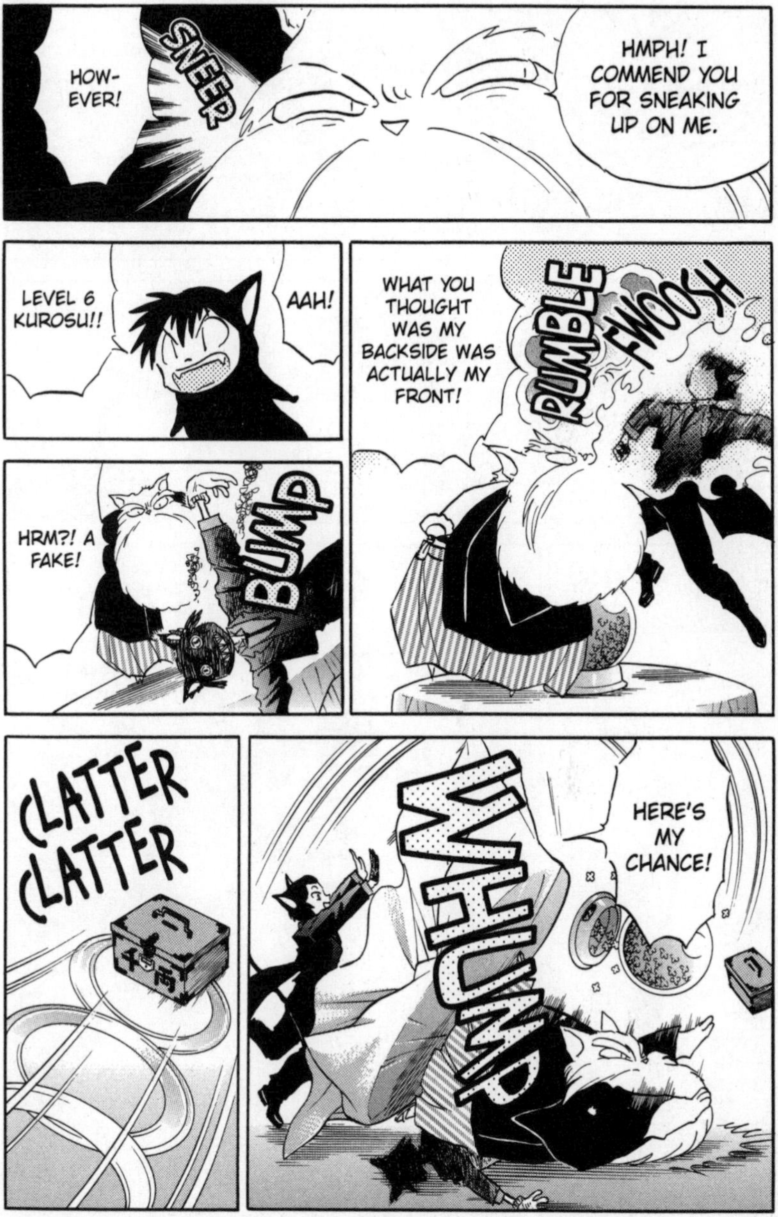
HMPH! I COMMEND YOU FOR SNEAKING UP ON ME.
SNEER
HOW-EVER!
WHAT YOU THOUGHT WAS MY BACKSIDE WAS ACTUALLY MY FRONT!
FWOOSH
RUMBLE
AAH!
LEVEL 6 KUROSU!!
BUMP
HRM?! A FAKE!
HERE'S MY CHANCE!
WHUMP
CLATTER CLATTER

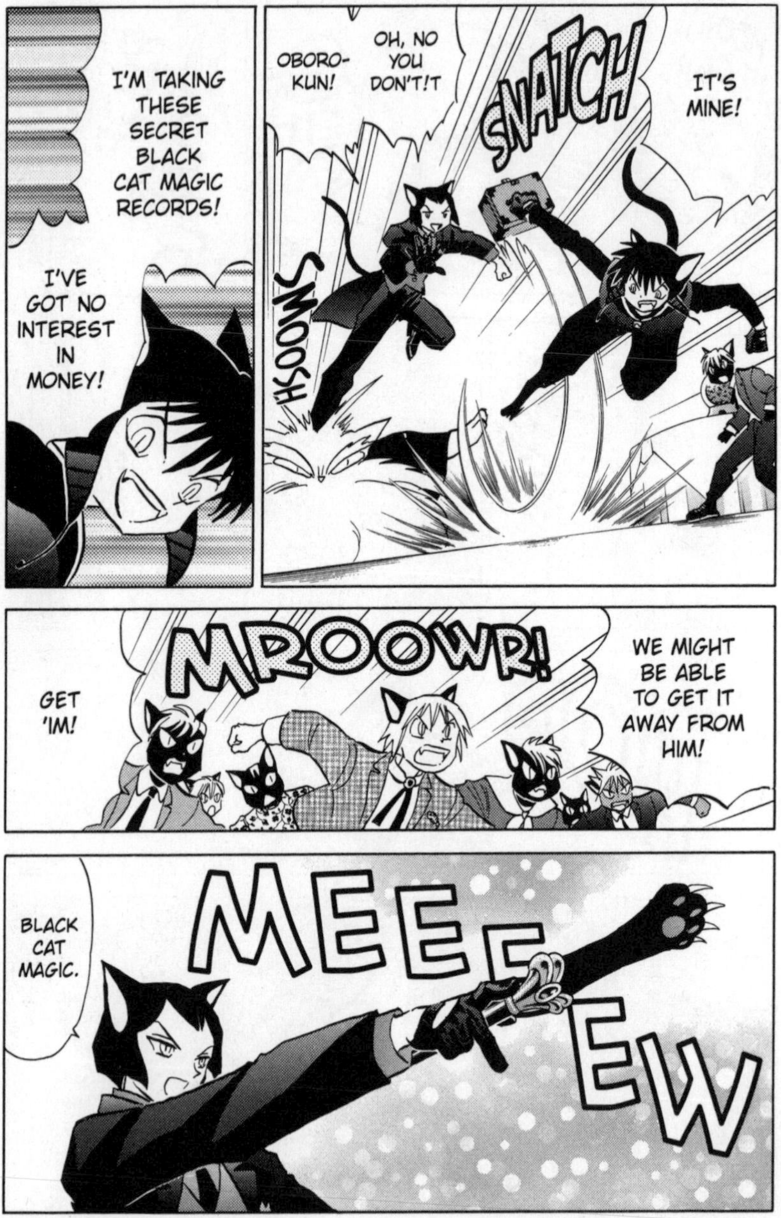
IT'S MINE!
SNATCH
OH, NO YOU DON'T!T
OBORO-KUN!
SWOOSH
I'M TAKING THESE SECRET BLACK CAT MAGIC RECORDS!
I'VE GOT NO INTEREST IN MONEY!
WE MIGHT BE ABLE TO GET IT AWAY FROM HIM!
MROOWR!
GET 'IM!
MEEEEEW
BLACK CAT MAGIC.

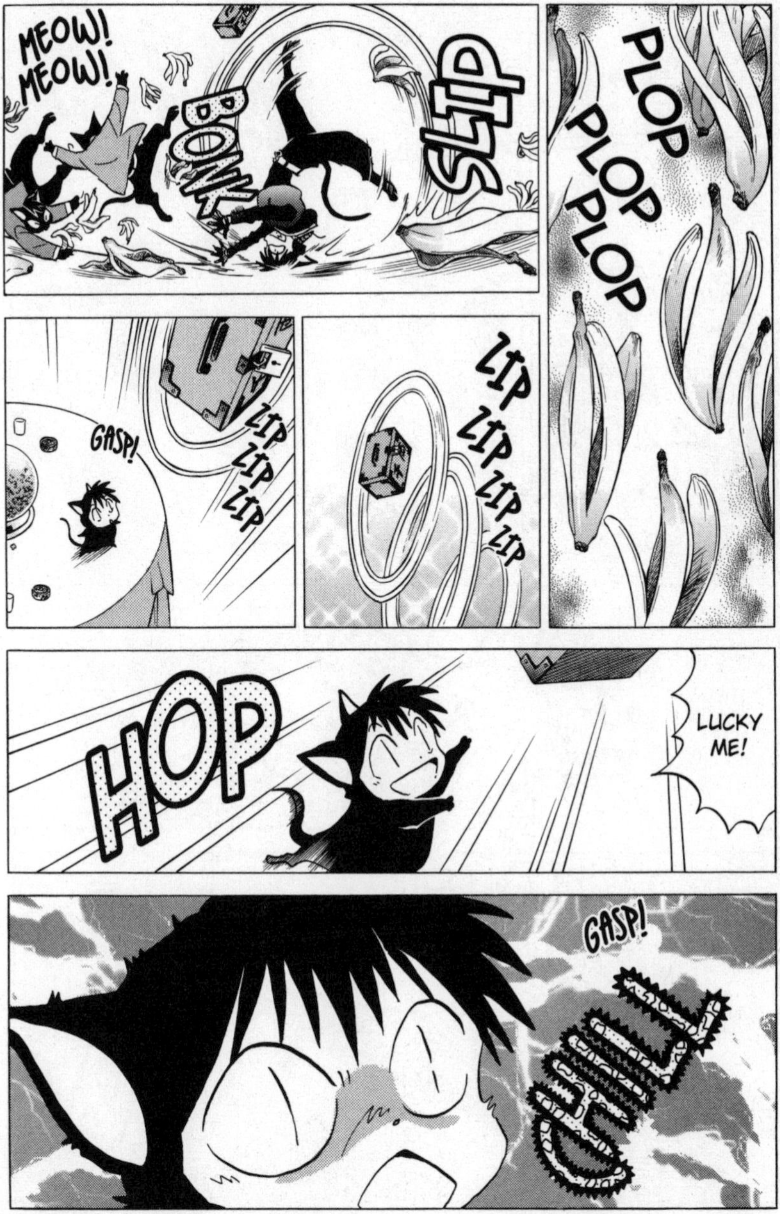
PLOP
PLOP
PLOP
SLIP
BONK
MEOW! MEOW!
ZIP ZIP ZIP ZIP ZIP
GASP!
ZIP ZIP ZIP
LUCKY ME!
HOP
GASP!
CHILL

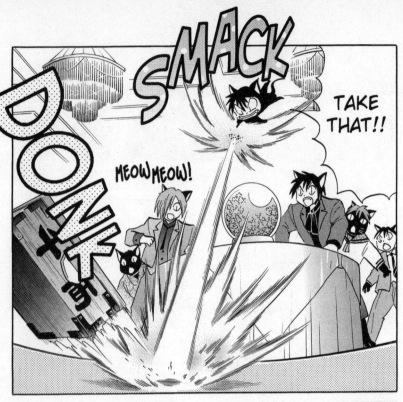

SMACK

DONK

TAKE THAT!!

MEOW MEOW!

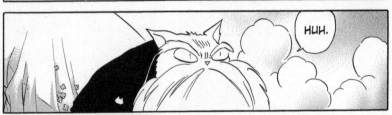

HUH.

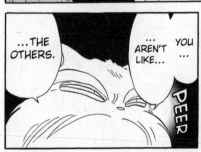

...THE OTHERS.

...AREN'T LIKE...

YOU...

PEER

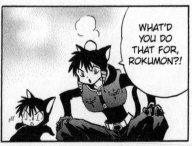

WHAT'D YOU DO THAT FOR, ROKUMON?!

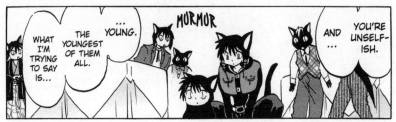

AND ...
YOU'RE UNSELF-ISH.
MURMUR
... YOUNG.
THE YOUNGEST OF THEM ALL.
WHAT I'M TRYING TO SAY IS...
...YOU ARE THE MOST SUITED FOR...
...LIVING THE REST OF YOUR LONG LIFE WITH MY INHERITANCE.
I WANT YOU...
...TO TAKE IT.
PUSH
BOWING
WHOA! WHAT A TURN OF EVENTS!
MURMUR
NO, THANK YOU.
I DECLINE.
SHOCK
TAKE IT.
SHOVE SHOVE

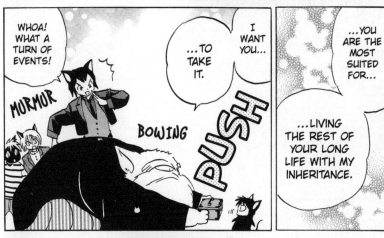

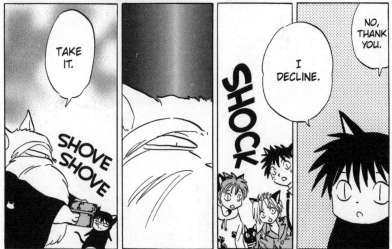

I'M TELLING YOU, I DON'T NEED IT.
PUSH PUSH
I INSIST.
IT'S ALL YOURS.
CLATTER
FWAP
FWAP FWAP FWAP
借用書
IOU
借用書
借用書
BAM
TROOP TROOP
KUROIDA-SAN! TODAY'S THE DAY YOU PAY BACK WHAT YOU OWE US!
TROOP
WE'RE GETTING BACK THE MONEY WE LOANED YOU AND YOUR PREDECESSOR. WITH INTEREST!
YOU'VE AVOIDED US FOR THE PAST HUNDRED YEARS!
御

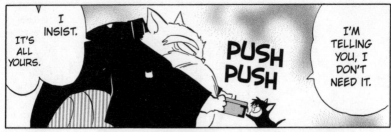

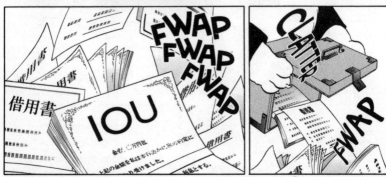

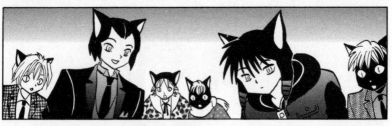

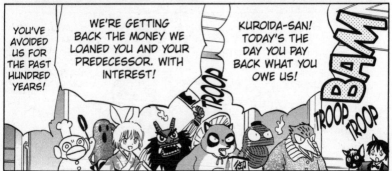

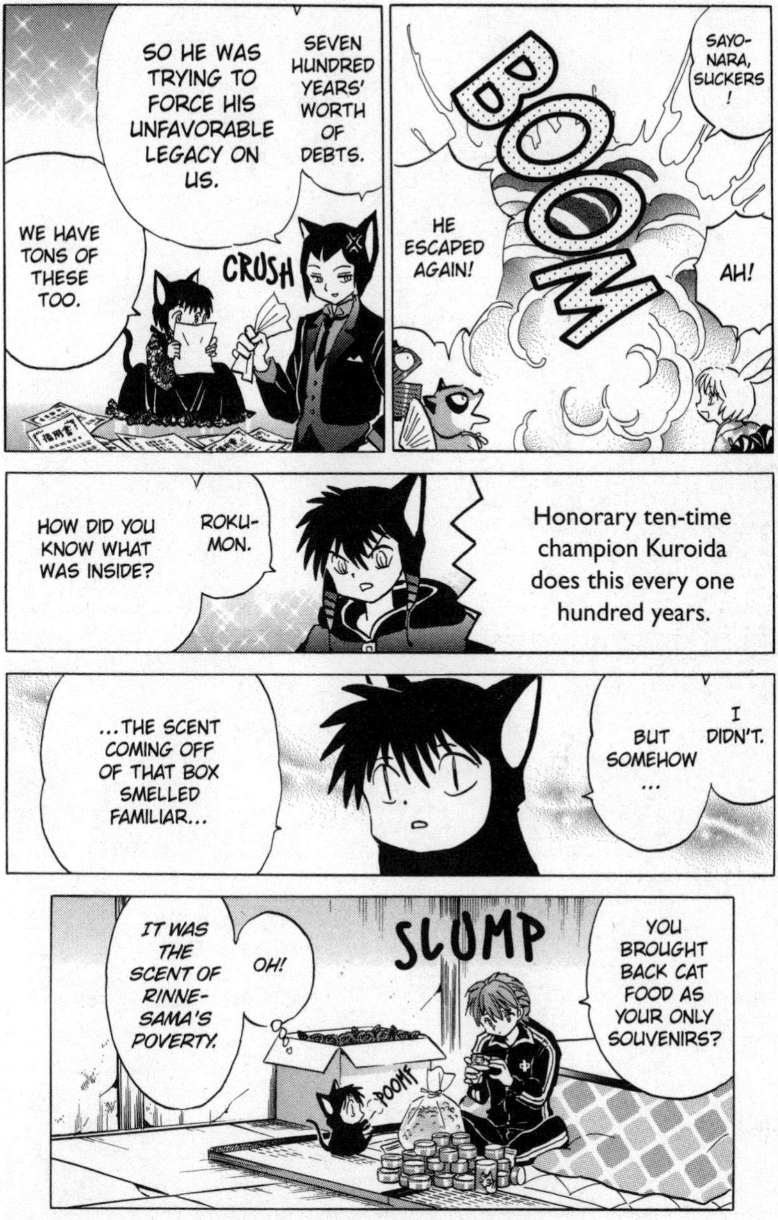
SAYONARA, SUCKERS!
BOOM
AH!
HE ESCAPED AGAIN!
SEVEN HUNDRED YEARS' WORTH OF DEBTS.
SO HE WAS TRYING TO FORCE HIS UNFAVORABLE LEGACY ON US.
CRUSH
WE HAVE TONS OF THESE TOO.
Honorary ten-time champion Kuroida does this every one hundred years.
ROKUMON.
HOW DID YOU KNOW WHAT WAS INSIDE?
I DIDN'T.
BUT SOMEHOW...
...THE SCENT COMING OFF OF THAT BOX SMELLED FAMILIAR...
YOU BROUGHT BACK CAT FOOD AS YOUR ONLY SOUVENIRS?
SLUMP
POOMF
OH!
IT WAS THE SCENT OF RINNE-SAMA'S POVERTY.

CHAPTER 131: DEMONS & SETSUBUN

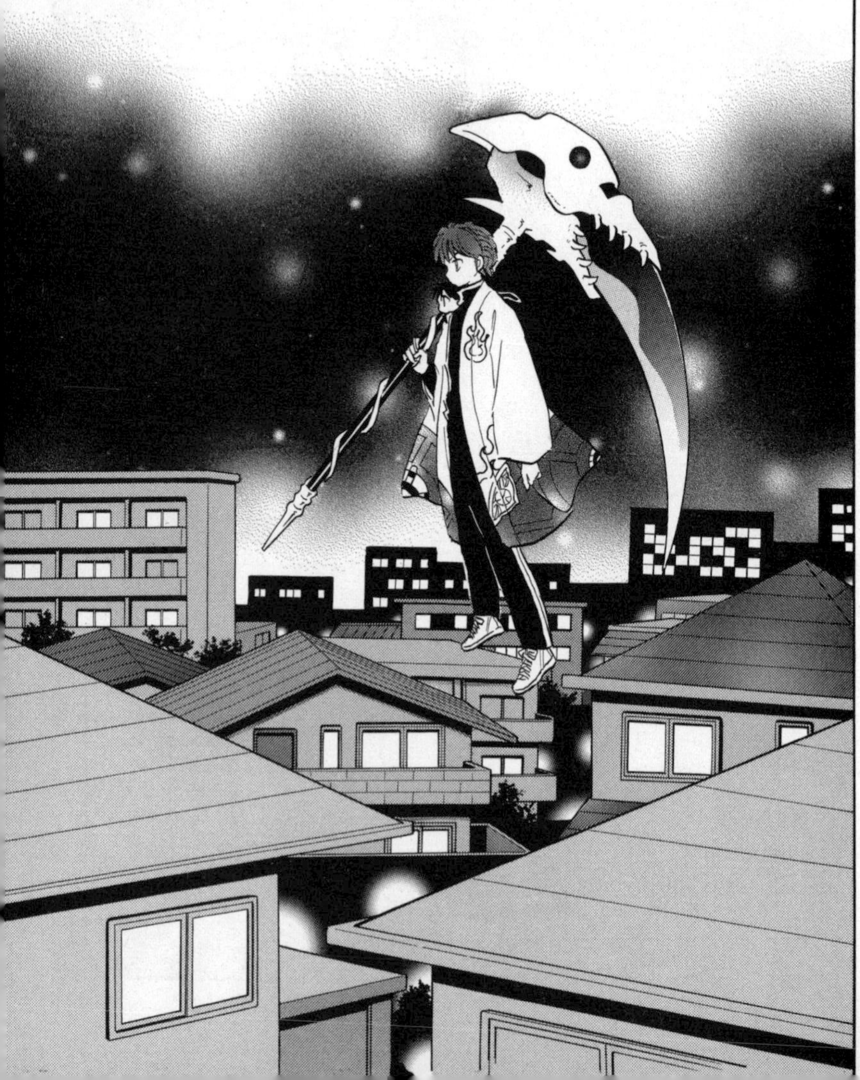

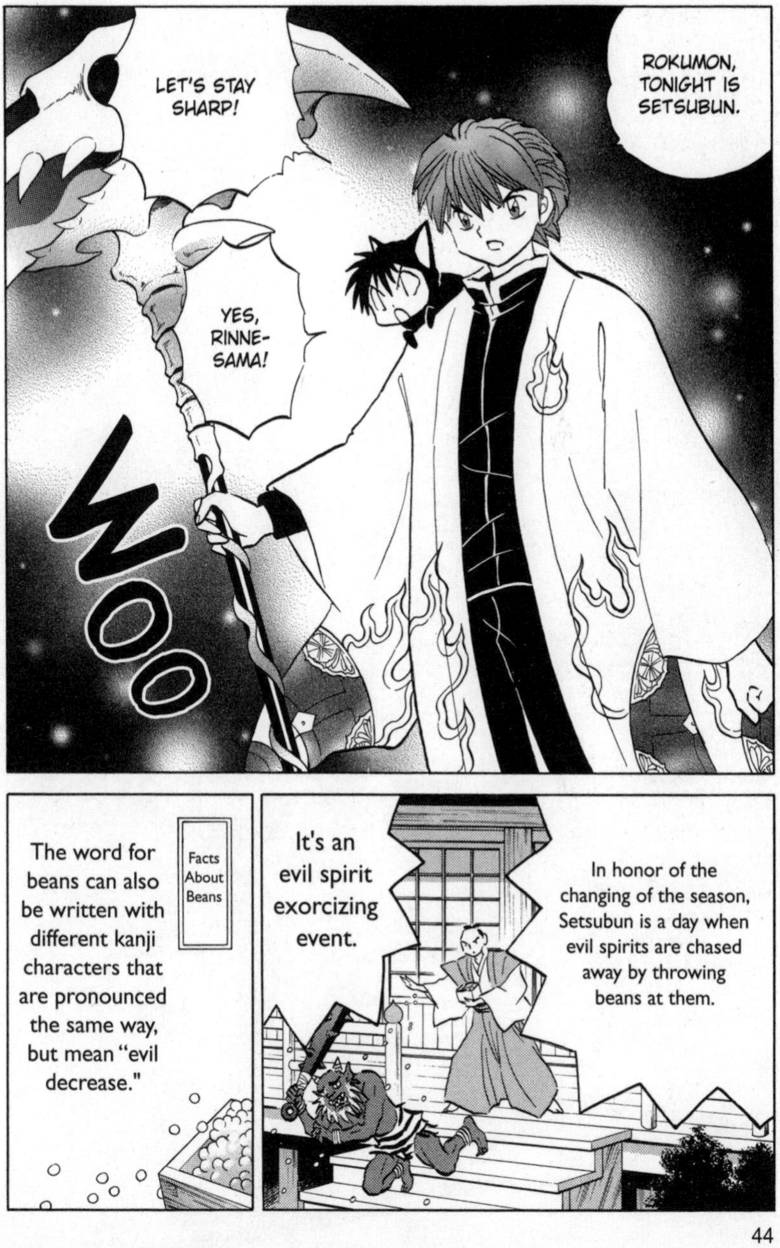
ROKUMON, TONIGHT IS SETSUBUN.
LET'S STAY SHARP!
YES, RINNE-SAMA!
WOO
In honor of the changing of the season, Setsubun is a day when evil spirits are chased away by throwing beans at them.
It's an evil spirit exorcizing event.
Facts About Beans
The word for beans can also be written with different kanji characters that are pronounced the same way, but mean "evil decrease."

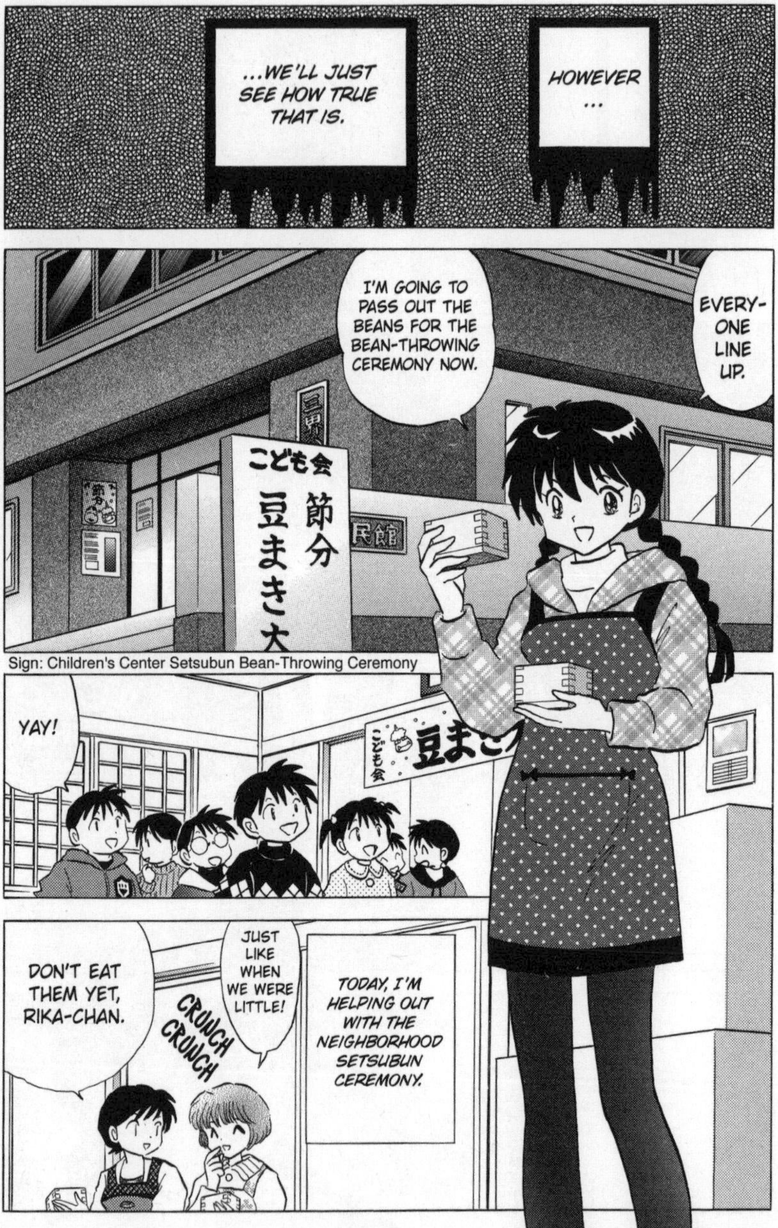
HOWEVER ...
...WE'LL JUST SEE HOW TRUE THAT IS.
EVERY-ONE LINE UP.
I'M GOING TO PASS OUT THE BEANS FOR THE BEAN-THROWING CEREMONY NOW.
こども会
節分
豆まき大
民館
Sign: Children's Center Setsubun Bean-Throwing Ceremony
こども会
豆ま
YAY!
TODAY, I'M HELPING OUT WITH THE NEIGHBORHOOD SETSUBUN CEREMONY.
JUST LIKE WHEN WE WERE LITTLE!
CRUNCH CRUNCH
DON'T EAT THEM YET, RIKA-CHAN.

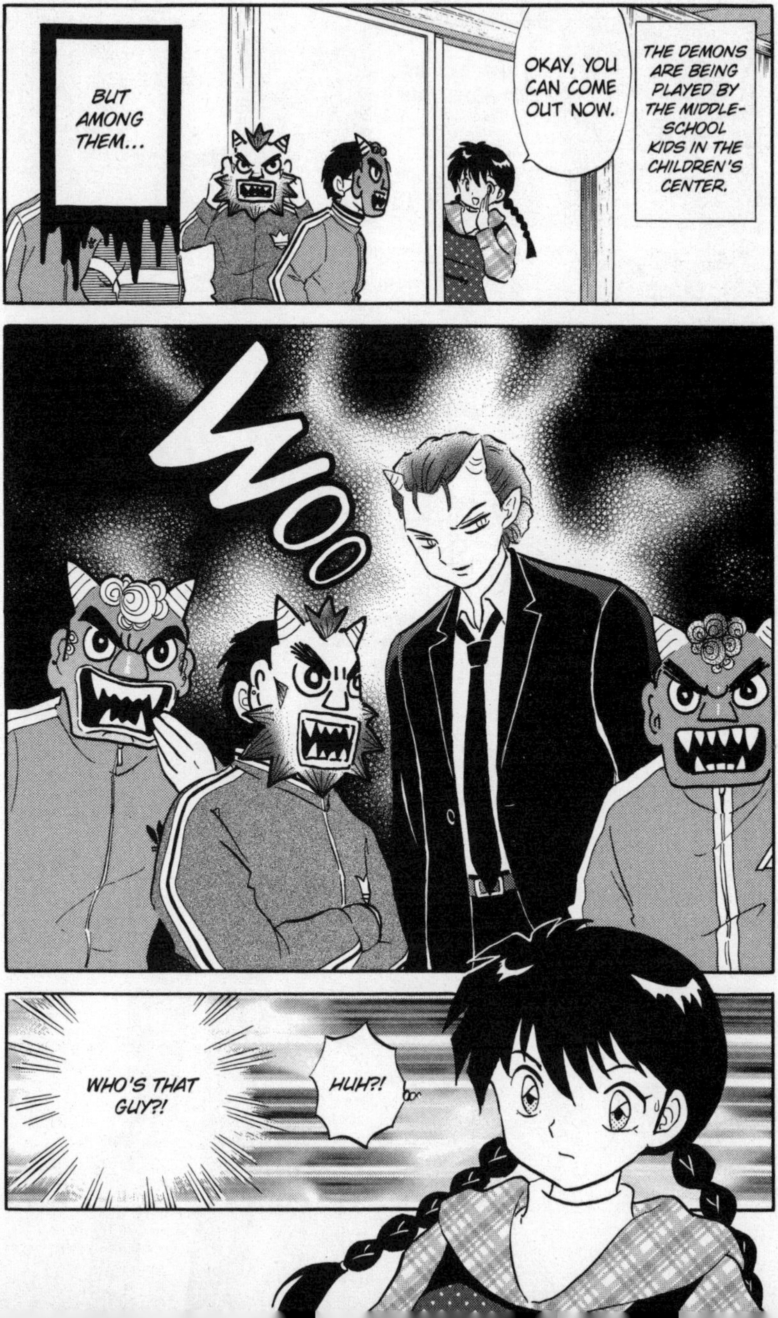
THE DEMONS ARE BEING PLAYED BY THE MIDDLE-SCHOOL KIDS IN THE CHILDREN'S CENTER.
OKAY, YOU CAN COME OUT NOW.
BUT AMONG THEM...
WOO
HUH?!
WHO'S THAT GUY?!

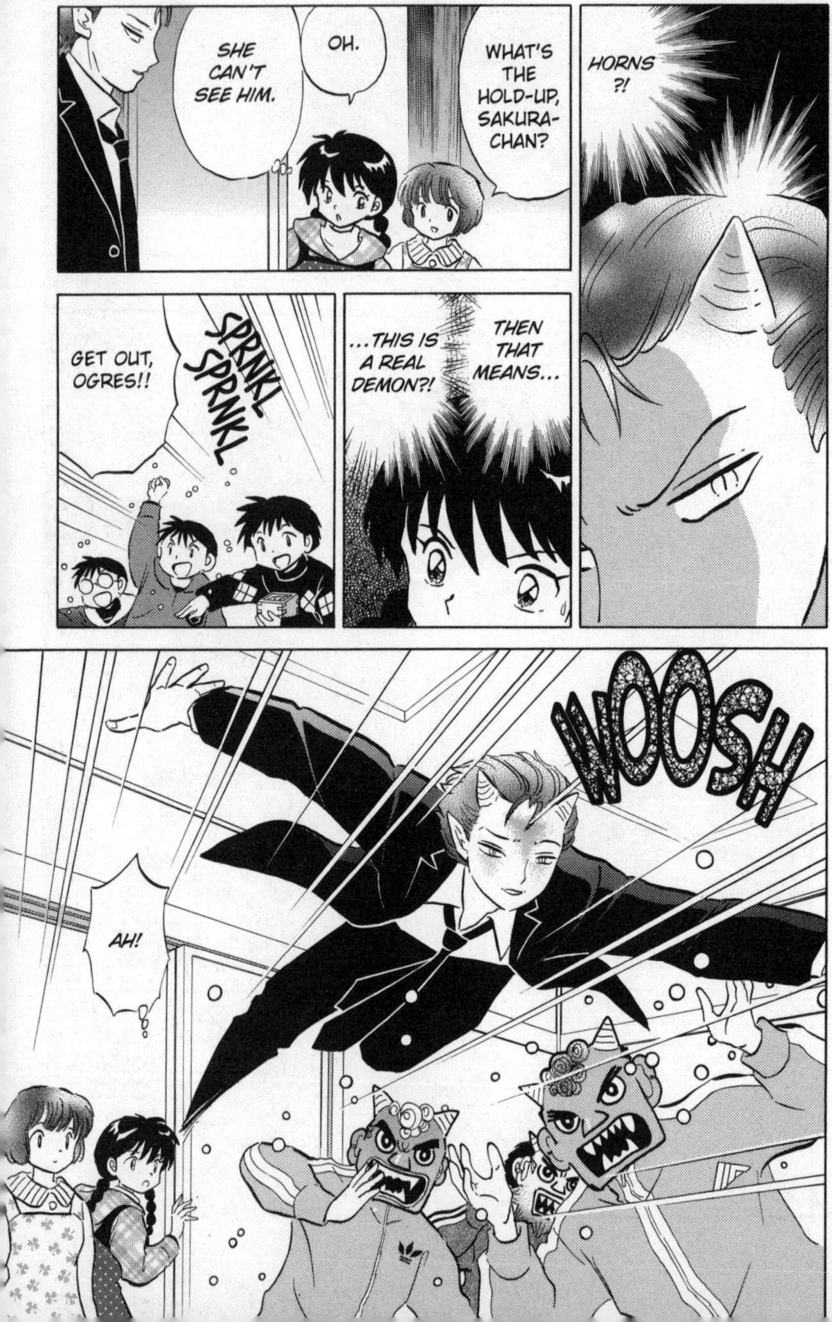
HORNS ?!
WHAT'S THE HOLD-UP, SAKURA-CHAN?
OH.
SHE CAN'T SEE HIM.
THEN THAT MEANS...
...THIS IS A REAL DEMON?!
SPRNKL SPRNKL
GET OUT, OGRES!!
WOOSH
AH!

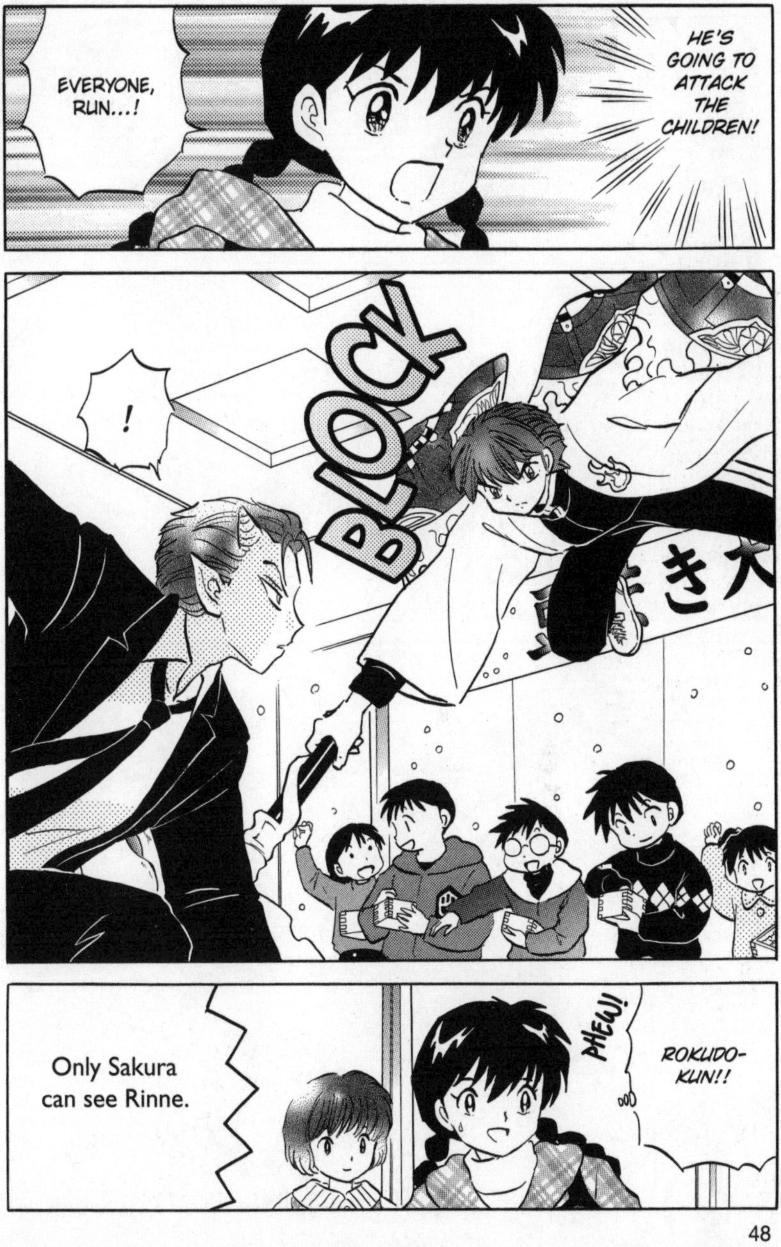
HE'S GOING TO ATTACK THE CHILDREN!
EVERYONE, RUN...!
BLOCK
!
ROKUDO-KUN!!
PHEW!
Only Sakura can see Rinne.

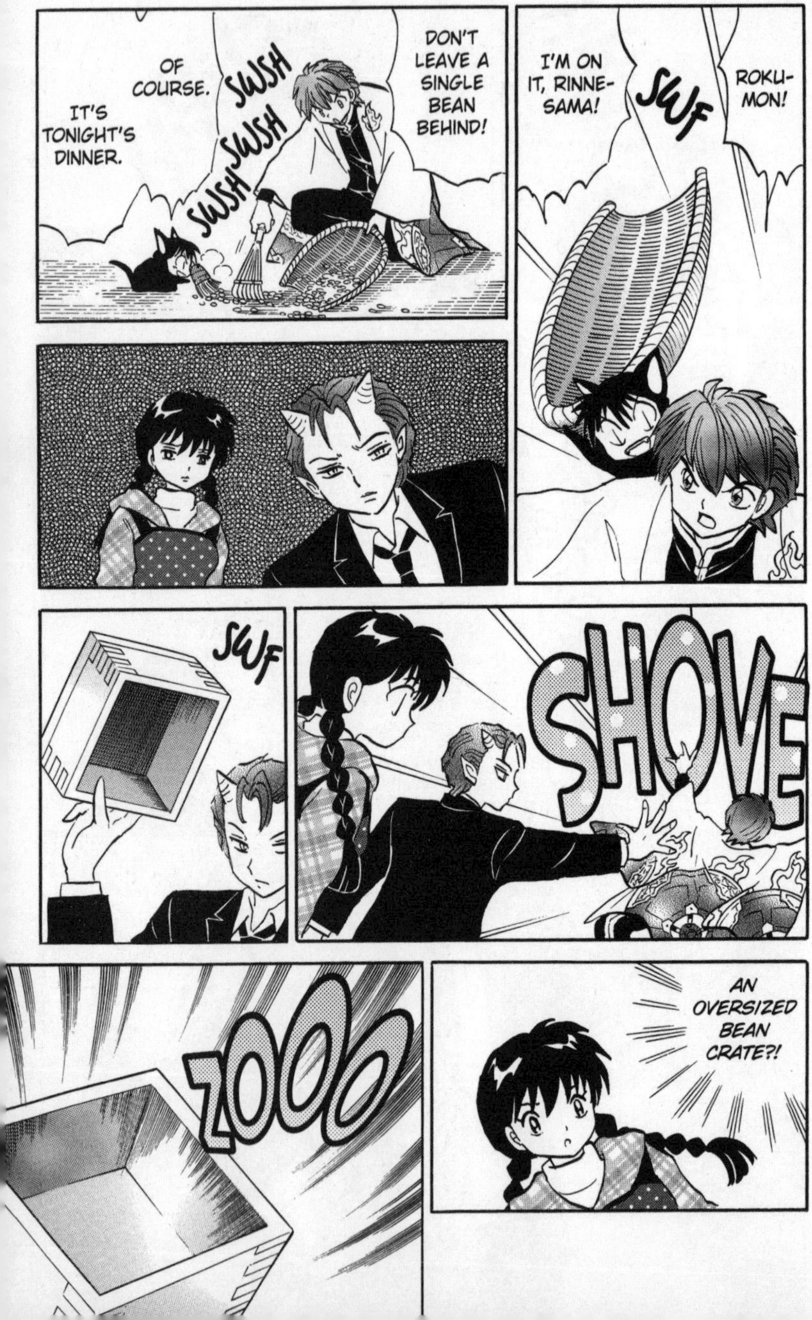

ROKU-MON!
SWF
I'M ON IT, RINNE-SAMA!
DON'T LEAVE A SINGLE BEAN BEHIND!
SWISH
SWISH
OF COURSE.
SWISH
IT'S TONIGHT'S DINNER.
SHOVE
SWF
AN OVERSIZED BEAN CRATE?!
ZOOOO

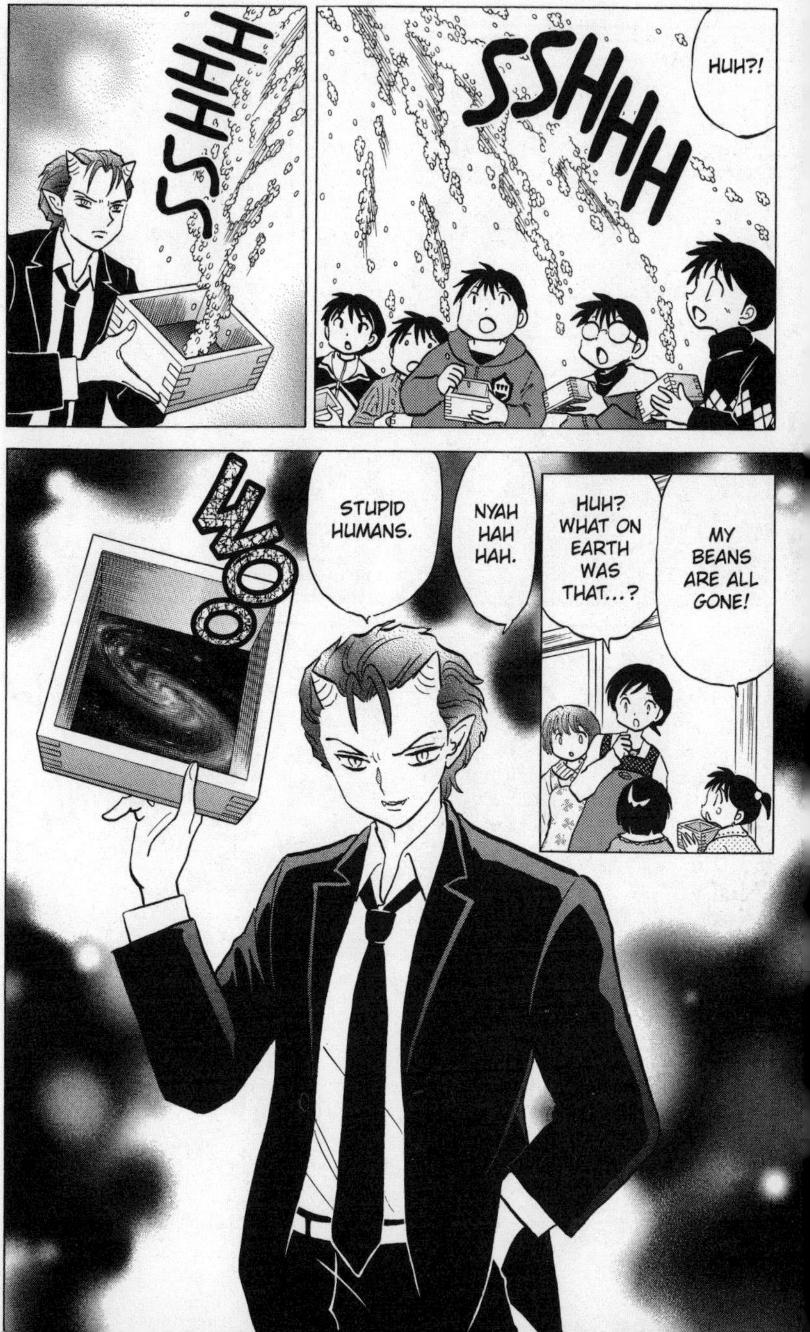
HUH?!
SSHHH
SSHHH
MY BEANS ARE ALL GONE!
HUH? WHAT ON EARTH WAS THAT...?
NYAH HAH HAH.
STUPID HUMANS.
WOO

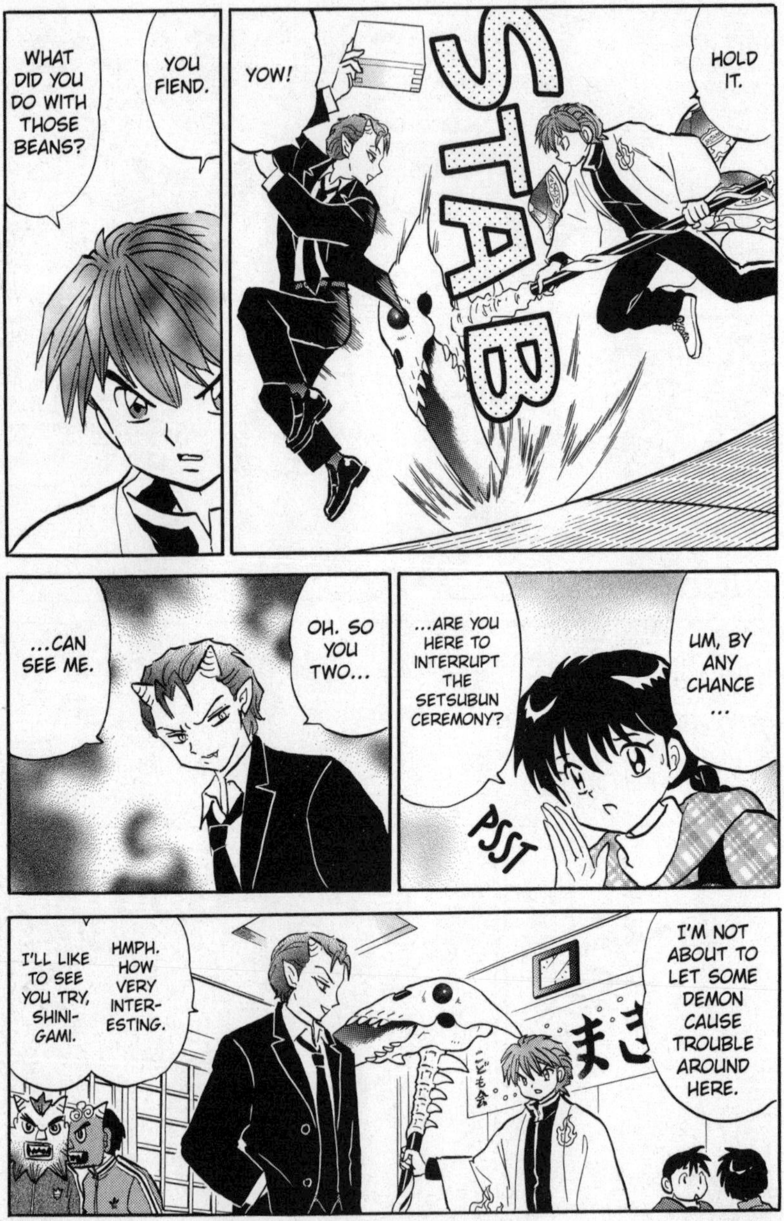
HOLD IT.
STAB
YOW!
YOU FIEND.
WHAT DID YOU DO WITH THOSE BEANS?
UM, BY ANY CHANCE ...
...ARE YOU HERE TO INTERRUPT THE SETSUBUN CEREMONY?
PSST
OH. SO YOU TWO...
...CAN SEE ME.
I'M NOT ABOUT TO LET SOME DEMON CAUSE TROUBLE AROUND HERE.
HMPH. HOW VERY INTER-ESTING.
I'LL LIKE TO SEE YOU TRY, SHINI-GAMI.

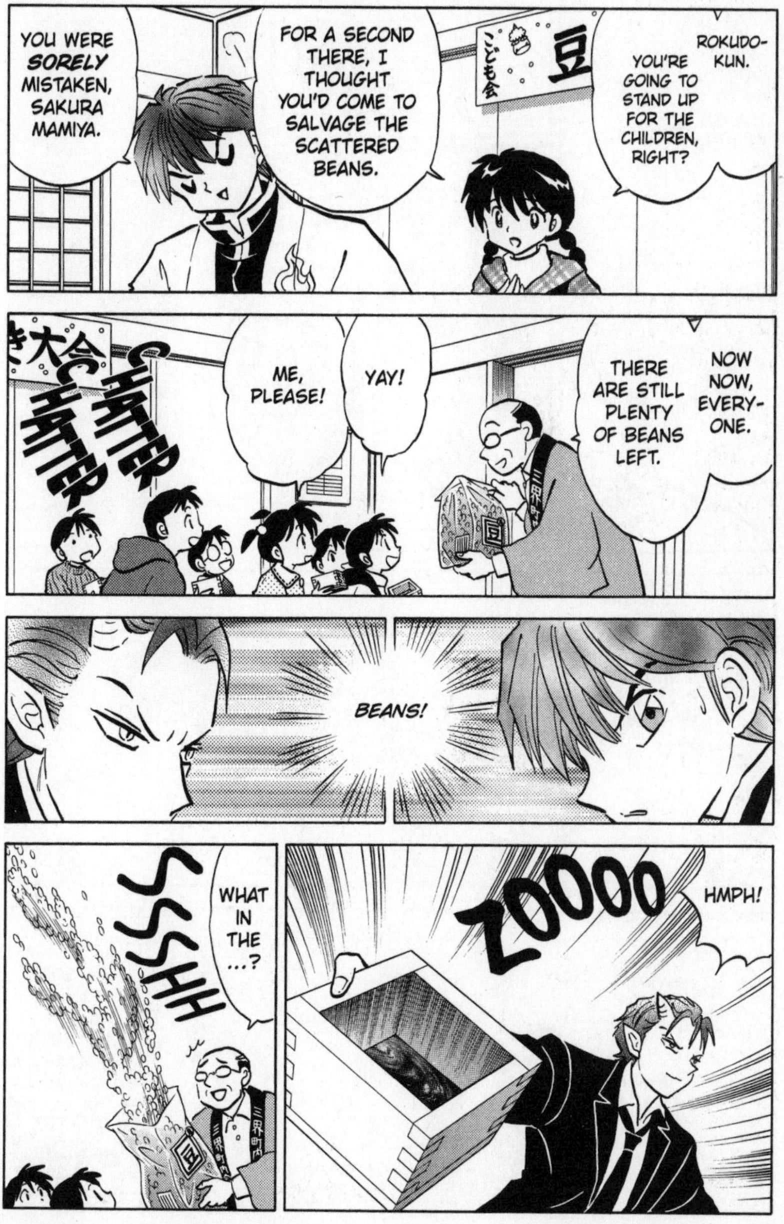

こども会
豆
ROKUDO-KUN.
YOU'RE GOING TO STAND UP FOR THE CHILDREN, RIGHT?
FOR A SECOND THERE, I THOUGHT YOU'D COME TO SALVAGE THE SCATTERED BEANS.
YOU WERE SORELY MISTAKEN, SAKURA MAMIYA.
NOW NOW, EVERYONE.
THERE ARE STILL PLENTY OF BEANS LEFT.
YAY!
ME, PLEASE!
CHATTER CHATTER
BEANS!
HMPH!
ZOOOO
WHAT IN THE ...?
SSSHH

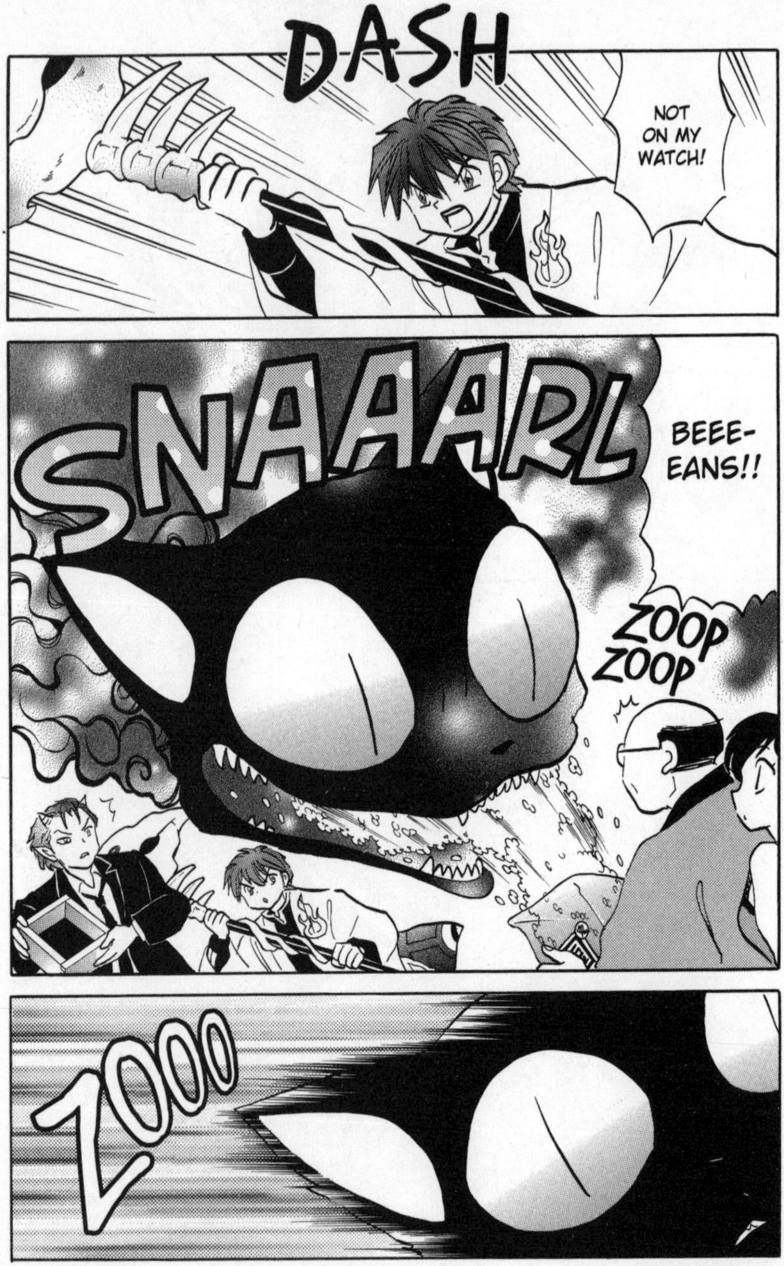
DASH
NOT ON MY WATCH!
SNAAARL
BEEE-EANS!!
ZOOP ZOOP
ZOOO

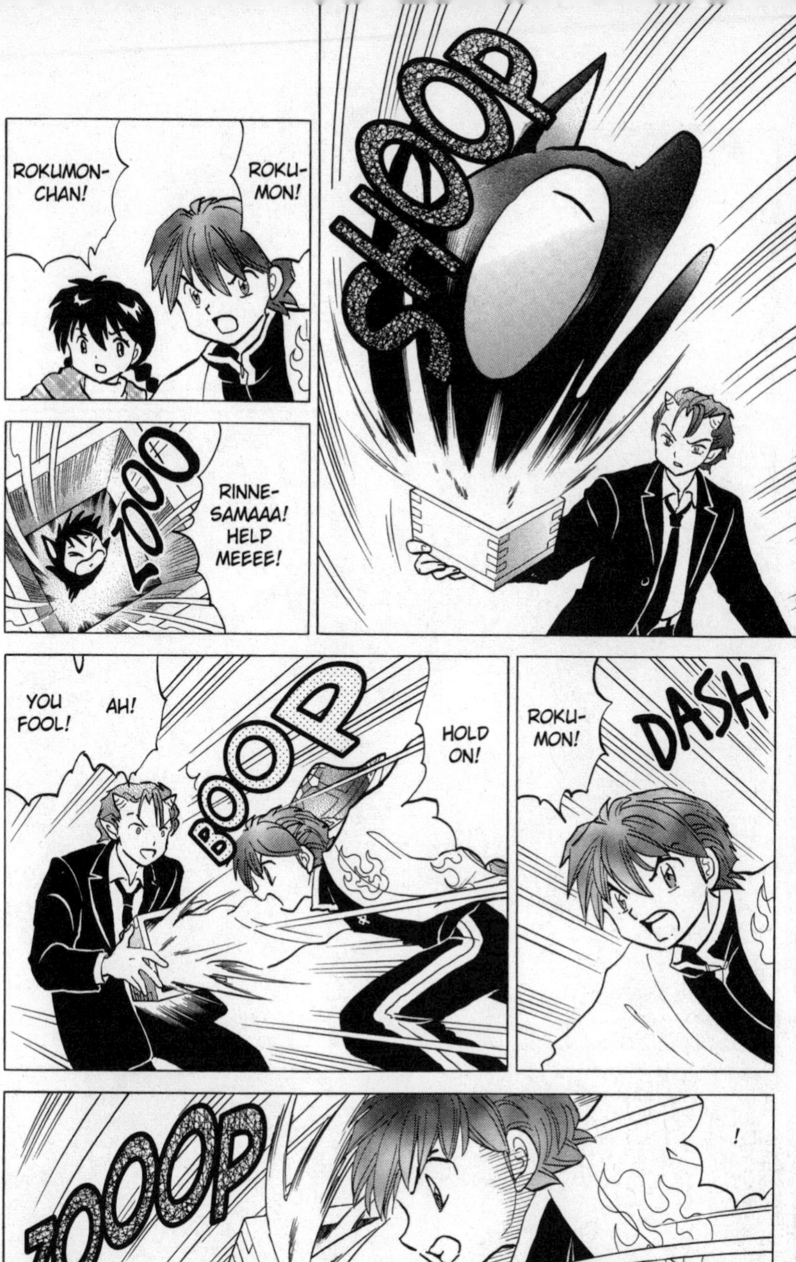
SHOOP
ROKU-MON!
ROKUMON-CHAN!
RINNE-SAMAAA! HELP MEEEE!
ZOOO
DASH
ROKU-MON!
HOLD ON!
BOOOP
AH!
YOU FOOL!
!
ZOOOOP

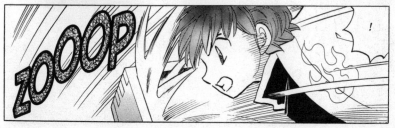

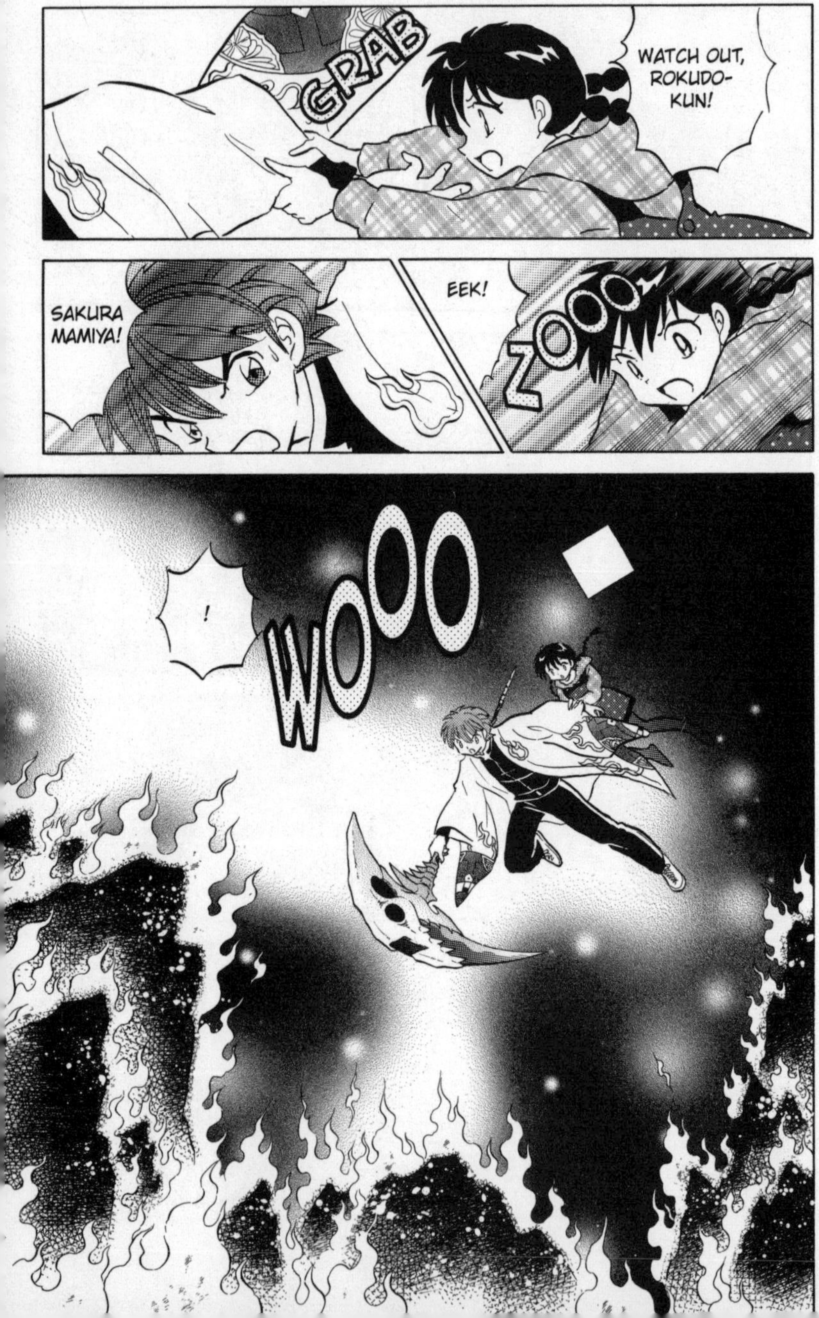
WATCH OUT, ROKUDO-KUN!
GRAB
EEK!
ZOOOO
SAKURA MAMIYA!
!
WOOO

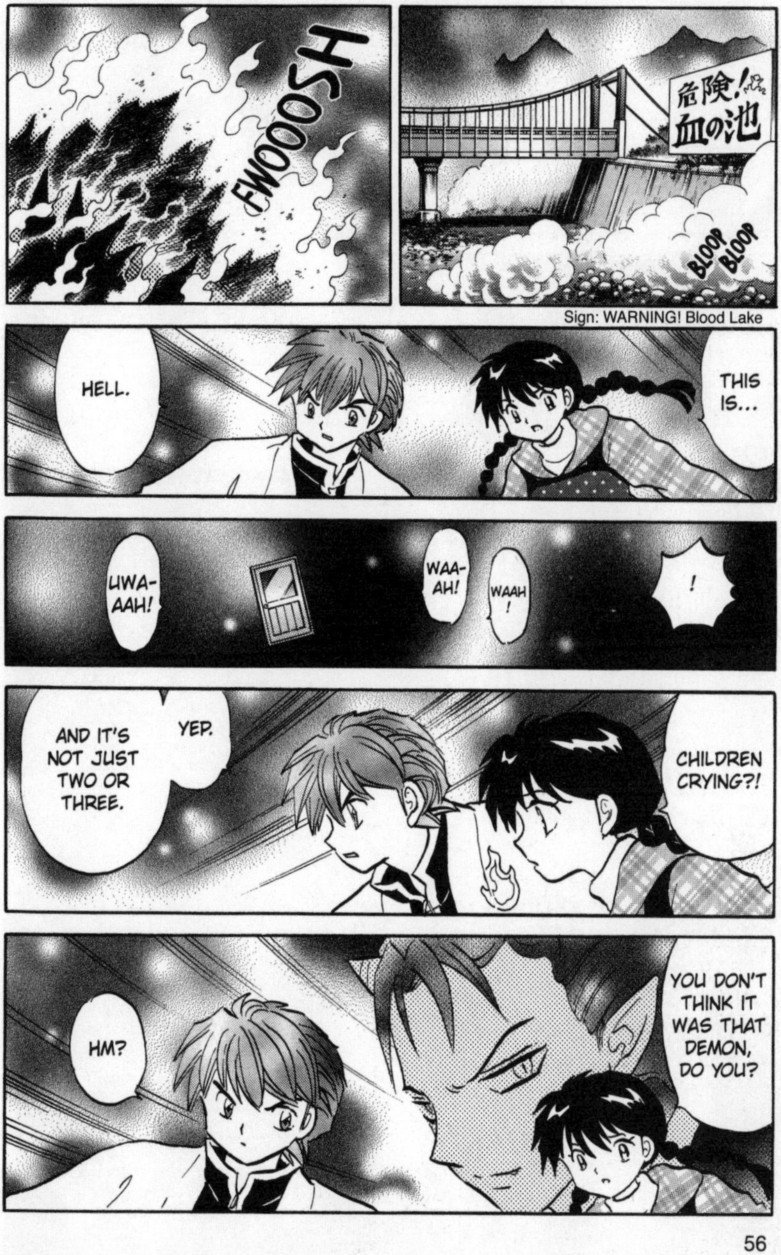
危険！血の池
BLOOP BLOOP
FWOOOSH
Sign: WARNING! Blood Lake
THIS IS...
HELL.
!
WAAH!
WAA-AH!
UWA-AAH!
CHILDREN CRYING?!
YEP.
AND IT'S NOT JUST TWO OR THREE.
YOU DON'T THINK IT WAS THAT DEMON, DO YOU?
HM?

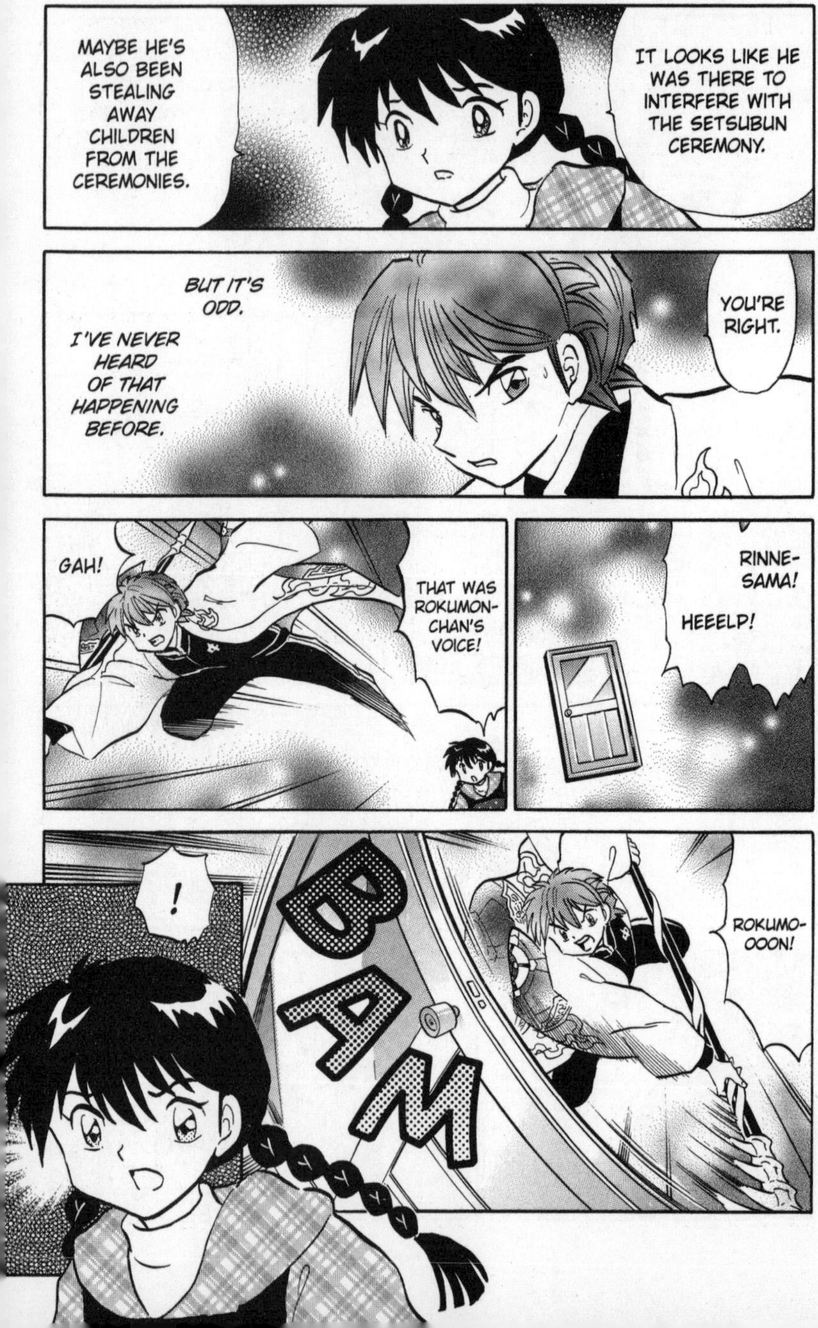
IT LOOKS LIKE HE WAS THERE TO INTERFERE WITH THE SETSUBUN CEREMONY.
MAYBE HE'S ALSO BEEN STEALING AWAY CHILDREN FROM THE CEREMONIES.
YOU'RE RIGHT.
BUT IT'S ODD.
I'VE NEVER HEARD OF THAT HAPPENING BEFORE.
RINNE-SAMA!
HEEELP!
THAT WAS ROKUMON-CHAN'S VOICE!
GAH!
ROKUMO-OOON!
BAM
!

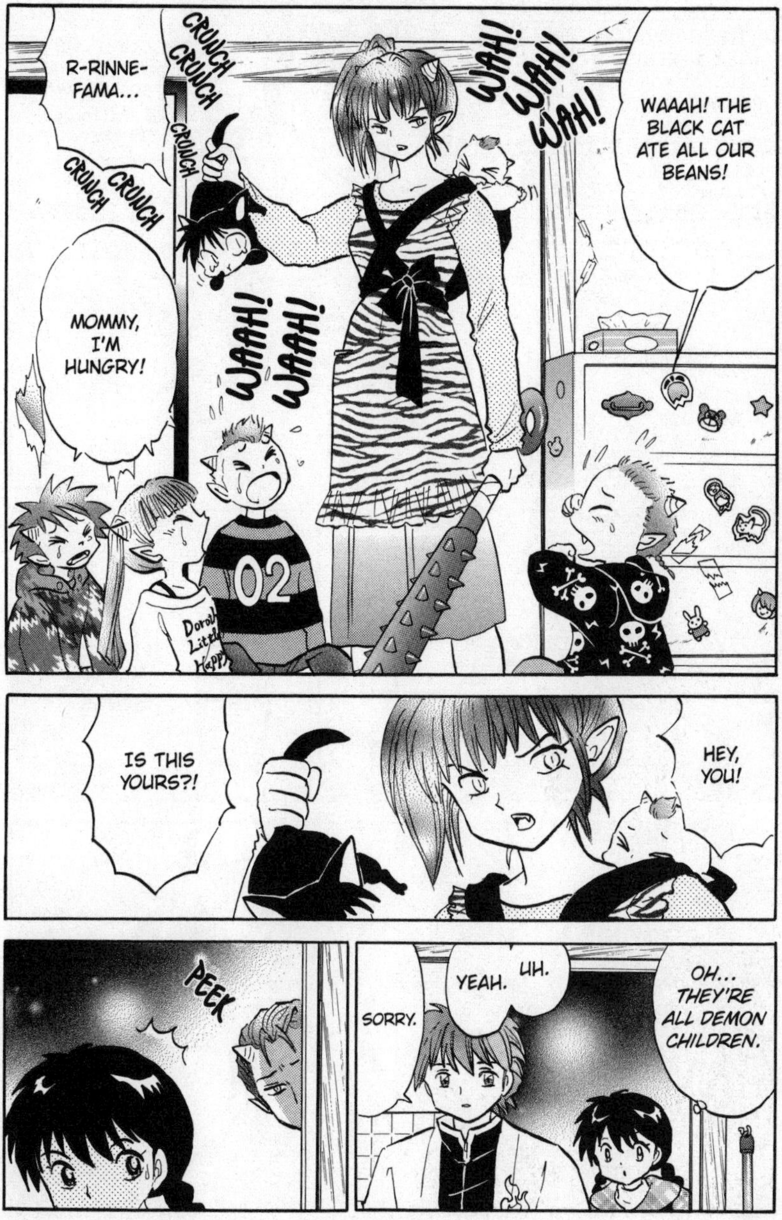
WAAAH! THE BLACK CAT ATE ALL OUR BEANS!
WAH! WAH! WAH!
CRUNCH CRUNCH CRUNCH
R-RINNE-FAMA...
CRUNCH CRUNCH CRUNCH
WAAAH! WAAAH!
MOMMY, I'M HUNGRY!
HEY, YOU!
IS THIS YOURS?!
OH... THEY'RE ALL DEMON CHILDREN.
UH.
YEAH.
SORRY.
PEEK

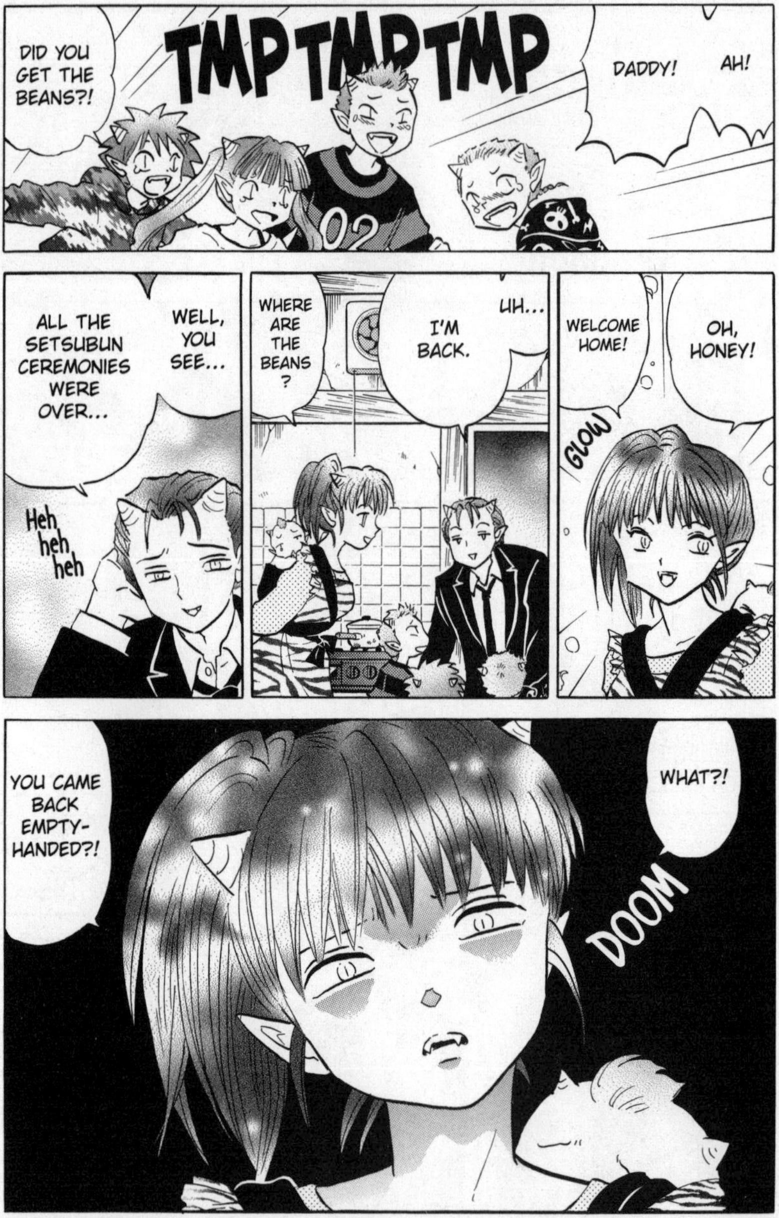
AH!
DADDY!
TMP TMP TMP
DID YOU GET THE BEANS?!
OH, HONEY!
WELCOME HOME!
GLOW
UH...
I'M BACK.
WHERE ARE THE BEANS?
WELL, YOU SEE...
ALL THE SETSUBUN CEREMONIES WERE OVER...
Heh heh heh
WHAT?!
DOOM
YOU CAME BACK EMPTY-HANDED?!

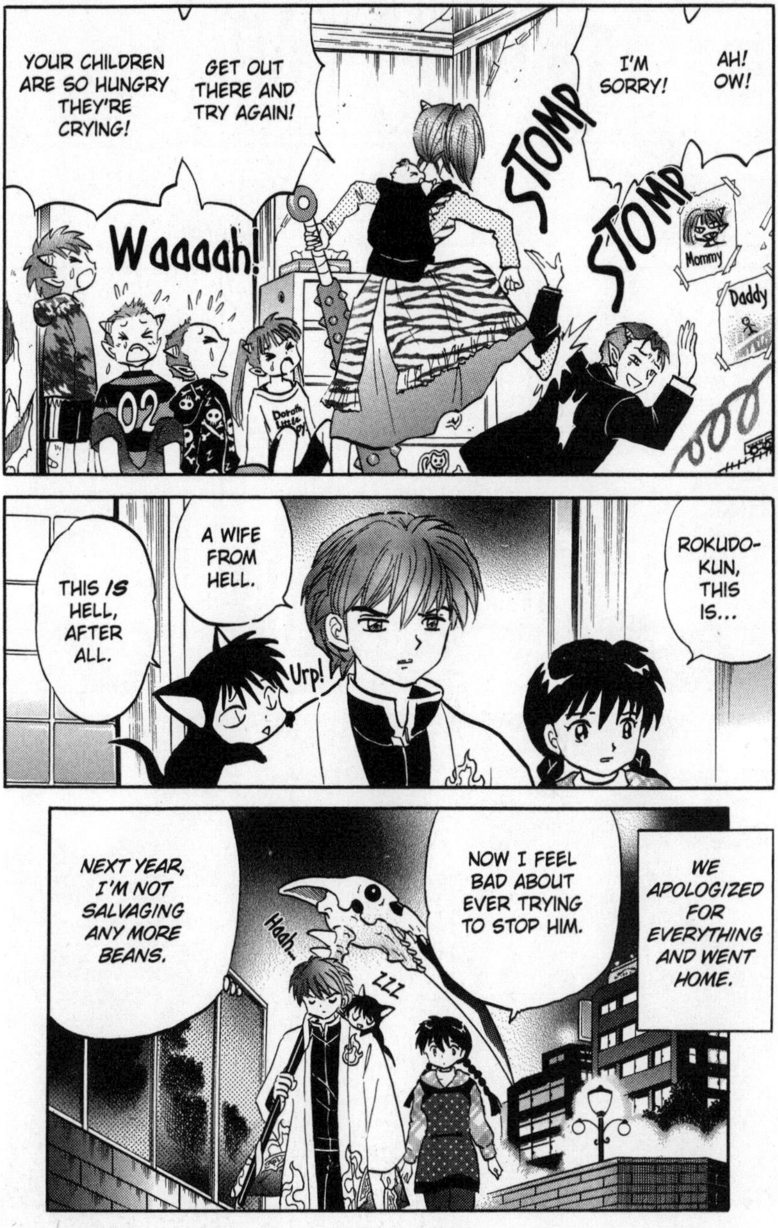
AH! OW!
I'M SORRY!
STOMP
STOMP
Mommy
Daddy
GET OUT THERE AND TRY AGAIN!
YOUR CHILDREN ARE SO HUNGRY THEY'RE CRYING!
Waaaah!
ROKUDO-KUN, THIS IS...
A WIFE FROM HELL.
THIS *IS* HELL, AFTER ALL.
Urp!
WE APOLOGIZED FOR EVERYTHING AND WENT HOME.
NOW I FEEL BAD ABOUT EVER TRYING TO STOP HIM.
NEXT YEAR, I'M NOT SALVAGING ANY MORE BEANS.
Haah...
ZZZ

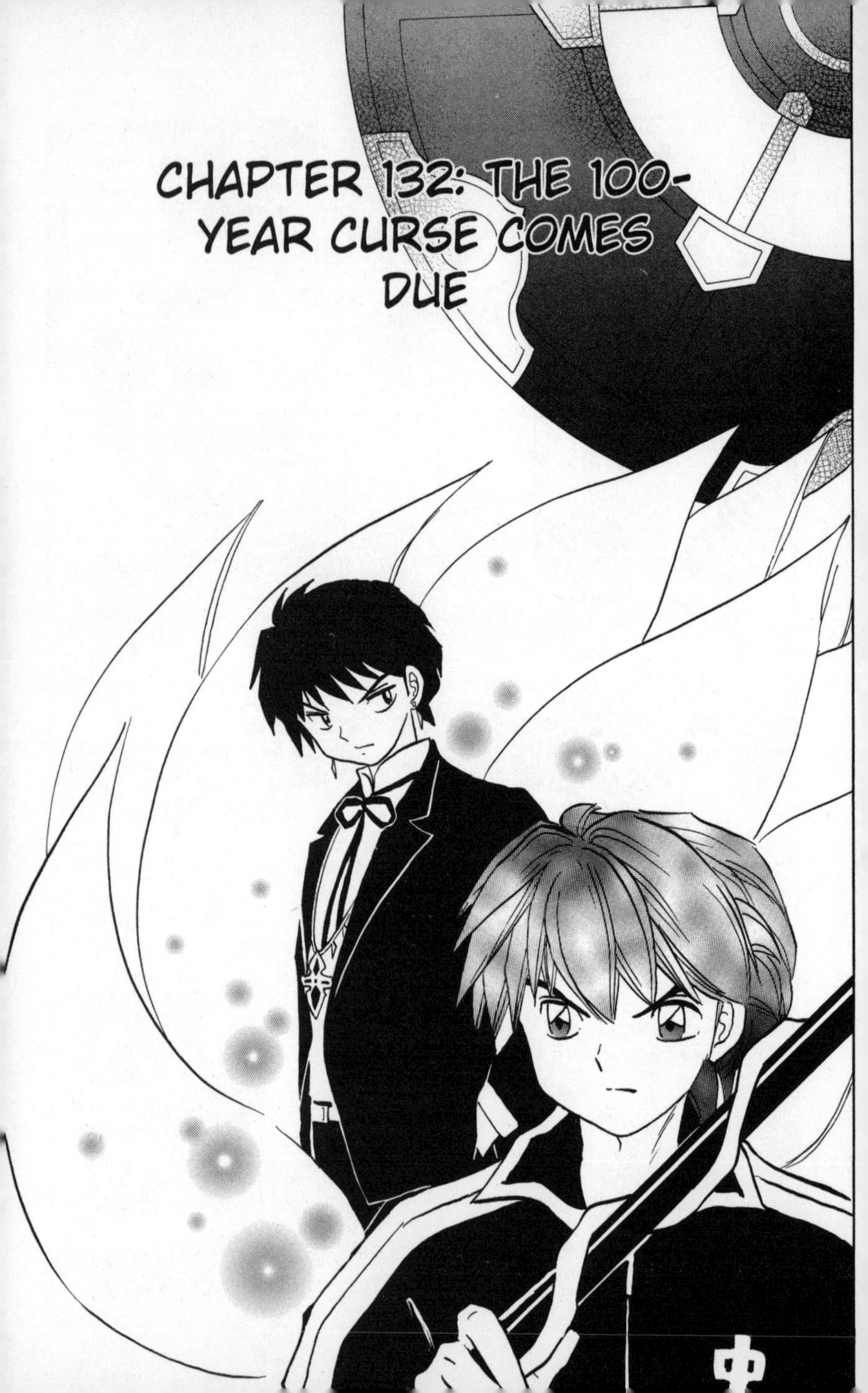
CHAPTER 132: THE 100-YEAR CURSE COMES DUE

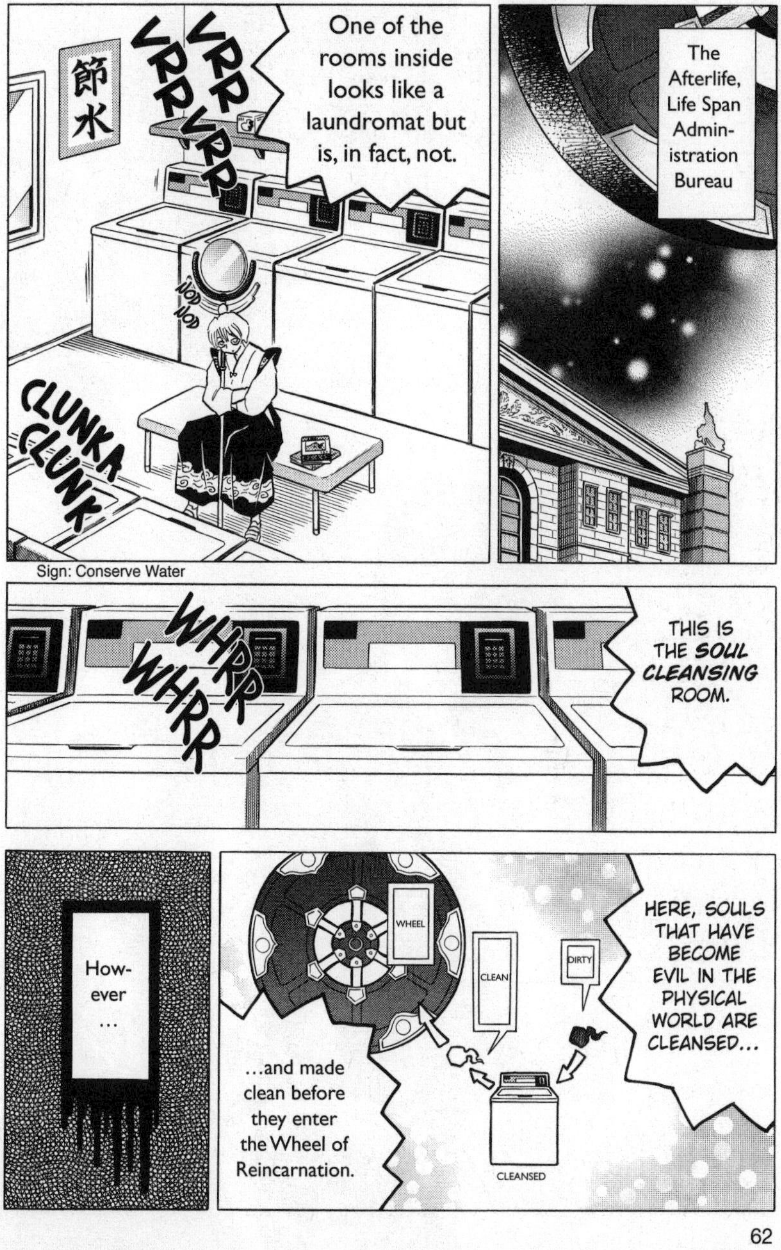
The Afterlife, Life Span Administration Bureau
One of the rooms inside looks like a laundromat but is, in fact, not.
VRR VRR
VRR VRR
節水
NOD NOD
CLUNKA CLUNK
THIS IS THE ***SOUL CLEANSING*** ROOM.
WHRR WHRR
HERE, SOULS THAT HAVE BECOME EVIL IN THE PHYSICAL WORLD ARE CLEANSED…
WHEEL
DIRTY
CLEAN
CLEANSED
…and made clean before they enter the Wheel of Reincarnation.
How-ever…
Sign: Conserve Water

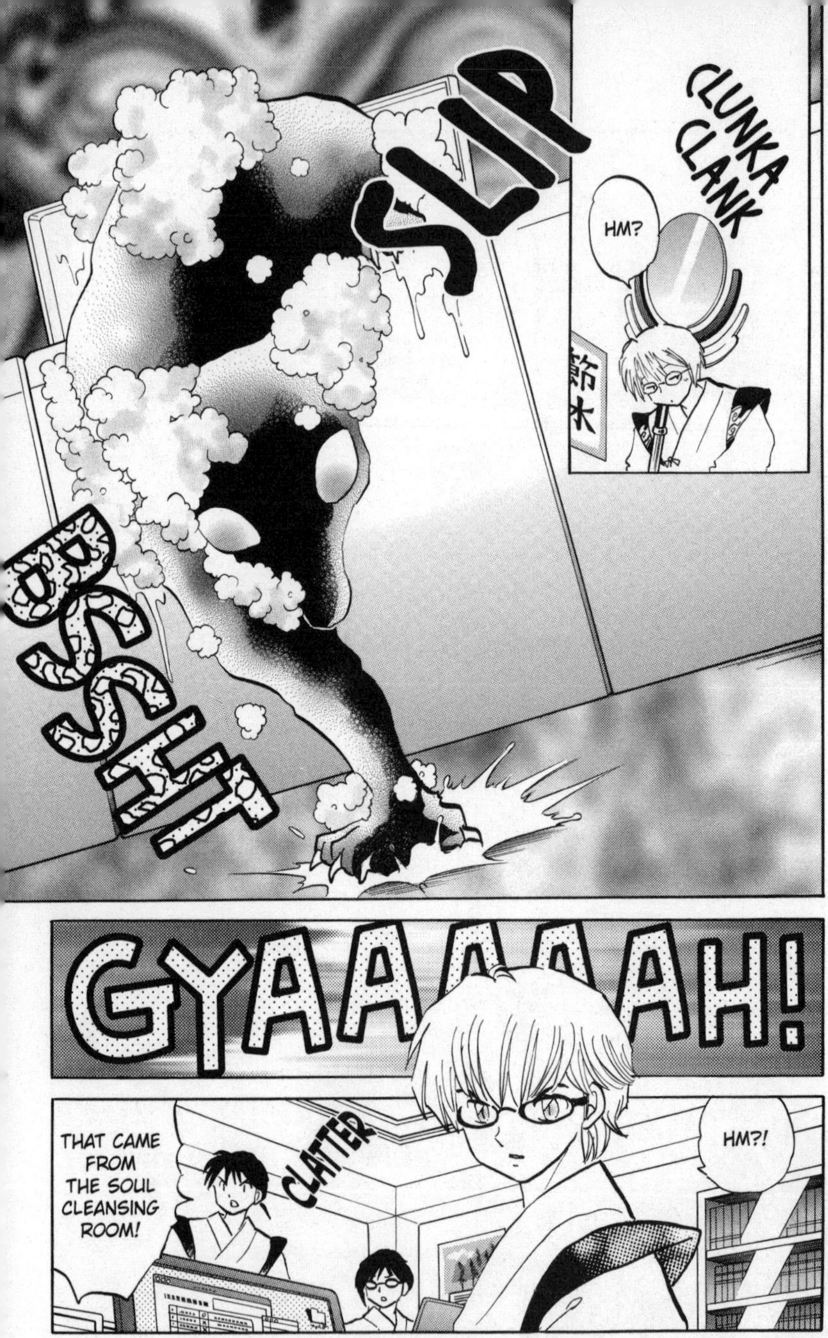
CLUNKA CLANK
HM?
節水
SLIP
BSSHT
GYAAAAAH!
HM?!
CLATTER
THAT CAME FROM THE SOUL CLEANSING ROOM!

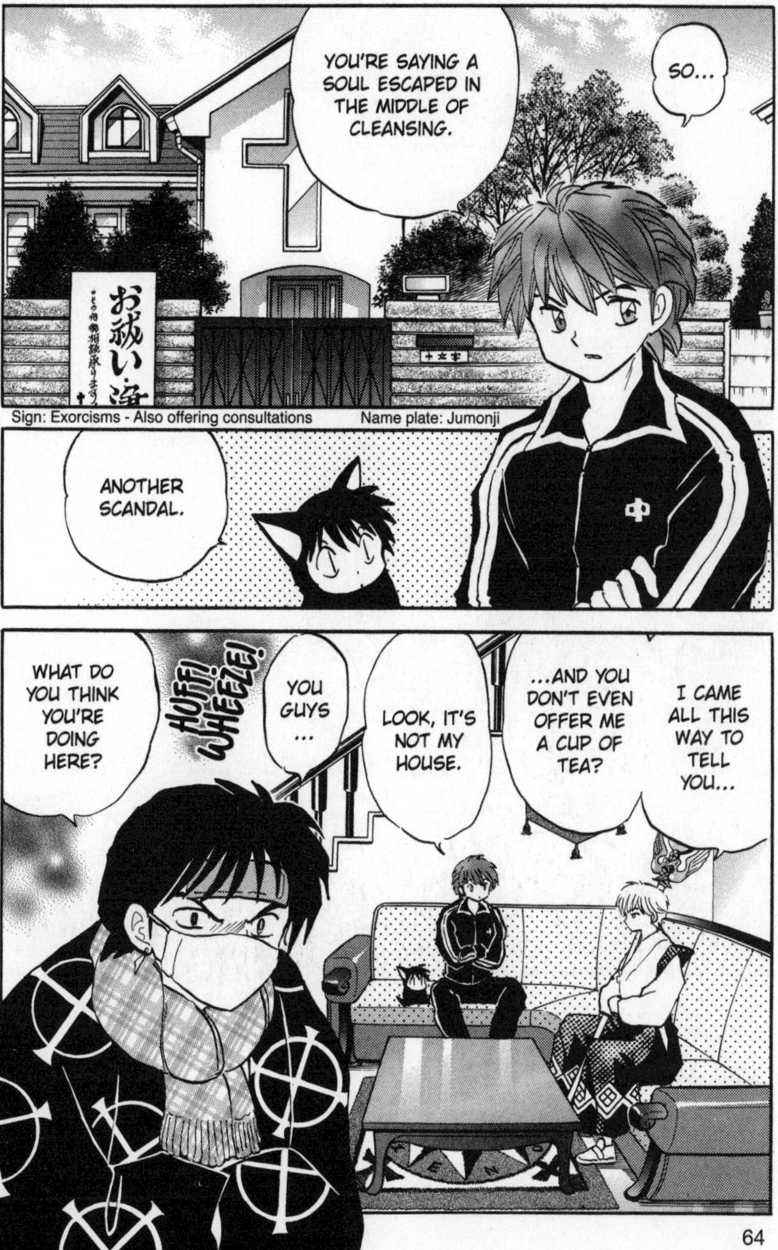
SO...
YOU'RE SAYING A SOUL ESCAPED IN THE MIDDLE OF CLEANSING.
Sign: Exorcisms - Also offering consultations
Name plate: Jumonji
ANOTHER SCANDAL.
I CAME ALL THIS WAY TO TELL YOU...
...AND YOU DON'T EVEN OFFER ME A CUP OF TEA?
LOOK, IT'S NOT MY HOUSE.
YOU GUYS...
HUFF! WHEEZE!
WHAT DO YOU THINK YOU'RE DOING HERE?

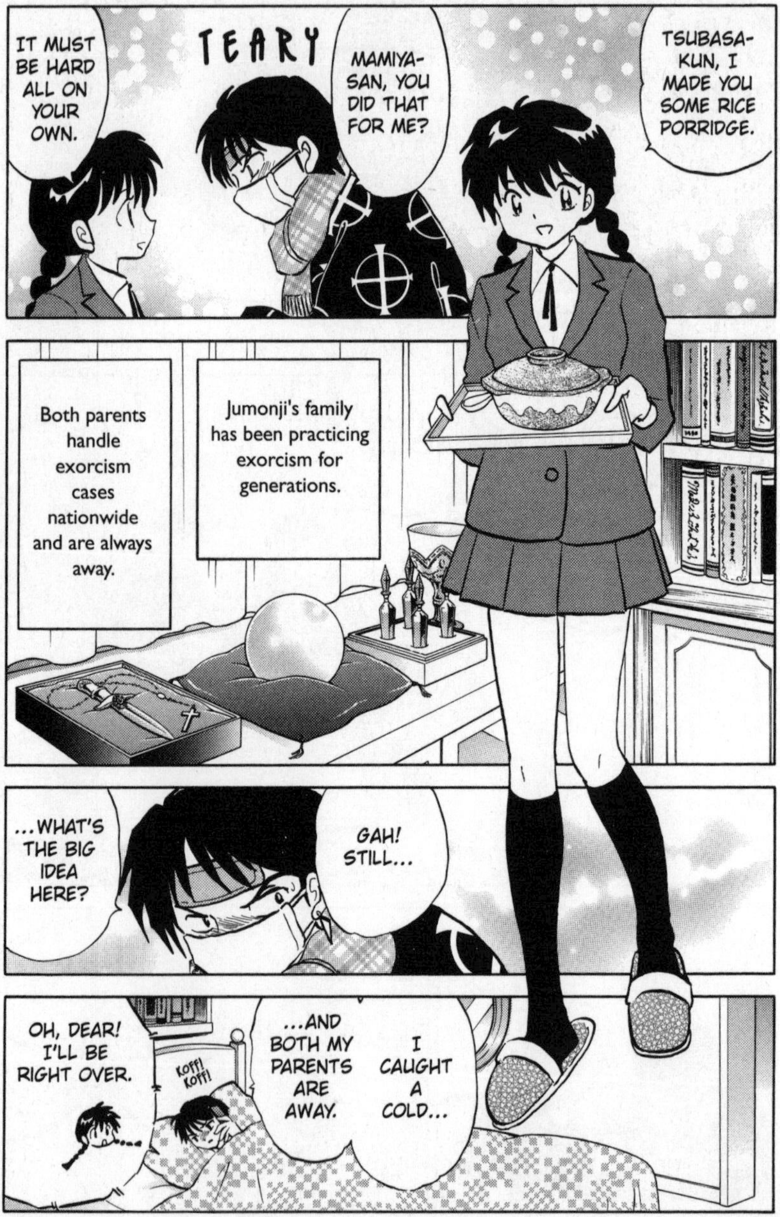
TSUBASA-KUN, I MADE YOU SOME RICE PORRIDGE.
MAMIYA-SAN, YOU DID THAT FOR ME?
TEARY
IT MUST BE HARD ALL ON YOUR OWN.
Jumonji's family has been practicing exorcism for generations.
Both parents handle exorcism cases nationwide and are always away.
GAH! STILL...
...WHAT'S THE BIG IDEA HERE?
I CAUGHT A COLD...
...AND BOTH MY PARENTS ARE AWAY.
KOFF! KOFF!
OH, DEAR! I'LL BE RIGHT OVER.

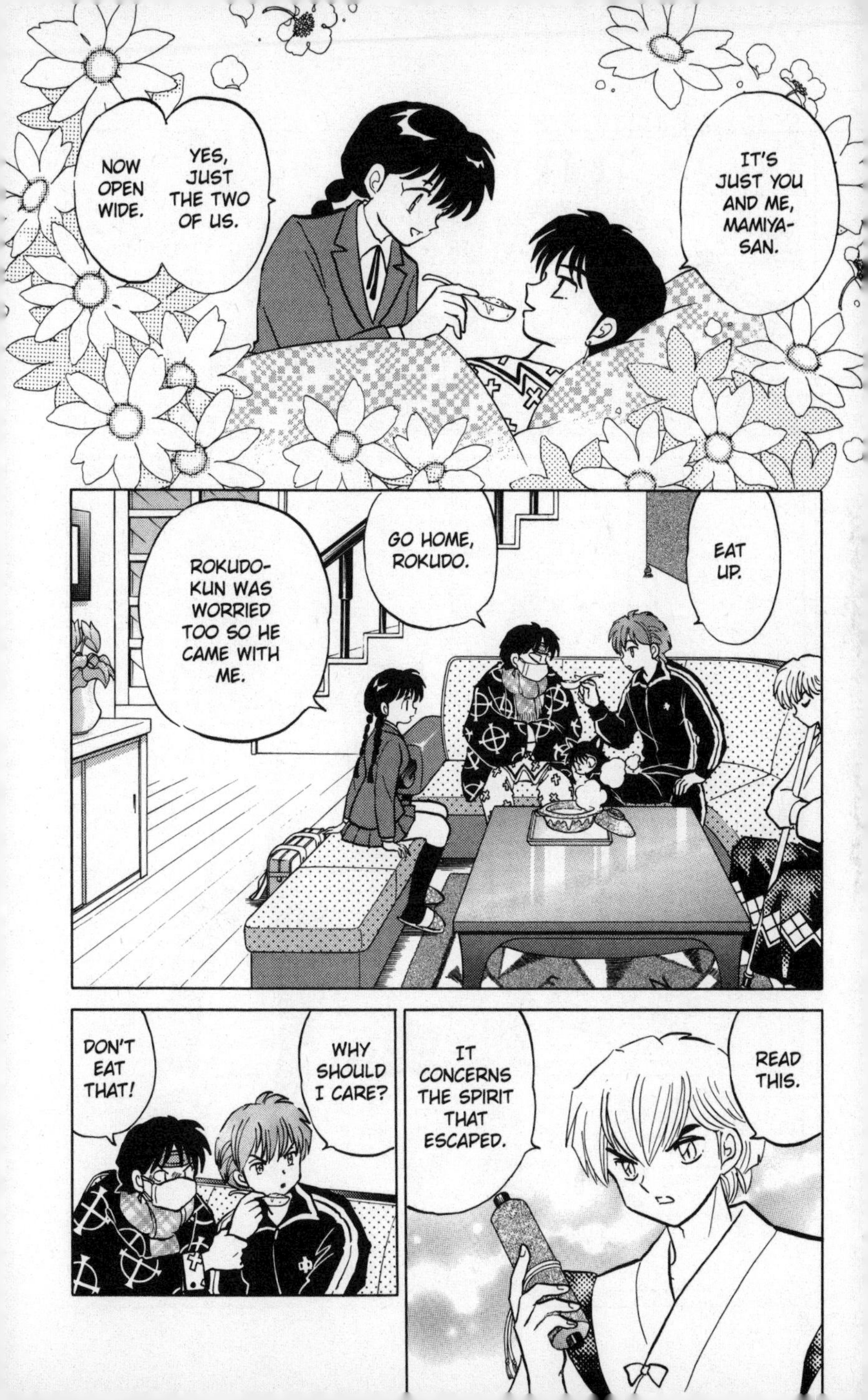
IT'S JUST YOU AND ME, MAMIYA-SAN.
YES, JUST THE TWO OF US.
NOW OPEN WIDE.
EAT UP.
GO HOME, ROKUDO.
ROKUDO-KUN WAS WORRIED TOO SO HE CAME WITH ME.
READ THIS.
IT CONCERNS THE SPIRIT THAT ESCAPED.
WHY SHOULD I CARE?
DON'T EAT THAT!

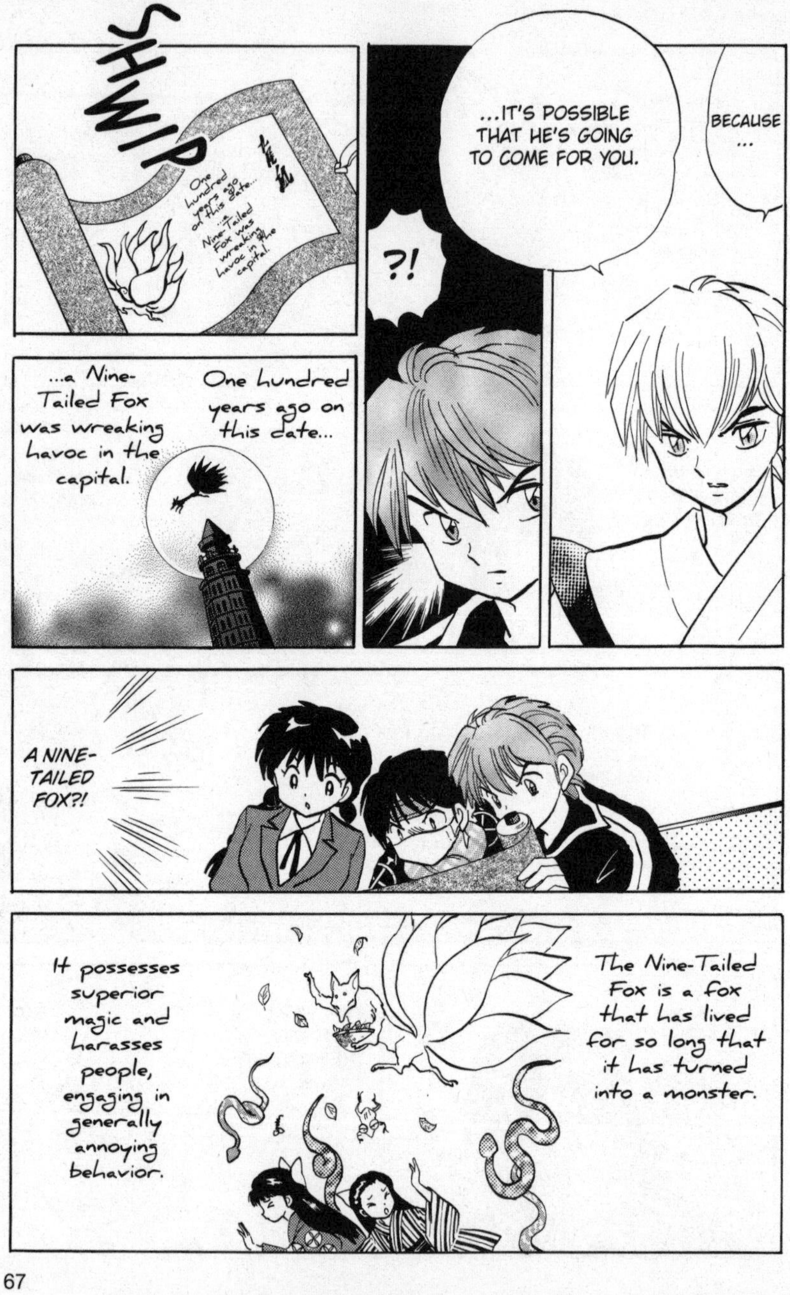
BECAUSE ...
...IT'S POSSIBLE THAT HE'S GOING TO COME FOR YOU.
?!
SHWIP
One hundred years ago on this date... ...a Nine-Tailed Fox was wreaking havoc in the capital.
One hundred years ago on this date...
...a Nine-Tailed Fox was wreaking havoc in the capital.
A NINE-TAILED FOX?!
The Nine-Tailed Fox is a fox that has lived for so long that it has turned into a monster.
It possesses superior magic and harasses people, engaging in generally annoying behavior.

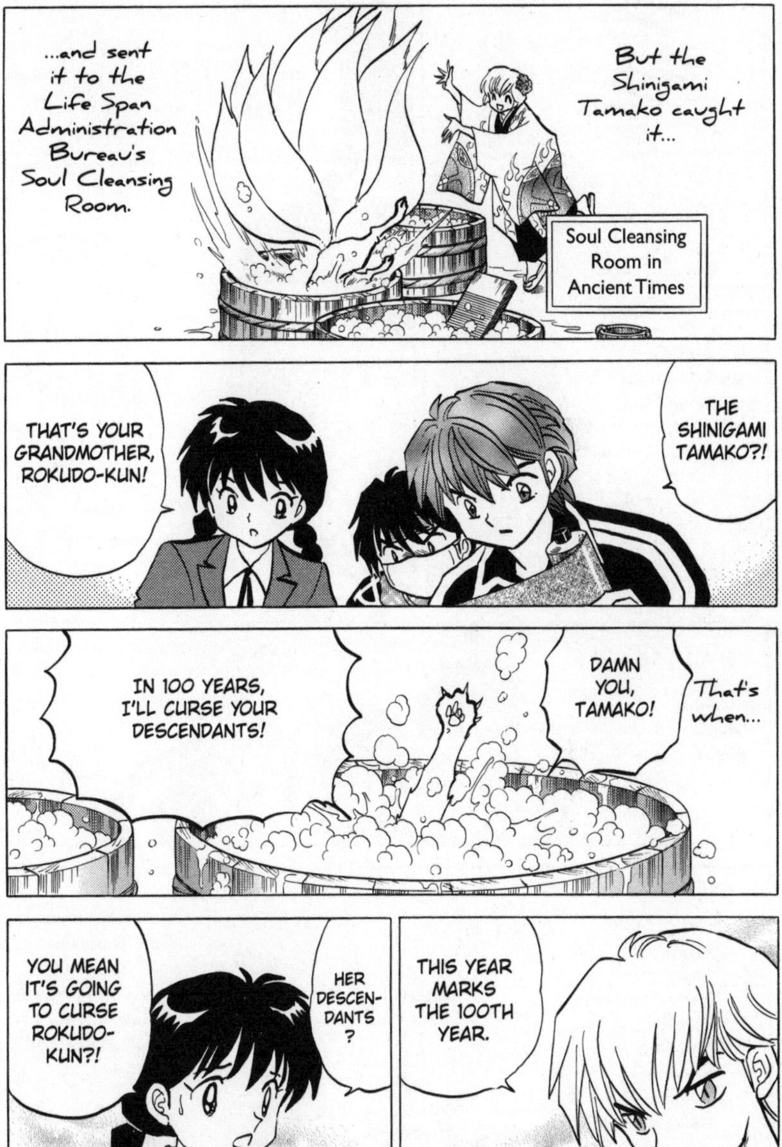
But the Shinigami Tamako caught it...
...and sent it to the Life Span Administration Bureau's Soul Cleansing Room.
Soul Cleansing Room in Ancient Times
THE SHINIGAMI TAMAKO?!
THAT'S YOUR GRANDMOTHER, ROKUDO-KUN!
That's when...
DAMN YOU, TAMAKO!
IN 100 YEARS, I'LL CURSE YOUR DESCENDANTS!
THIS YEAR MARKS THE 100TH YEAR.
HER DESCEN-DANTS?
YOU MEAN IT'S GOING TO CURSE ROKUDO-KUN?!

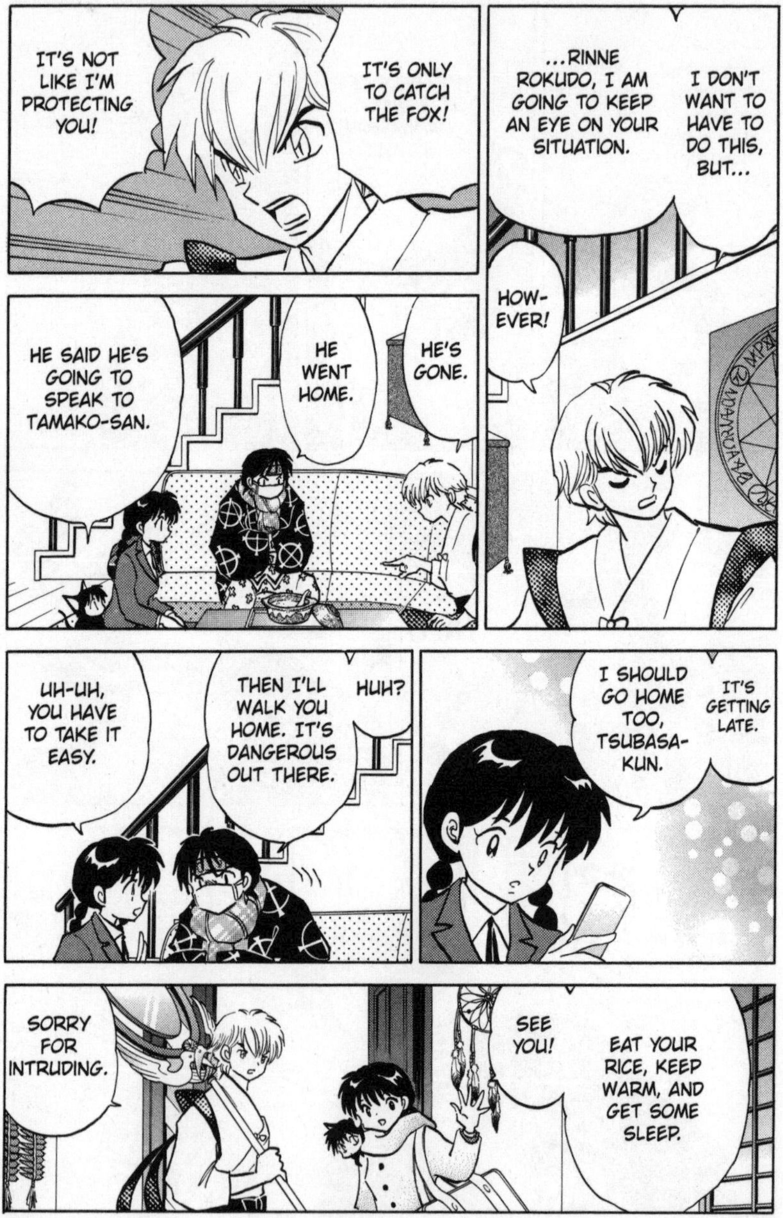
I DON'T WANT TO HAVE TO DO THIS, BUT...
...RINNE ROKUDO, I AM GOING TO KEEP AN EYE ON YOUR SITUATION.
HOW-EVER!
IT'S ONLY TO CATCH THE FOX!
IT'S NOT LIKE I'M PROTECTING YOU!
HE'S GONE.
HE WENT HOME.
HE SAID HE'S GOING TO SPEAK TO TAMAKO-SAN.
IT'S GETTING LATE.
I SHOULD GO HOME TOO, TSUBASA-KUN.
HUH?
THEN I'LL WALK YOU HOME. IT'S DANGEROUS OUT THERE.
UH-UH, YOU HAVE TO TAKE IT EASY.
EAT YOUR RICE, KEEP WARM, AND GET SOME SLEEP.
SEE YOU!
SORRY FOR INTRUDING.

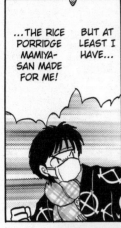

HAAH...
WHAT GIVES?
GRR
I BARELY GOT TO SPEAK TO MAMIYA-SAN AT ALL!
BUT AT LEAST I HAVE...
...THE RICE PORRIDGE MAMIYA-SAN MADE FOR ME!
SLURP SLURP
ROKUDO, YOU LITTLE...
EMPTY
TODAY'S THE DAY...
SHI'ING
...YOU DON'T GET AWAY WITH IT!

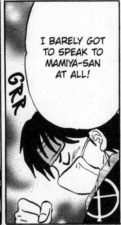

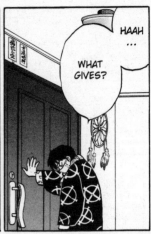

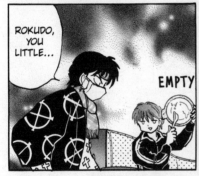

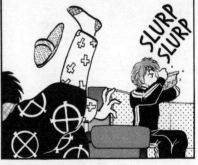

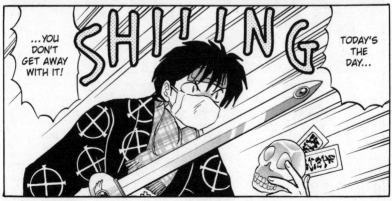

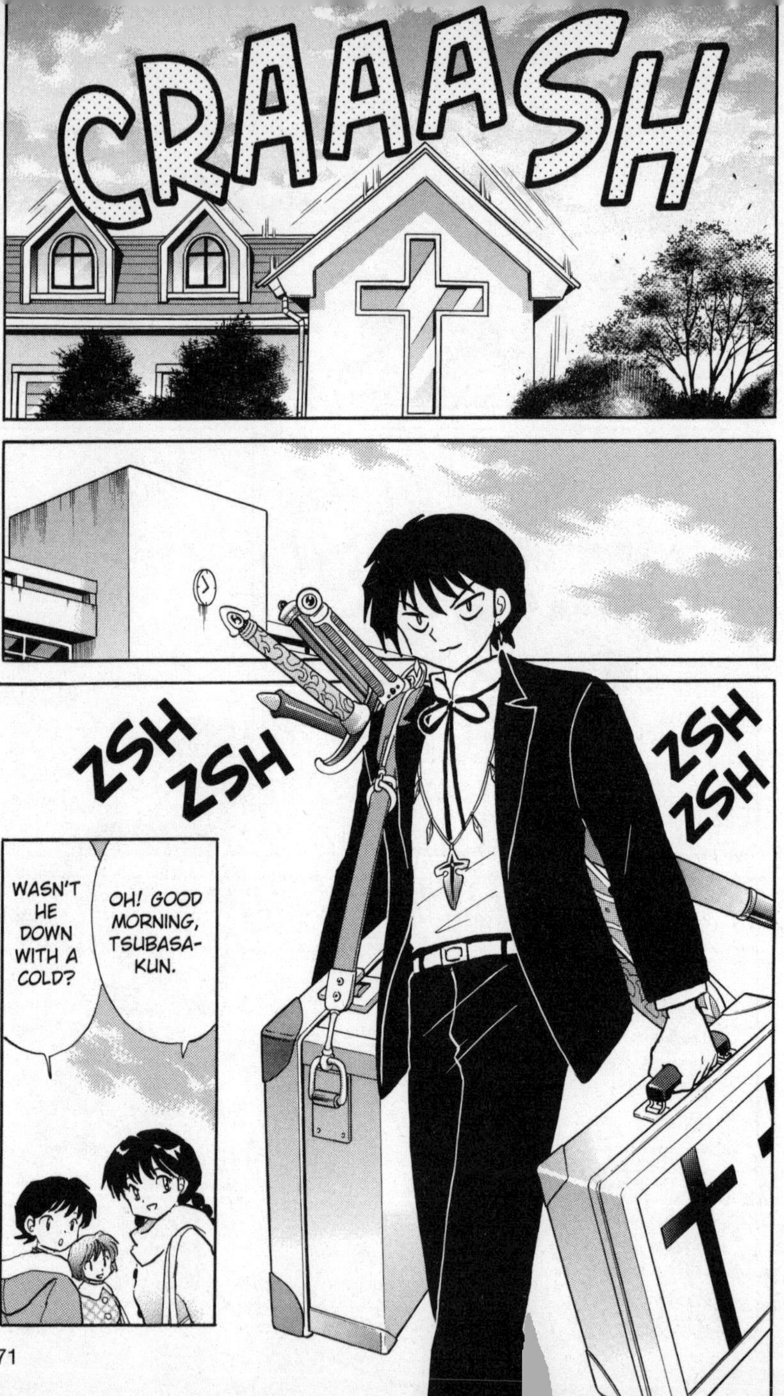
CRAAASH
ZSH ZSH
ZSH ZSH
OH! GOOD MORNING, TSUBASA-KUN.
WASN'T HE DOWN WITH A COLD?

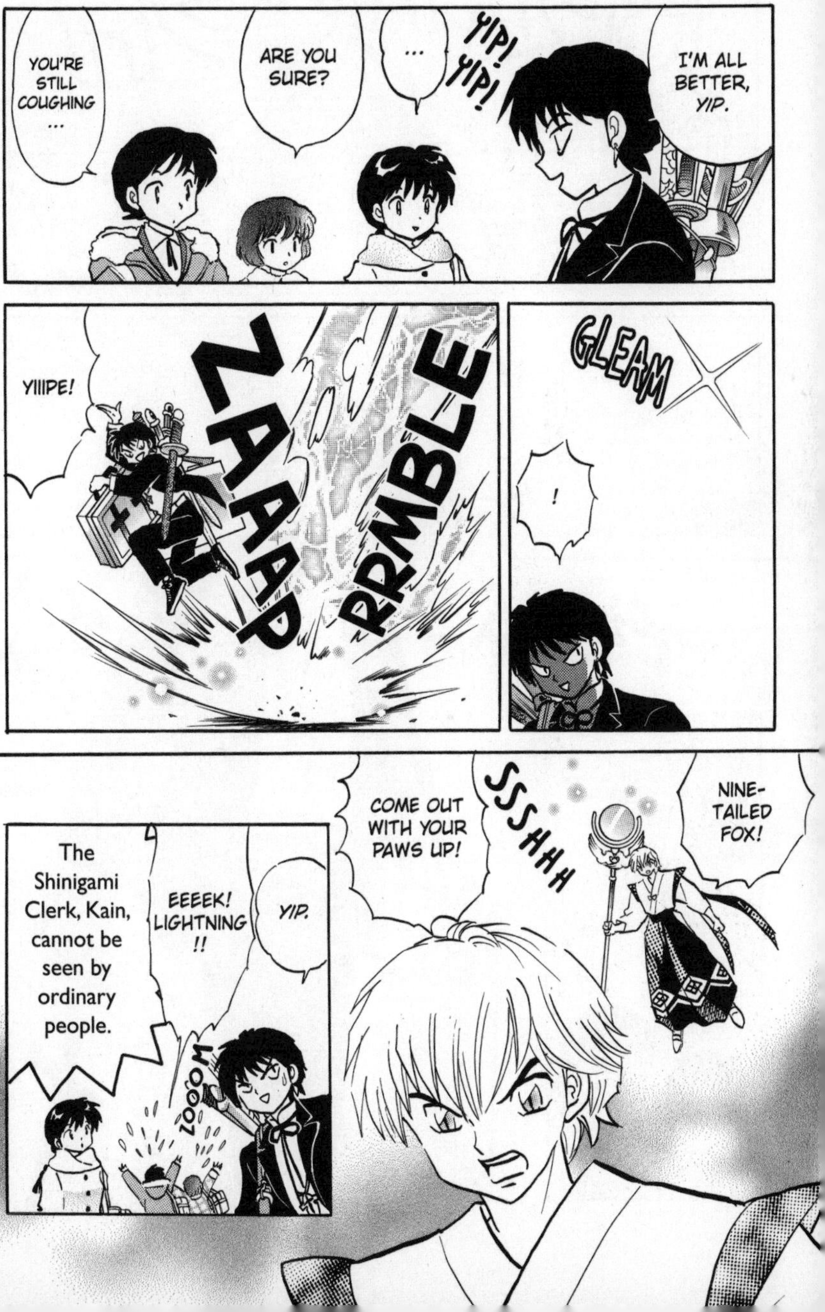
I'M ALL BETTER, YIP.
YIP! YIP!
...
ARE YOU SURE?
YOU'RE STILL COUGHING ...
GLEAM
!
RRMBLE
ZAAAP
YIIIPE!
NINE-TAILED FOX!
SSSHHH
COME OUT WITH YOUR PAWS UP!
YIP.
EEEEK! LIGHTNING !!
ZOOOM
The Shinigami Clerk, Kain, cannot be seen by ordinary people.

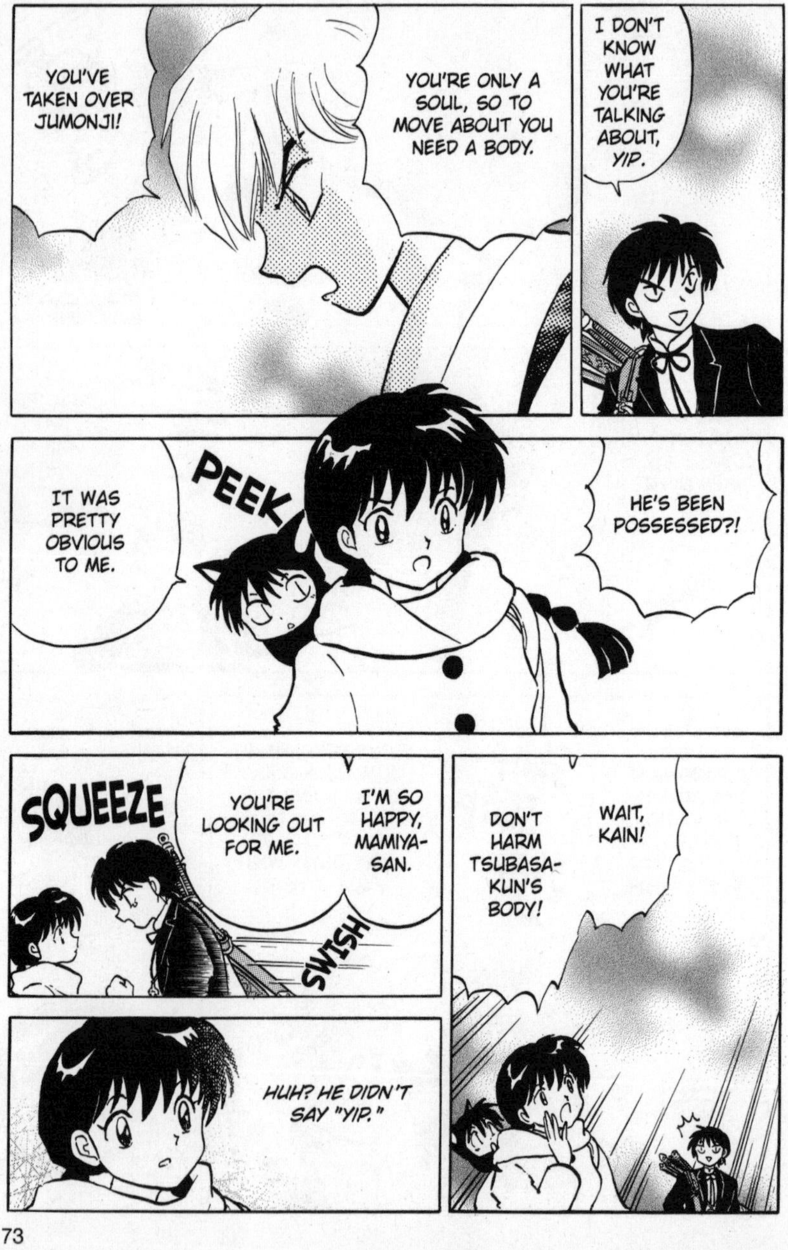
I DON'T KNOW WHAT YOU'RE TALKING ABOUT, YIP.
YOU'RE ONLY A SOUL, SO TO MOVE ABOUT YOU NEED A BODY.
YOU'VE TAKEN OVER JUMONJI!
HE'S BEEN POSSESSED?!
PEEK
IT WAS PRETTY OBVIOUS TO ME.
WAIT, KAIN!
DON'T HARM TSUBASA-KUN'S BODY!
I'M SO HAPPY, MAMIYA-SAN.
YOU'RE LOOKING OUT FOR ME.
SQUEEZE
SWISH
HUH? HE DIDN'T SAY "YIP."

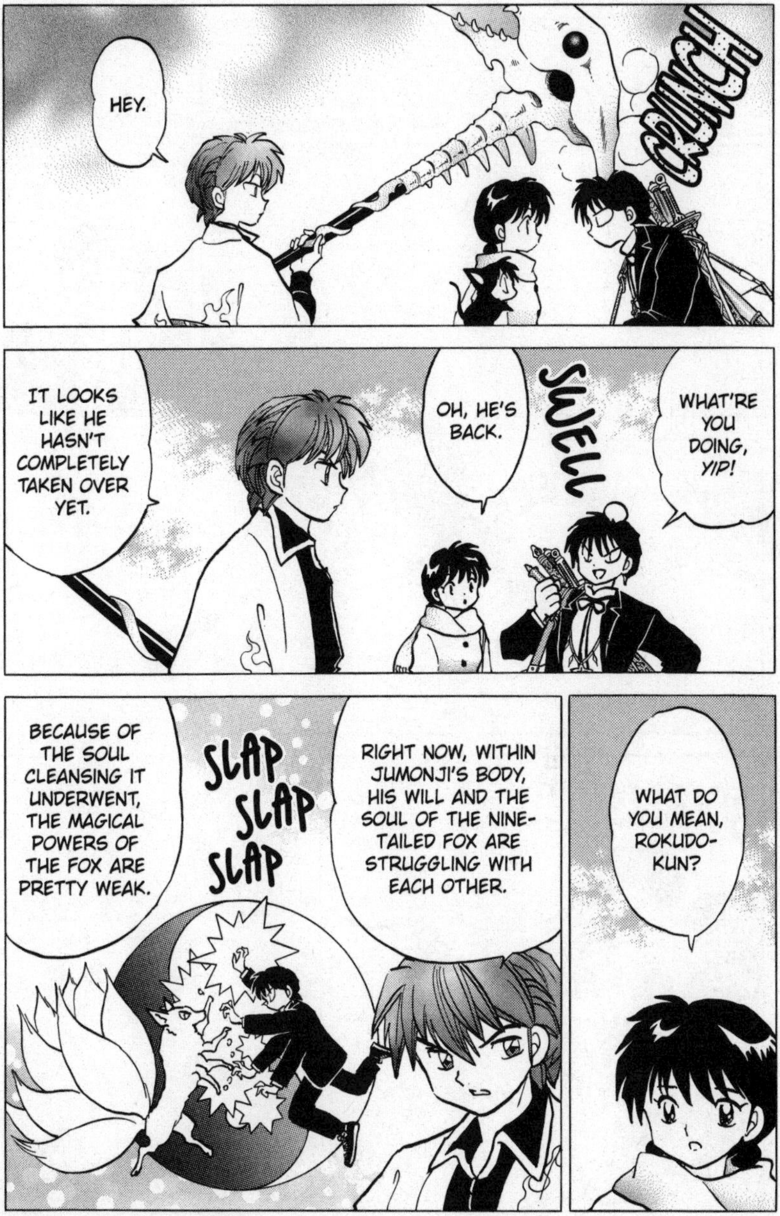
CRUNCH
HEY.
WHAT'RE YOU DOING, YIP!
SWELL
OH, HE'S BACK.
IT LOOKS LIKE HE HASN'T COMPLETELY TAKEN OVER YET.
WHAT DO YOU MEAN, ROKUDO-KUN?
RIGHT NOW, WITHIN JUMONJI'S BODY, HIS WILL AND THE SOUL OF THE NINE-TAILED FOX ARE STRUGGLING WITH EACH OTHER.
SLAP SLAP SLAP
BECAUSE OF THE SOUL CLEANSING IT UNDERWENT, THE MAGICAL POWERS OF THE FOX ARE PRETTY WEAK.

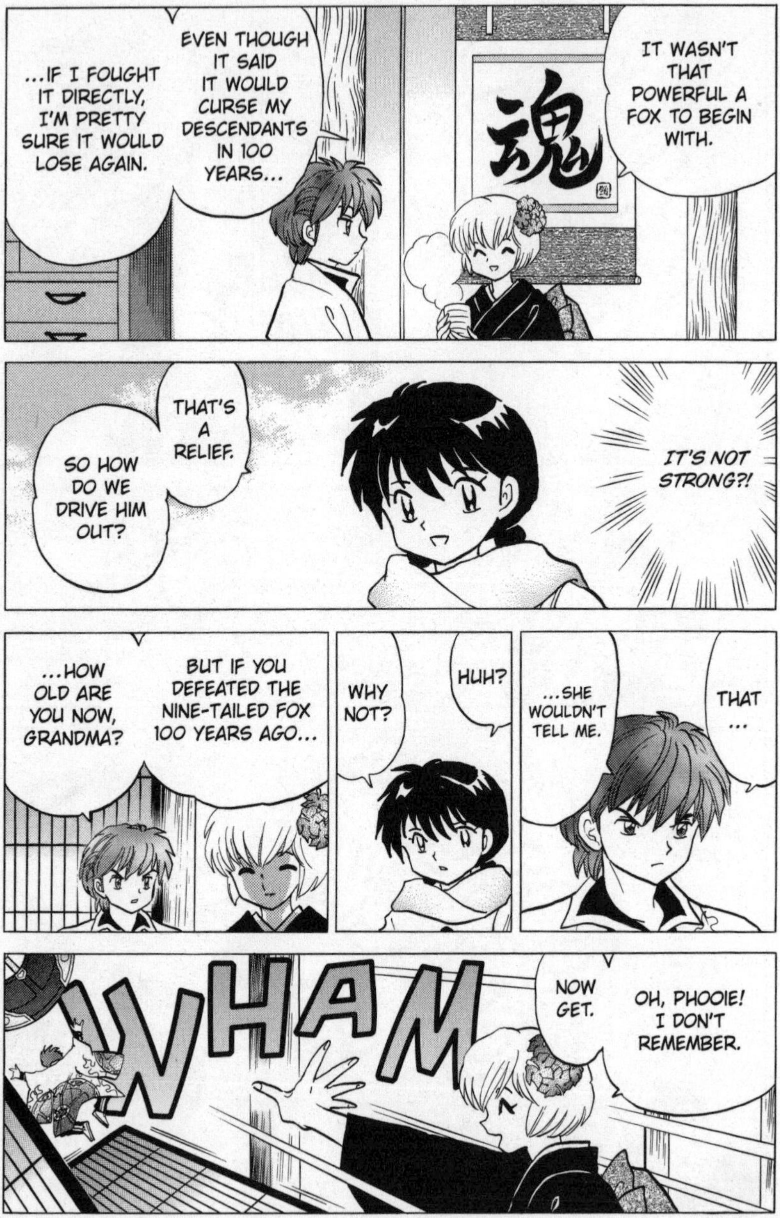
IT WASN'T THAT POWERFUL A FOX TO BEGIN WITH.
EVEN THOUGH IT SAID IT WOULD CURSE MY DESCENDANTS IN 100 YEARS...
...IF I FOUGHT IT DIRECTLY, I'M PRETTY SURE IT WOULD LOSE AGAIN.
IT'S NOT STRONG?!
THAT'S A RELIEF.
SO HOW DO WE DRIVE HIM OUT?
THAT...
...SHE WOULDN'T TELL ME.
HUH?
WHY NOT?
BUT IF YOU DEFEATED THE NINE-TAILED FOX 100 YEARS AGO...
...HOW OLD ARE YOU NOW, GRANDMA?
OH, PHOOIE! I DON'T REMEMBER.
NOW GET.
WHAM

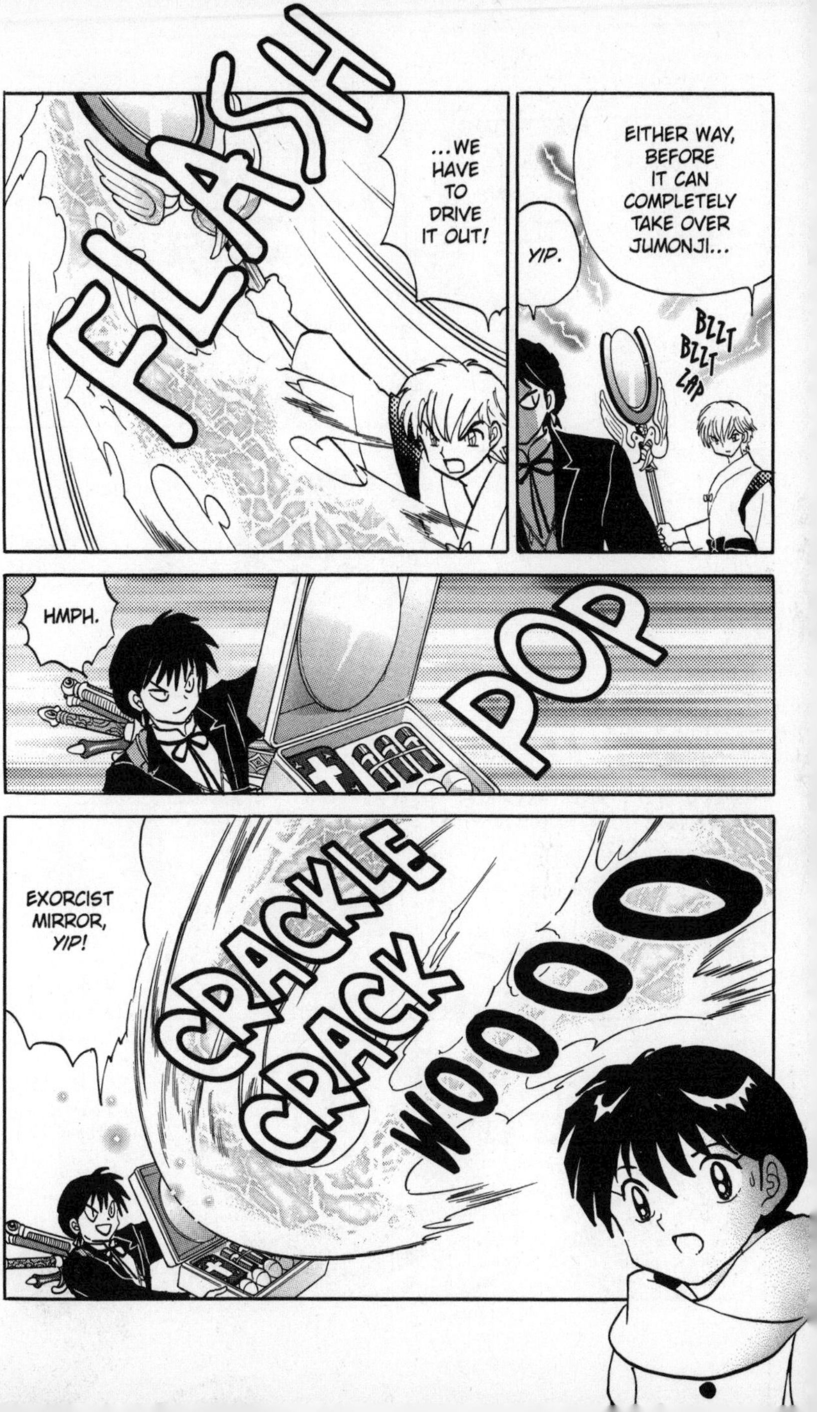
EITHER WAY, BEFORE IT CAN COMPLETELY TAKE OVER JUMONJI...
YIP.
BZZT
BZZT
ZAP
...WE HAVE TO DRIVE IT OUT!
FLASH
POP
HMPH.
WOOOO
CRACKLE
CRACK
EXORCIST MIRROR, YIP!

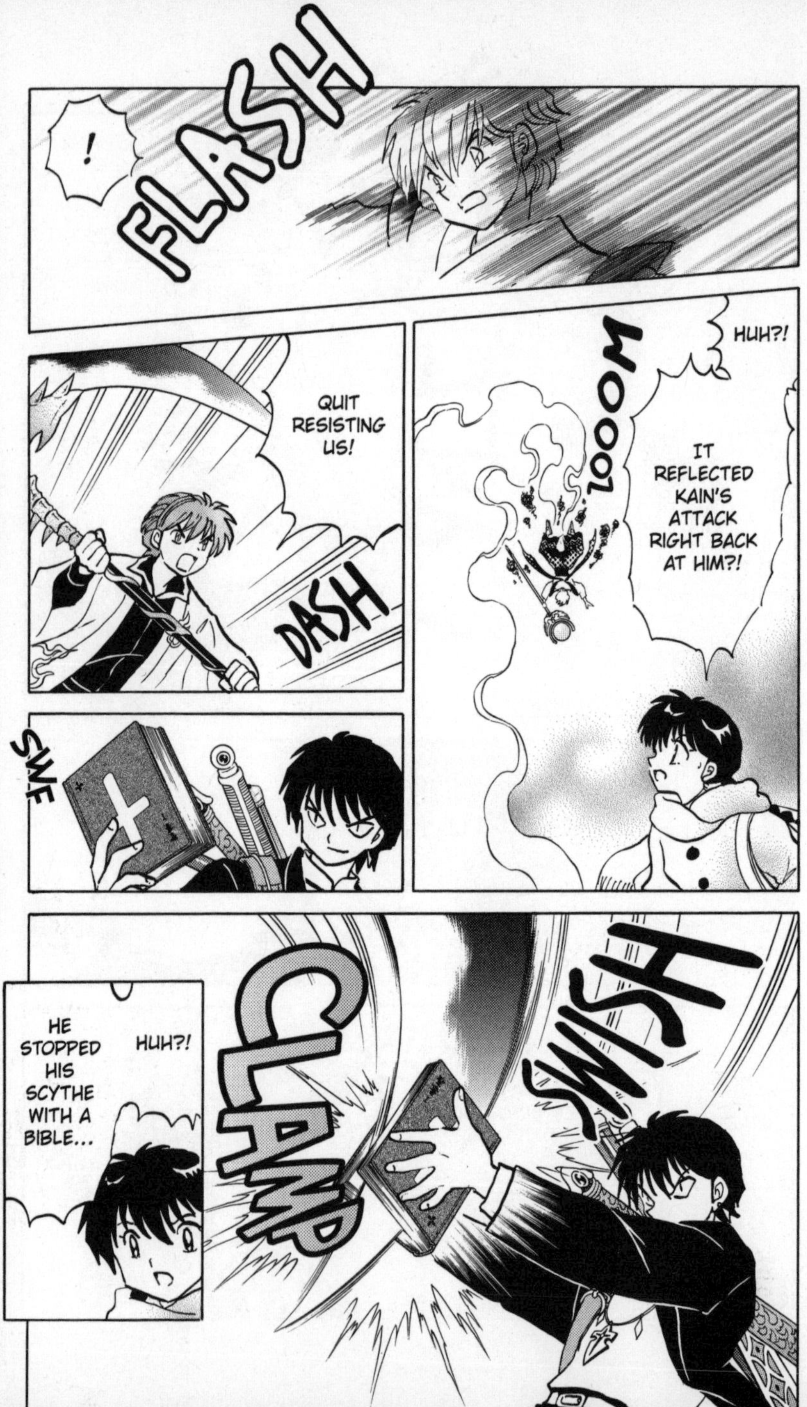
FLASH
!
HUH?!
WOOOM
IT REFLECTED KAIN'S ATTACK RIGHT BACK AT HIM?!
QUIT RESISTING US!
DASH
SWF
SWISH
CLAMP
HUH?!
HE STOPPED HIS SCYTHE WITH A BIBLE...

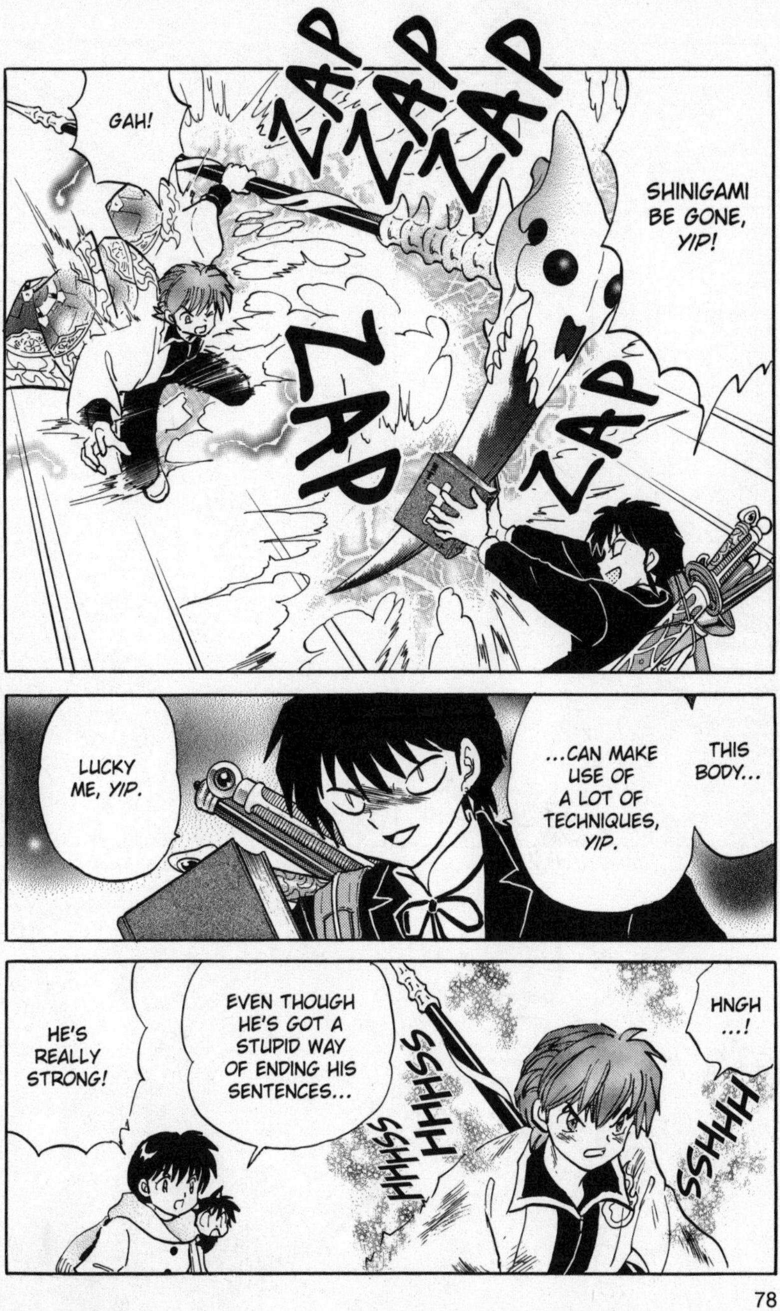
SHINIGAMI BE GONE, YIP!
ZAP ZAP ZAP
ZAP ZAP
ZAP
GAH!
THIS BODY...
...CAN MAKE USE OF A LOT OF TECHNIQUES, YIP.
LUCKY ME, YIP.
HNGH ...!
SSHHH
HHHSS
HHHSS
EVEN THOUGH HE'S GOT A STUPID WAY OF ENDING HIS SENTENCES...
HE'S REALLY STRONG!

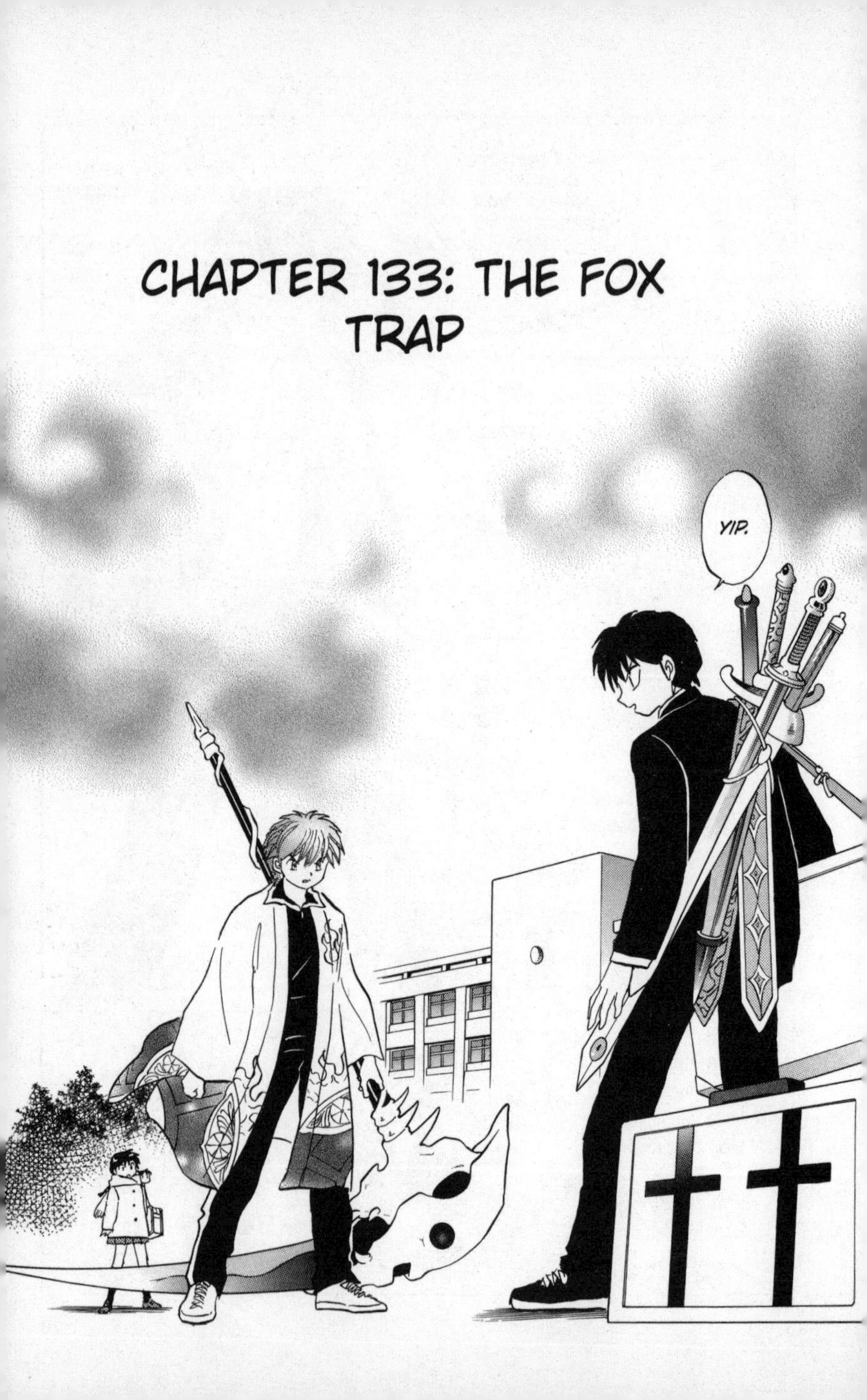
CHAPTER 133: THE FOX TRAP
YIP.

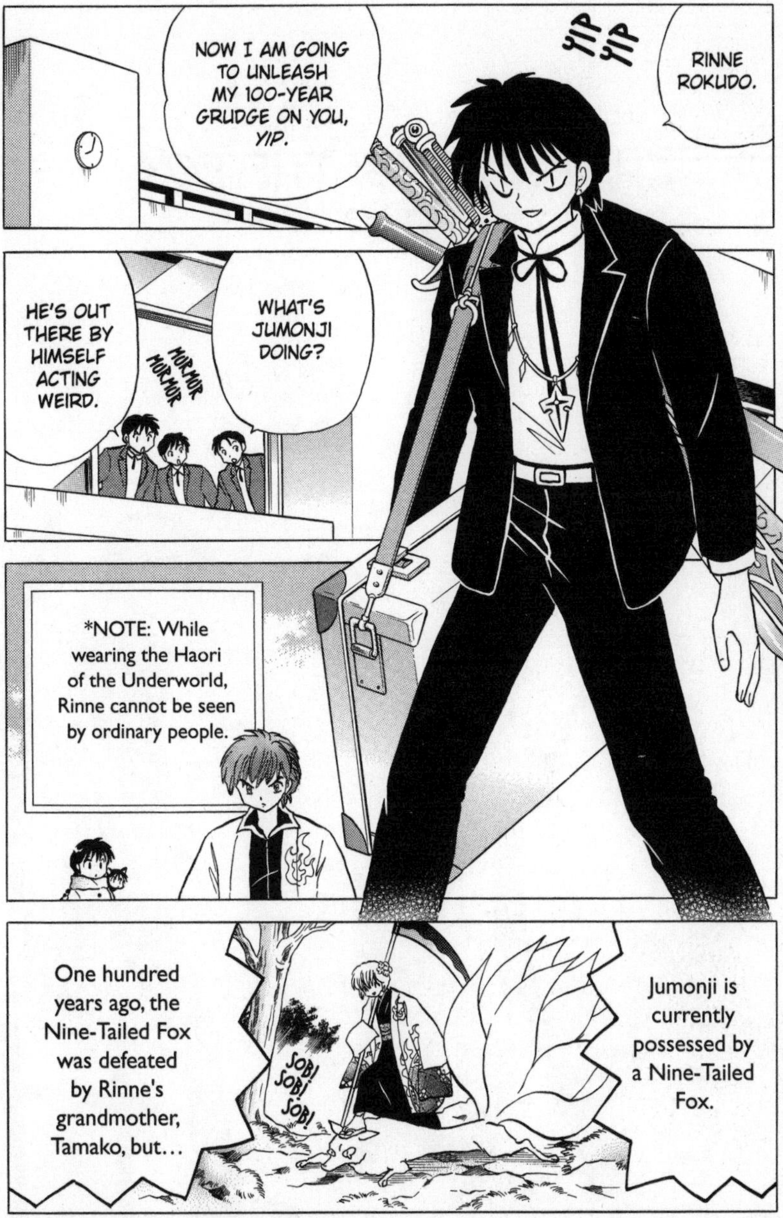
RINNE ROKUDO.
YIP YIP
NOW I AM GOING TO UNLEASH MY 100-YEAR GRUDGE ON YOU, YIP.
WHAT'S JUMONJI DOING?
MOR MOR MOR MOR
HE'S OUT THERE BY HIMSELF ACTING WEIRD.
*NOTE: While wearing the Haori of the Underworld, Rinne cannot be seen by ordinary people.
Jumonji is currently possessed by a Nine-Tailed Fox.
SOB! SOB! SOB!
One hundred years ago, the Nine-Tailed Fox was defeated by Rinne's grandmother, Tamako, but…

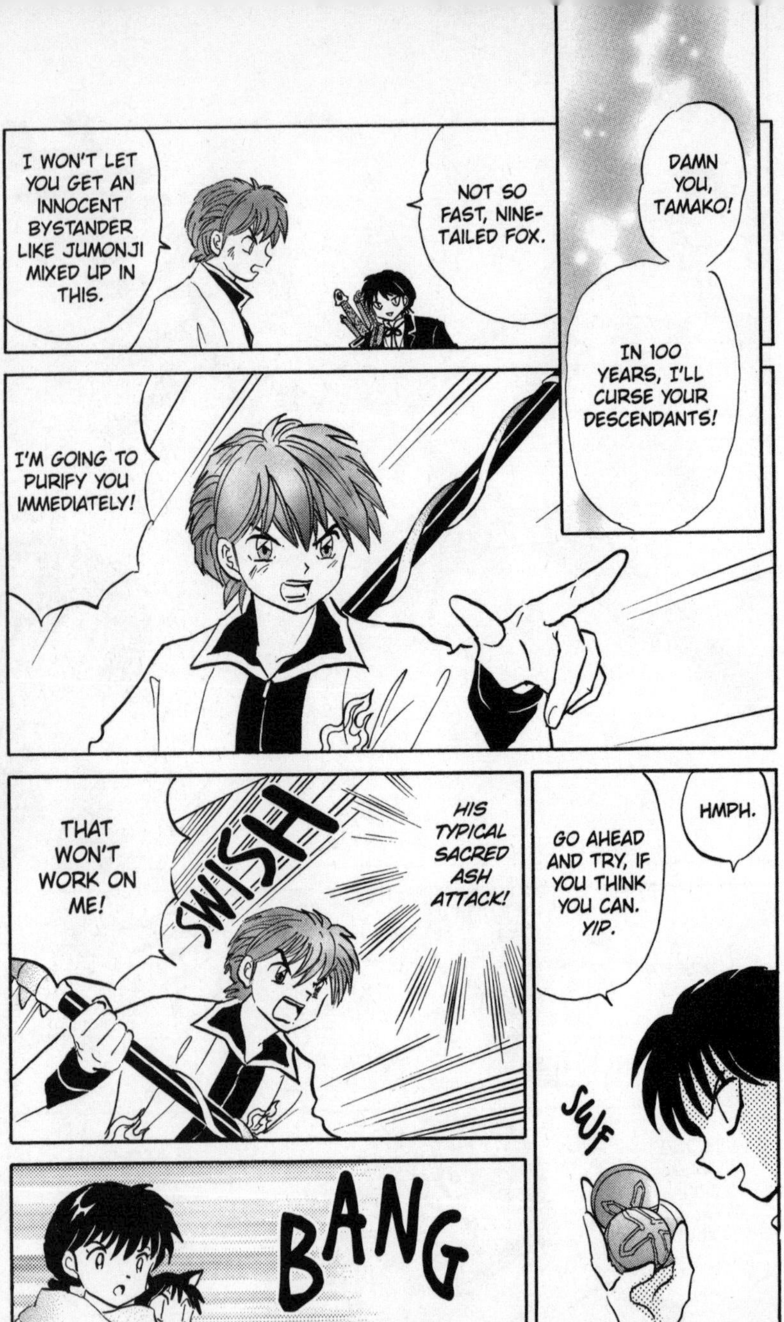
DAMN YOU, TAMAKO!
IN 100 YEARS, I'LL CURSE YOUR DESCENDANTS!
NOT SO FAST, NINE-TAILED FOX.
I WON'T LET YOU GET AN INNOCENT BYSTANDER LIKE JUMONJI MIXED UP IN THIS.
I'M GOING TO PURIFY YOU IMMEDIATELY!
HMPH.
GO AHEAD AND TRY, IF YOU THINK YOU CAN. YIP.
SWF
HIS TYPICAL SACRED ASH ATTACK!
SWISH
THAT WON'T WORK ON ME!
BANG

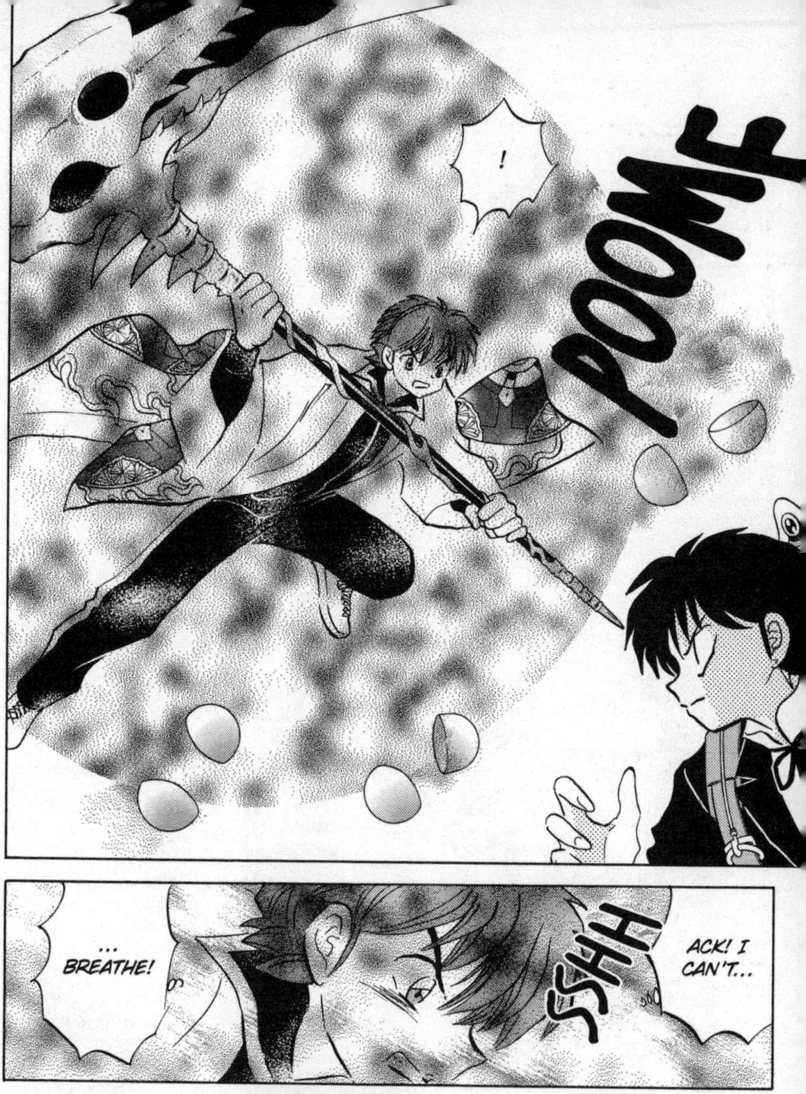
!
POOMF
ACK! I CAN'T...
SSHH
... BREATHE!
THE SACRED ASHES FORMED A BALL?!
IT'S NOT LIKE HIS TYPICAL ATTACK AT ALL!

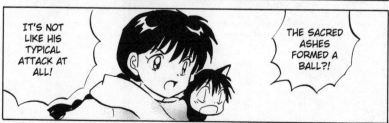

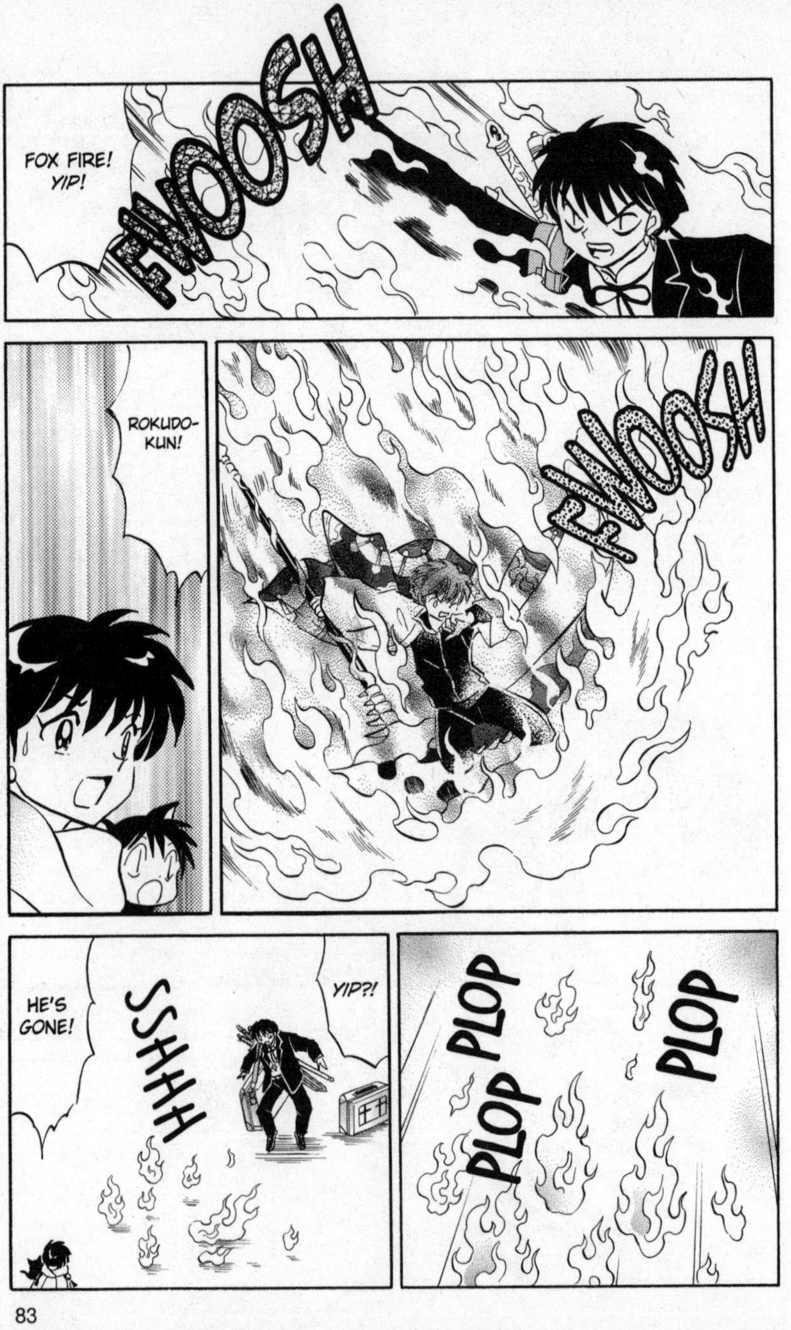
FWOOSH
FOX FIRE! YIP!
FWOOSH
ROKUDO-KUN!
PLOP
PLOP
PLOP
YIP?!
SSHHH
HE'S GONE!

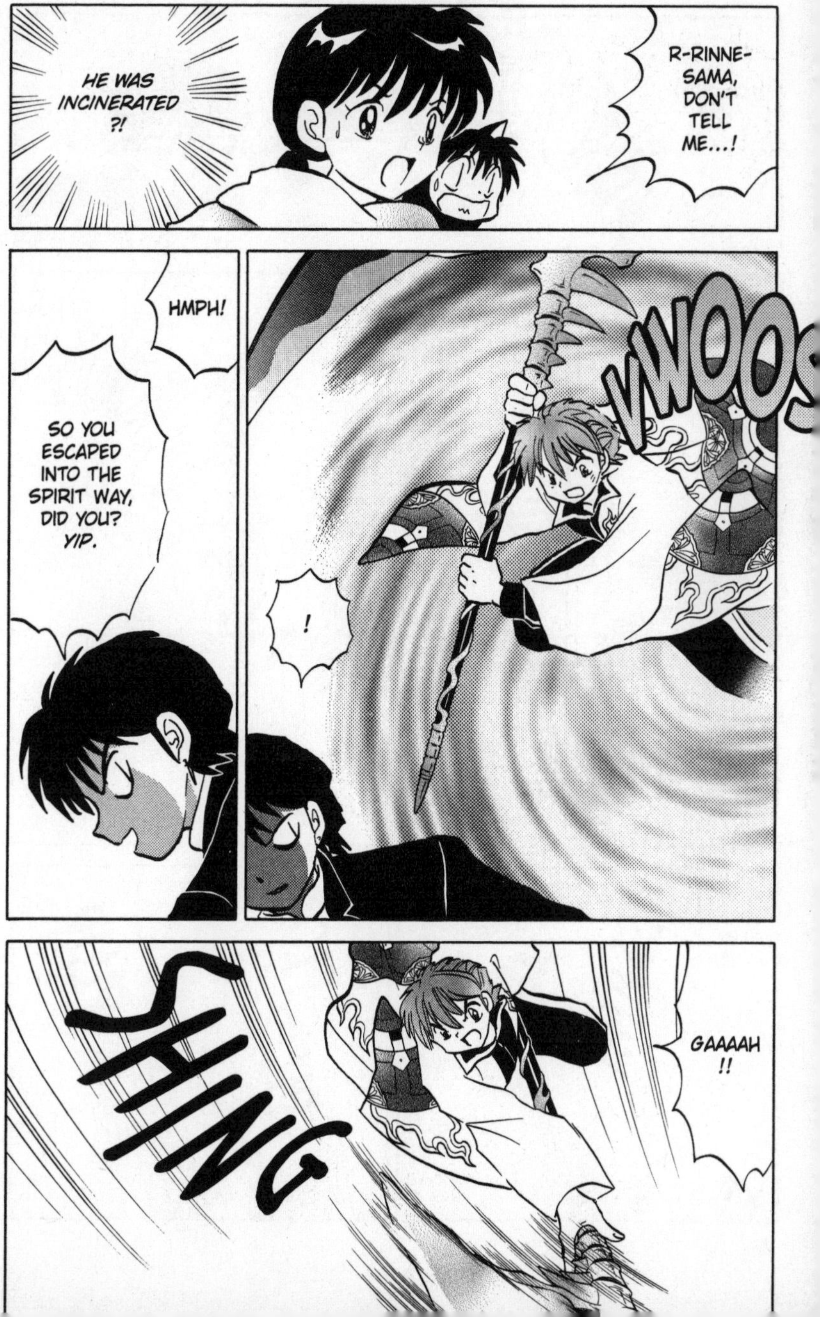
R-RINNE-SAMA, DON'T TELL ME...!
HE WAS INCINERATED?!
VWOOS
!
HMPH!
SO YOU ESCAPED INTO THE SPIRIT WAY, DID YOU? YIP.
GAAAAH!!
SHING

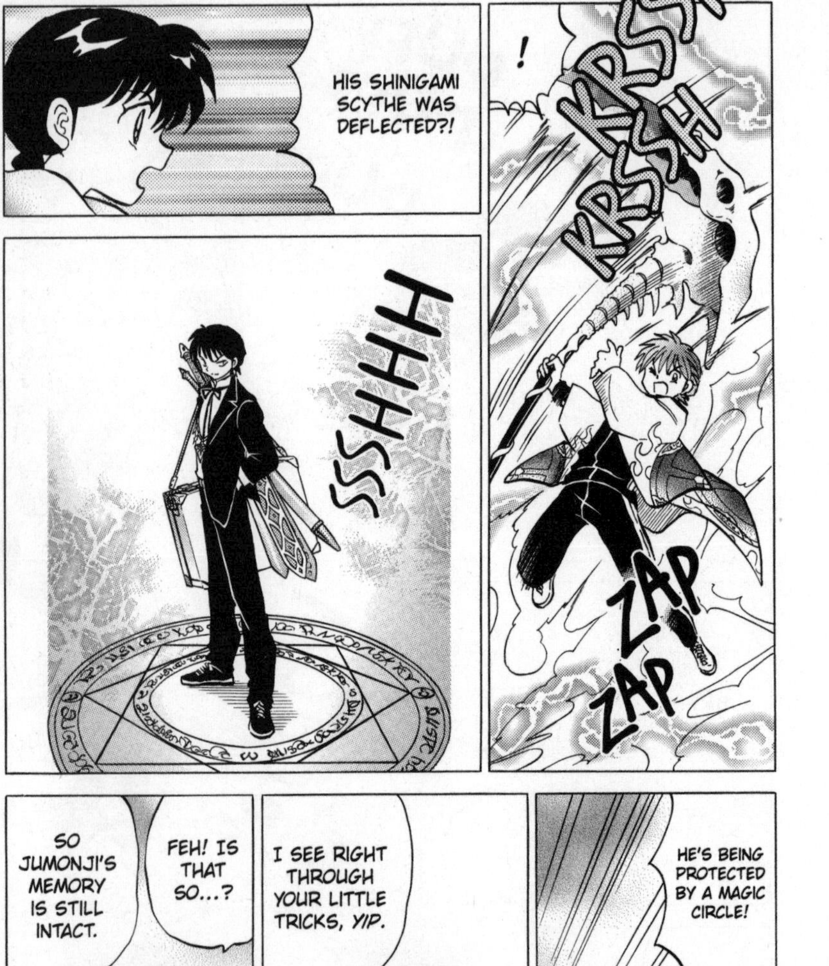
!
KRSSH
KRSSH
ZAP
ZAP
HIS SHINIGAMI SCYTHE WAS DEFLECTED?!
SSSHHHH
HE'S BEING PROTECTED BY A MAGIC CIRCLE!
I SEE RIGHT THROUGH YOUR LITTLE TRICKS, *YIP*.
FEH! IS THAT SO...?
SO JUMONJI'S MEMORY IS STILL INTACT.

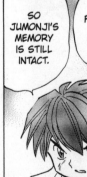

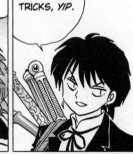

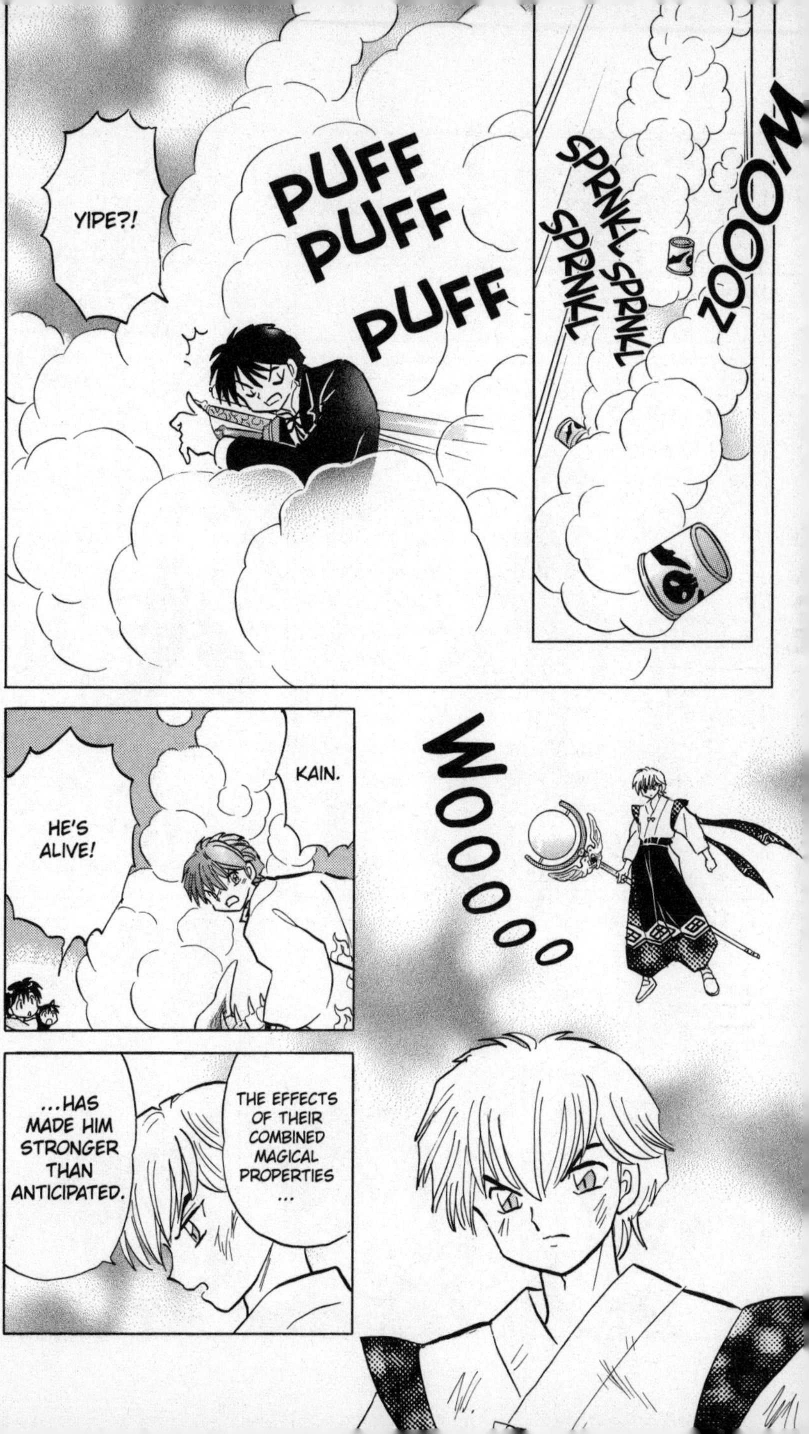
ZOOOM
SPRNKL SPRNKL
SPRNKL
PUFF
PUFF
PUFF
YIPE?!
WOOOOOO
KAIN.
HE'S ALIVE!
THE EFFECTS OF THEIR COMBINED MAGICAL PROPERTIES ...
...HAS MADE HIM STRONGER THAN ANTICIPATED.

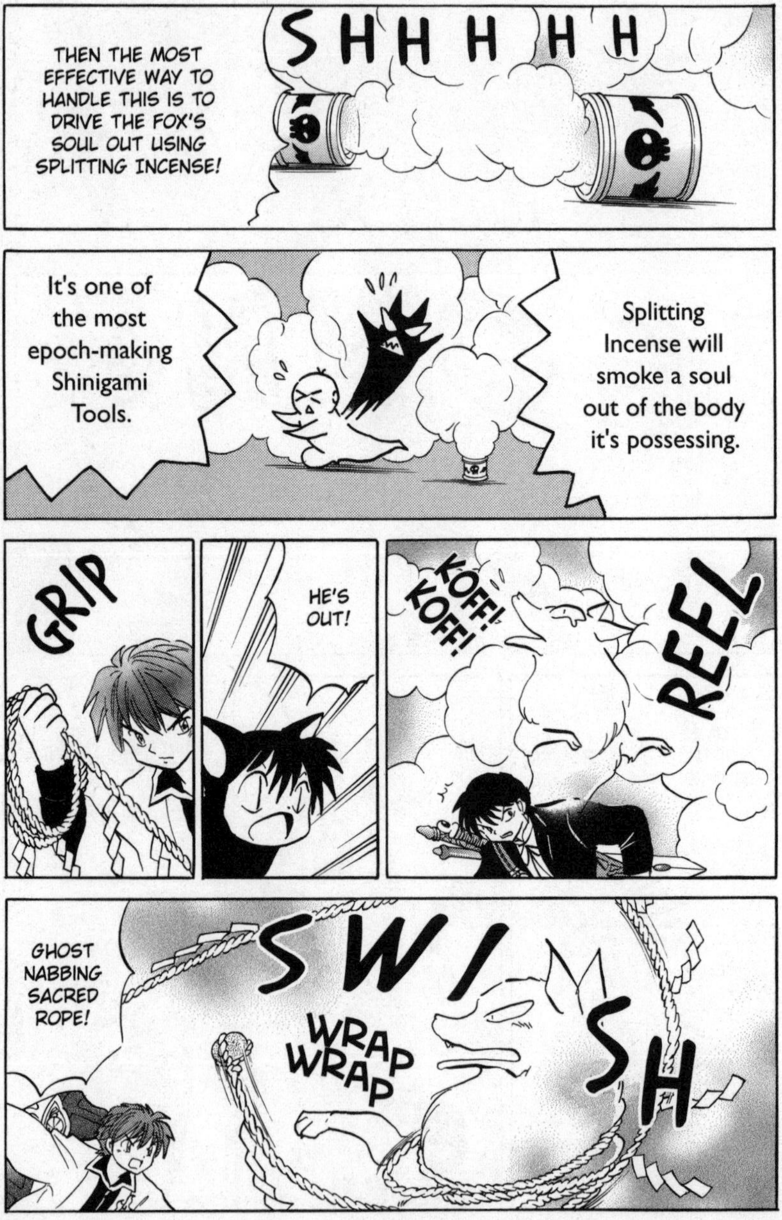
SHHHHH
THEN THE MOST EFFECTIVE WAY TO HANDLE THIS IS TO DRIVE THE FOX'S SOUL OUT USING SPLITTING INCENSE!
Splitting Incense will smoke a soul out of the body it's possessing.
It's one of the most epoch-making Shinigami Tools.
REEL
KOFF! KOFF!
HE'S OUT!
GRIP
SWISH
WRAP WRAP
GHOST NABBING SACRED ROPE!

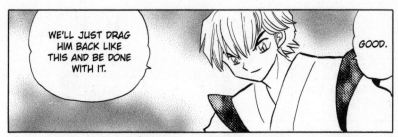

GOOD.
WE'LL JUST DRAG HIM BACK LIKE THIS AND BE DONE WITH IT.
GONNG
WHAT?!
THE SPLITTING INCENSE DIDN'T WORK?!
GLARE
POWER STONE!
COME FORTH, SPIRITS!
SHWF

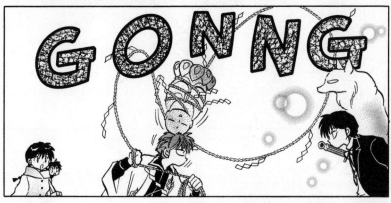

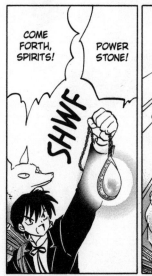

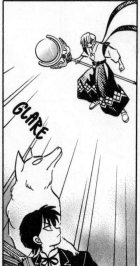

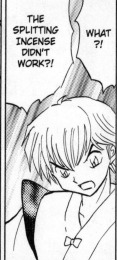

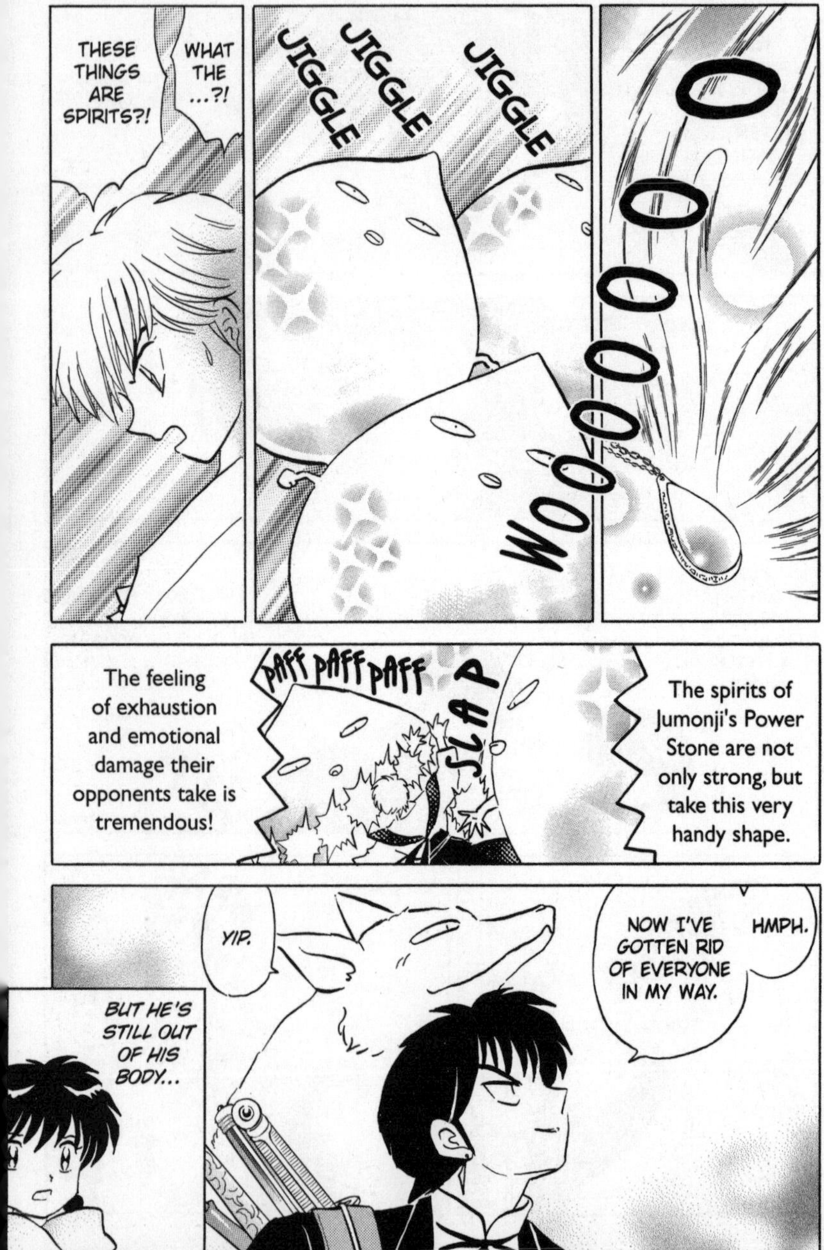
WOOOOOOOOO
JIGGLE
JIGGLE
JIGGLE
WHAT THE ...?!
THESE THINGS ARE SPIRITS?!
The spirits of Jumonji's Power Stone are not only strong, but take this very handy shape.
SLAP
PAFF PAFF PAFF
The feeling of exhaustion and emotional damage their opponents take is tremendous!
HMPH.
NOW I'VE GOTTEN RID OF EVERYONE IN MY WAY.
YIP.
BUT HE'S STILL OUT OF HIS BODY...

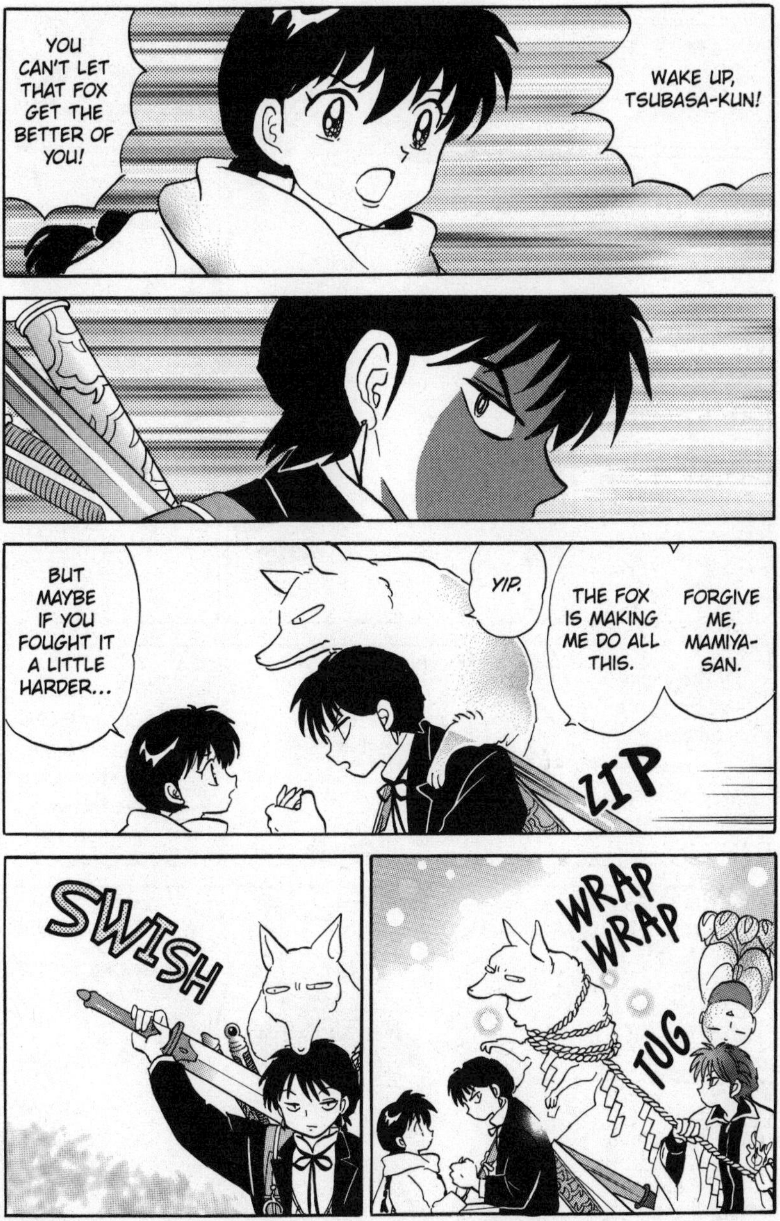
WAKE UP, TSUBASA-KUN!
YOU CAN'T LET THAT FOX GET THE BETTER OF YOU!
FORGIVE ME, MAMIYA-SAN.
THE FOX IS MAKING ME DO ALL THIS.
YIP.
BUT MAYBE IF YOU FOUGHT IT A LITTLE HARDER...
ZIP
WRAP WRAP
TUG
SWISH

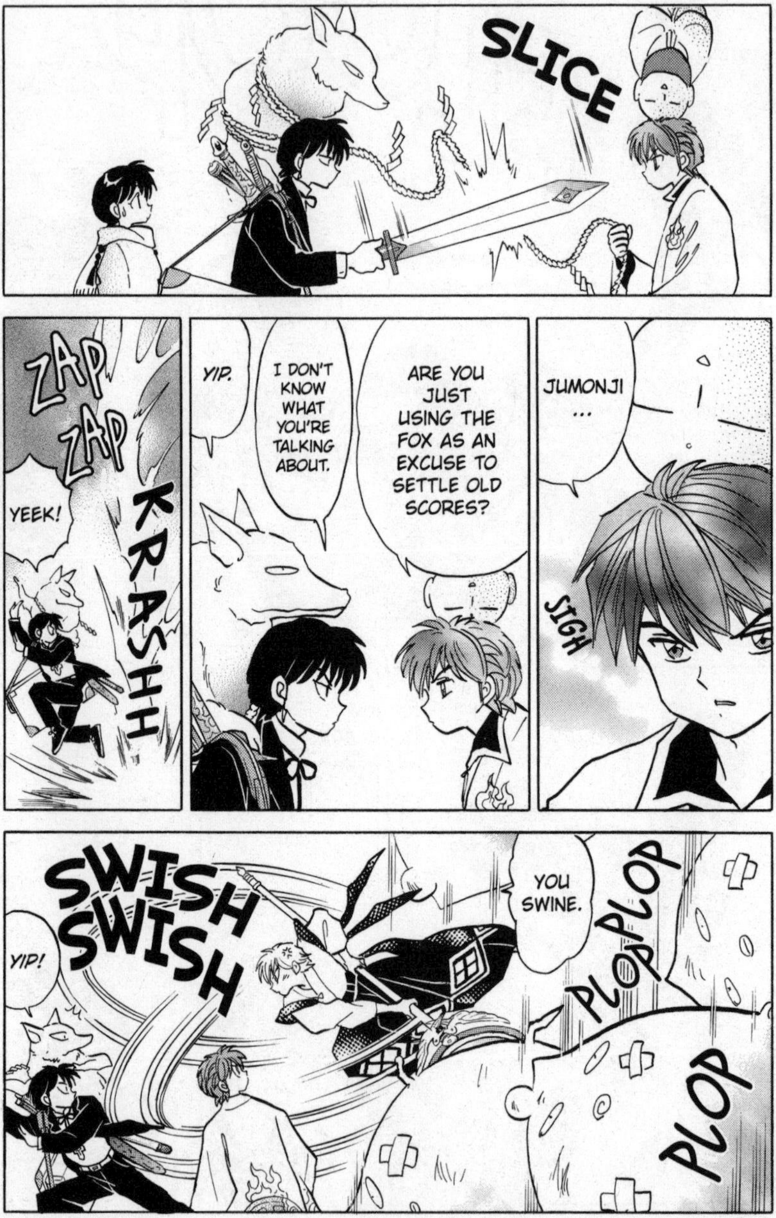
SLICE
JUMONJI...
SIGH
ARE YOU JUST USING THE FOX AS AN EXCUSE TO SETTLE OLD SCORES?
I DON'T KNOW WHAT YOU'RE TALKING ABOUT.
YIP.
ZAP ZAP
KRASHH
YEEK!
YOU SWINE.
PLOP PLOP
PLOP
SWISH SWISH
YIP!

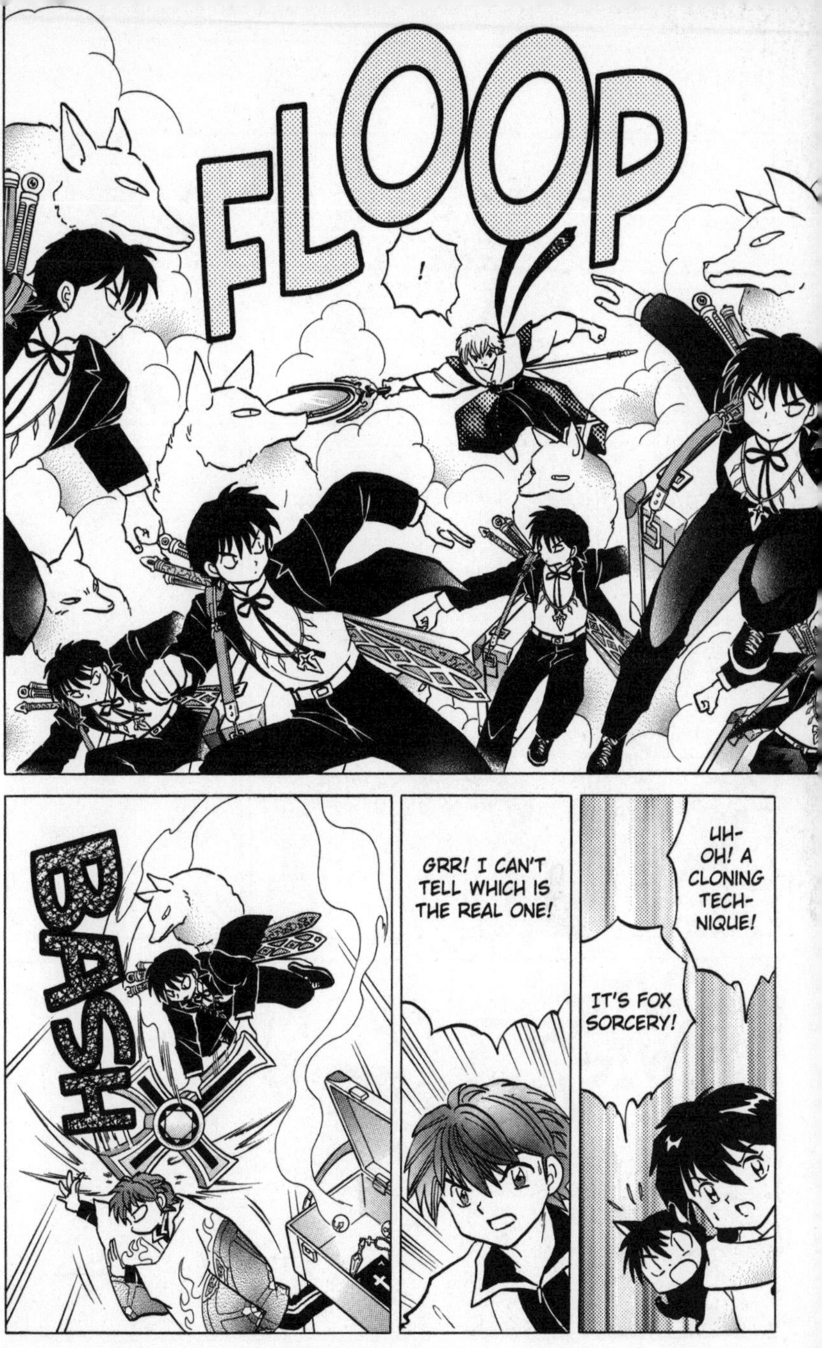
FLOOP
!
UH-OH! A CLONING TECH-NIQUE!
IT'S FOX SORCERY!
GRR! I CAN'T TELL WHICH IS THE REAL ONE!
BASH

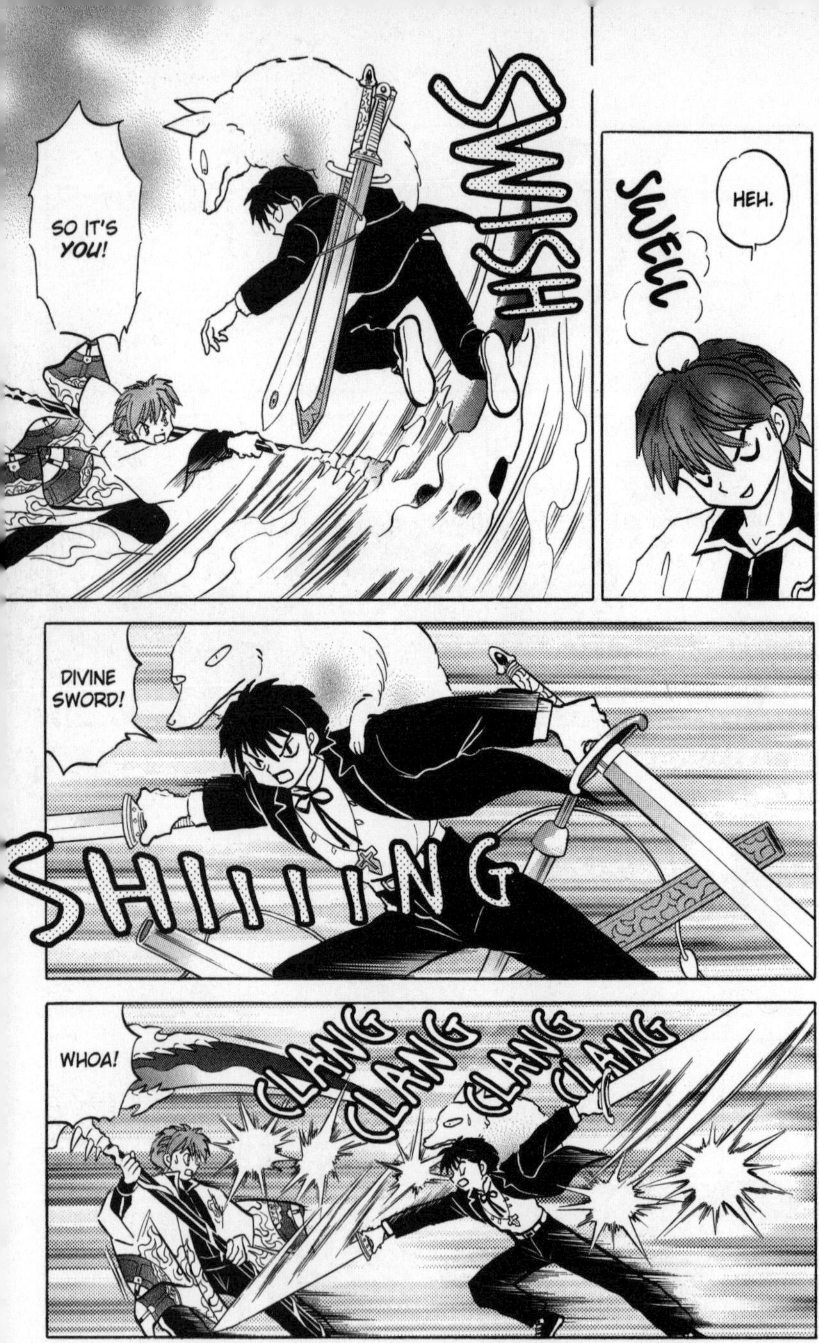
HEH.
SWELL
SWISH
SO IT'S *YOU!*
DIVINE SWORD!
SHIIIIING
WHOA!
CLANG
CLANG
CLANG
CLANG

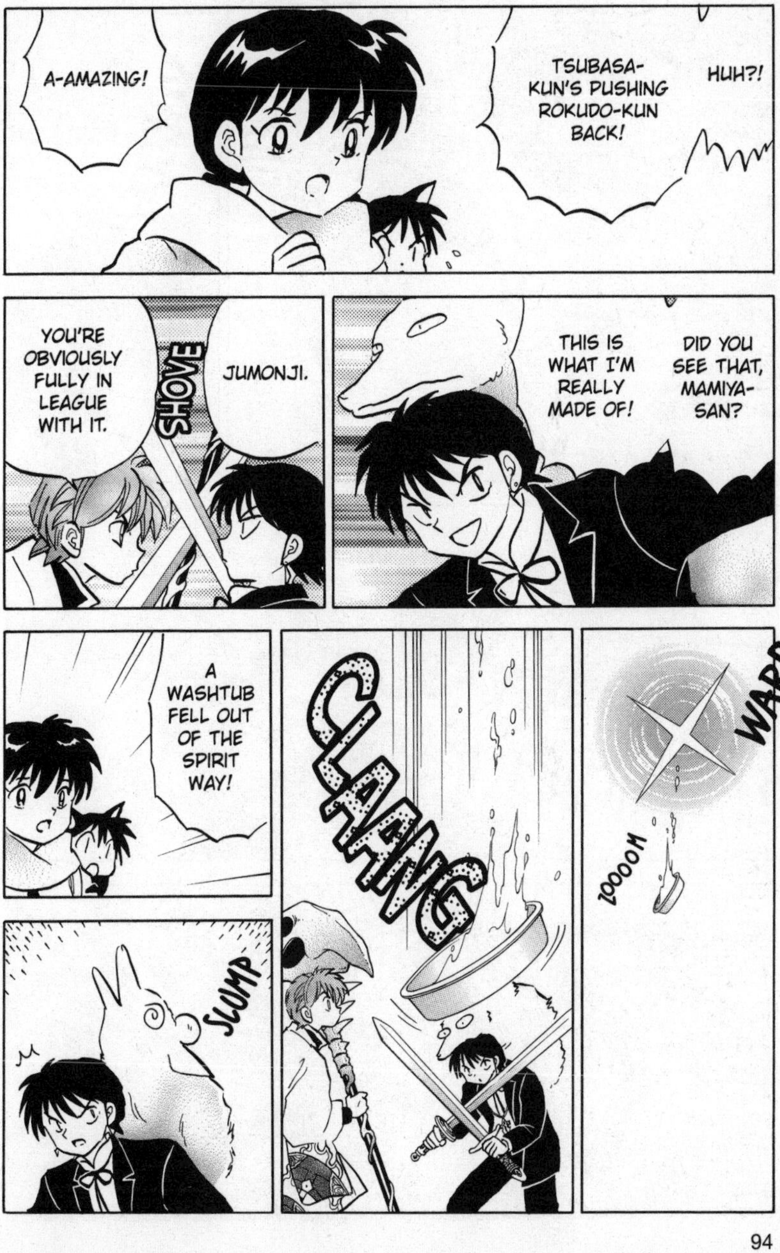
HUH?!
TSUBASA-KUN'S PUSHING ROKUDO-KUN BACK!
A-AMAZING!
DID YOU SEE THAT, MAMIYA-SAN?
THIS IS WHAT I'M REALLY MADE OF!
JUMONJI.
SHOVE
YOU'RE OBVIOUSLY FULLY IN LEAGUE WITH IT.
WARP
ZOOOOM
CLAANG
A WASHTUB FELL OUT OF THE SPIRIT WAY!
SLUMP

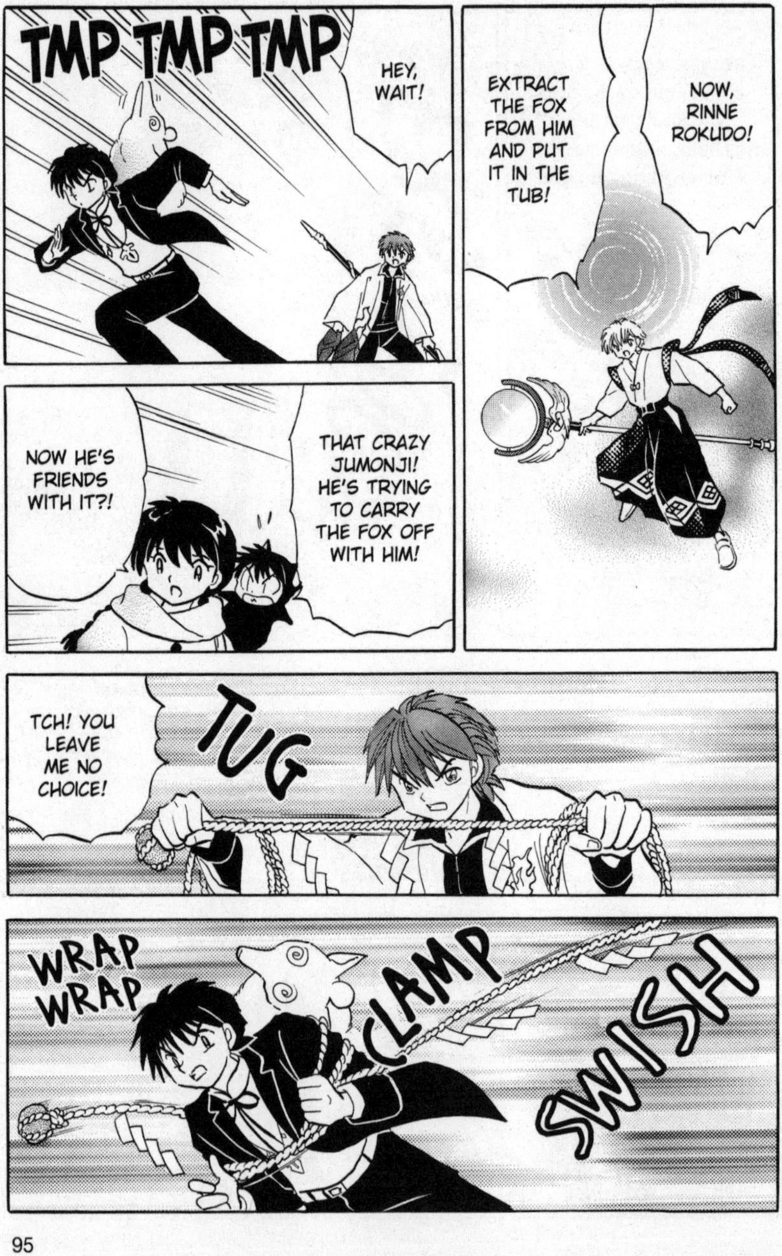
NOW, RINNE ROKUDO!
EXTRACT THE FOX FROM HIM AND PUT IT IN THE TUB!
HEY, WAIT!
TMP TMP TMP
THAT CRAZY JUMONJI! HE'S TRYING TO CARRY THE FOX OFF WITH HIM!
NOW HE'S FRIENDS WITH IT?!
TUG
TCH! YOU LEAVE ME NO CHOICE!
SWISH
CLAMP
WRAP WRAP

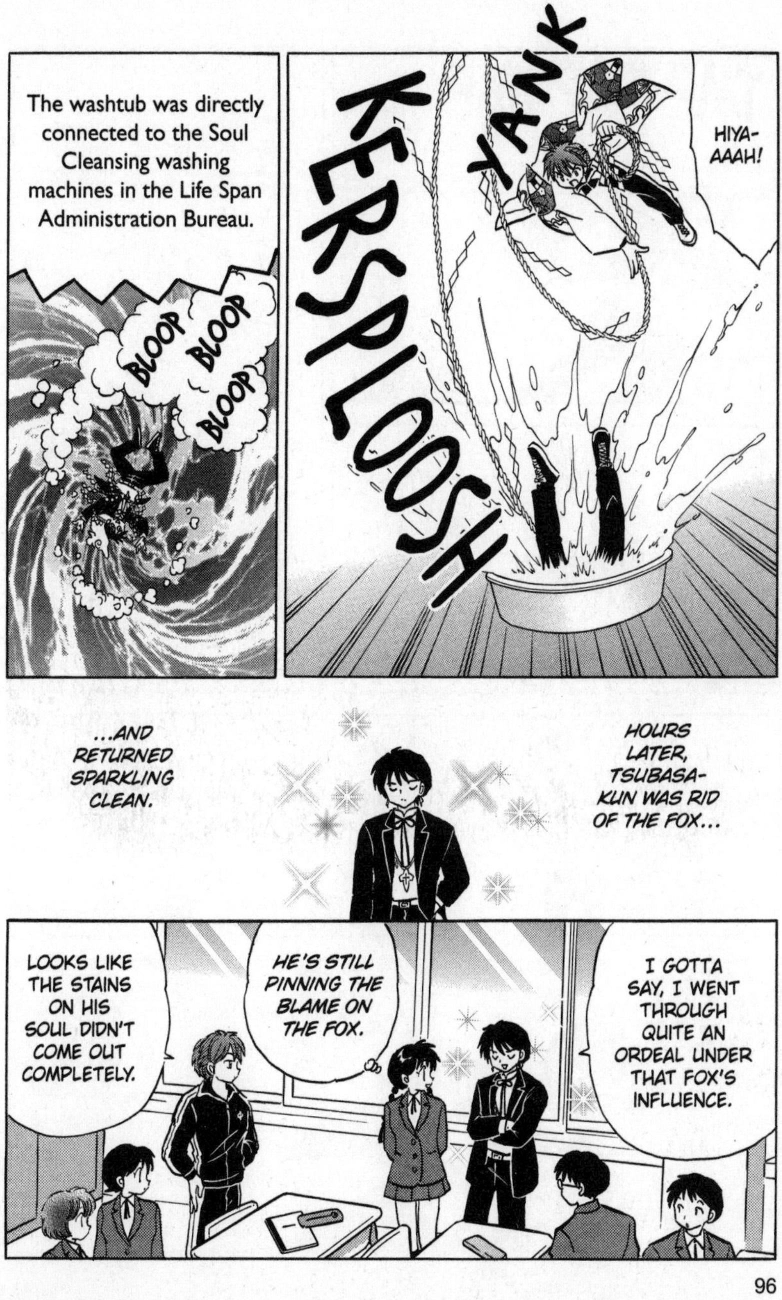
YANK
KERSPLOOSH
HIYA-AAAH!
The washtub was directly connected to the Soul Cleansing washing machines in the Life Span Administration Bureau.
BLOOP BLOOP BLOOP BLOOP
HOURS LATER, TSUBASA-KUN WAS RID OF THE FOX...
...AND RETURNED SPARKLING CLEAN.
I GOTTA SAY, I WENT THROUGH QUITE AN ORDEAL UNDER THAT FOX'S INFLUENCE.
HE'S STILL PINNING THE BLAME ON THE FOX.
LOOKS LIKE THE STAINS ON HIS SOUL DIDN'T COME OUT COMPLETELY.

CHAPTER 134: THE MYSTERIOUS TRANSFER STUDENT

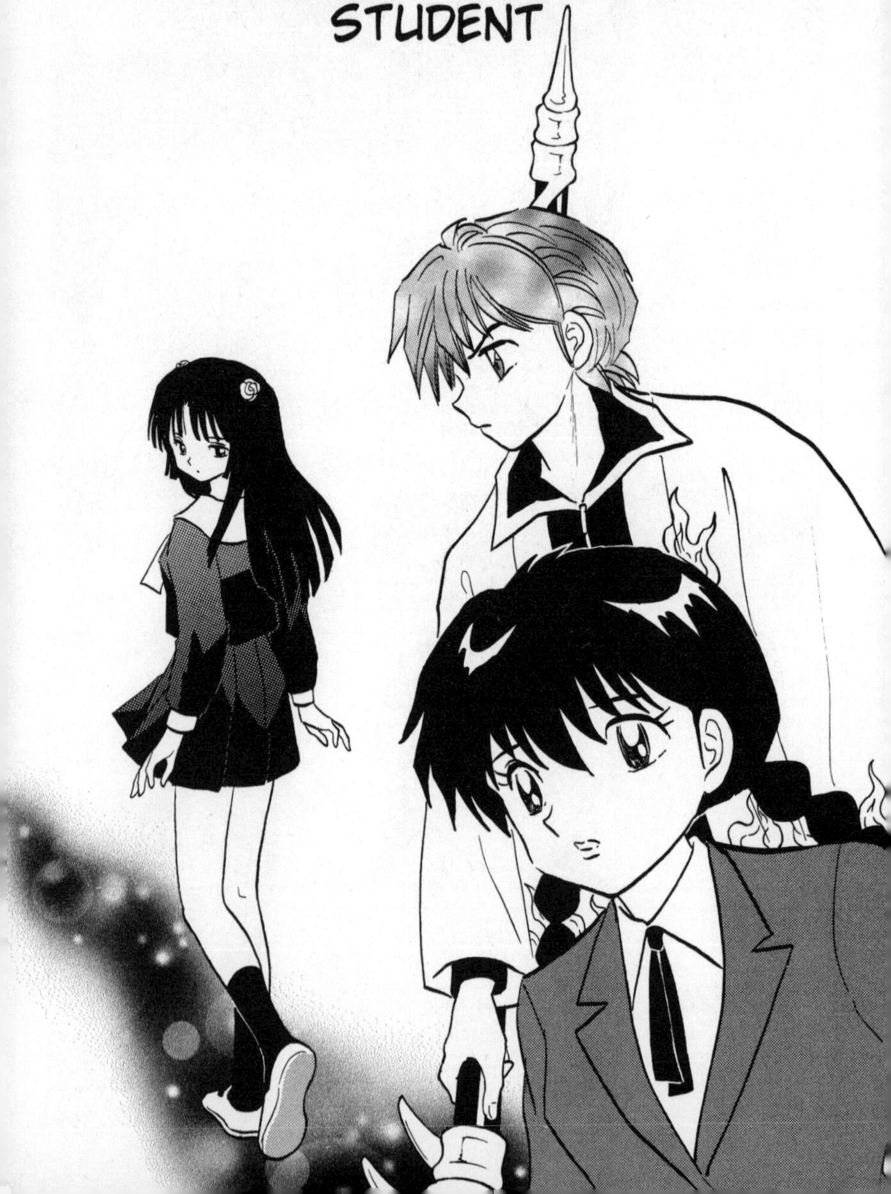

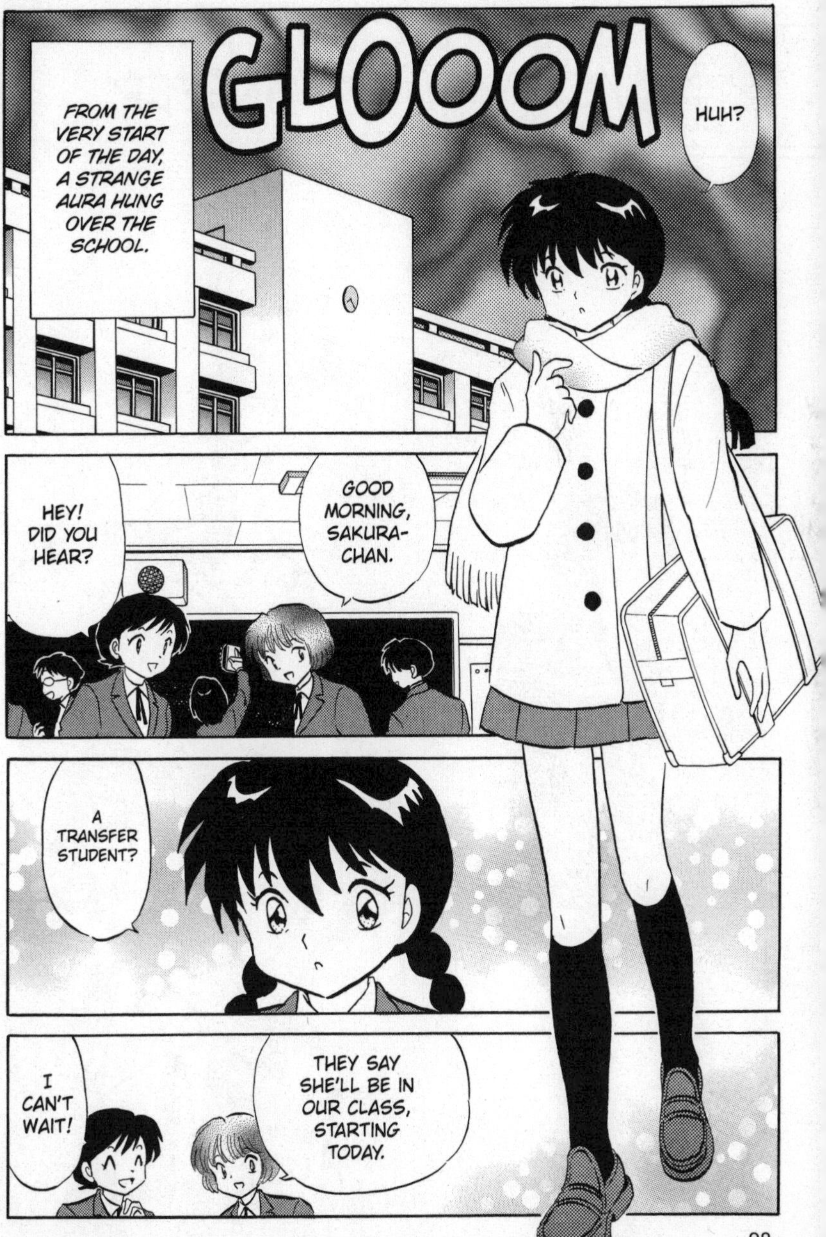
HUH?
GLOOOM
FROM THE VERY START OF THE DAY, A STRANGE AURA HUNG OVER THE SCHOOL.
GOOD MORNING, SAKURA-CHAN.
HEY! DID YOU HEAR?
A TRANSFER STUDENT?
THEY SAY SHE'LL BE IN OUR CLASS, STARTING TODAY.
I CAN'T WAIT!

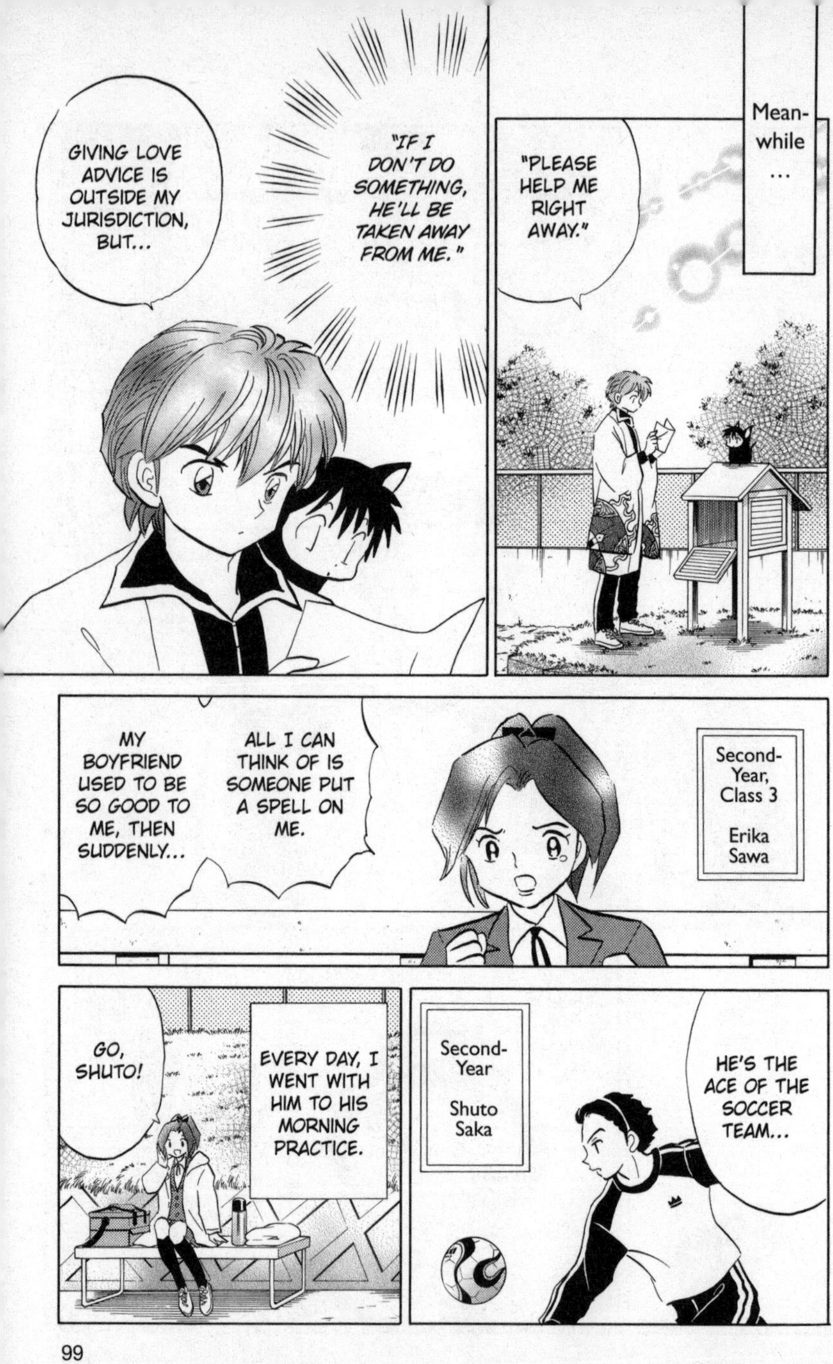
Mean-
while
...
"PLEASE HELP ME RIGHT AWAY."
"IF I DON'T DO SOMETHING, HE'LL BE TAKEN AWAY FROM ME."
GIVING LOVE ADVICE IS OUTSIDE MY JURISDICTION, BUT...
Second-Year, Class 3
Erika Sawa
ALL I CAN THINK OF IS SOMEONE PUT A SPELL ON ME.
MY BOYFRIEND USED TO BE SO GOOD TO ME, THEN SUDDENLY...
Second-Year
Shuto Saka
HE'S THE ACE OF THE SOCCER TEAM...
EVERY DAY, I WENT WITH HIM TO HIS MORNING PRACTICE.
GO, SHUTO!

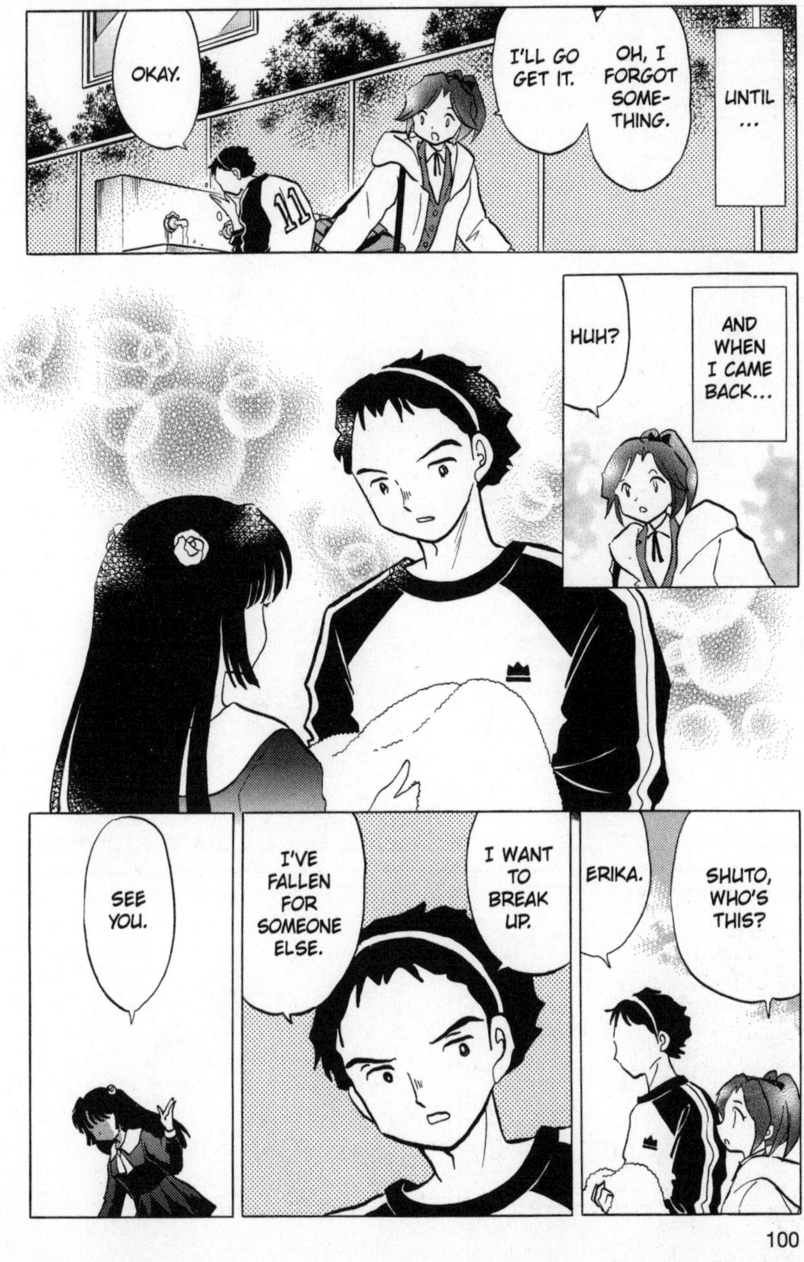
UNTIL ...
OH, I FORGOT SOMETHING.
I'LL GO GET IT.
OKAY.
AND WHEN I CAME BACK...
HUH?
SHUTO, WHO'S THIS?
ERIKA.
I WANT TO BREAK UP.
I'VE FALLEN FOR SOMEONE ELSE.
SEE YOU.

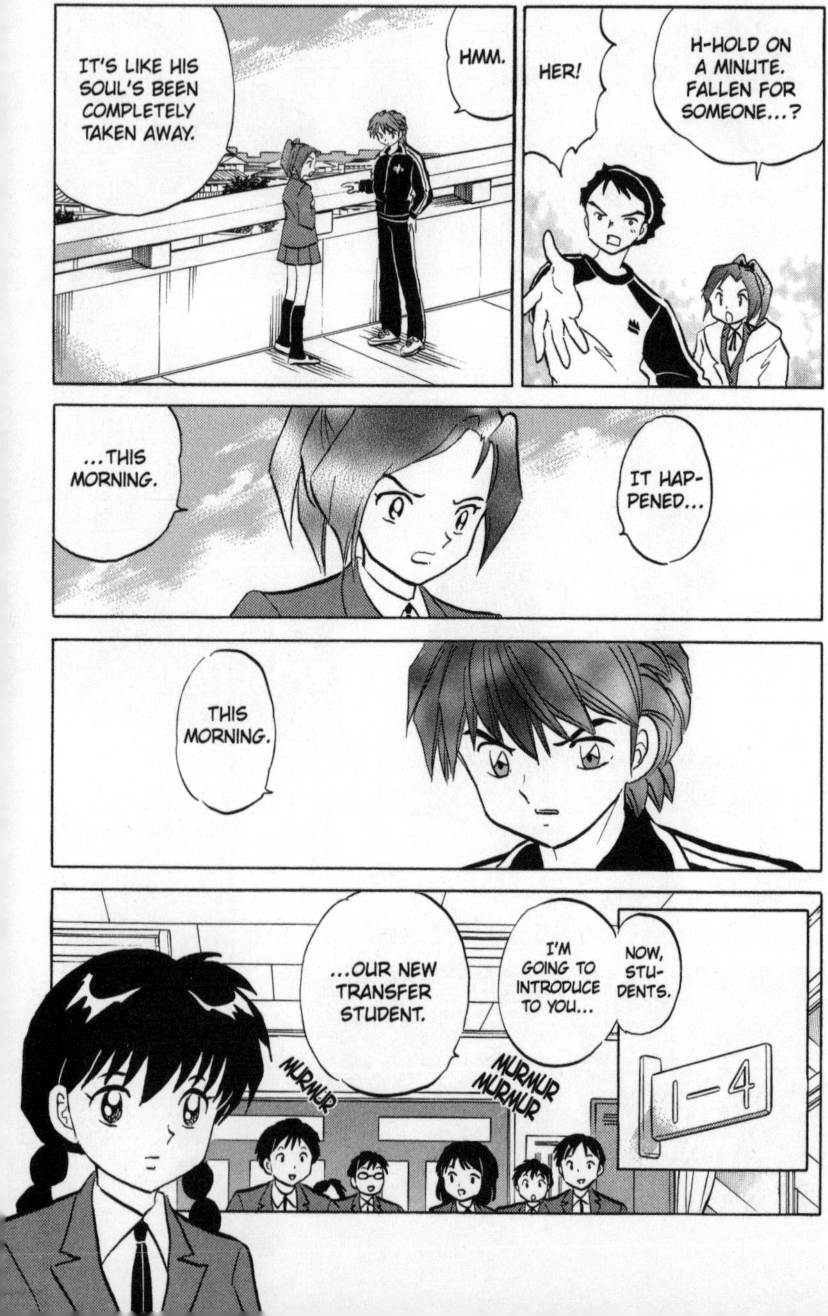
H-HOLD ON A MINUTE. FALLEN FOR SOMEONE...?
HER!
HMM.
IT'S LIKE HIS SOUL'S BEEN COMPLETELY TAKEN AWAY.
IT HAPPENED...
...THIS MORNING.
THIS MORNING.
NOW, STUDENTS.
I'M GOING TO INTRODUCE TO YOU...
...OUR NEW TRANSFER STUDENT.
1-4
MURMUR MURMUR
MURMUR

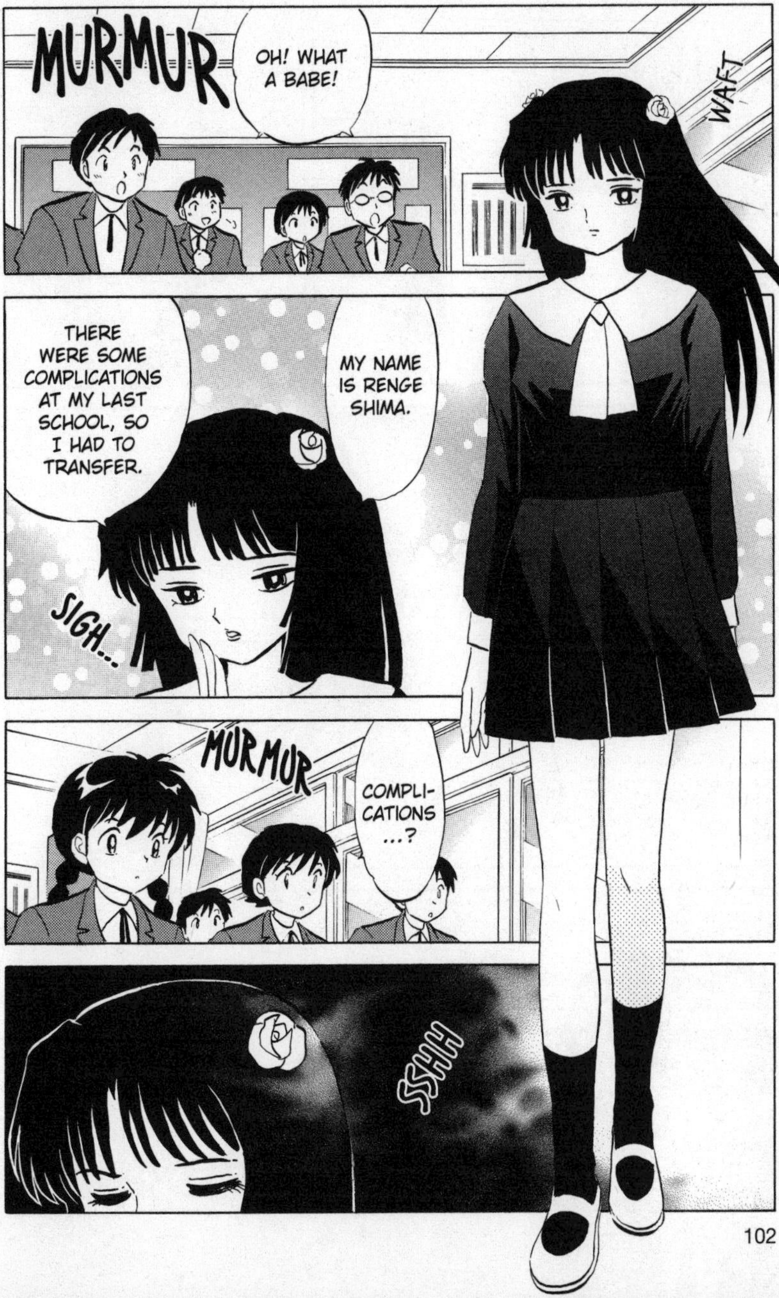
WAFT
OH! WHAT A BABE!
MURMUR
MY NAME IS RENGE SHIMA.
THERE WERE SOME COMPLICATIONS AT MY LAST SCHOOL, SO I HAD TO TRANSFER.
SIGH...
COMPLI-CATIONS ...?
MURMUR
SSHH

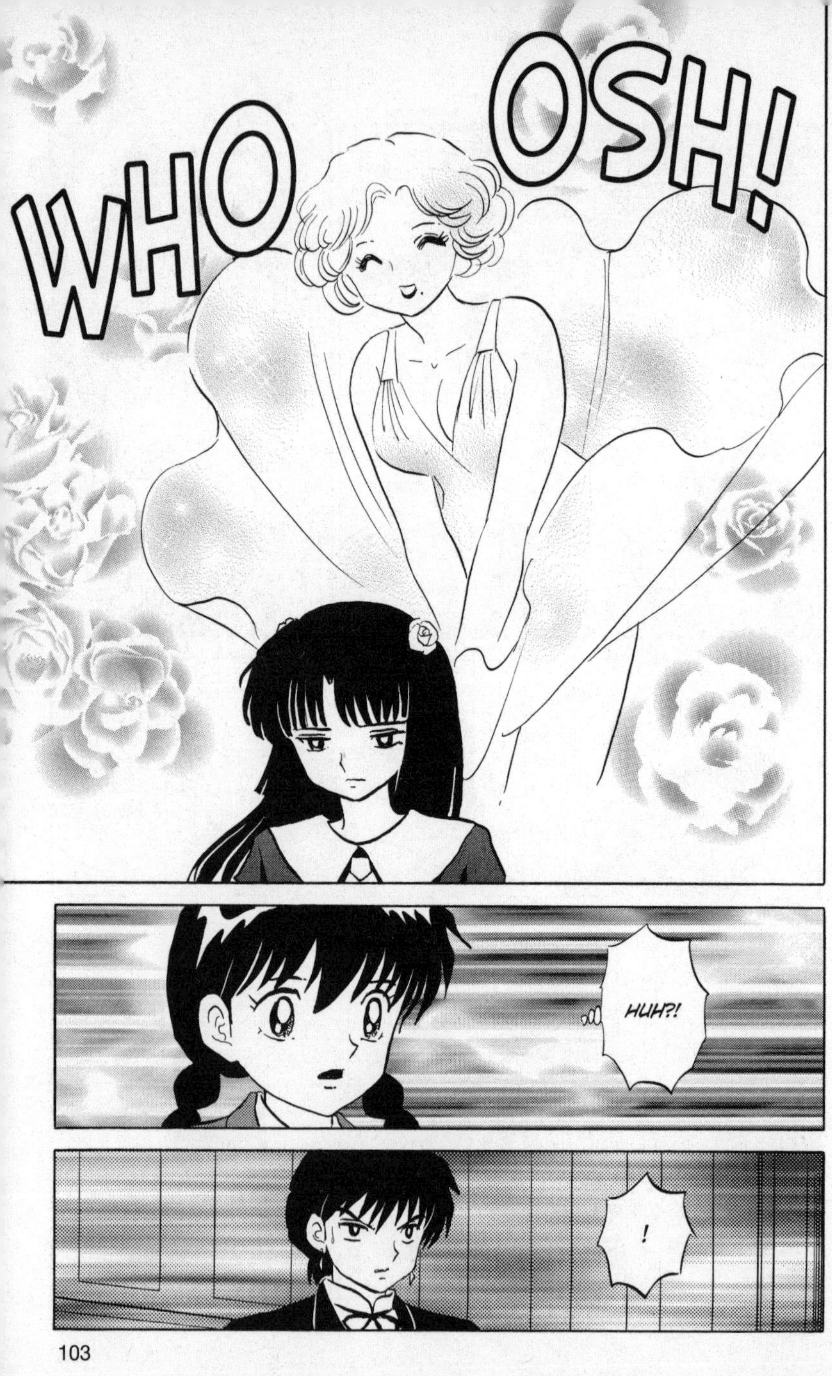
WHOOSH!
HUH?!
!

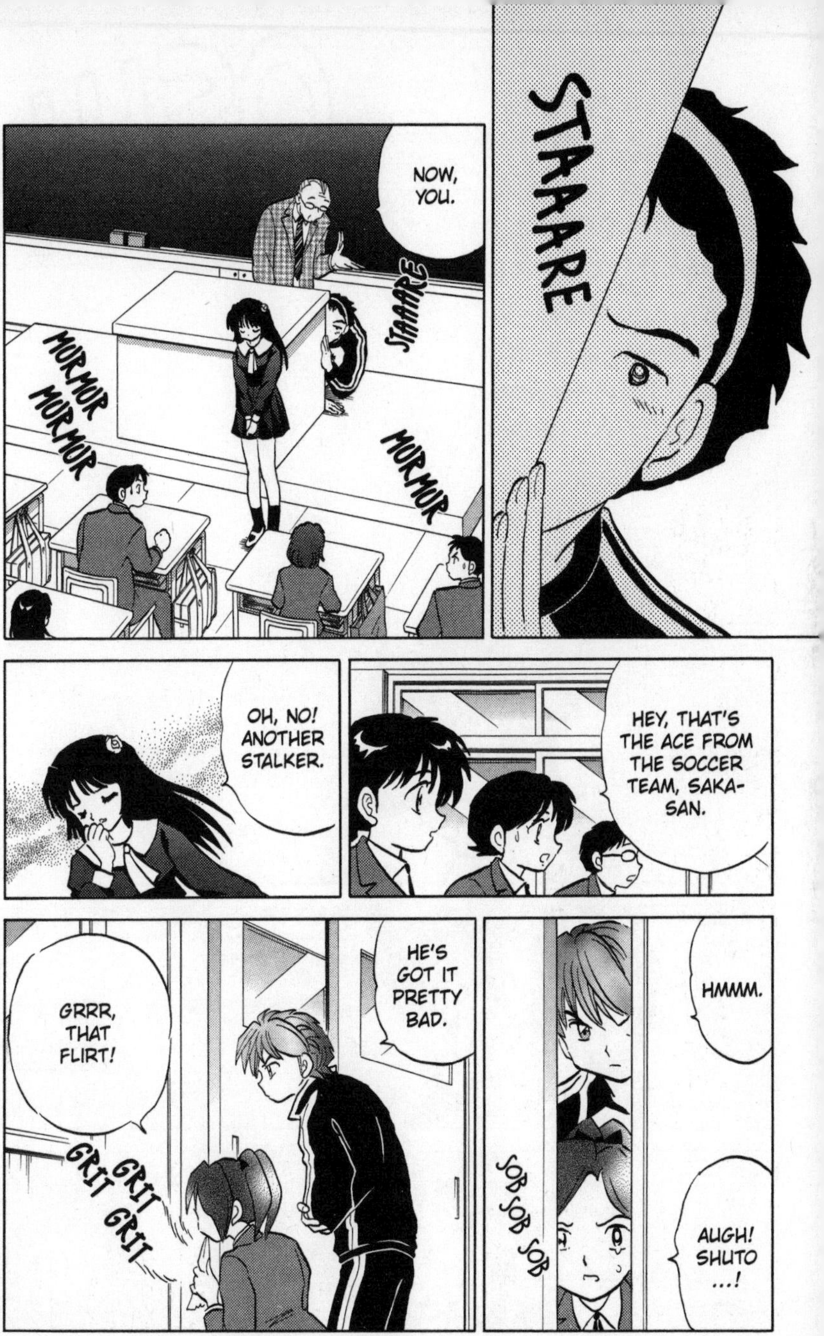
STAAARE
NOW, YOU.
STAAARE
MURMUR MURMUR MURMUR
MURMUR
HEY, THAT'S THE ACE FROM THE SOCCER TEAM, SAKA-SAN.
OH, NO! ANOTHER STALKER.
HMMM.
AUGH! SHUTO ...!
SOB SOB SOB
HE'S GOT IT PRETTY BAD.
GRRR, THAT FLIRT!
GRIT GRIT GRIT

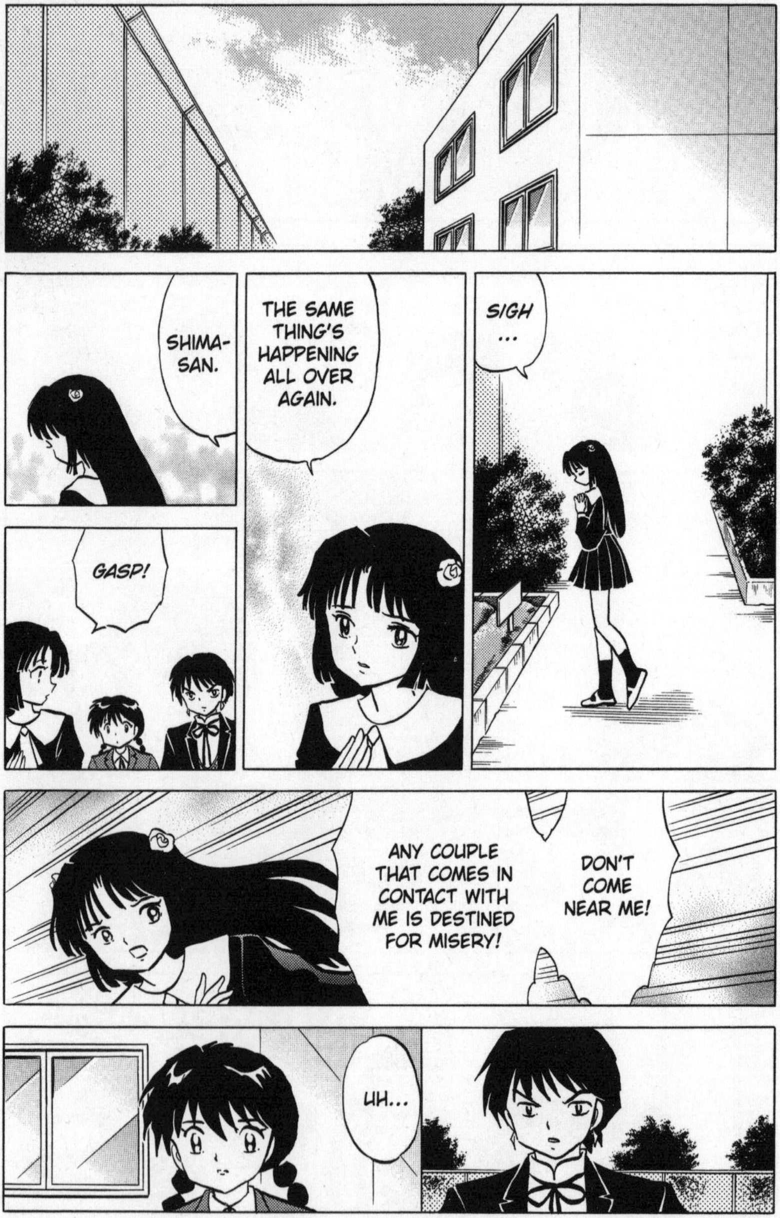
SIGH ...
THE SAME THING'S HAPPENING ALL OVER AGAIN.
SHIMA-SAN.
GASP!
DON'T COME NEAR ME!
ANY COUPLE THAT COMES IN CONTACT WITH ME IS DESTINED FOR MISERY!
UH...

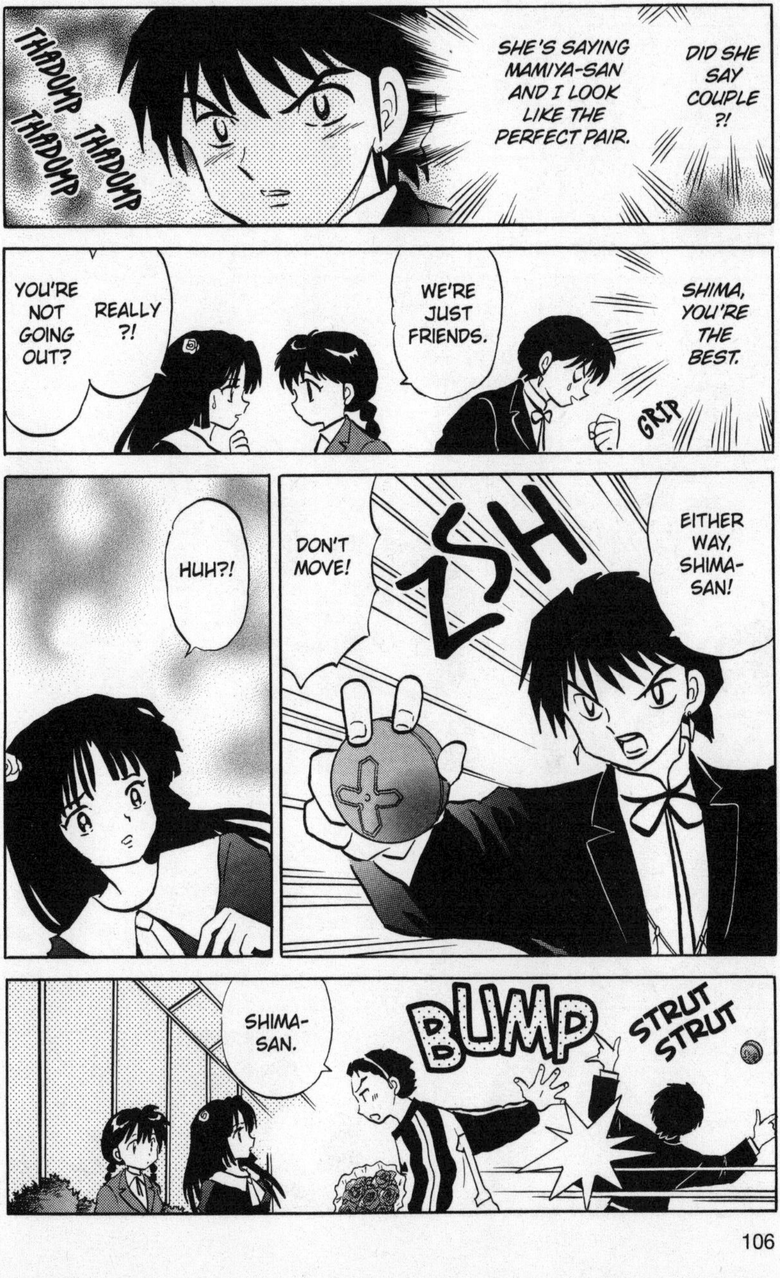
DID SHE SAY COUPLE ?!
SHE'S SAYING MAMIYA-SAN AND I LOOK LIKE THE PERFECT PAIR.
THADUMP THADUMP THADUMP
SHIMA, YOU'RE THE BEST.
GRIP
WE'RE JUST FRIENDS.
REALLY ?!
YOU'RE NOT GOING OUT?
EITHER WAY, SHIMA-SAN!
ZSH
DON'T MOVE!
HUH?!
STRUT STRUT
BUMP
SHIMA-SAN.

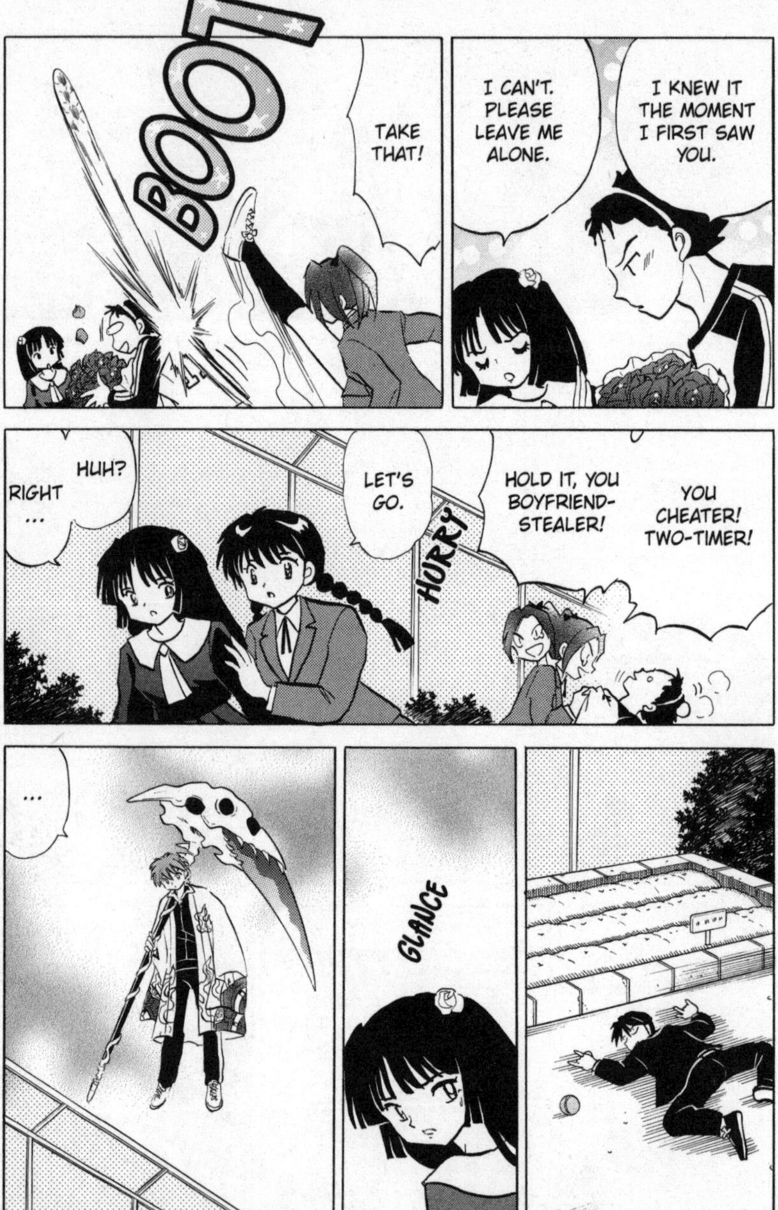
I KNEW IT THE MOMENT I FIRST SAW YOU.
I CAN'T. PLEASE LEAVE ME ALONE.
TAKE THAT!
BOOT
YOU CHEATER! TWO-TIMER!
HOLD IT, YOU BOYFRIEND-STEALER!
HURRY
LET'S GO.
HUH?
RIGHT ...
GLANCE
...

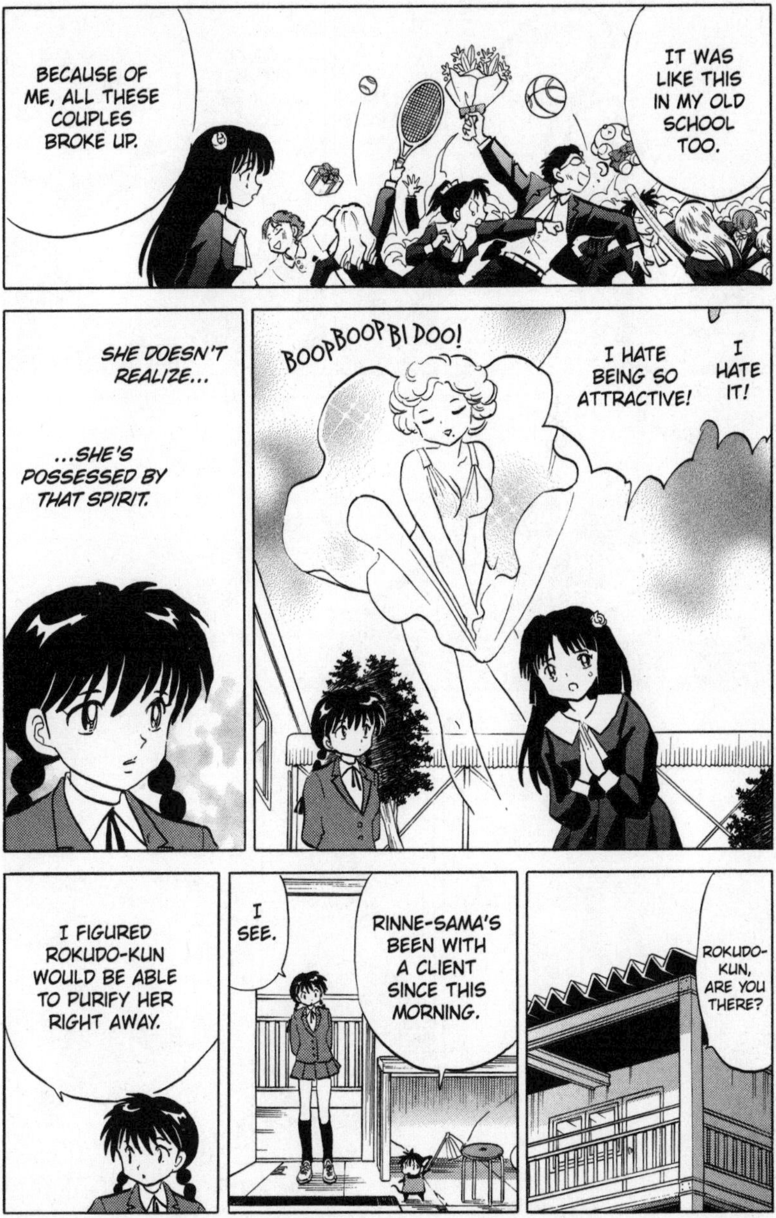
IT WAS LIKE THIS IN MY OLD SCHOOL TOO.
BECAUSE OF ME, ALL THESE COUPLES BROKE UP.
I HATE IT!
I HATE BEING SO ATTRACTIVE!
BOOPBOOPBI DOO!
SHE DOESN'T REALIZE...
...SHE'S POSSESSED BY THAT SPIRIT.
ROKUDO-KUN, ARE YOU THERE?
RINNE-SAMA'S BEEN WITH A CLIENT SINCE THIS MORNING.
I SEE.
I FIGURED ROKUDO-KUN WOULD BE ABLE TO PURIFY HER RIGHT AWAY.

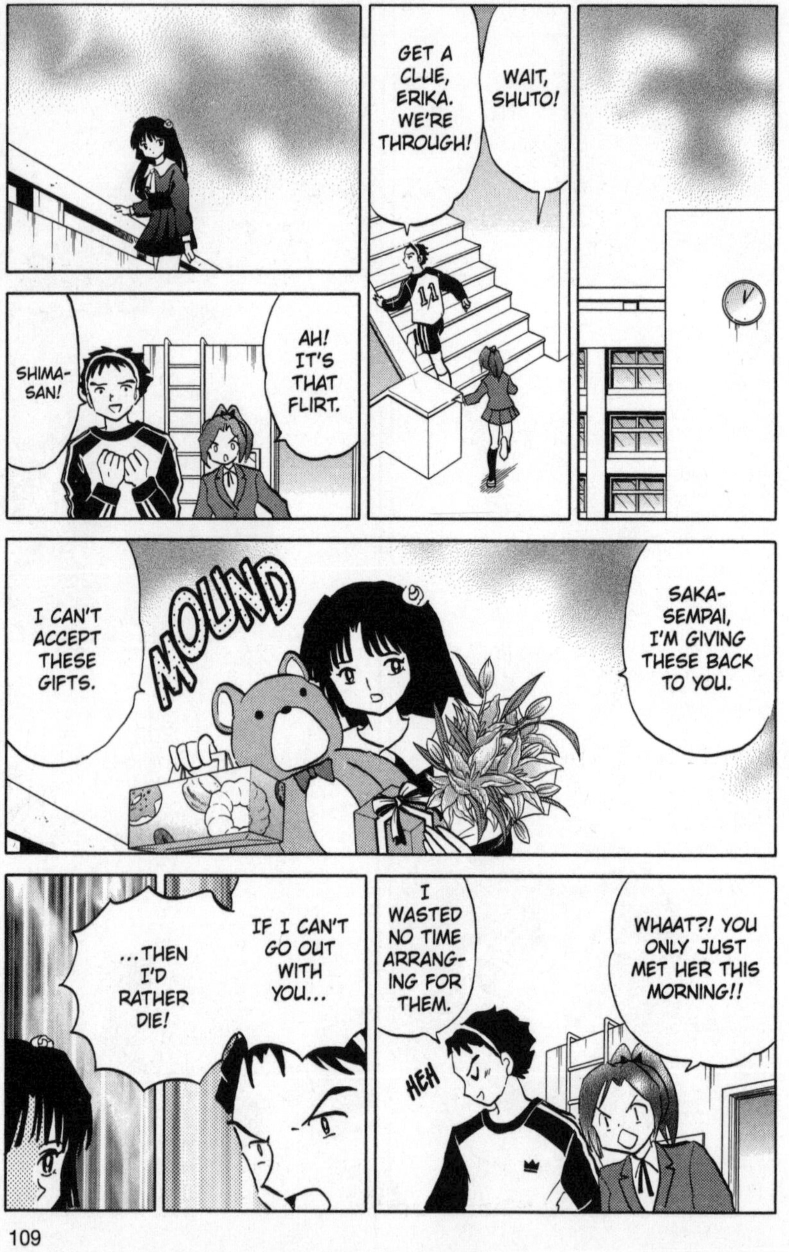
WAIT, SHUTO!
GET A CLUE, ERIKA. WE'RE THROUGH!
AH! IT'S THAT FLIRT.
SHIMA-SAN!
SAKA-SEMPAI, I'M GIVING THESE BACK TO YOU.
MOUND
I CAN'T ACCEPT THESE GIFTS.
WHAAT?! YOU ONLY JUST MET HER THIS MORNING!!
I WASTED NO TIME ARRANGING FOR THEM.
HEH
IF I CAN'T GO OUT WITH YOU...
...THEN I'D RATHER DIE!

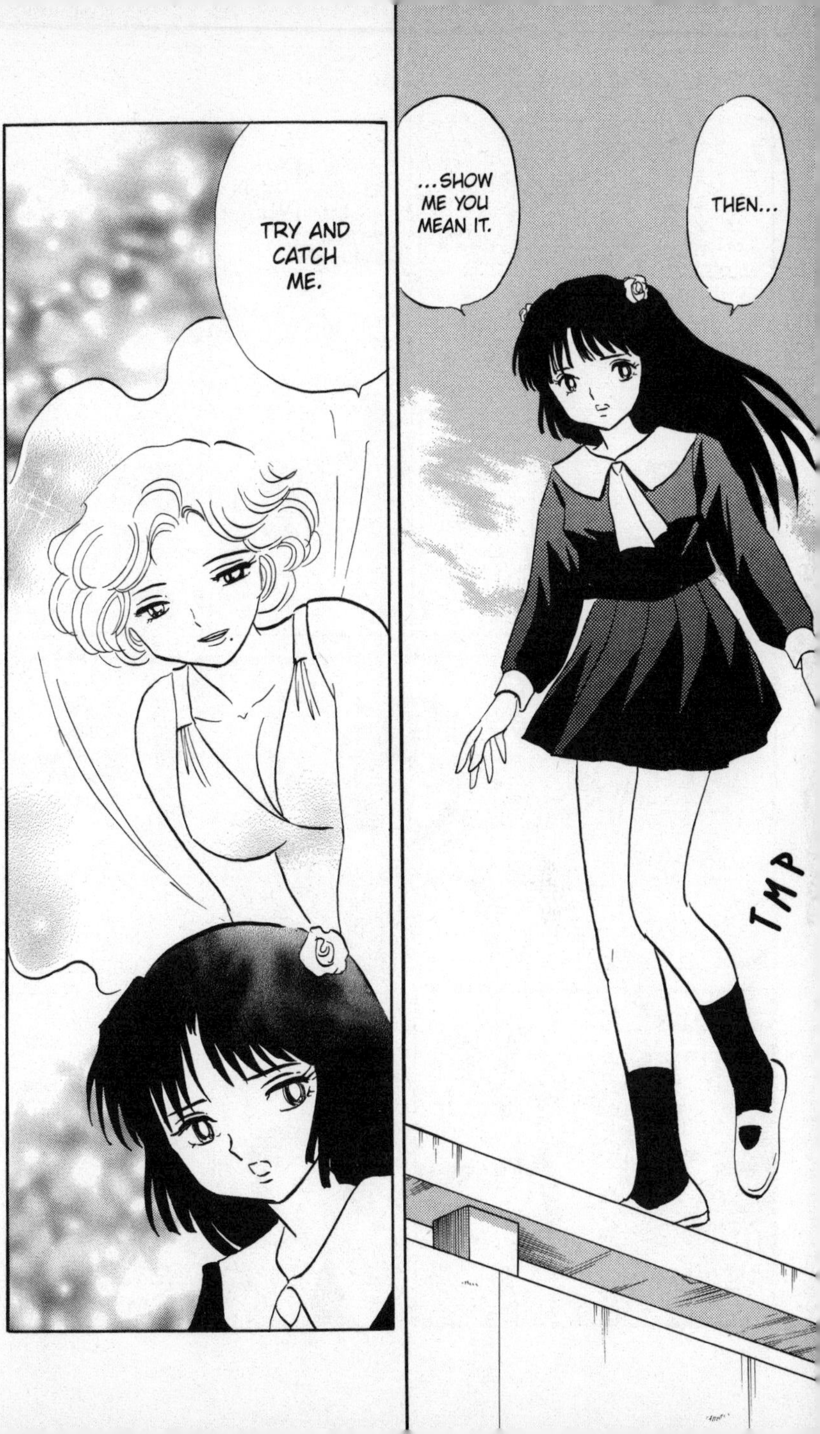
THEN...
...SHOW ME YOU MEAN IT.
TMP
TRY AND CATCH ME.

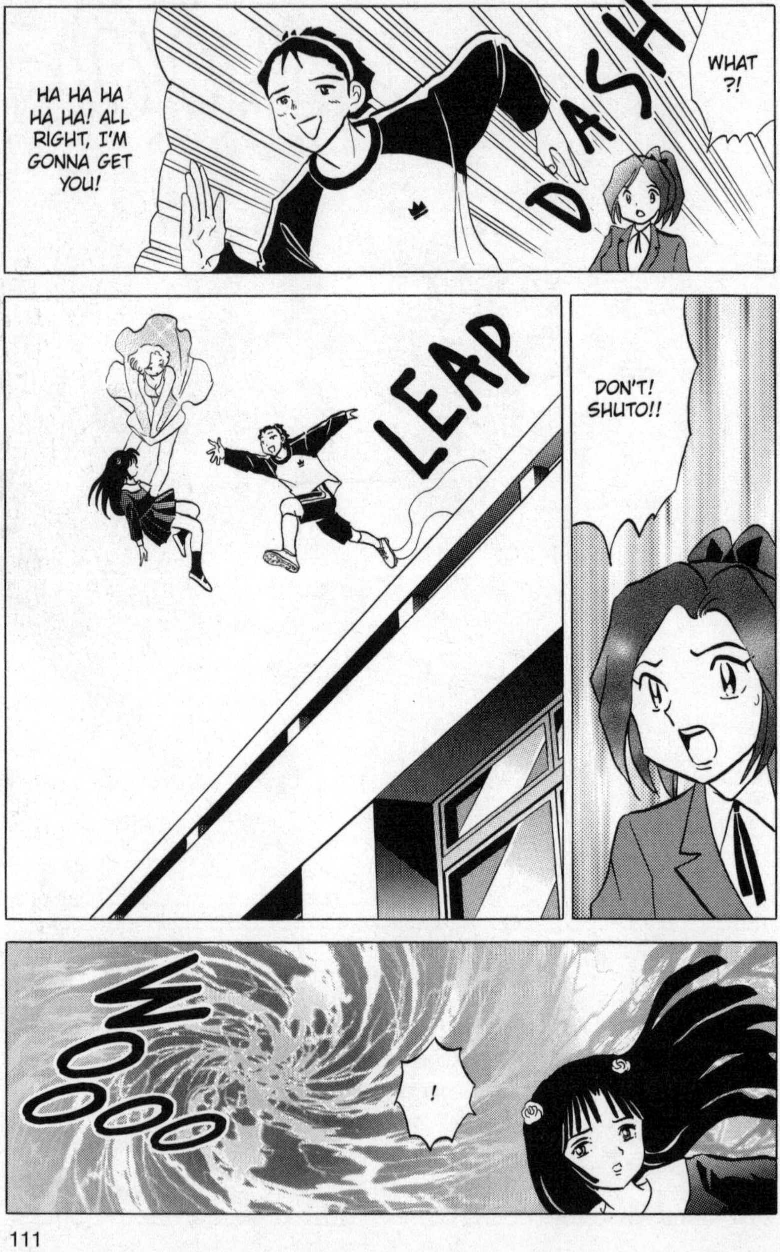
WHAT ?!
DASH
HA HA HA HA HA! ALL RIGHT, I'M GONNA GET YOU!
DON'T! SHUTO!!
LEAP
!
WOOOO

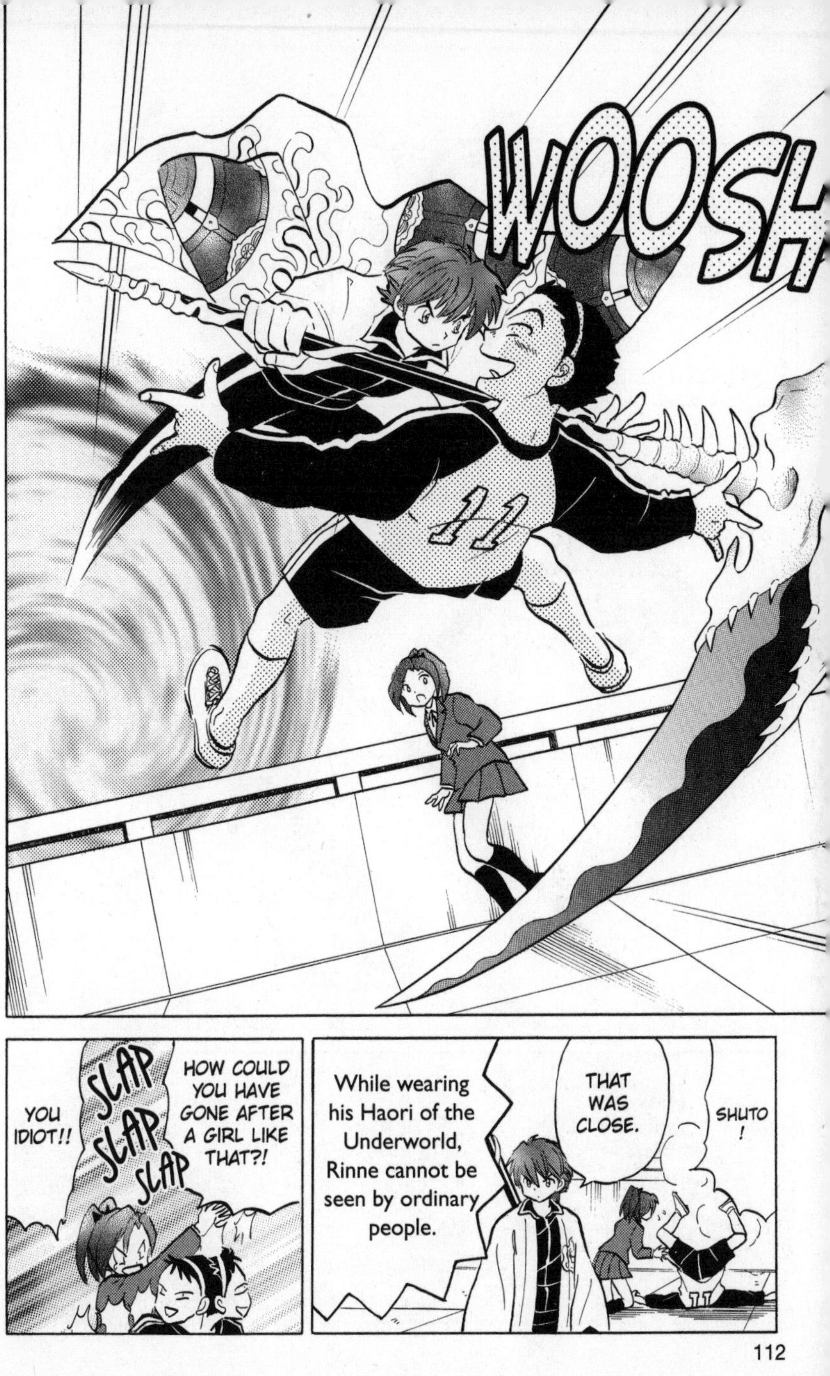
WOOSH
SHUTO!
THAT WAS CLOSE.
While wearing his Haori of the Underworld, Rinne cannot be seen by ordinary people.
HOW COULD YOU HAVE GONE AFTER A GIRL LIKE THAT?!
SLAP SLAP SLAP
YOU IDIOT!!

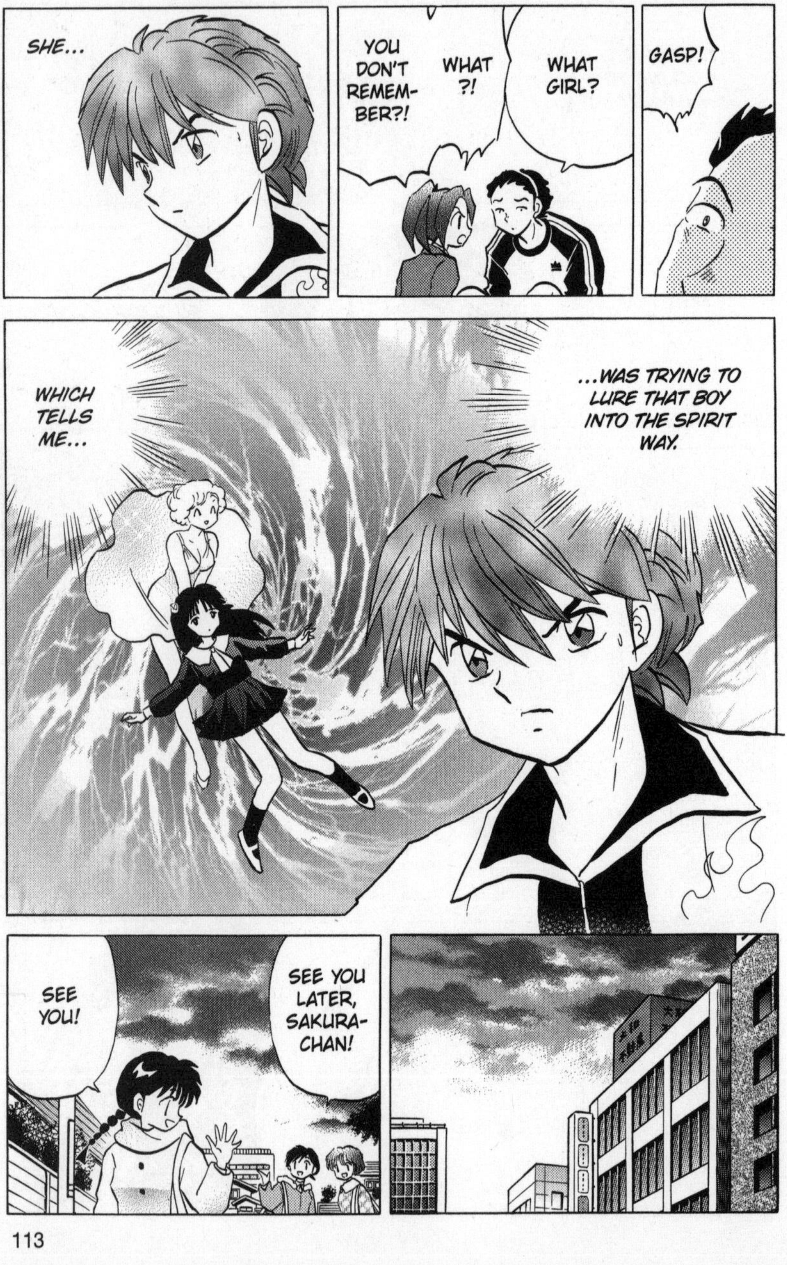
GASP!
WHAT GIRL?
WHAT ?!
YOU DON'T REMEM-BER?!
SHE…
WHICH TELLS ME…
…WAS TRYING TO LURE THAT BOY INTO THE SPIRIT WAY.
SEE YOU LATER, SAKURA-CHAN!
SEE YOU!

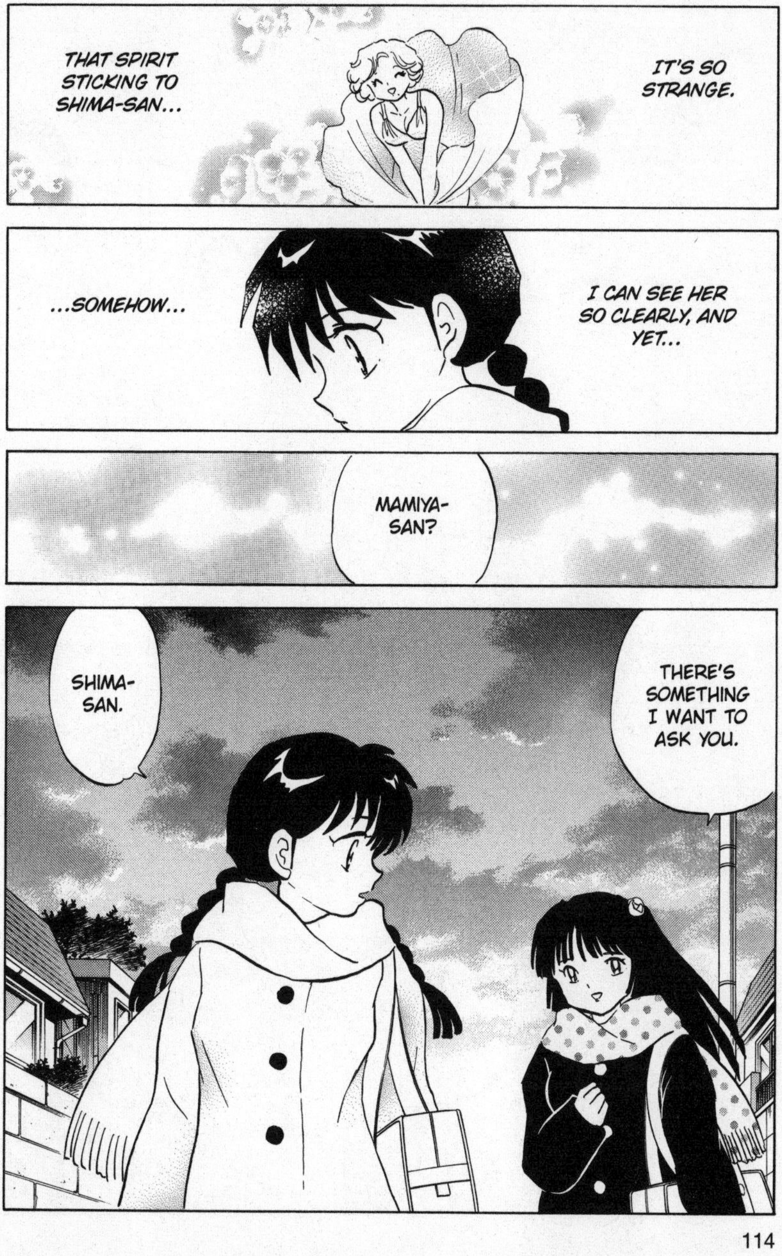
IT'S SO STRANGE.
THAT SPIRIT STICKING TO SHIMA-SAN...
I CAN SEE HER SO CLEARLY, AND YET...
...SOMEHOW...
MAMIYA-SAN?
THERE'S SOMETHING I WANT TO ASK YOU.
SHIMA-SAN.

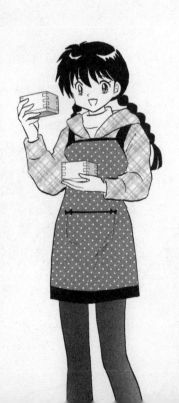

CHAPTER 135: THE TRUTH ABOUT RENGE

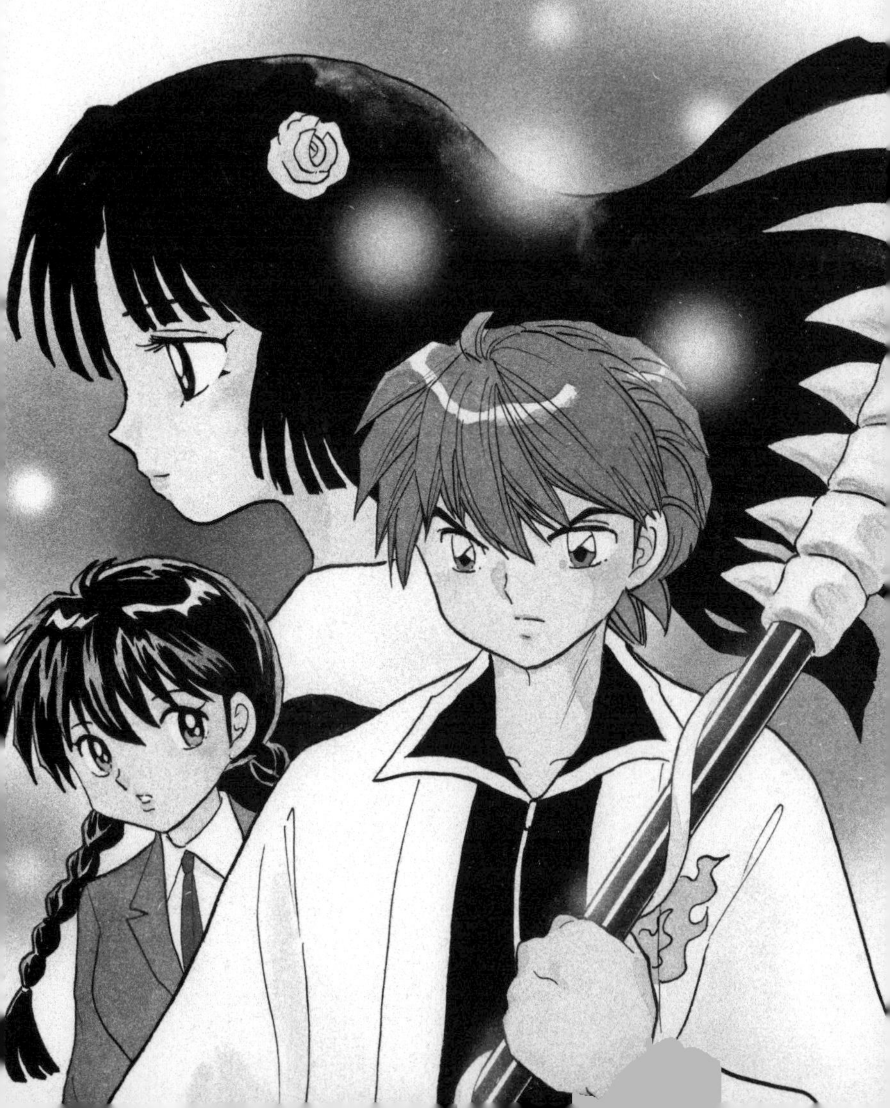

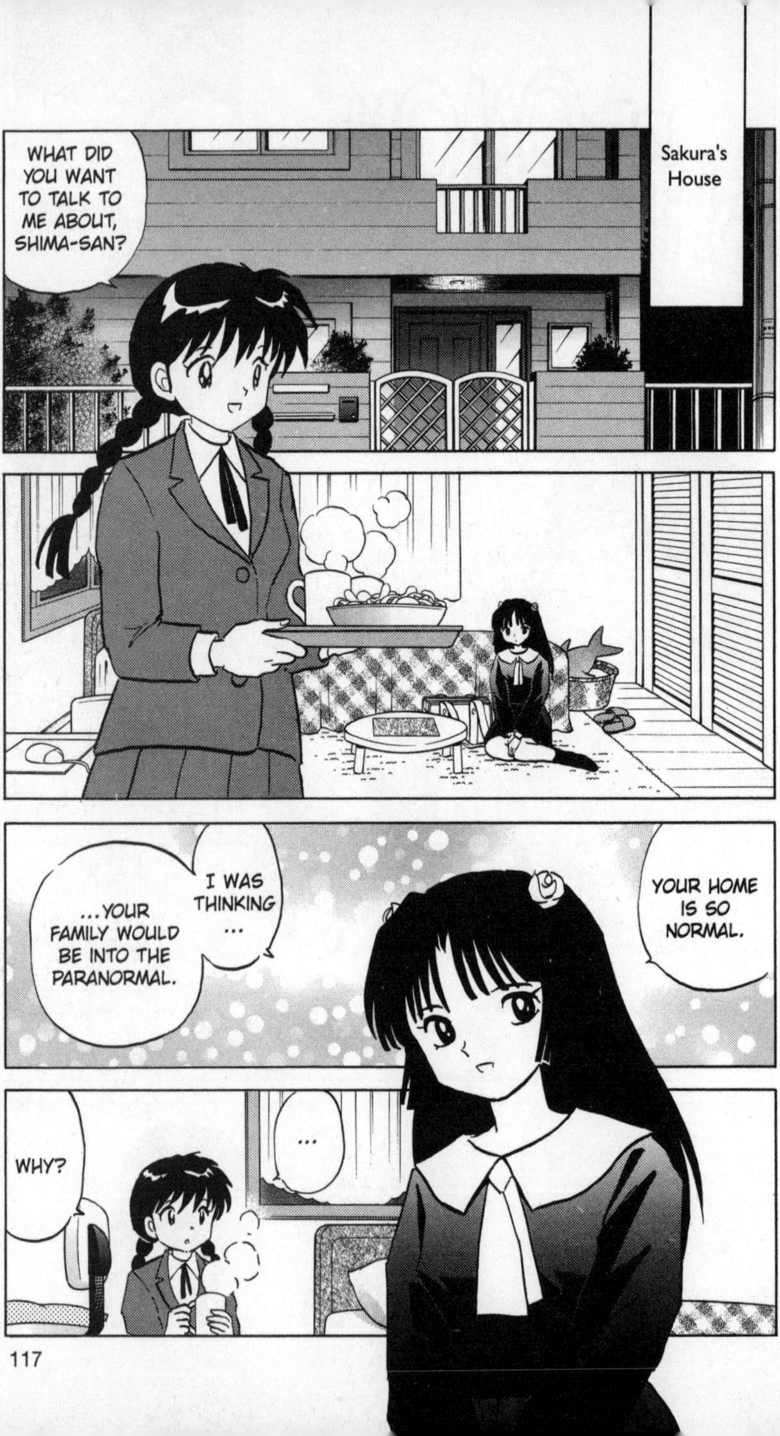
Sakura's House
WHAT DID YOU WANT TO TALK TO ME ABOUT, SHIMA-SAN?
YOUR HOME IS SO NORMAL.
I WAS THINKING ...
...YOUR FAMILY WOULD BE INTO THE PARANORMAL.
...
WHY?

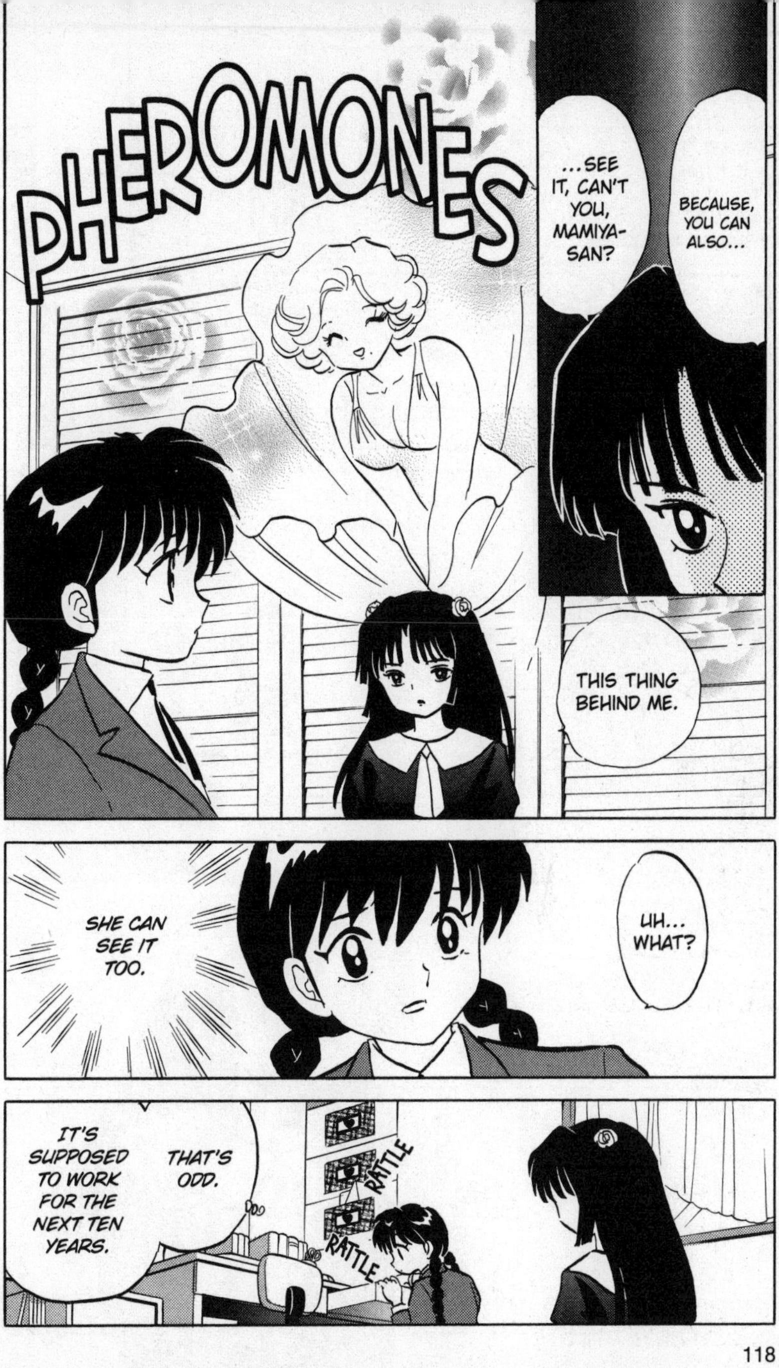
BECAUSE, YOU CAN ALSO...
...SEE IT, CAN'T YOU, MAMIYA-SAN?
THIS THING BEHIND ME.
PHEROMONES
UH... WHAT?
SHE CAN SEE IT TOO.
RATTLE
RATTLE
THAT'S ODD.
IT'S SUPPOSED TO WORK FOR THE NEXT TEN YEARS.

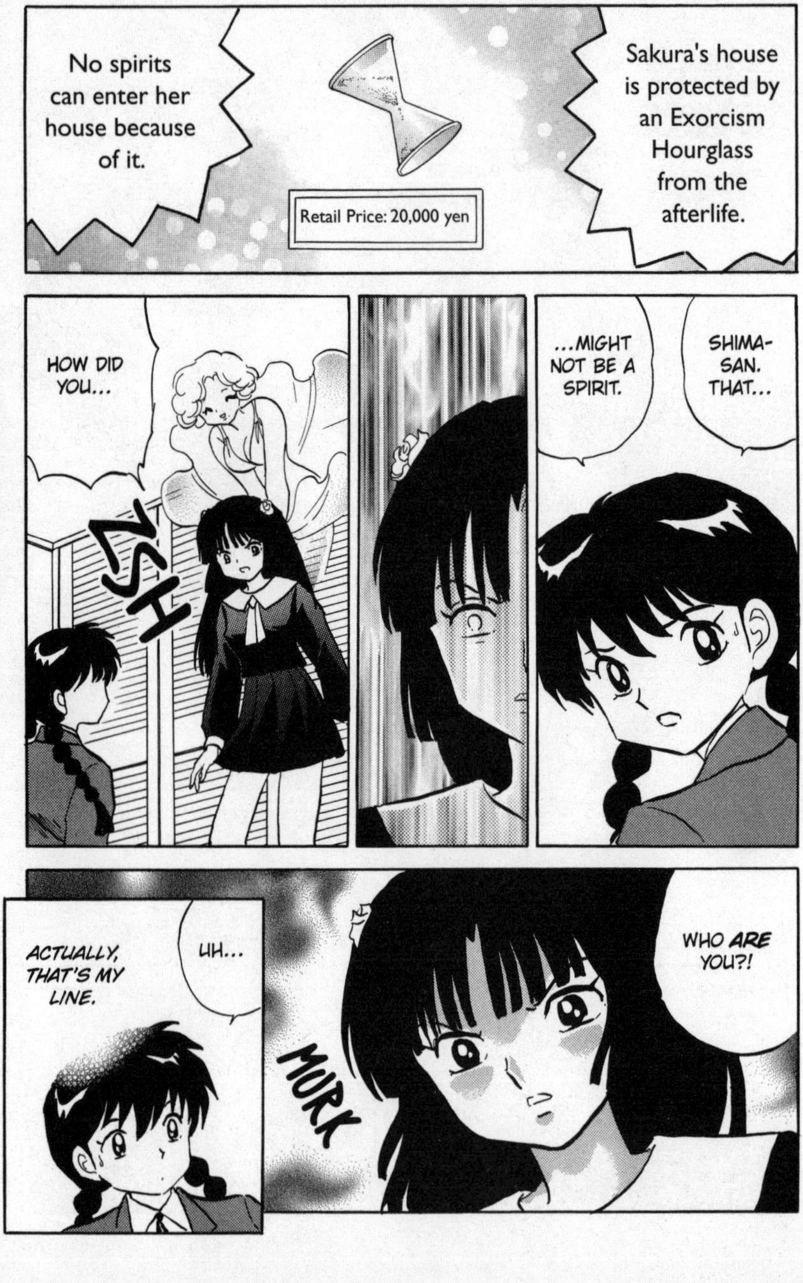
Sakura's house is protected by an Exorcism Hourglass from the afterlife.
No spirits can enter her house because of it.
Retail Price: 20,000 yen
SHIMA-SAN. THAT...
...MIGHT NOT BE A SPIRIT.
HOW DID YOU...
ZSH
WHO *ARE* YOU?!
MURK
UH...
ACTUALLY, THAT'S MY LINE.

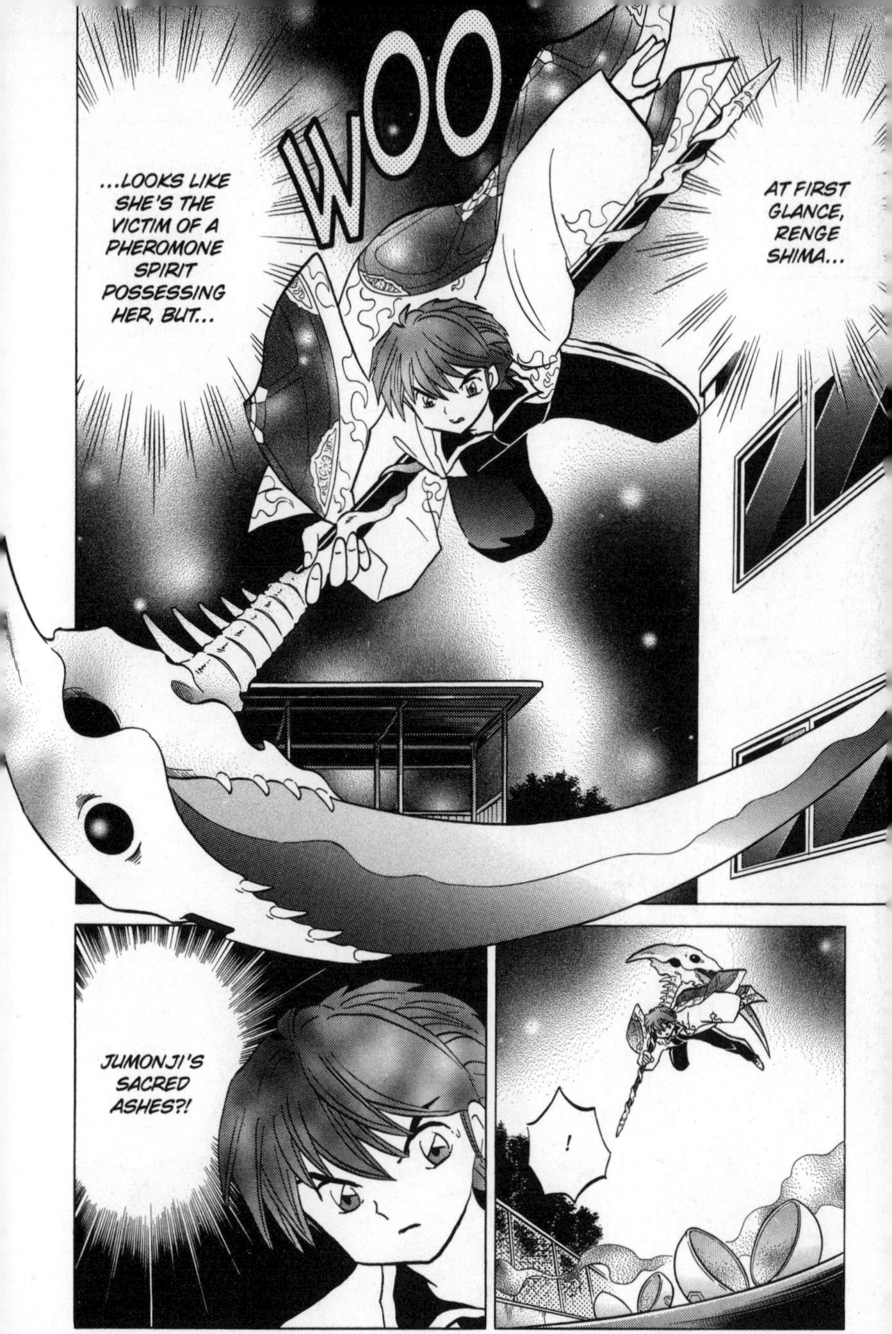
WOO
AT FIRST GLANCE, RENGE SHIMA...
...LOOKS LIKE SHE'S THE VICTIM OF A PHEROMONE SPIRIT POSSESSING HER, BUT...
!
JUMONJI'S SACRED ASHES?!

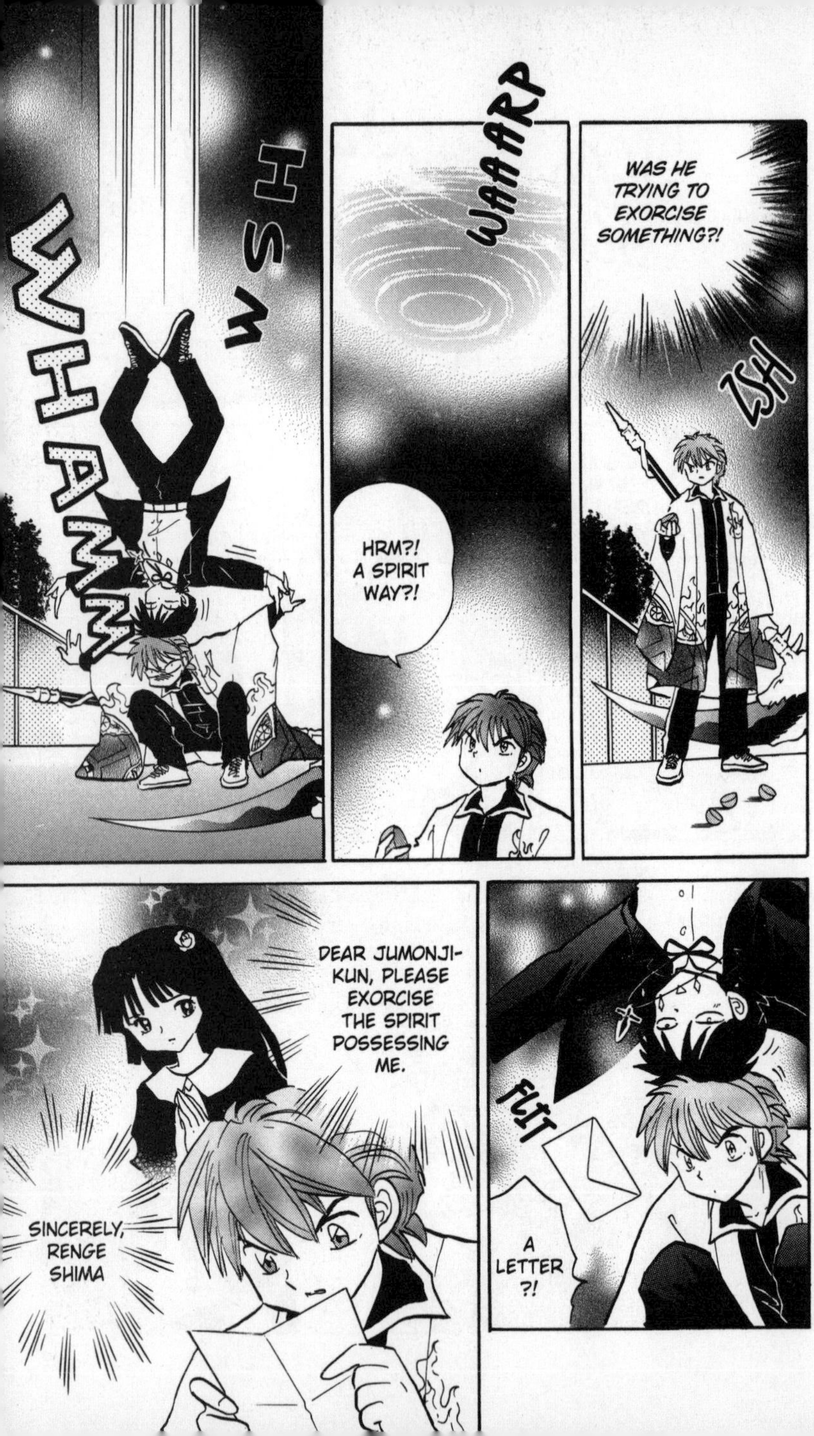
WAS HE TRYING TO EXORCISE SOMETHING?!
ZSH
WAARP
HRM?! A SPIRIT WAY?!
WSH
WHAMM
FLIT
A LETTER?!
DEAR JUMONJI-KUN, PLEASE EXORCISE THE SPIRIT POSSESSING ME.
SINCERELY, RENGE SHIMA

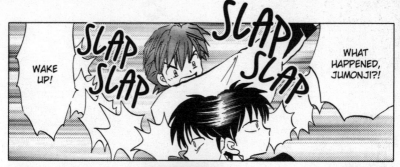

WHAT HAPPENED, JUMONJI?!
SLAP SLAP
SLAP SLAP
WAKE UP!
GOOD MORN-ING.
I'M FINE.
TH-THIS IS...
HIS SOUL'S BEEN COMPLETELY SUCKED OUT OF HIM?
HE'S BEEN REDUCED TO THE LEVEL OF A MYNA BIRD.
GOOD MORN-ING.
CHILL
!
THREE PEOPLE IN ONE CLASS...

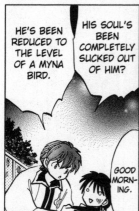

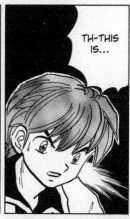

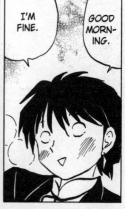

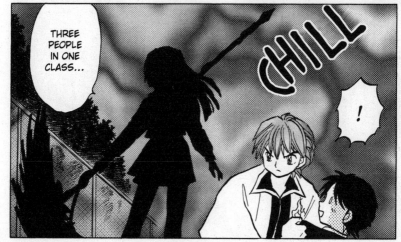

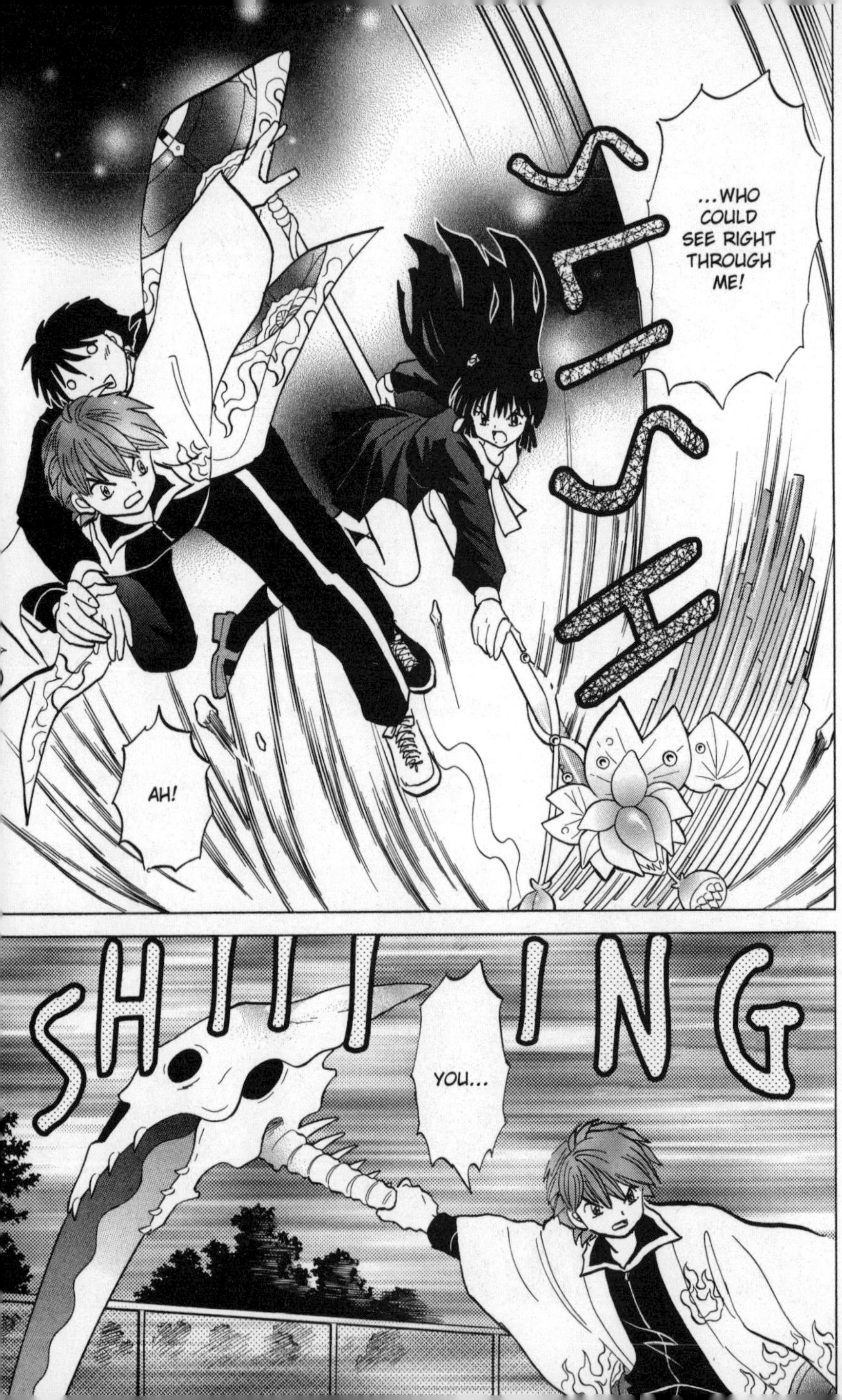
...WHO COULD SEE RIGHT THROUGH ME!
AH!
SHIIING
YOU...

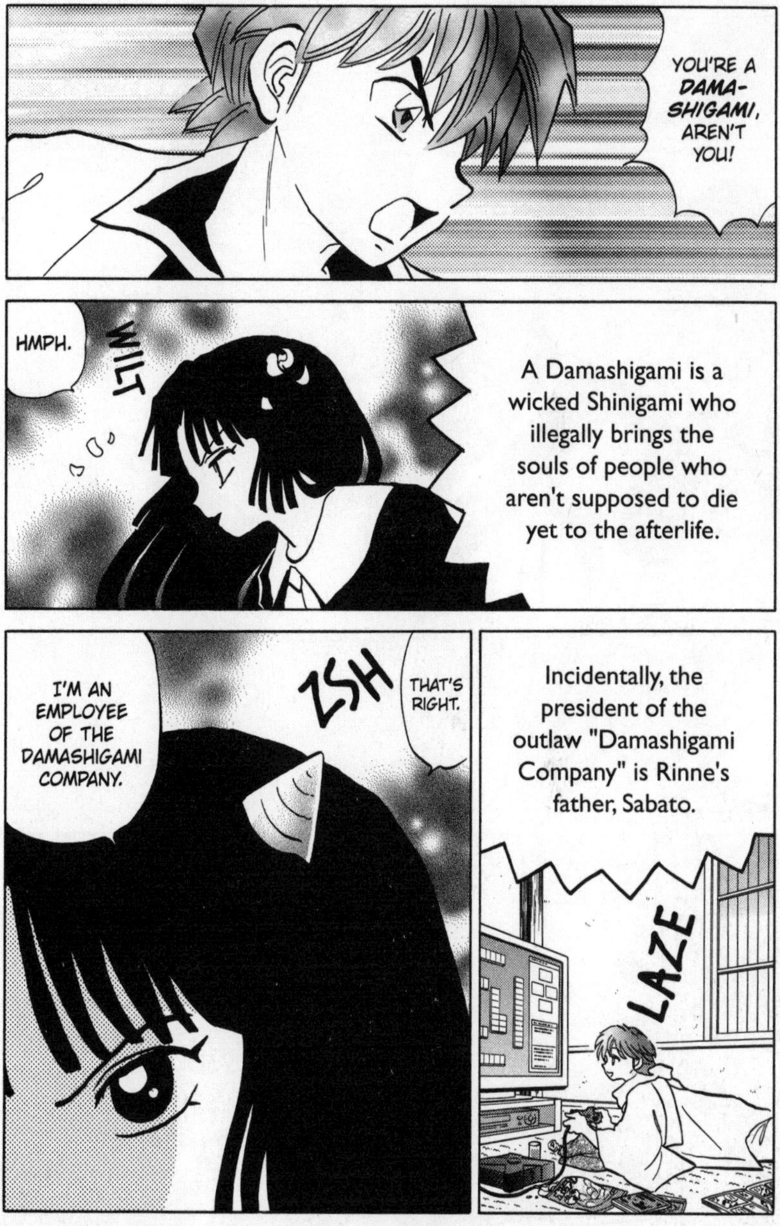

YOU'RE A *DAMASHIGAMI*, AREN'T YOU!
A Damashigami is a wicked Shinigami who illegally brings the souls of people who aren't supposed to die yet to the afterlife.
WILT
HMPH.
Incidentally, the president of the outlaw "Damashigami Company" is Rinne's father, Sabato.
LAZE
THAT'S RIGHT.
ZSH
I'M AN EMPLOYEE OF THE DAMASHIGAMI COMPANY.

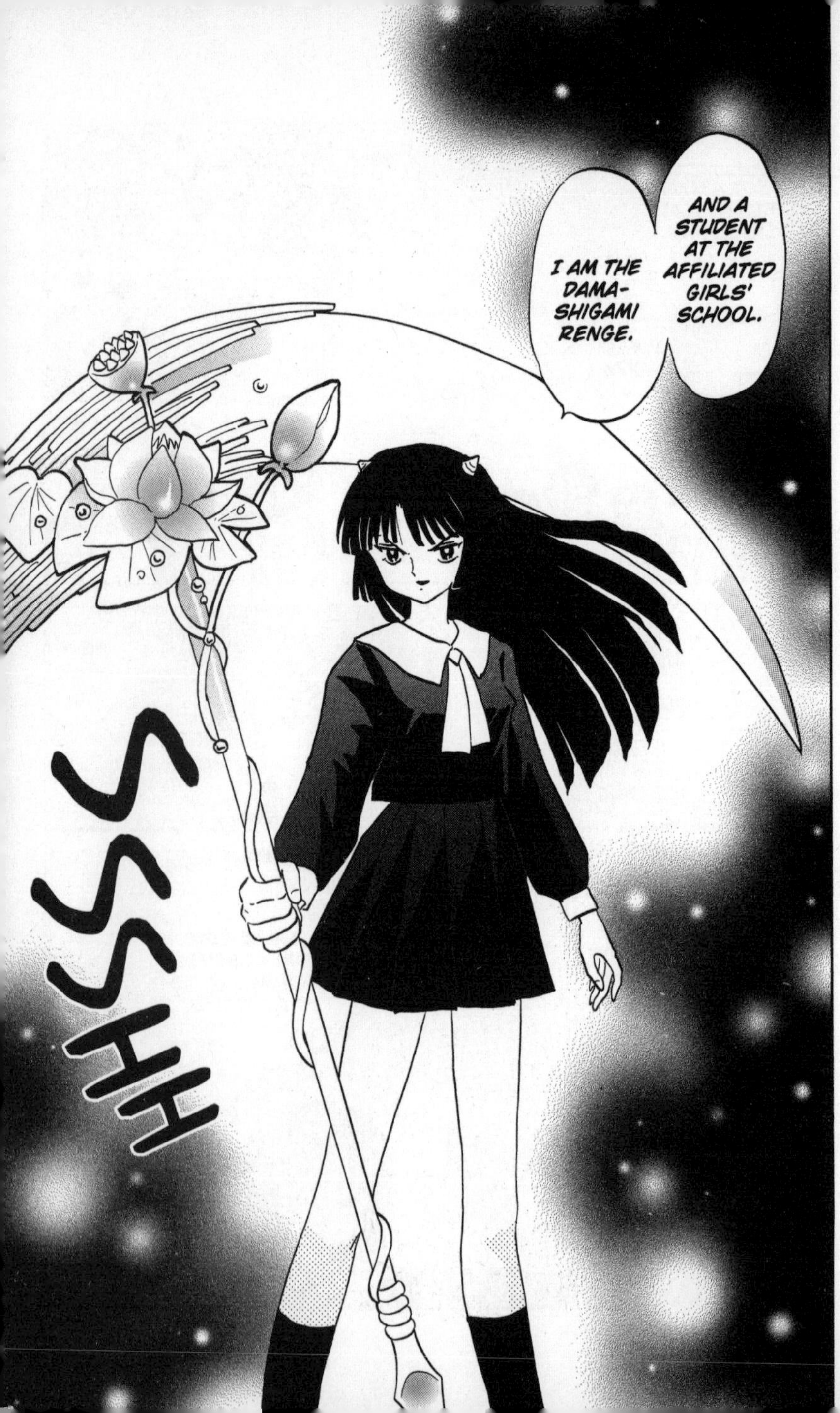
AND A STUDENT AT THE AFFILIATED GIRLS' SCHOOL.
I AM THE DAMA-SHIGAMI RENGE.
SSSHHH

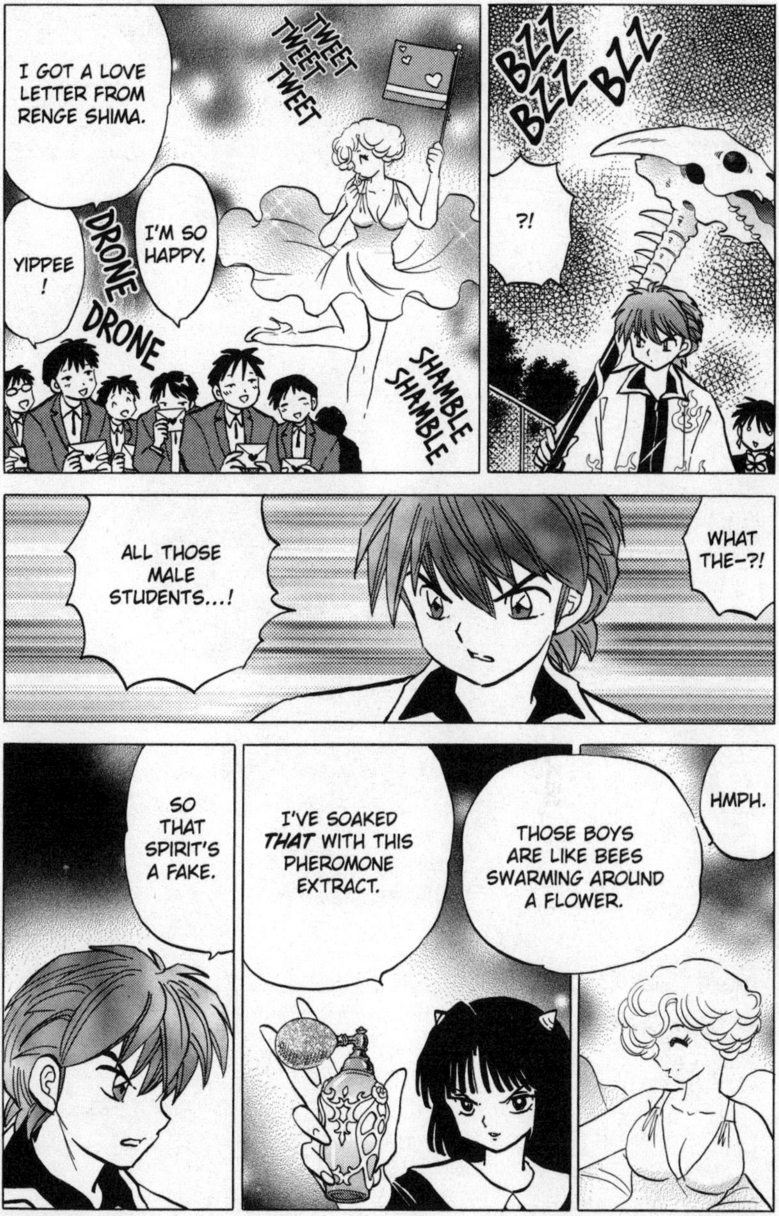
BZZ BZZ BZZ
?!
TWEET TWEET TWEET
I GOT A LOVE LETTER FROM RENGE SHIMA.
I'M SO HAPPY.
YIPPEE!
DRONE DRONE
SHAMBLE SHAMBLE
WHAT THE-?!
ALL THOSE MALE STUDENTS...!
HMPH.
THOSE BOYS ARE LIKE BEES SWARMING AROUND A FLOWER.
I'VE SOAKED THAT WITH THIS PHEROMONE EXTRACT.
SO THAT SPIRIT'S A FAKE.

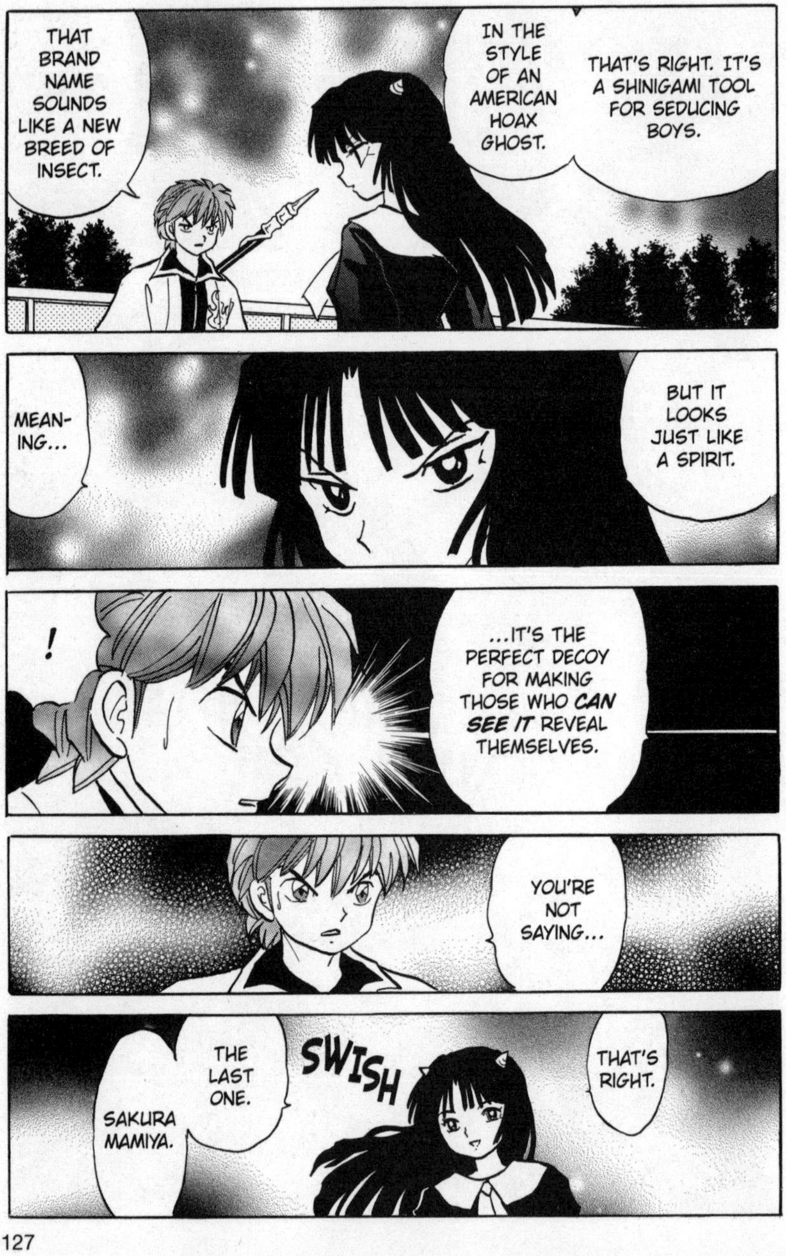
THAT'S RIGHT. IT'S A SHINIGAMI TOOL FOR SEDUCING BOYS.
IN THE STYLE OF AN AMERICAN HOAX GHOST.
THAT BRAND NAME SOUNDS LIKE A NEW BREED OF INSECT.
BUT IT LOOKS JUST LIKE A SPIRIT.
MEAN-ING...
...IT'S THE PERFECT DECOY FOR MAKING THOSE WHO *CAN SEE IT* REVEAL THEMSELVES.
!
YOU'RE NOT SAYING...
THAT'S RIGHT.
SWISH
THE LAST ONE.
SAKURA MAMIYA.

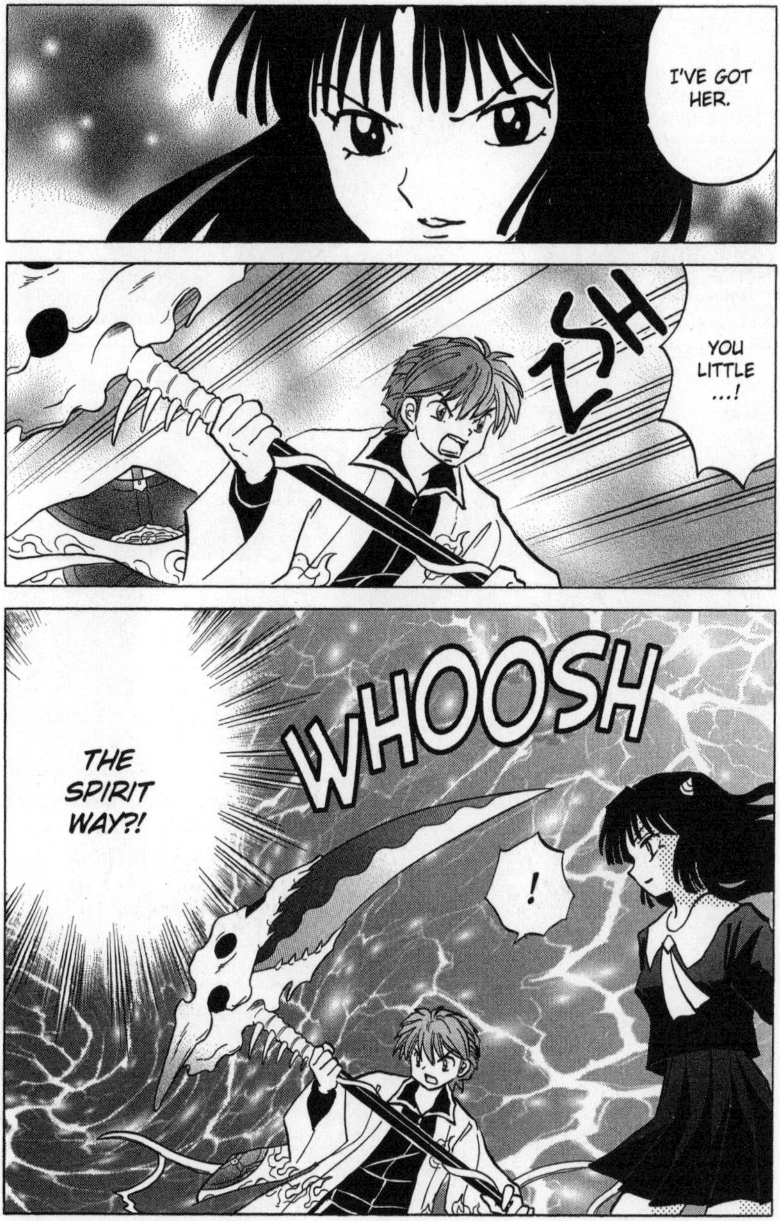
I'VE GOT HER.
YOU LITTLE ...!
ZSH
WHOOSH
!
THE SPIRIT WAY?!

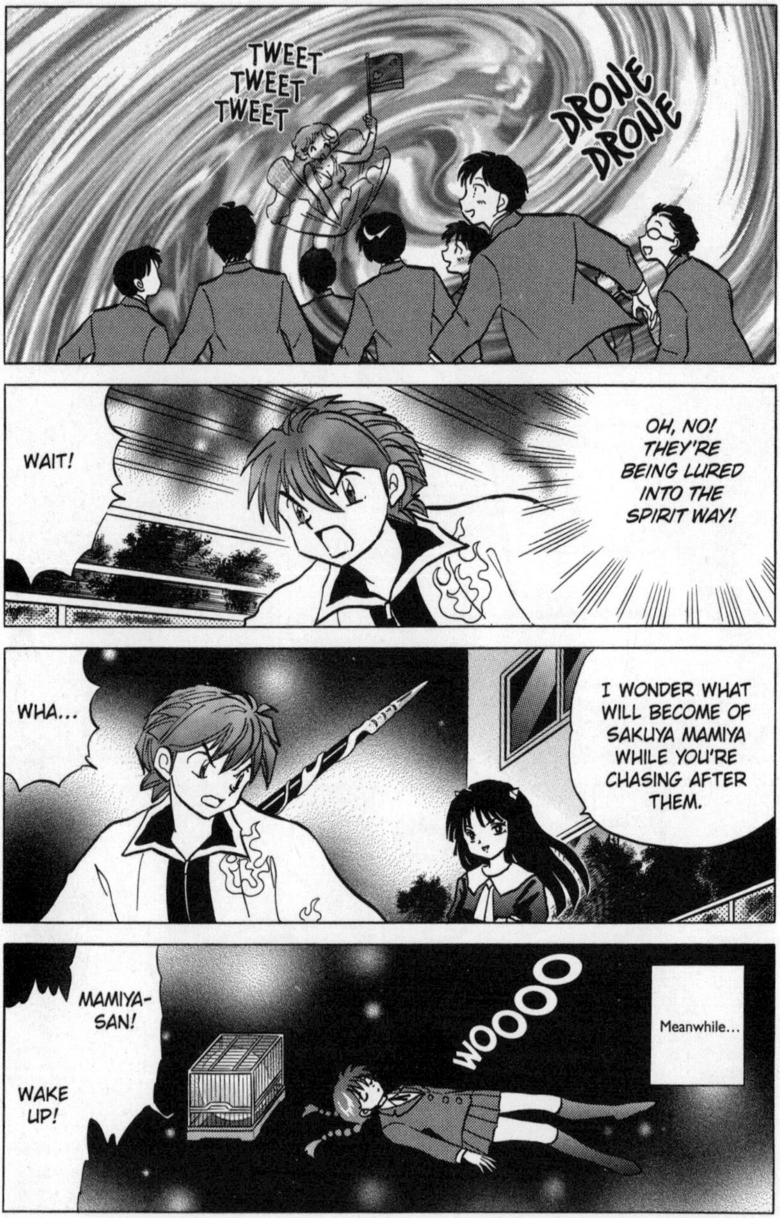
DRONE DRONE
TWEET TWEET TWEET
OH, NO! THEY'RE BEING LURED INTO THE SPIRIT WAY!
WAIT!
I WONDER WHAT WILL BECOME OF SAKUYA MAMIYA WHILE YOU'RE CHASING AFTER THEM.
WHA...
Meanwhile...
WOOOO
MAMIYA-SAN!
WAKE UP!

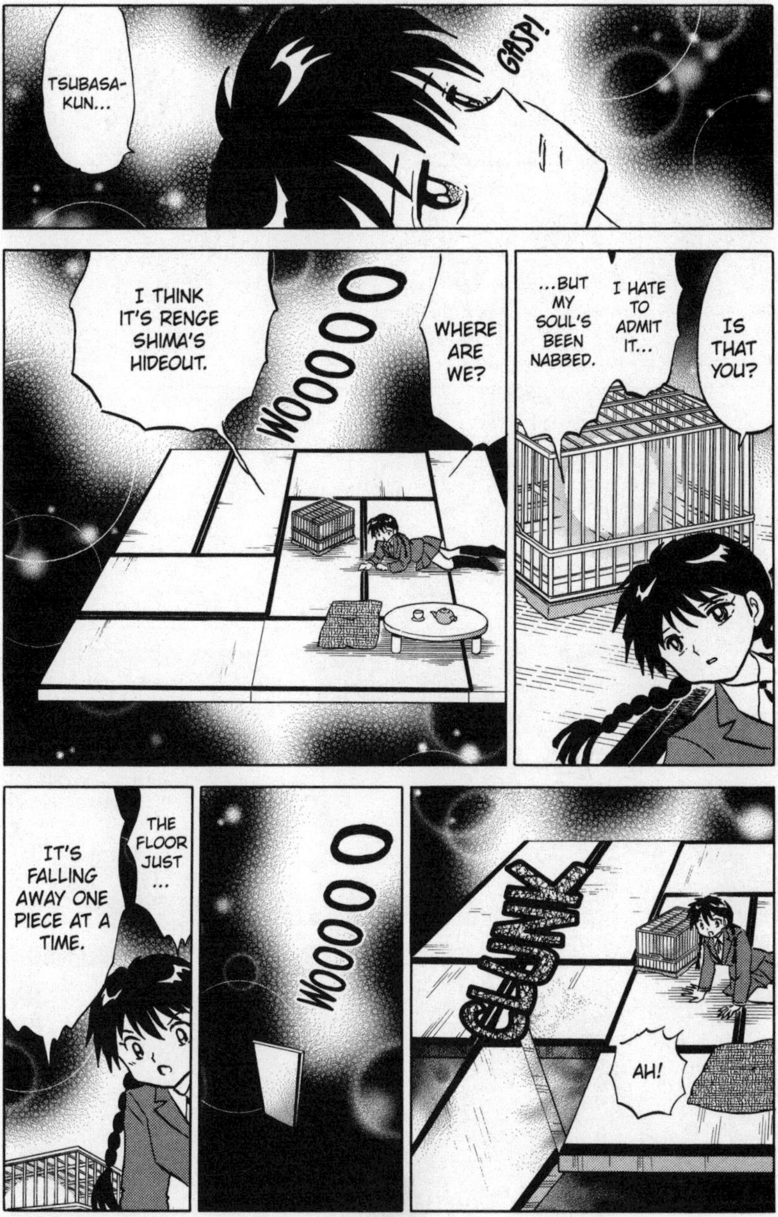
GASP!
TSUBASA-KUN...
IS THAT YOU?
I HATE TO ADMIT IT...
...BUT MY SOUL'S BEEN NABBED.
WHERE ARE WE?
WOOOOOM
I THINK IT'S RENGE SHIMA'S HIDEOUT.
CLUNK
AH!
WOOOOOM
THE FLOOR JUST ...
IT'S FALLING AWAY ONE PIECE AT A TIME.

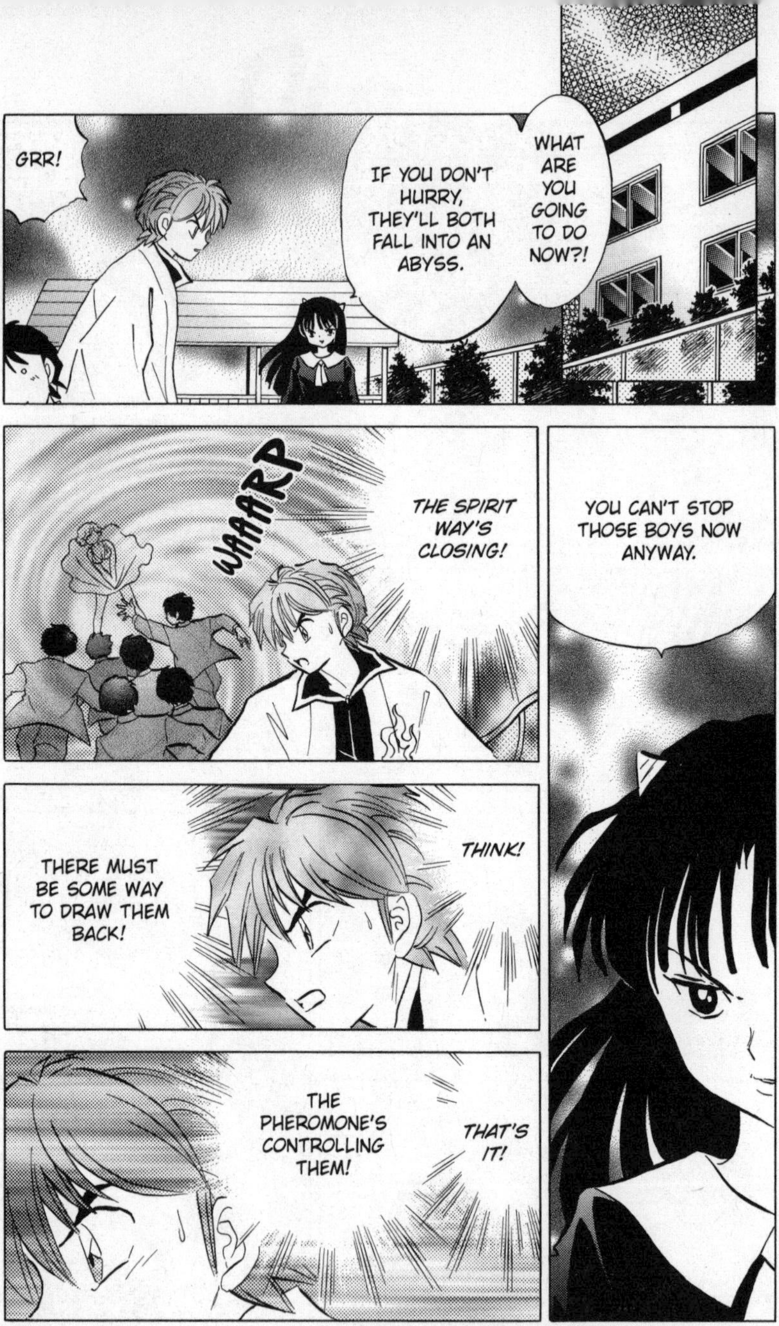
WHAT ARE YOU GOING TO DO NOW?!
IF YOU DON'T HURRY, THEY'LL BOTH FALL INTO AN ABYSS.
GRR!
YOU CAN'T STOP THOSE BOYS NOW ANYWAY.
THE SPIRIT WAY'S CLOSING!
WAAARP
THINK!
THERE MUST BE SOME WAY TO DRAW THEM BACK!
THAT'S IT!
THE PHEROMONE'S CONTROLLING THEM!

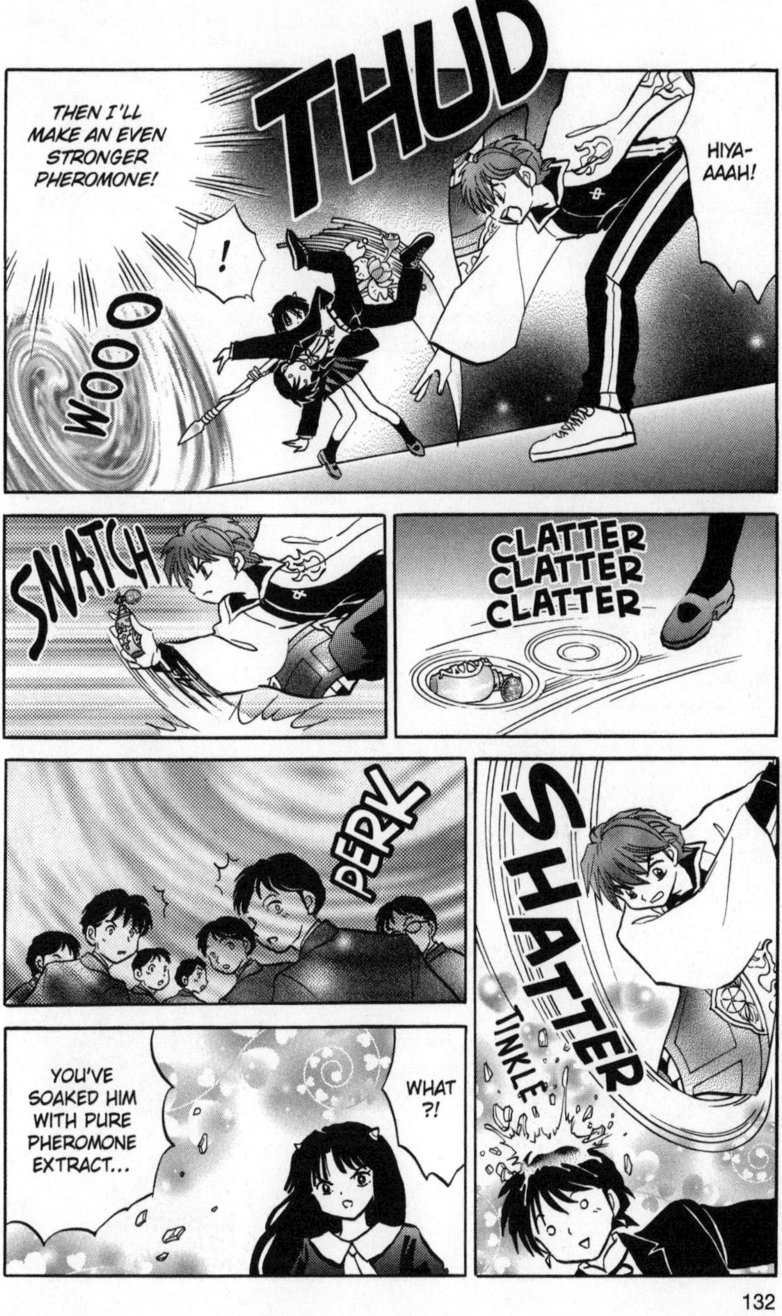
HIYA-AAAH!
THUD
THEN I'LL MAKE AN EVEN STRONGER PHEROMONE!
!
WOOO
CLATTER CLATTER CLATTER
SNATCH
SHATTER
TINKLE
PERK
WHAT ?!
YOU'VE SOAKED HIM WITH PURE PHEROMONE EXTRACT...

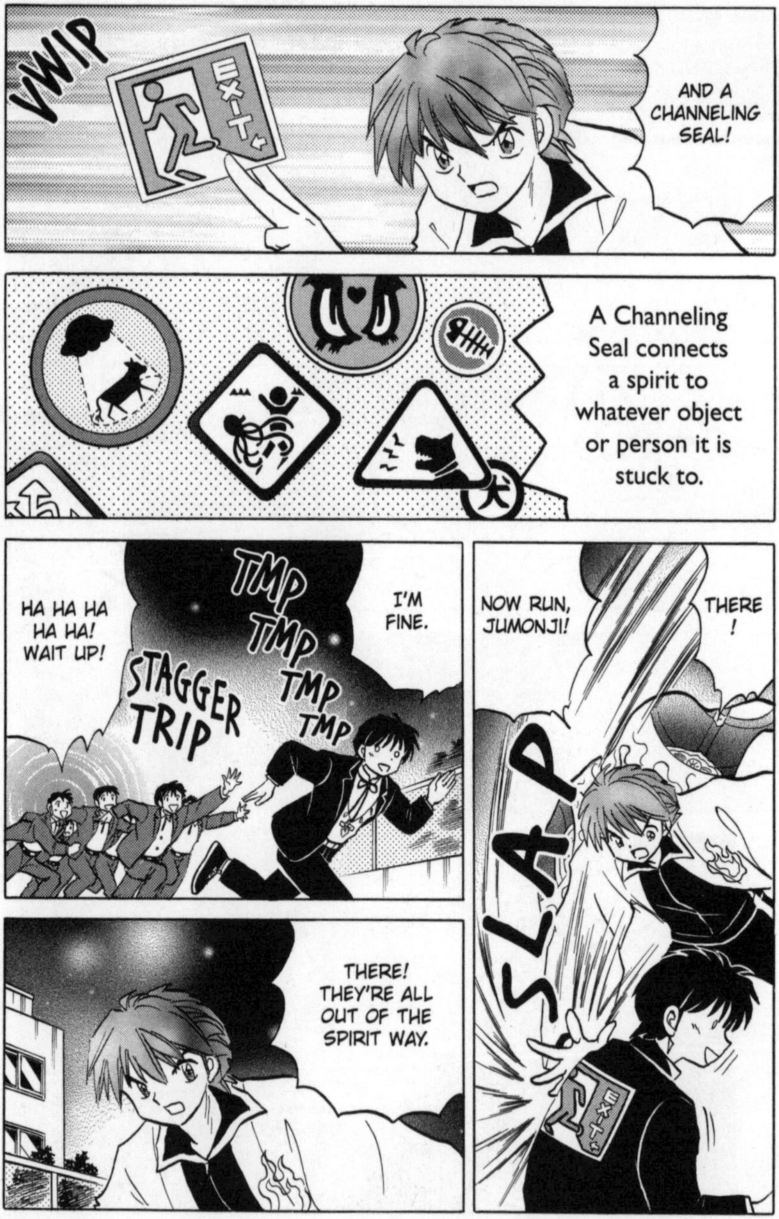
VWIP
AND A CHANNELING SEAL!
A Channeling Seal connects a spirit to whatever object or person it is stuck to.
THERE!
NOW RUN, JUMONJI!
SLAP
TMP TMP TMP TMP
I'M FINE.
HA HA HA HA HA! WAIT UP!
STAGGER TRIP
THERE! THEY'RE ALL OUT OF THE SPIRIT WAY.

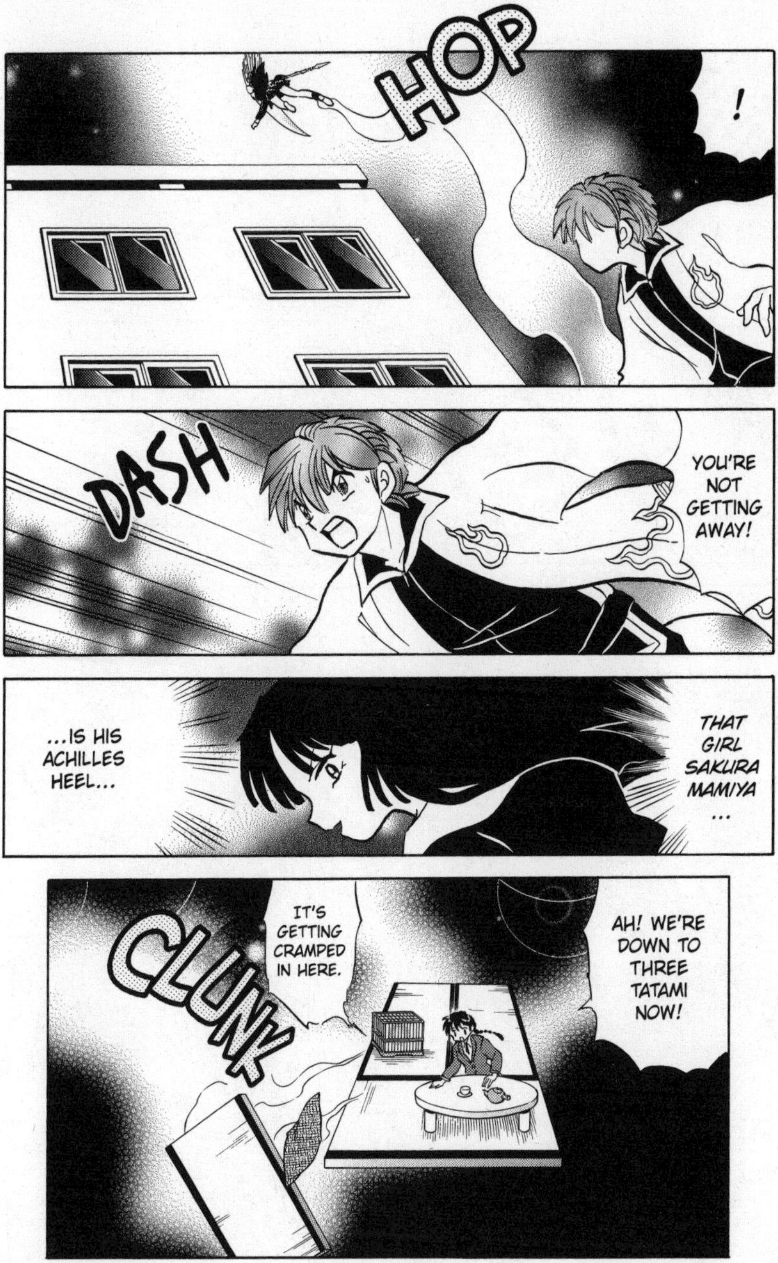
HOP
!
YOU'RE NOT GETTING AWAY!
DASH
THAT GIRL SAKURA MAMIYA ...
...IS HIS ACHILLES HEEL...
AH! WE'RE DOWN TO THREE TATAMI NOW!
IT'S GETTING CRAMPED IN HERE.
CLUNK

CHAPTER 136: THE ONE-HUNDREDTH SOUL

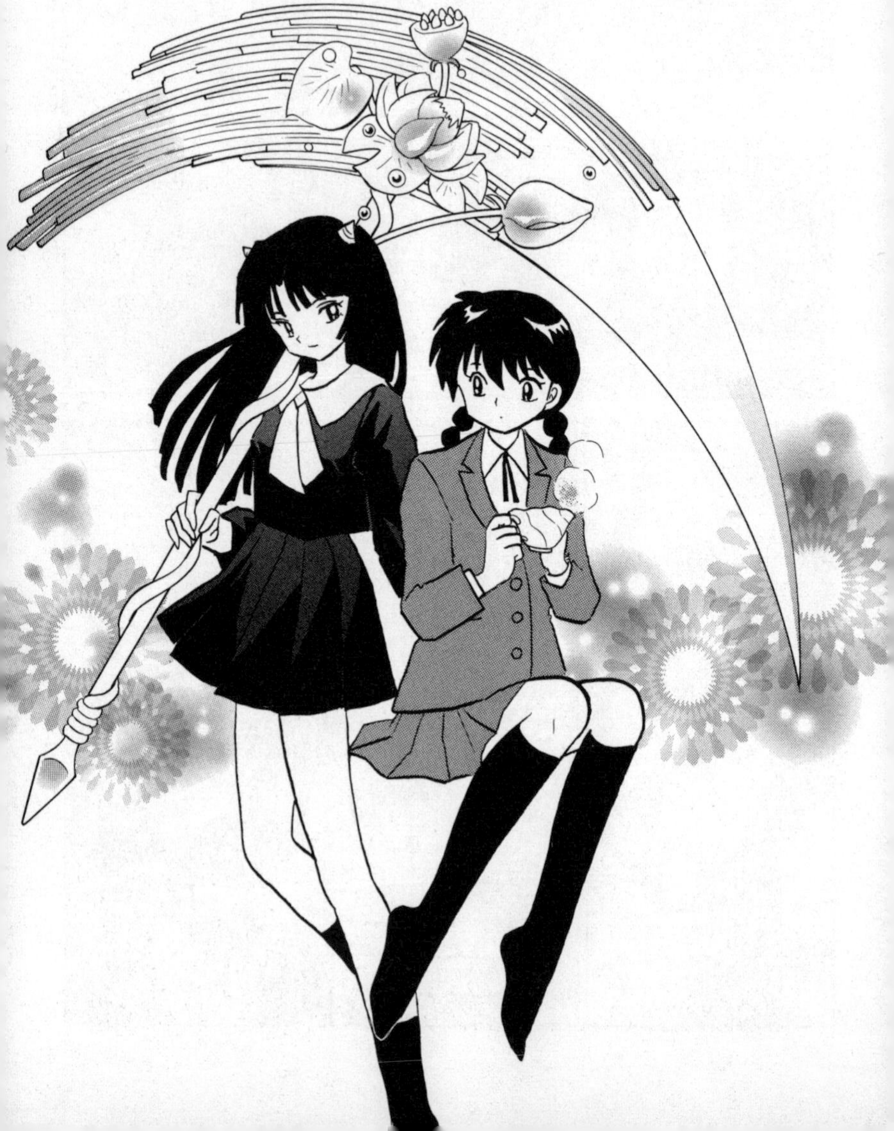

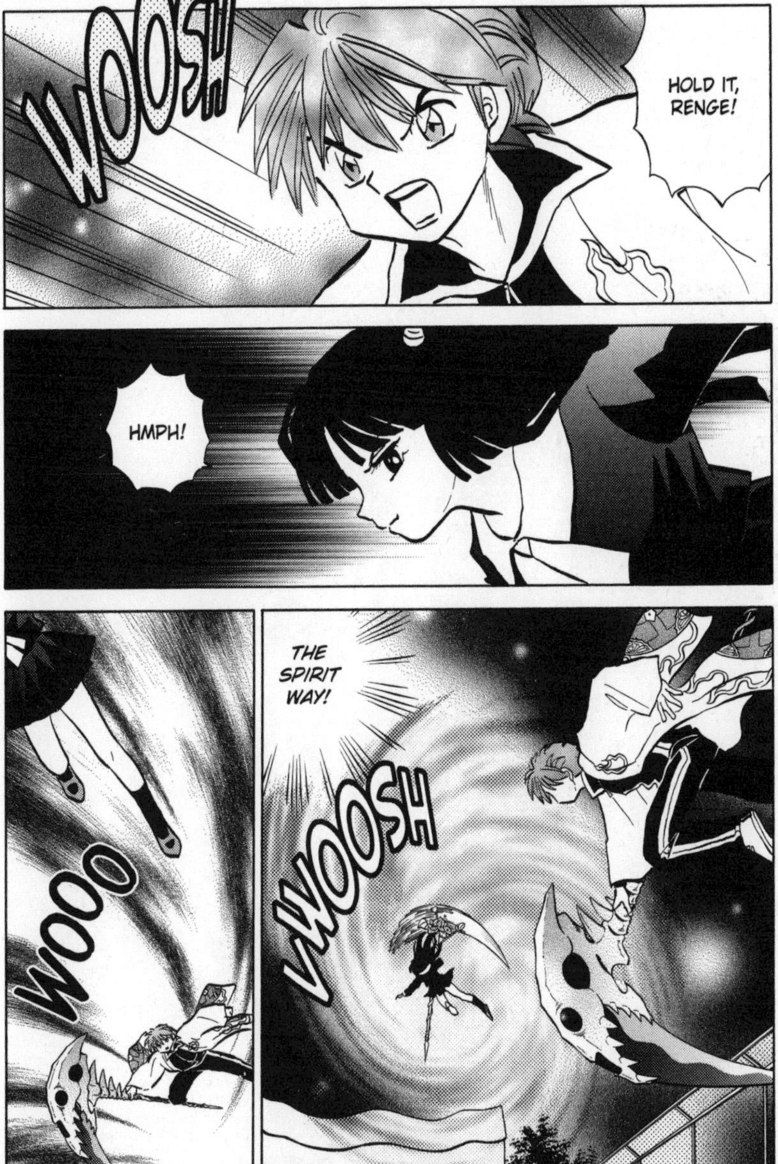
HOLD IT, RENGE!
WOOSH!
HMPH!
THE SPIRIT WAY!
WOOSH
WOOO

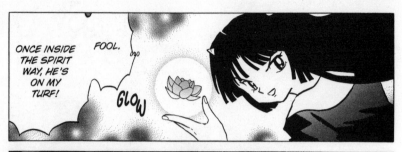

ONCE INSIDE THE SPIRIT WAY, HE'S ON MY TURF!

FOOL.

GLOW

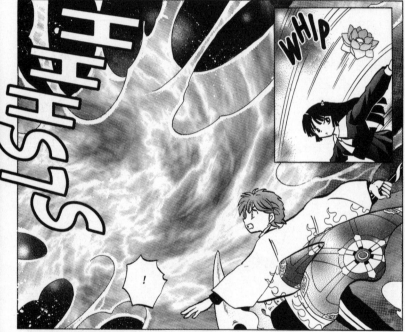

SHHHH

WHIP

!

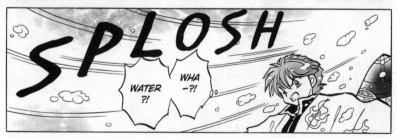

SPLOSH

WATER ?!

WHA -?!

137

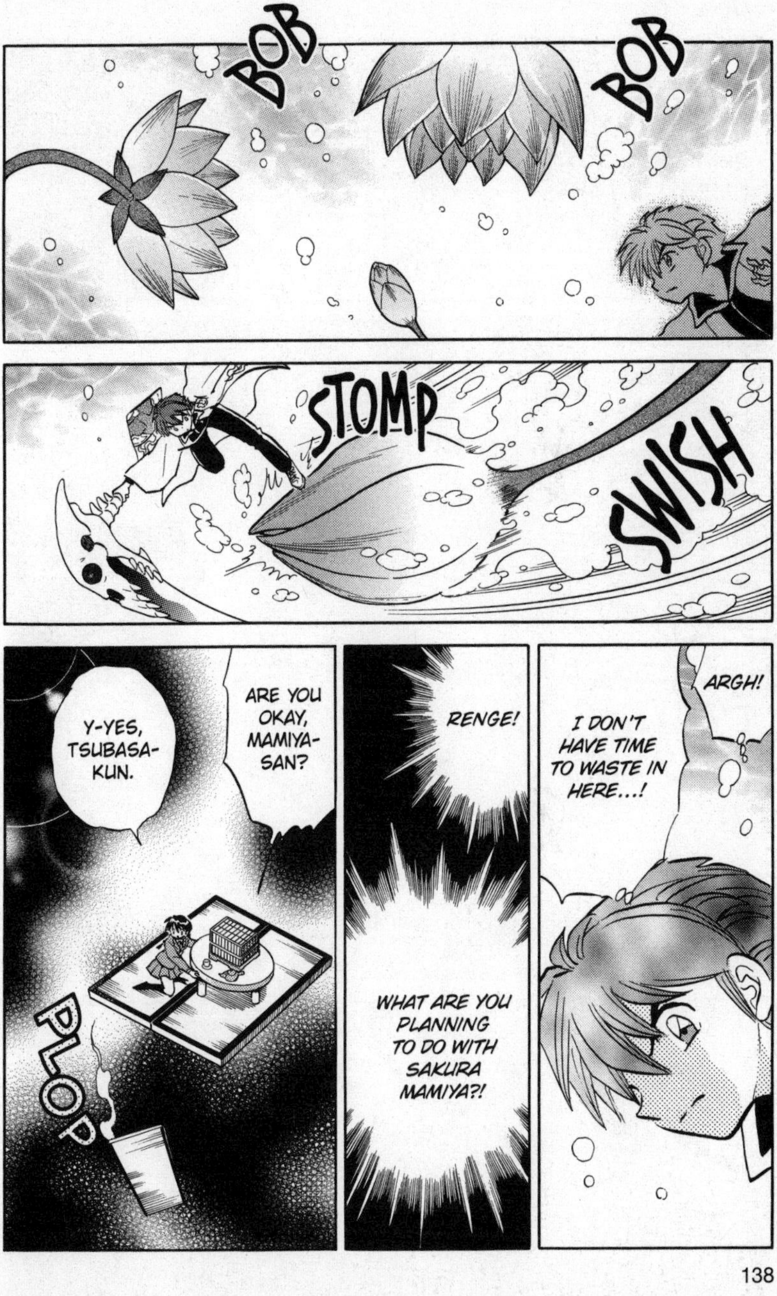
BOB
BOB
SWISH
STOMP
ARGH!
I DON'T HAVE TIME TO WASTE IN HERE...!
RENGE!
WHAT ARE YOU PLANNING TO DO WITH SAKURA MAMIYA?!
ARE YOU OKAY, MAMIYA-SAN?
Y-YES, TSUBASA-KUN.
PLOP

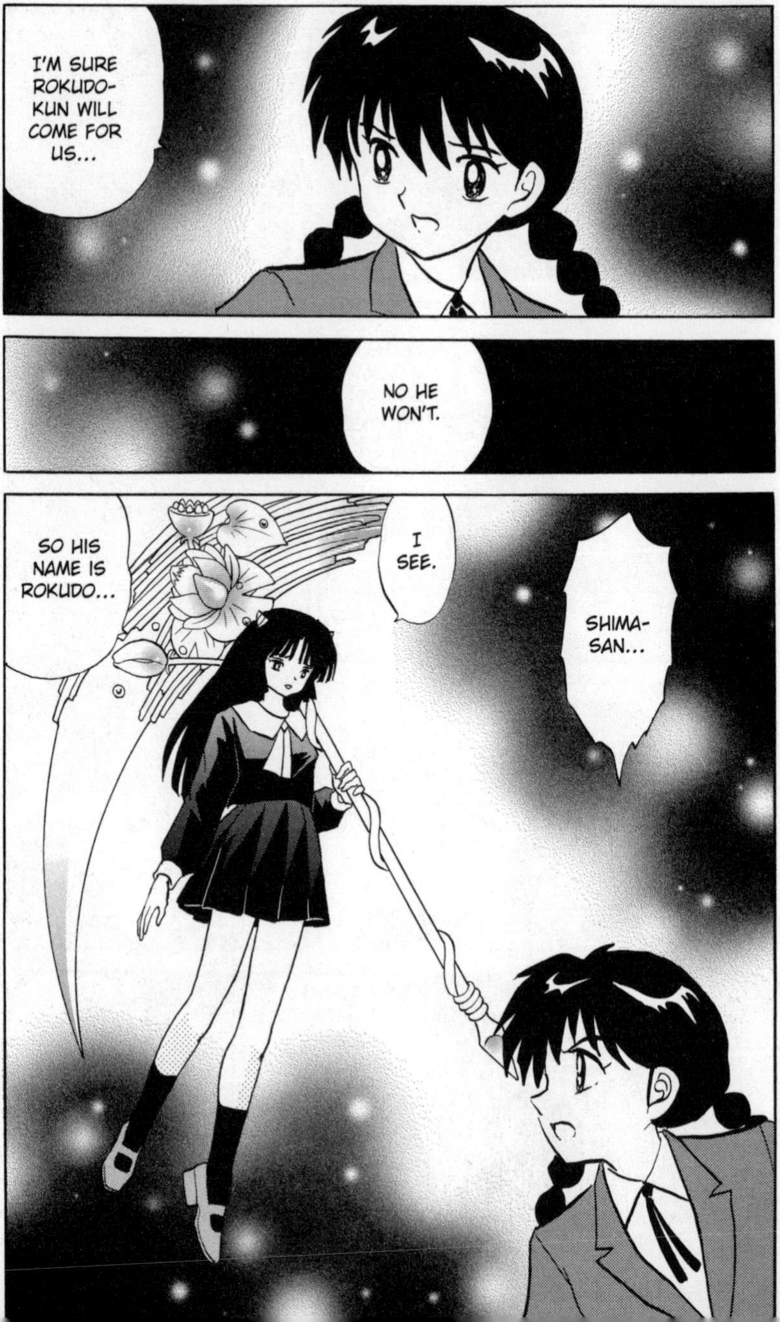
I'M SURE ROKUDO-KUN WILL COME FOR US...
NO HE WON'T.
SHIMA-SAN...
I SEE.
SO HIS NAME IS ROKUDO...

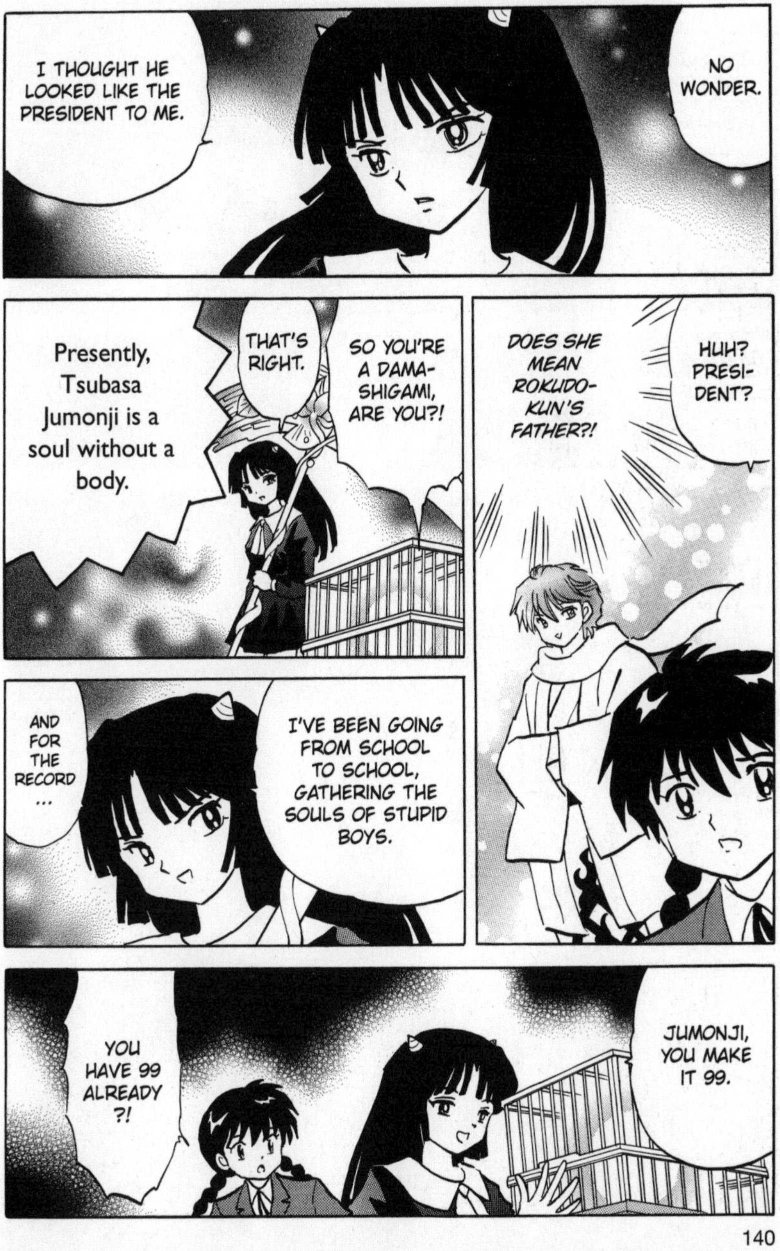
NO WONDER.
I THOUGHT HE LOOKED LIKE THE PRESIDENT TO ME.
HUH? PRESI-DENT?
DOES SHE MEAN ROKUDO-KUN'S FATHER?!
SO YOU'RE A DAMA-SHIGAMI, ARE YOU?!
THAT'S RIGHT.
Presently, Tsubasa Jumonji is a soul without a body.
I'VE BEEN GOING FROM SCHOOL TO SCHOOL, GATHERING THE SOULS OF STUPID BOYS.
AND FOR THE RECORD ...
JUMONJI, YOU MAKE IT 99.
YOU HAVE 99 ALREADY ?!

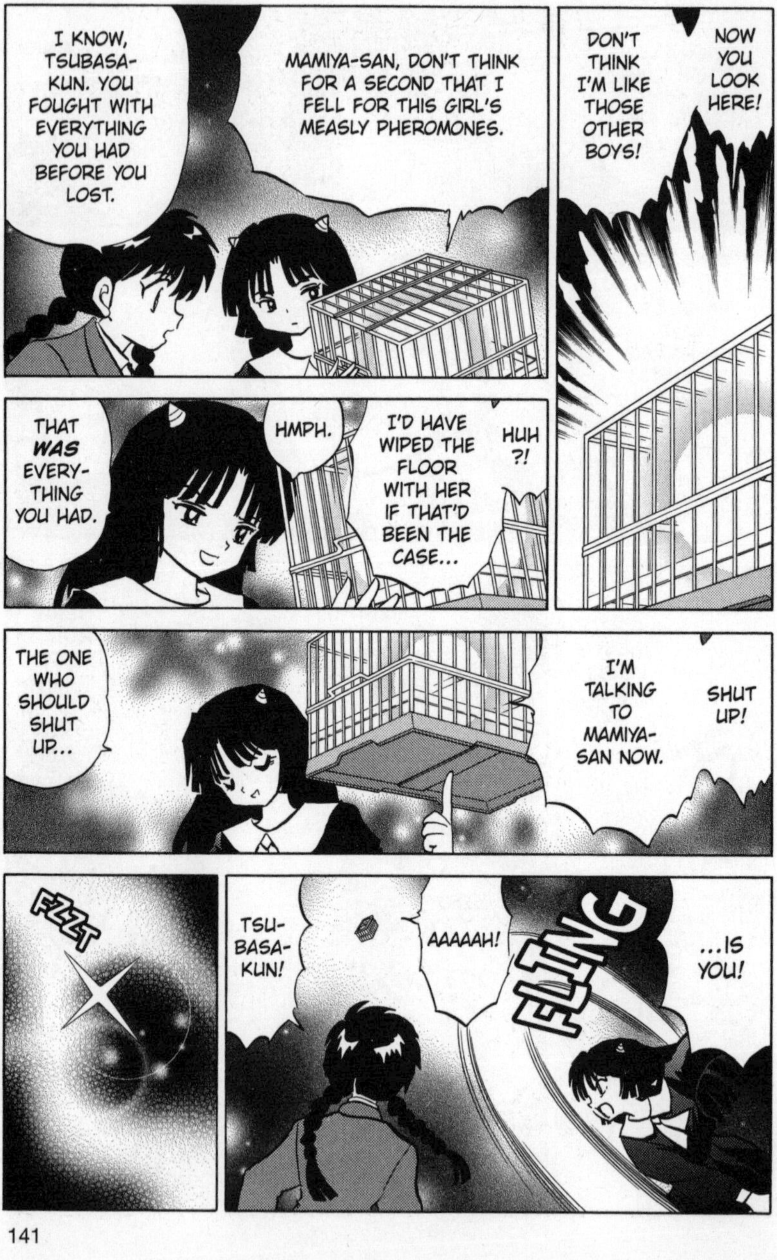
NOW YOU LOOK HERE!
DON'T THINK I'M LIKE THOSE OTHER BOYS!
MAMIYA-SAN, DON'T THINK FOR A SECOND THAT I FELL FOR THIS GIRL'S MEASLY PHEROMONES.
I KNOW, TSUBASA-KUN. YOU FOUGHT WITH EVERYTHING YOU HAD BEFORE YOU LOST.
HUH?!
I'D HAVE WIPED THE FLOOR WITH HER IF THAT'D BEEN THE CASE...
HMPH.
THAT *WAS* EVERY-THING YOU HAD.
SHUT UP!
I'M TALKING TO MAMIYA-SAN NOW.
THE ONE WHO SHOULD SHUT UP...
...IS YOU!
FLING
AAAAAH!
TSU-BASA-KUN!
FZZT

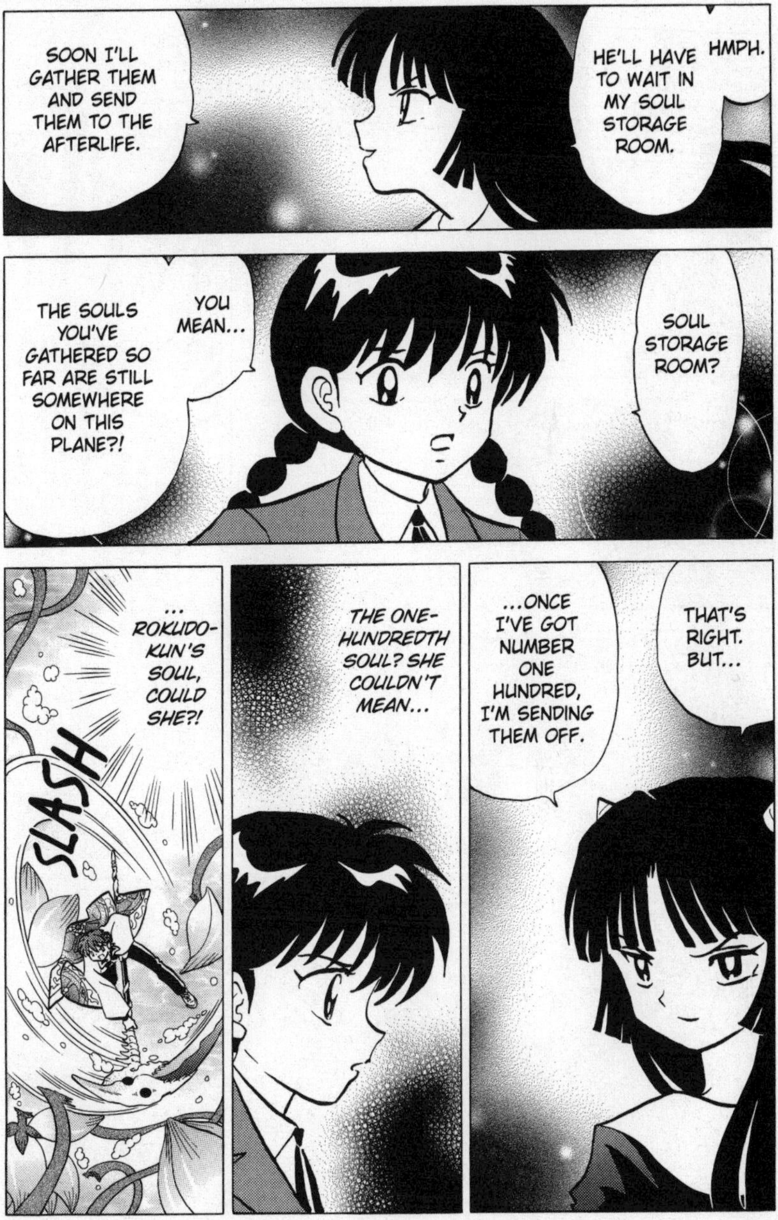
HMPH.
HE'LL HAVE TO WAIT IN MY SOUL STORAGE ROOM.
SOON I'LL GATHER THEM AND SEND THEM TO THE AFTERLIFE.
SOUL STORAGE ROOM?
YOU MEAN...
THE SOULS YOU'VE GATHERED SO FAR ARE STILL SOMEWHERE ON THIS PLANE?!
THAT'S RIGHT. BUT...
...ONCE I'VE GOT NUMBER ONE HUNDRED, I'M SENDING THEM OFF.
THE ONE-HUNDREDTH SOUL? SHE COULDN'T MEAN...
... ROKUDO-KUN'S SOUL, COULD SHE?!
SLASH

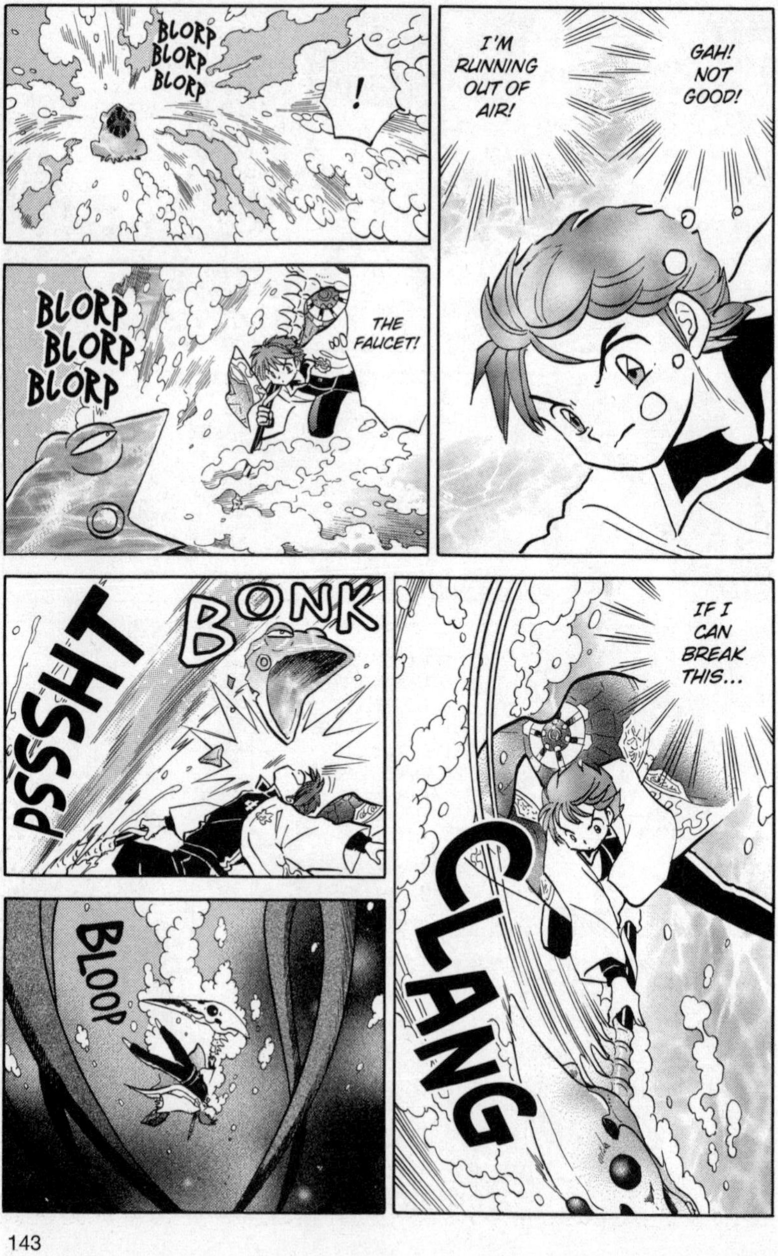
GAH! NOT GOOD!
I'M RUNNING OUT OF AIR!
!
BLORP BLORP BLORP
THE FAUCET!
BLORP BLORP BLORP
IF I CAN BREAK THIS...
CLANG
BONK
PSSSHT
BLOOP

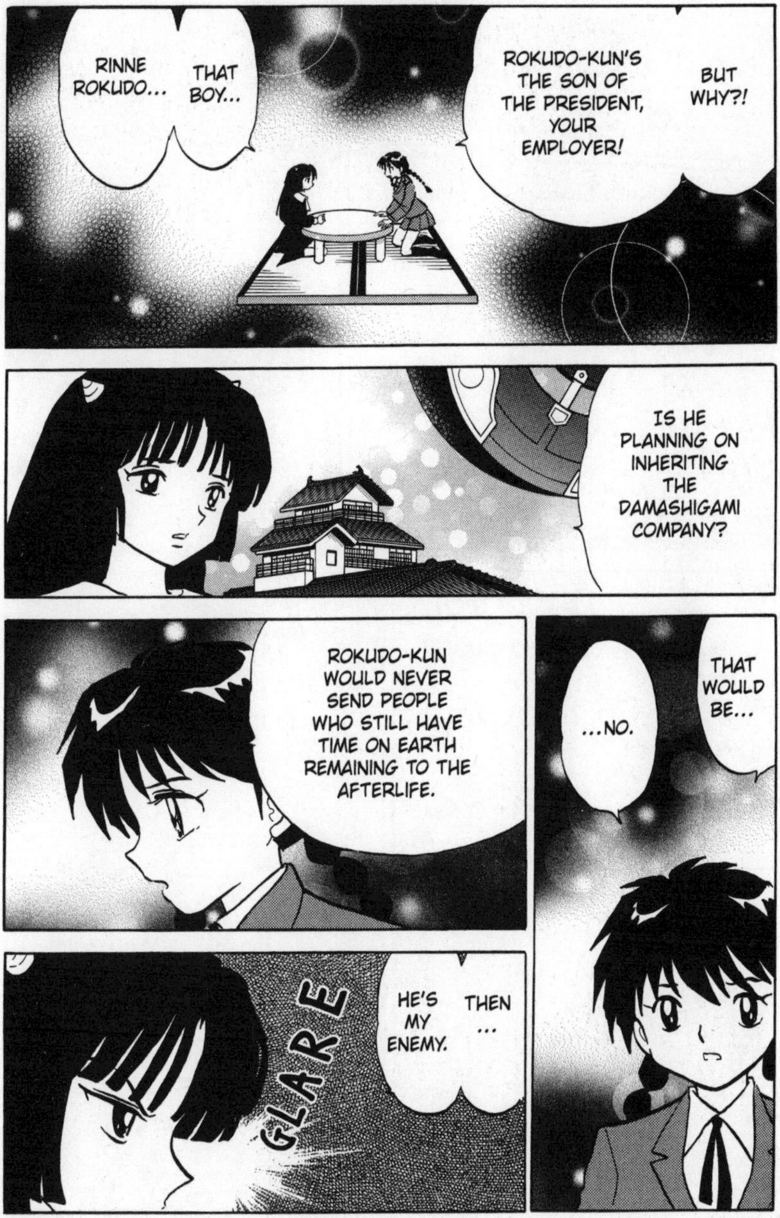
BUT WHY?!
ROKUDO-KUN'S THE SON OF THE PRESIDENT, YOUR EMPLOYER!
THAT BOY...
RINNE ROKUDO...
IS HE PLANNING ON INHERITING THE DAMASHIGAMI COMPANY?
THAT WOULD BE...
...NO.
ROKUDO-KUN WOULD NEVER SEND PEOPLE WHO STILL HAVE TIME ON EARTH REMAINING TO THE AFTERLIFE.
THEN...
HE'S MY ENEMY.
GLARE

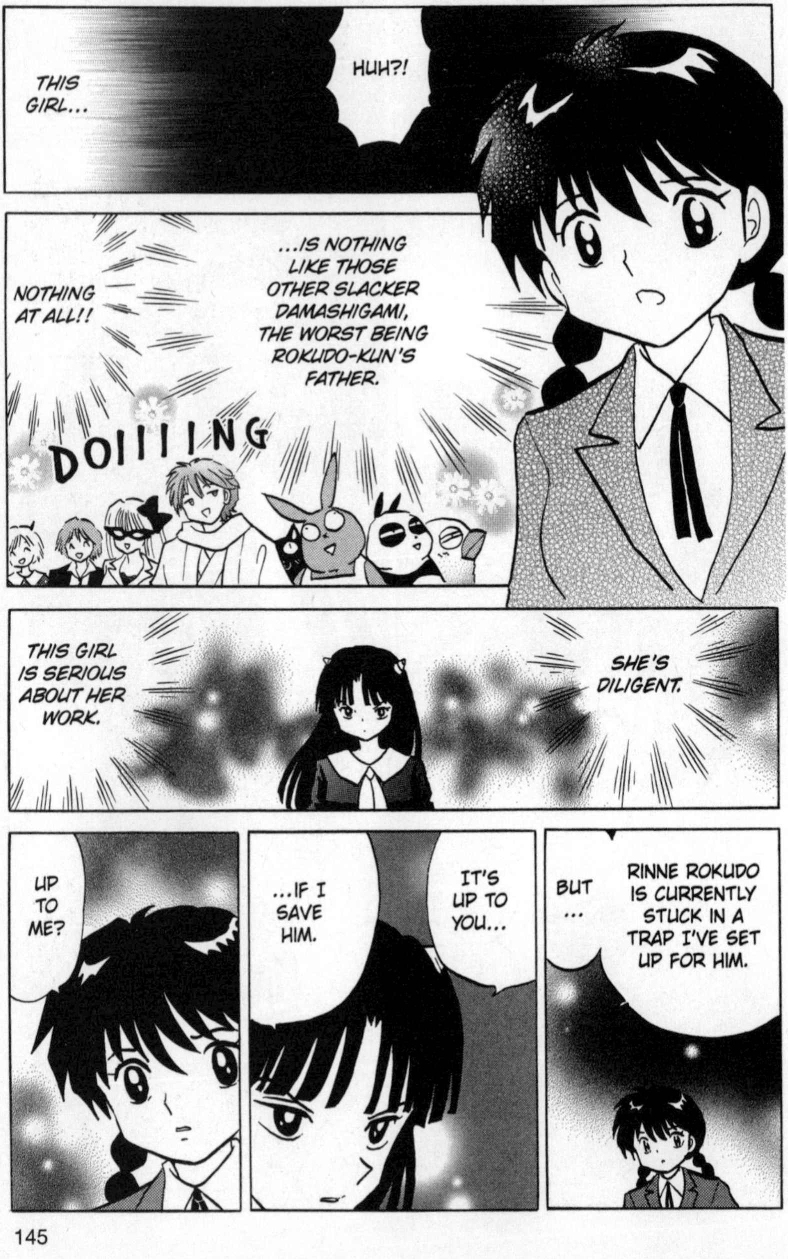
HUH?!
THIS GIRL...
...IS NOTHING LIKE THOSE OTHER SLACKER DAMASHIGAMI, THE WORST BEING ROKUDO-KUN'S FATHER.
NOTHING AT ALL!!
DOIIING
SHE'S DILIGENT.
THIS GIRL IS SERIOUS ABOUT HER WORK.
RINNE ROKUDO IS CURRENTLY STUCK IN A TRAP I'VE SET UP FOR HIM.
BUT...
IT'S UP TO YOU...
...IF I SAVE HIM.
UP TO ME?

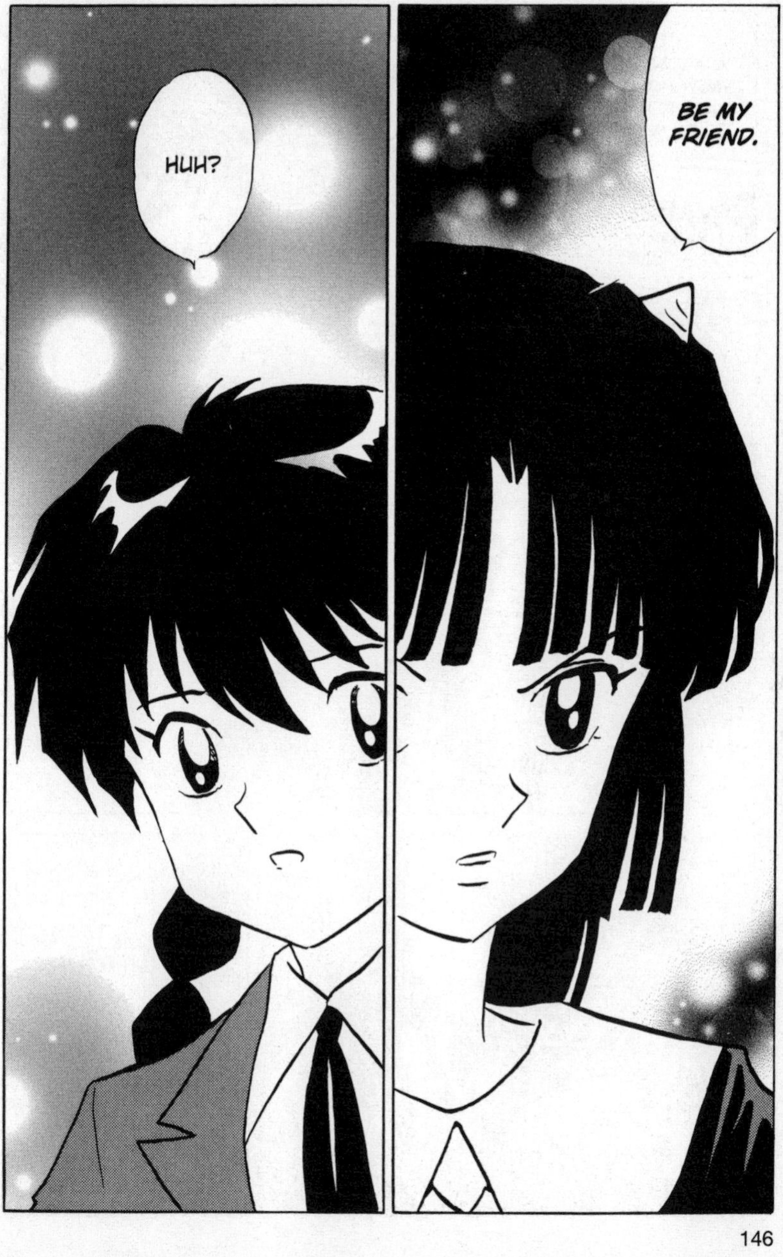
BE MY FRIEND.
HUH?

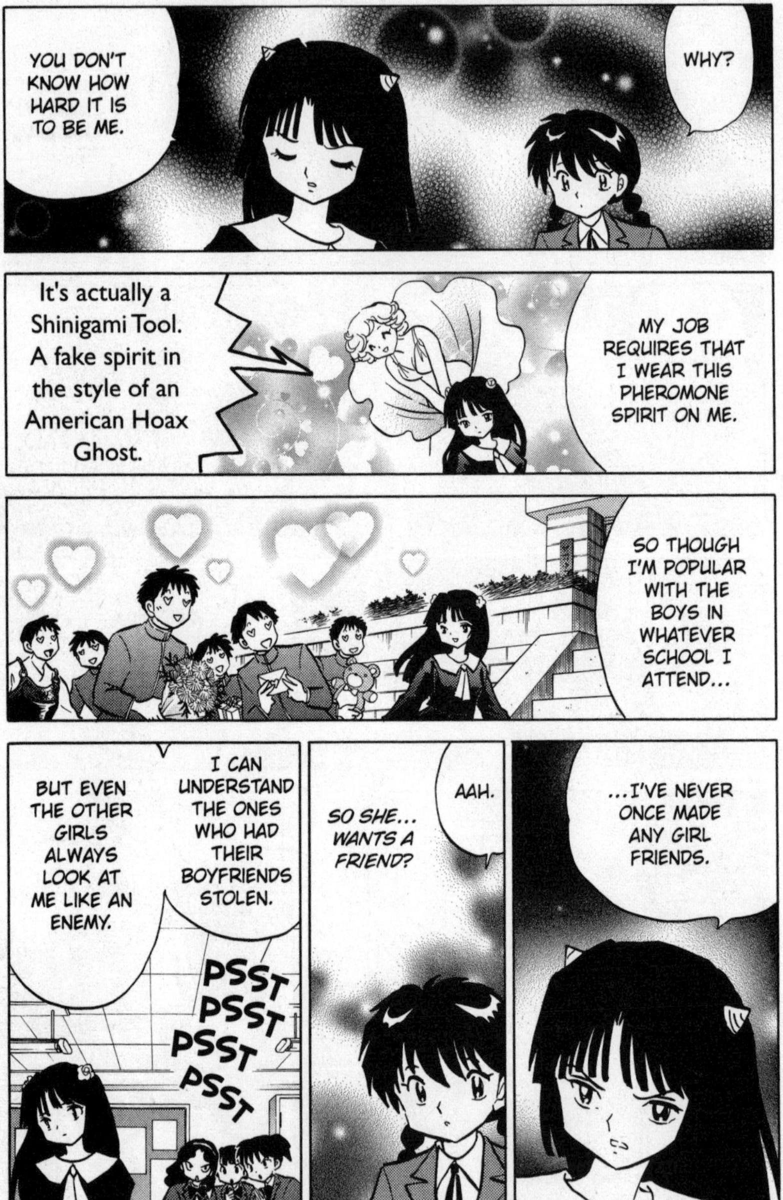
WHY?
YOU DON'T KNOW HOW HARD IT IS TO BE ME.
MY JOB REQUIRES THAT I WEAR THIS PHEROMONE SPIRIT ON ME.
It's actually a Shinigami Tool. A fake spirit in the style of an American Hoax Ghost.
SO THOUGH I'M POPULAR WITH THE BOYS IN WHATEVER SCHOOL I ATTEND...
...I'VE NEVER ONCE MADE ANY GIRL FRIENDS.
AAH.
SO SHE... WANTS A FRIEND?
I CAN UNDERSTAND THE ONES WHO HAD THEIR BOYFRIENDS STOLEN.
BUT EVEN THE OTHER GIRLS ALWAYS LOOK AT ME LIKE AN ENEMY.
PSST
PSST
PSST
PSST

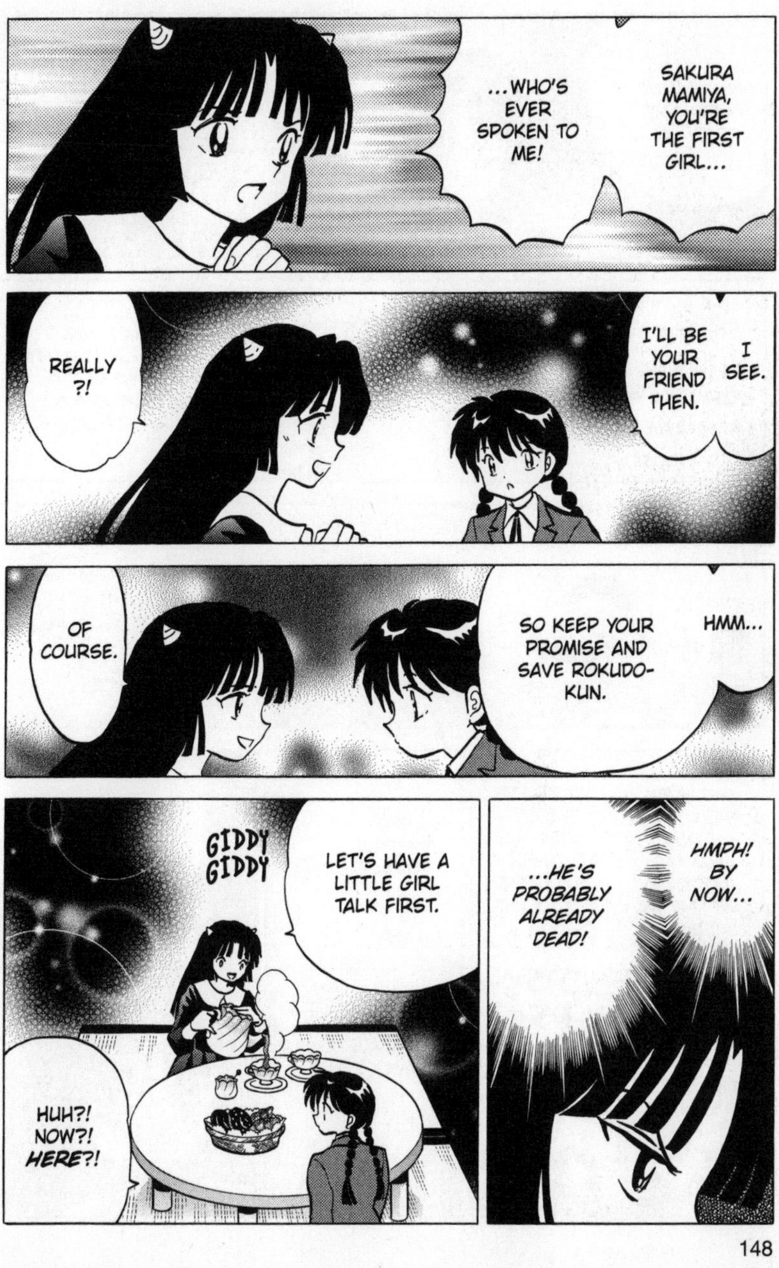
SAKURA MAMIYA, YOU'RE THE FIRST GIRL...
...WHO'S EVER SPOKEN TO ME!
I SEE.
I'LL BE YOUR FRIEND THEN.
REALLY?!
HMM...
SO KEEP YOUR PROMISE AND SAVE ROKUDO-KUN.
OF COURSE.
HMPH! BY NOW...
...HE'S PROBABLY ALREADY DEAD!
LET'S HAVE A LITTLE GIRL TALK FIRST.
GIDDY GIDDY
HUH?! NOW?! *HERE*?!

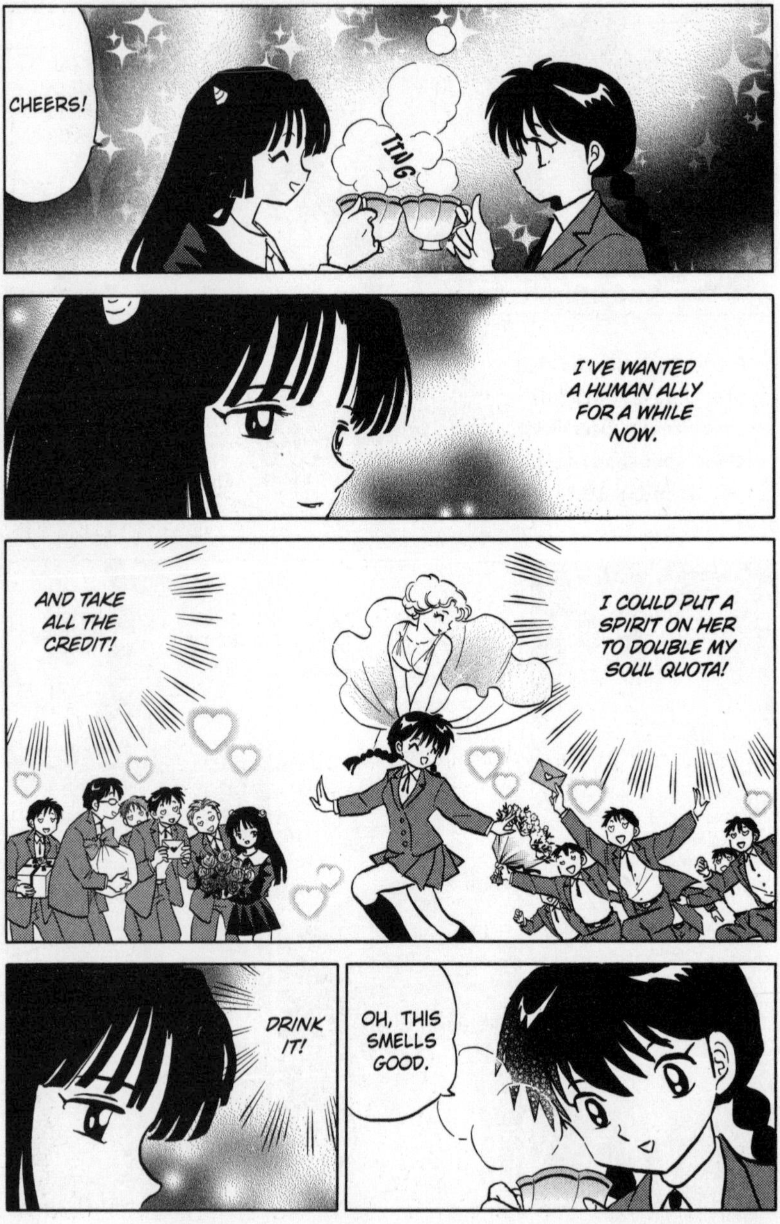
CHEERS!
TING
I'VE WANTED A HUMAN ALLY FOR A WHILE NOW.
I COULD PUT A SPIRIT ON HER TO DOUBLE MY SOUL QUOTA!
AND TAKE ALL THE CREDIT!
OH, THIS SMELLS GOOD.
DRINK IT!

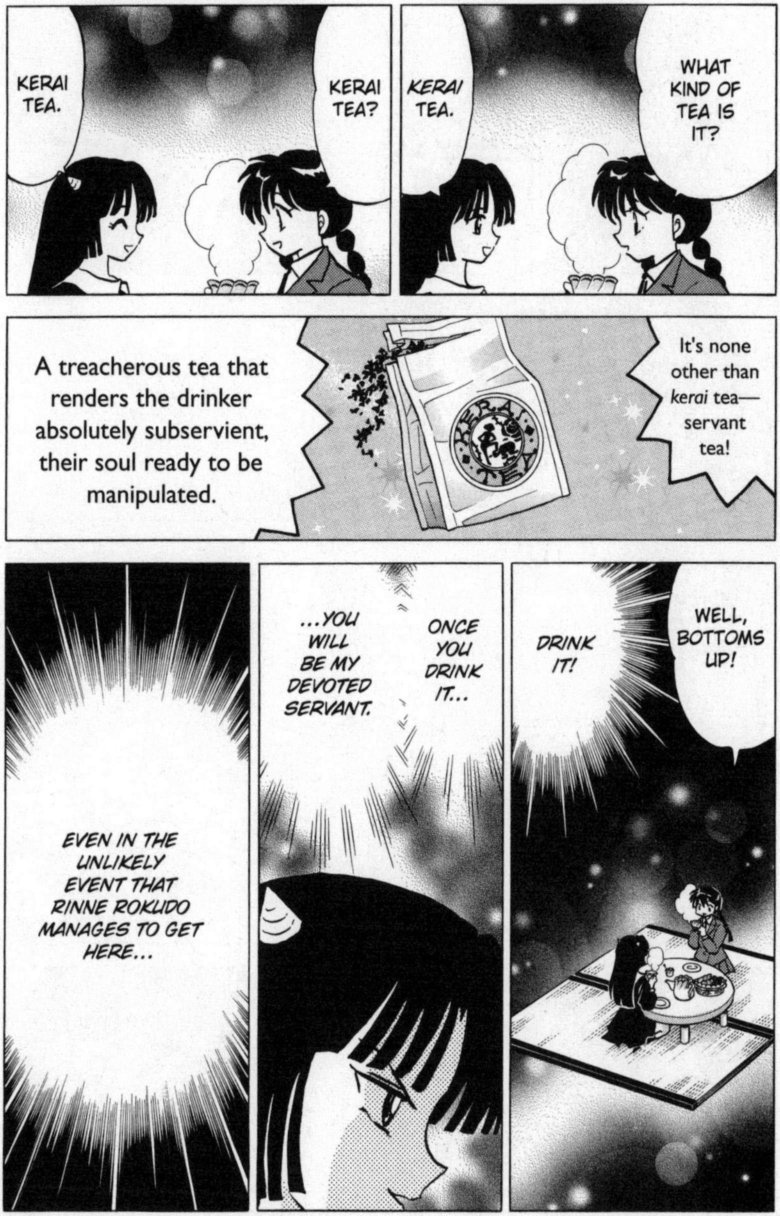
WHAT KIND OF TEA IS IT?
KERAI TEA.
KERAI TEA?
KERAI TEA.
It's none other than *kerai* tea—servant tea!
A treacherous tea that renders the drinker absolutely subservient, their soul ready to be manipulated.
WELL, BOTTOMS UP!
DRINK IT!
ONCE YOU DRINK IT...
...YOU WILL BE MY DEVOTED SERVANT.
EVEN IN THE UNLIKELY EVENT THAT RINNE ROKUDO MANAGES TO GET HERE...

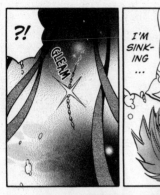

?!

GLEAM

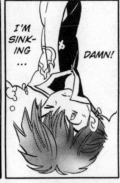

I'M SINK-ING...

DAMN!

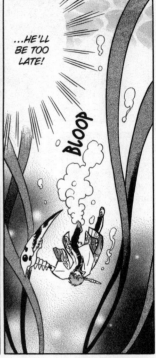

...HE'LL BE TOO LATE!

BLOOP

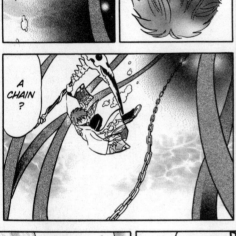

A CHAIN?

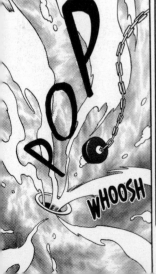

POP

WHOOSH

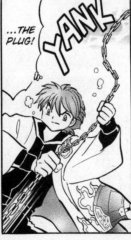

...THE PLUG!

YANK

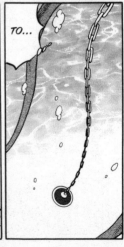

TO...

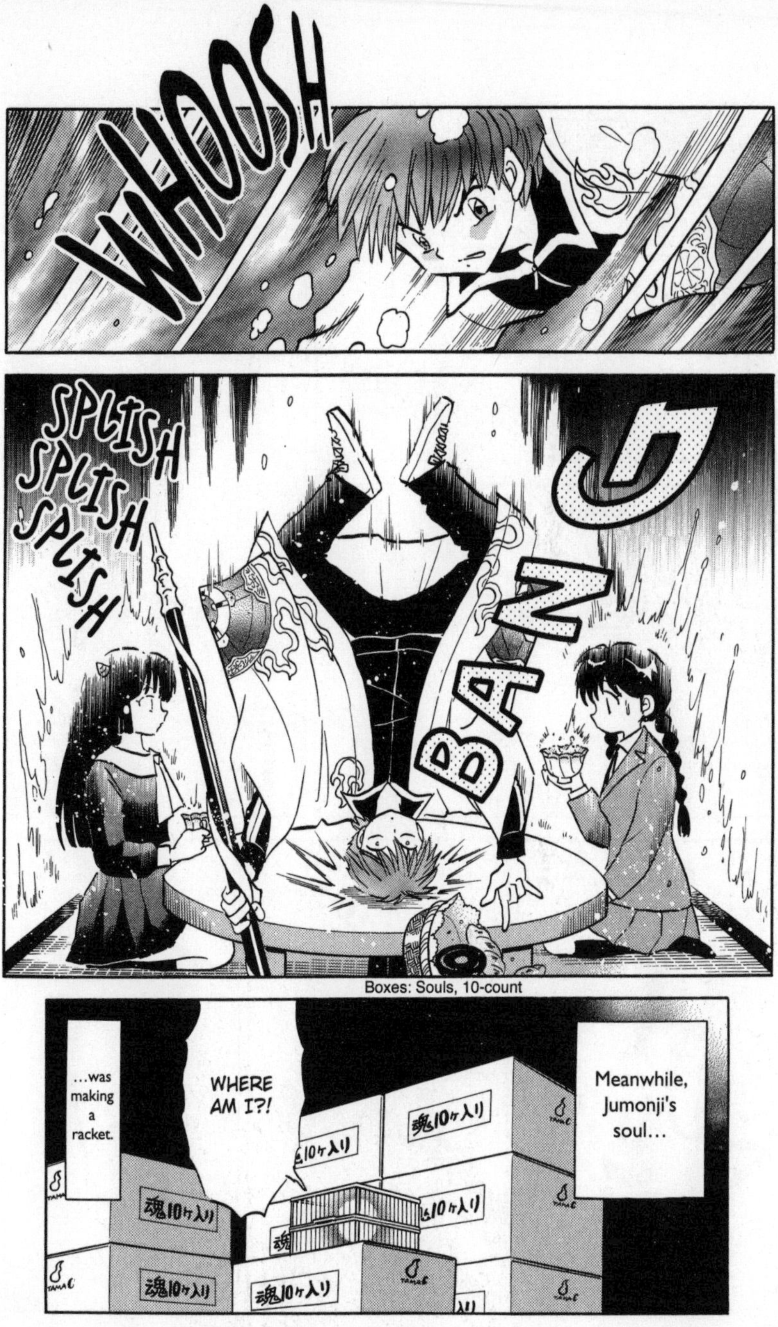
WHOOSH
SPLISH SPLISH SPLISH
BANG
Boxes: Souls, 10-count
魂10ヶ入り
Meanwhile, Jumonji's soul…
WHERE AM I?!
…was making a racket.

CHAPTER 137: AIMING FOR THE TOP

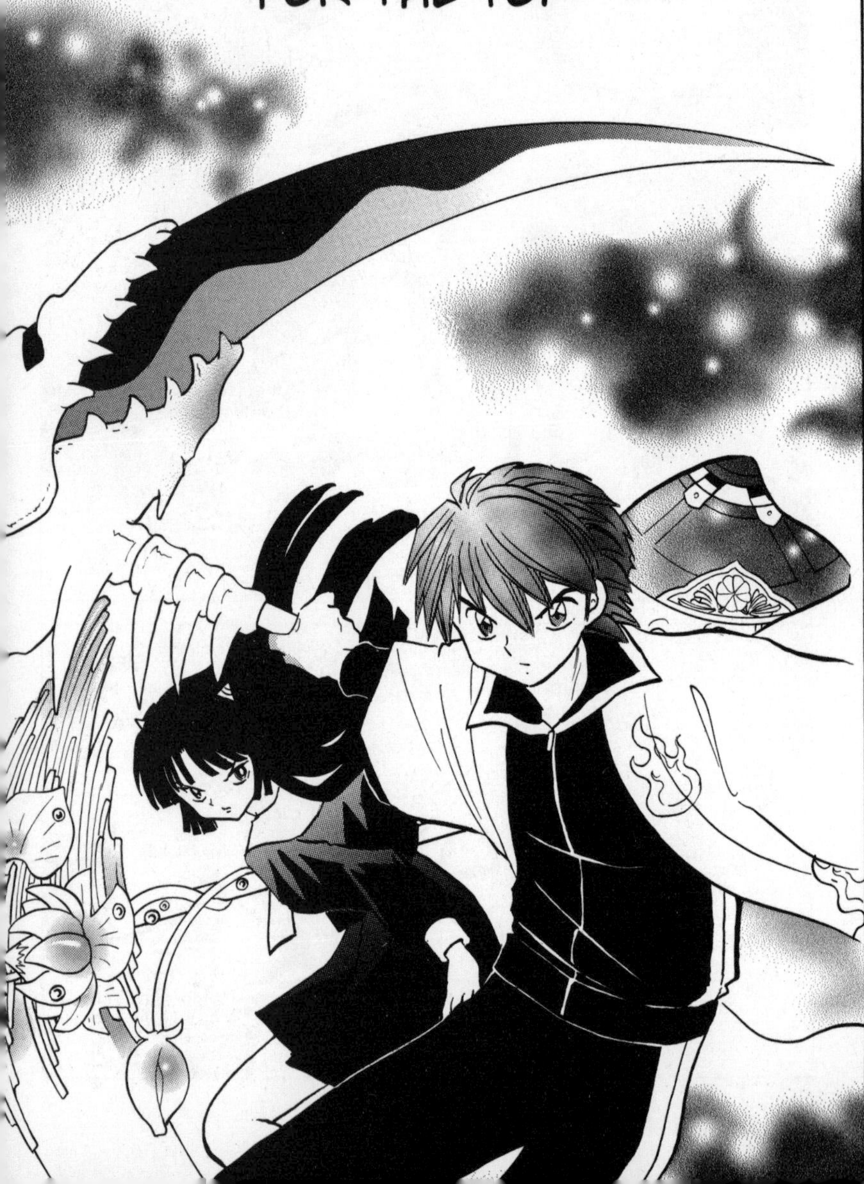

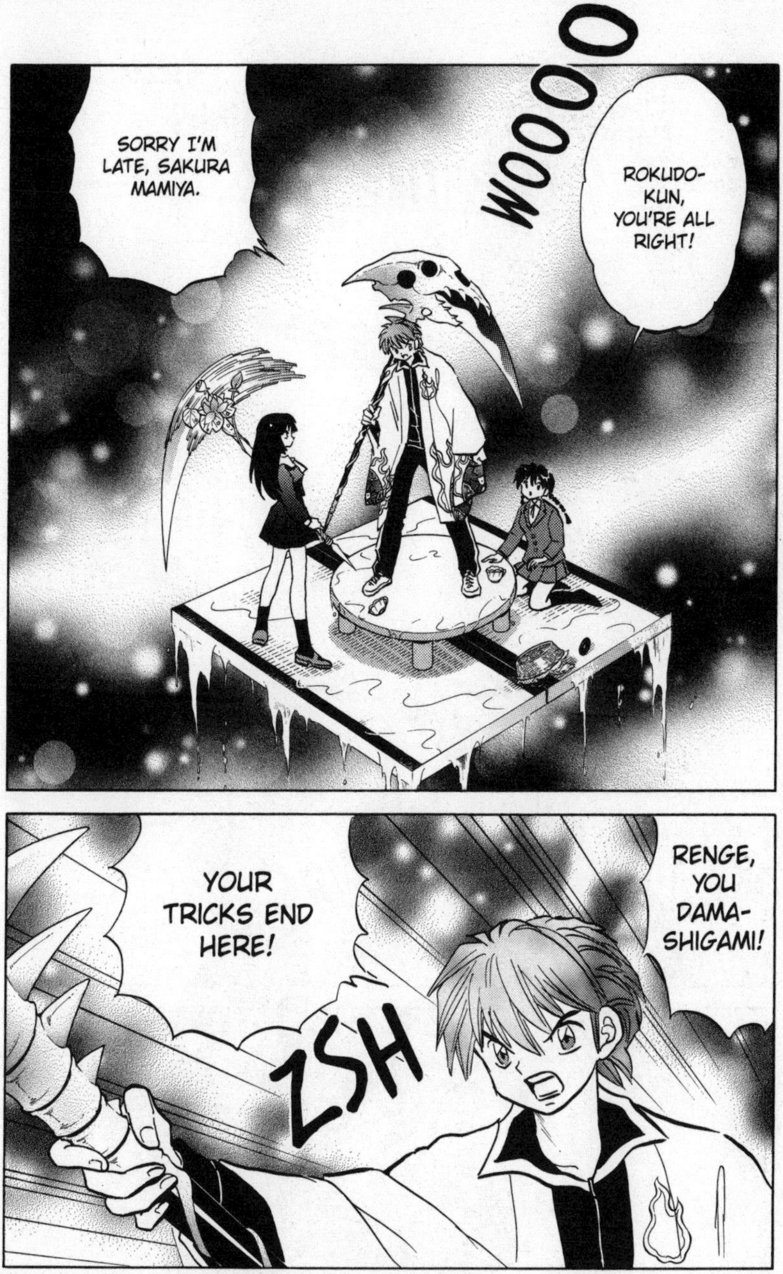
WOOOOM
ROKUDO-KUN, YOU'RE ALL RIGHT!
SORRY I'M LATE, SAKURA MAMIYA.
RENGE, YOU DAMA-SHIGAMI!
YOUR TRICKS END HERE!
ZSH

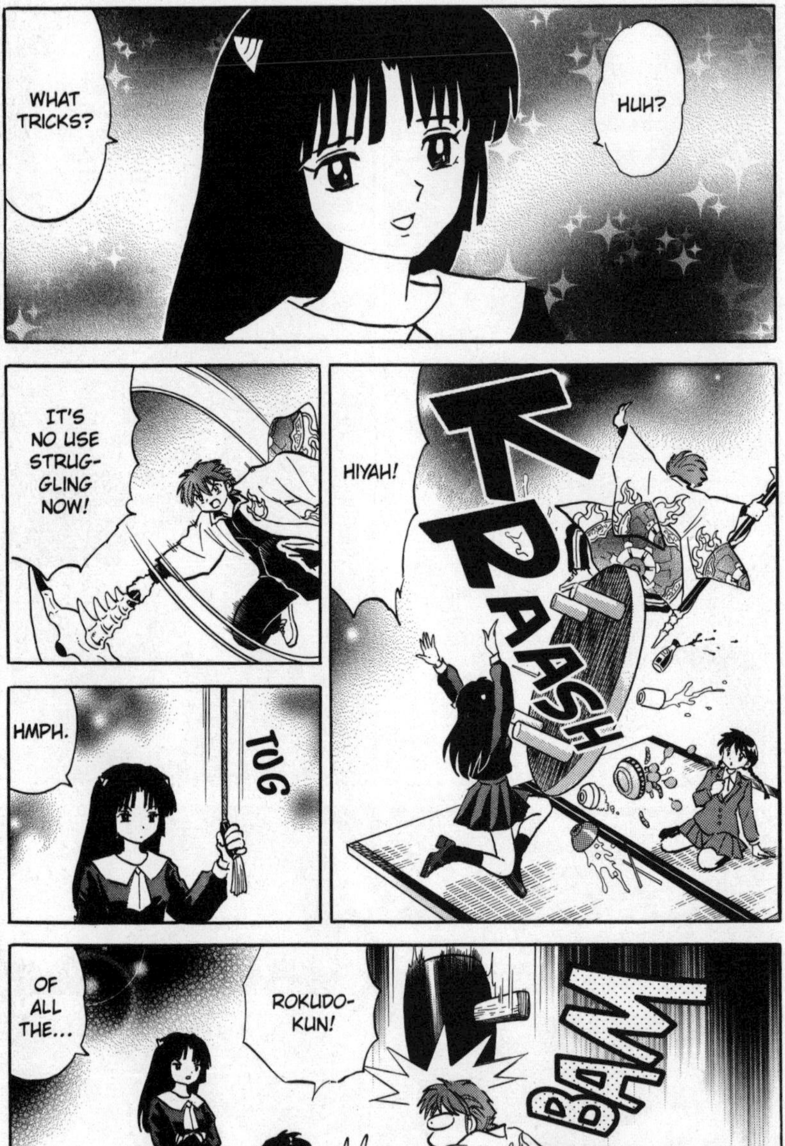
HUH?
WHAT TRICKS?
KRAASH!
HIYAH!
IT'S NO USE STRUG-GLING NOW!
TUG
HMPH.
BAM
ROKUDO-KUN!
OF ALL THE...

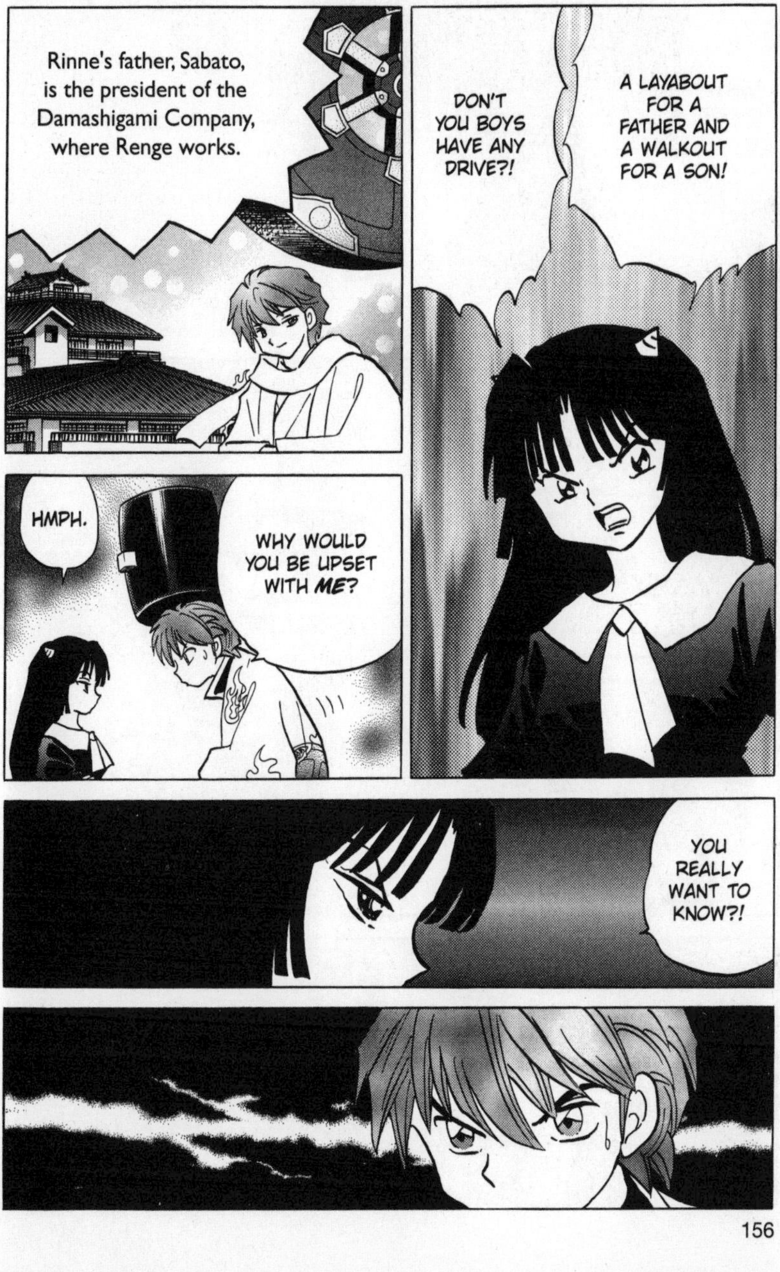
A LAYABOUT FOR A FATHER AND A WALKOUT FOR A SON!
DON'T YOU BOYS HAVE ANY DRIVE?!
Rinne's father, Sabato, is the president of the Damashigami Company, where Renge works.
WHY WOULD YOU BE UPSET WITH *ME*?
HMPH.
YOU REALLY WANT TO KNOW?!

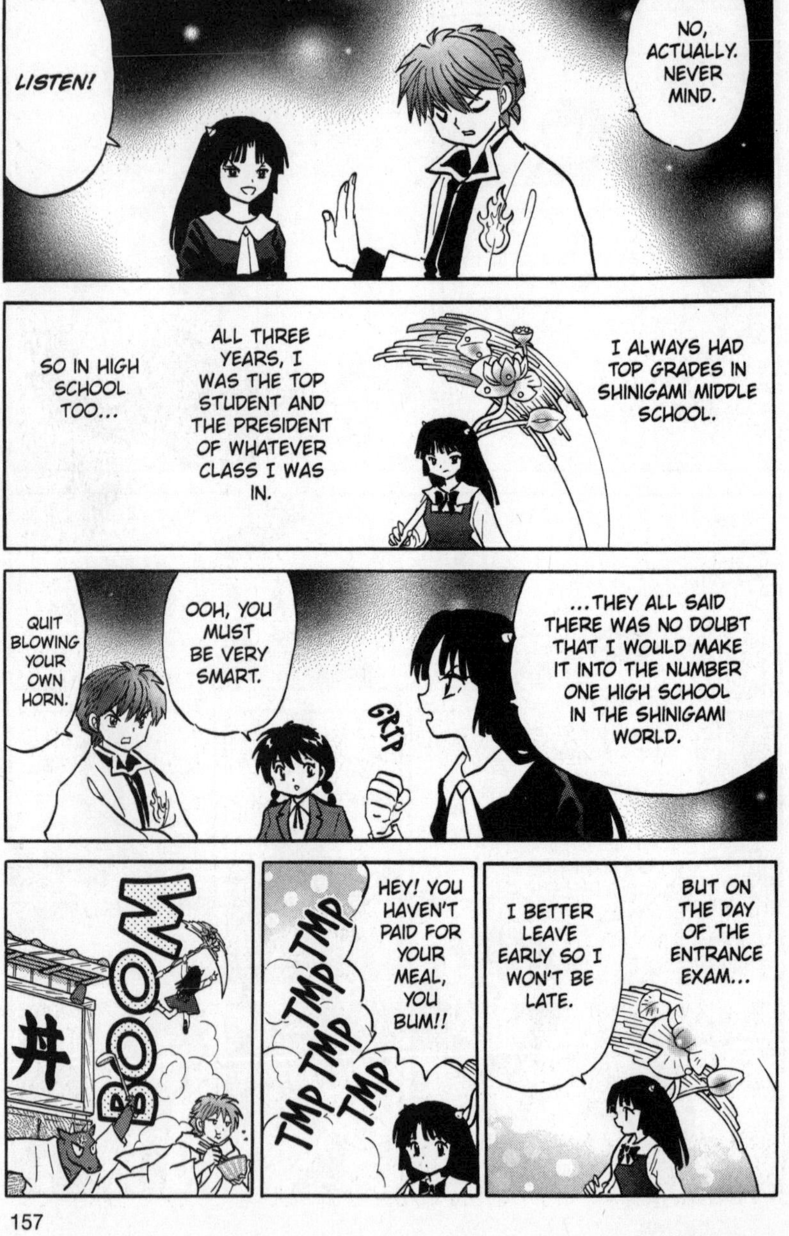
NO, ACTUALLY. NEVER MIND.
LISTEN!
I ALWAYS HAD TOP GRADES IN SHINIGAMI MIDDLE SCHOOL.
ALL THREE YEARS, I WAS THE TOP STUDENT AND THE PRESIDENT OF WHATEVER CLASS I WAS IN.
SO IN HIGH SCHOOL TOO...
...THEY ALL SAID THERE WAS NO DOUBT THAT I WOULD MAKE IT INTO THE NUMBER ONE HIGH SCHOOL IN THE SHINIGAMI WORLD.
GRIP
OOH, YOU MUST BE VERY SMART.
QUIT BLOWING YOUR OWN HORN.
BUT ON THE DAY OF THE ENTRANCE EXAM...
I BETTER LEAVE EARLY SO I WON'T BE LATE.
HEY! YOU HAVEN'T PAID FOR YOUR MEAL, YOU BUM!!
TMP TMP TMP TMP TMP
BOOM
丼

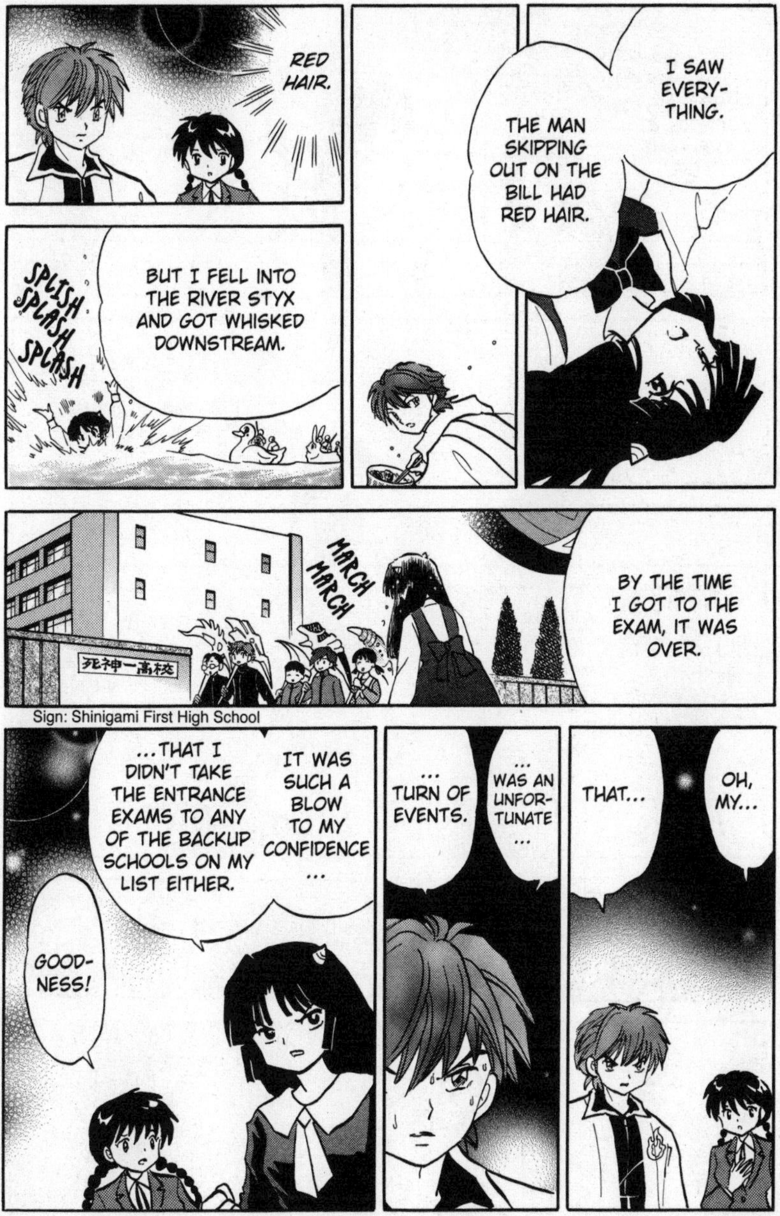
I SAW EVERY-THING.
THE MAN SKIPPING OUT ON THE BILL HAD RED HAIR.
RED HAIR.
SPLISH SPLASH SPLASH
BUT I FELL INTO THE RIVER STYX AND GOT WHISKED DOWNSTREAM.
BY THE TIME I GOT TO THE EXAM, IT WAS OVER.
MARCH MARCH
死神一高校
OH, MY...
THAT...
...WAS AN UNFOR-TUNATE...
...TURN OF EVENTS.
IT WAS SUCH A BLOW TO MY CONFIDENCE...
...THAT I DIDN'T TAKE THE ENTRANCE EXAMS TO ANY OF THE BACKUP SCHOOLS ON MY LIST EITHER.
GOOD-NESS!
Sign: Shinigami First High School

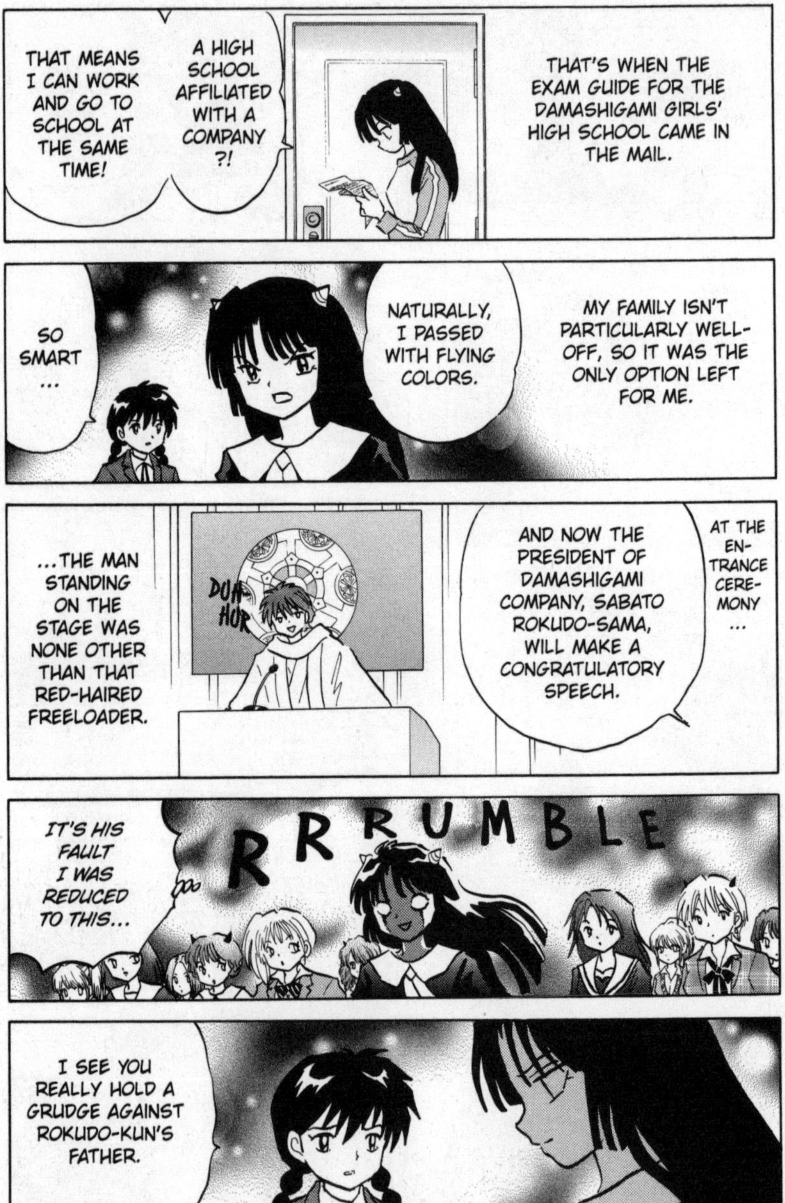
THAT'S WHEN THE EXAM GUIDE FOR THE DAMASHIGAMI GIRLS' HIGH SCHOOL CAME IN THE MAIL.
A HIGH SCHOOL AFFILIATED WITH A COMPANY ?!
THAT MEANS I CAN WORK AND GO TO SCHOOL AT THE SAME TIME!
MY FAMILY ISN'T PARTICULARLY WELL-OFF, SO IT WAS THE ONLY OPTION LEFT FOR ME.
NATURALLY, I PASSED WITH FLYING COLORS.
SO SMART ...
AT THE EN-TRANCE CERE-MONY ...
AND NOW THE PRESIDENT OF DAMASHIGAMI COMPANY, SABATO ROKUDO-SAMA, WILL MAKE A CONGRATULATORY SPEECH.
DUH HUR
...THE MAN STANDING ON THE STAGE WAS NONE OTHER THAN THAT RED-HAIRED FREELOADER.
RRRUMBLE
IT'S HIS FAULT I WAS REDUCED TO THIS...
I SEE YOU REALLY HOLD A GRUDGE AGAINST ROKUDO-KUN'S FATHER.

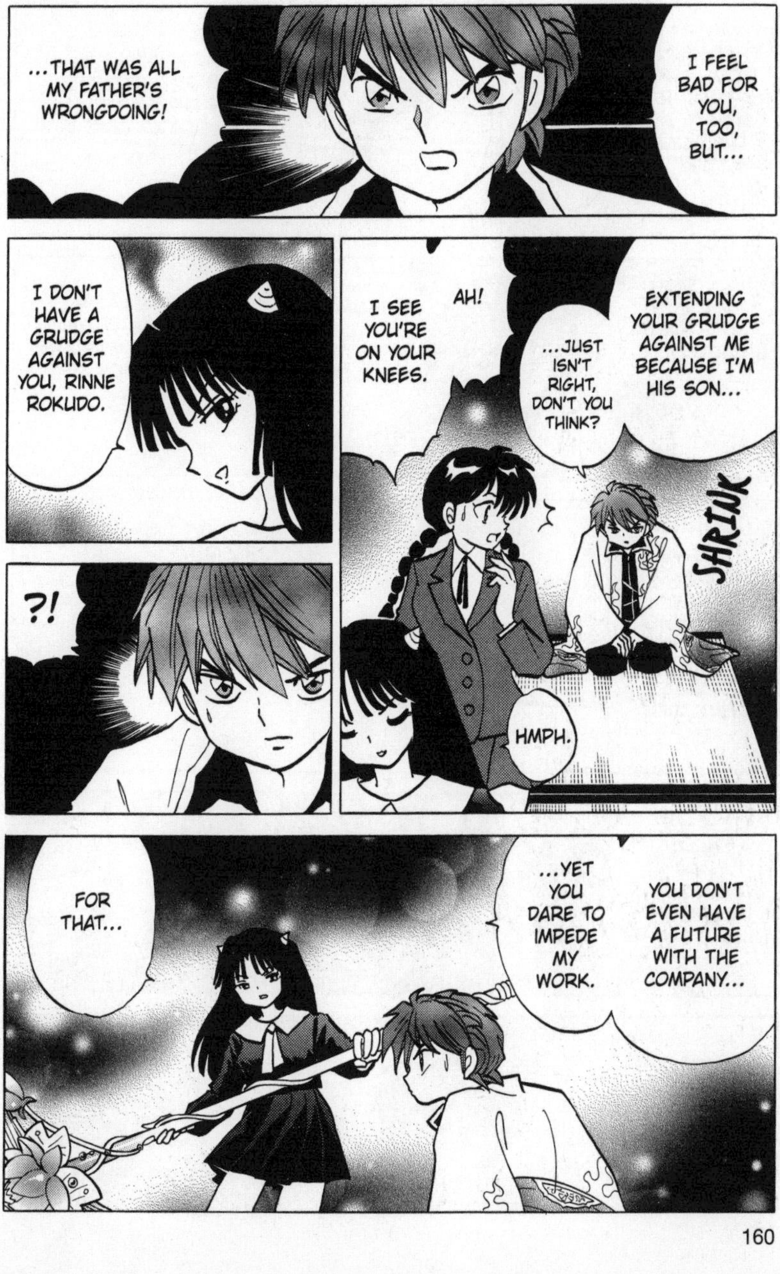
I FEEL BAD FOR YOU, TOO, BUT...
...THAT WAS ALL MY FATHER'S WRONGDOING!
EXTENDING YOUR GRUDGE AGAINST ME BECAUSE I'M HIS SON...
...JUST ISN'T RIGHT, DON'T YOU THINK?
AH!
I SEE YOU'RE ON YOUR KNEES.
SHRINK
HMPH.
I DON'T HAVE A GRUDGE AGAINST YOU, RINNE ROKUDO.
?!
YOU DON'T EVEN HAVE A FUTURE WITH THE COMPANY...
...YET YOU DARE TO IMPEDE MY WORK.
FOR THAT...

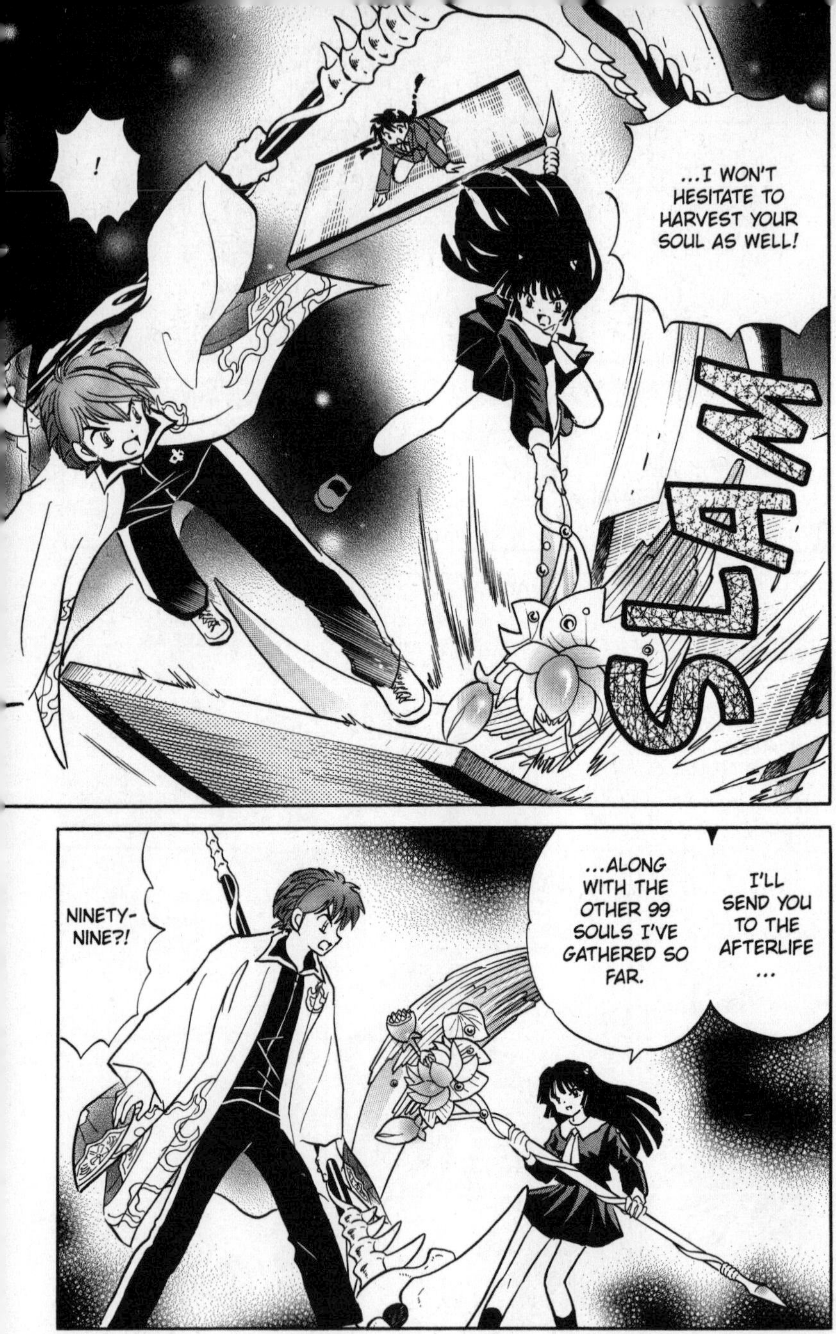
...I WON'T HESITATE TO HARVEST YOUR SOUL AS WELL!
SLAM
!
I'LL SEND YOU TO THE AFTERLIFE ...
...ALONG WITH THE OTHER 99 SOULS I'VE GATHERED SO FAR.
NINETY-NINE?!

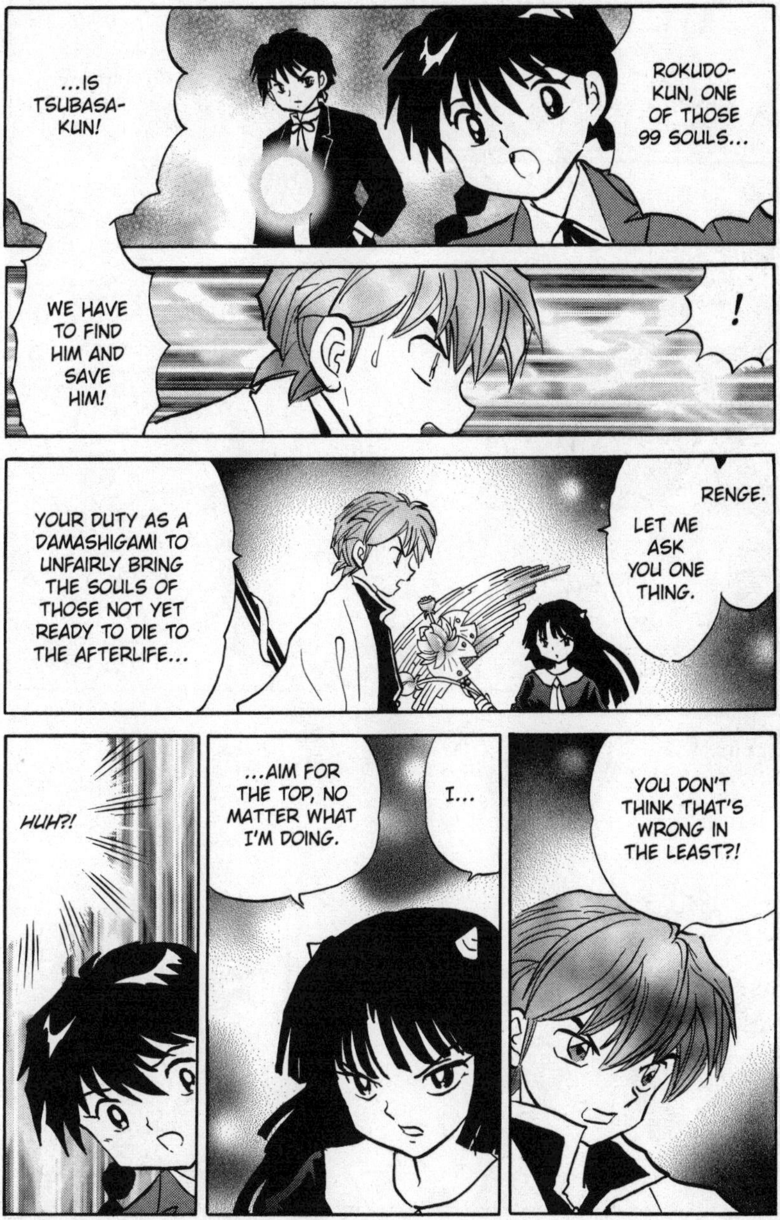
ROKUDO-KUN, ONE OF THOSE 99 SOULS...
...IS TSUBASA-KUN!
!
WE HAVE TO FIND HIM AND SAVE HIM!
RENGE.
LET ME ASK YOU ONE THING.
YOUR DUTY AS A DAMASHIGAMI TO UNFAIRLY BRING THE SOULS OF THOSE NOT YET READY TO DIE TO THE AFTERLIFE...
YOU DON'T THINK THAT'S WRONG IN THE LEAST?!
I...
...AIM FOR THE TOP, NO MATTER WHAT I'M DOING.
HUH?!

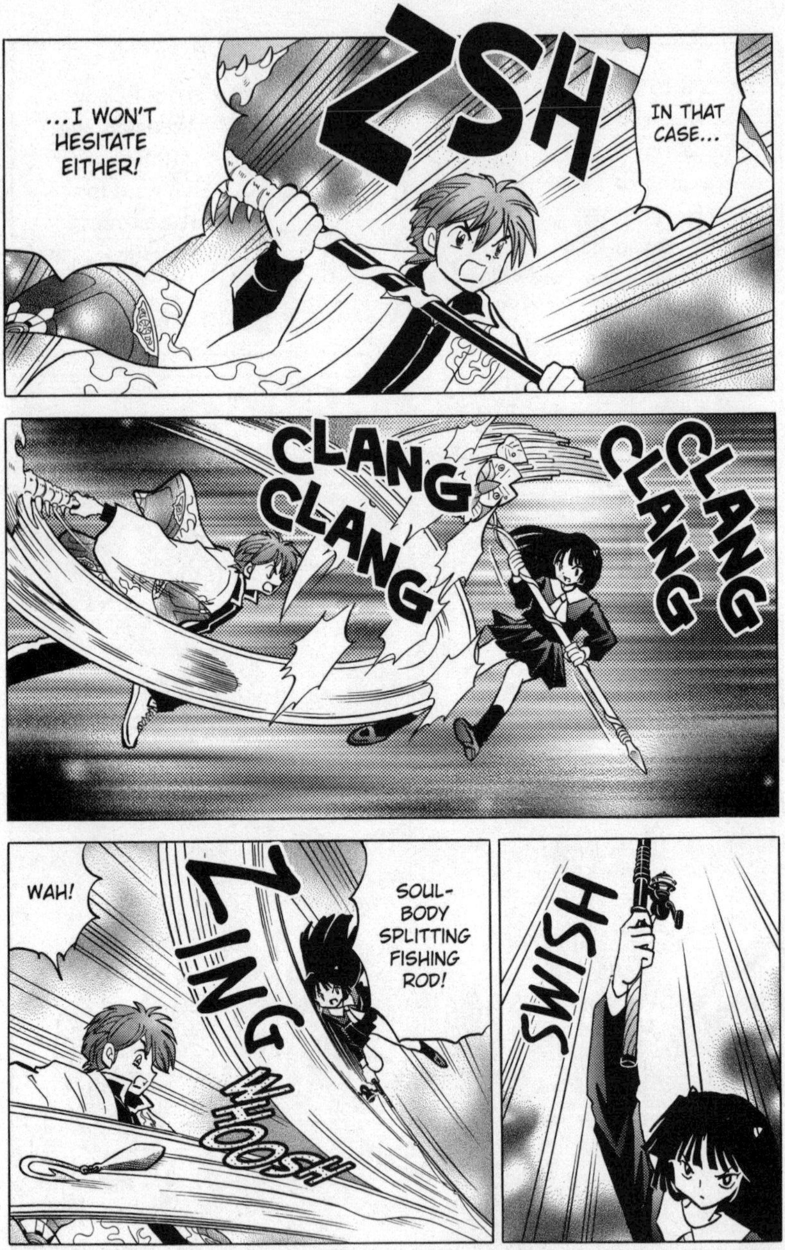
IN THAT CASE...
ZSH
...I WON'T HESITATE EITHER!
CLANG CLANG
CLANG CLANG
SWISH
SOUL-BODY SPLITTING FISHING ROD!
ZING
WAH!
WHOOSH

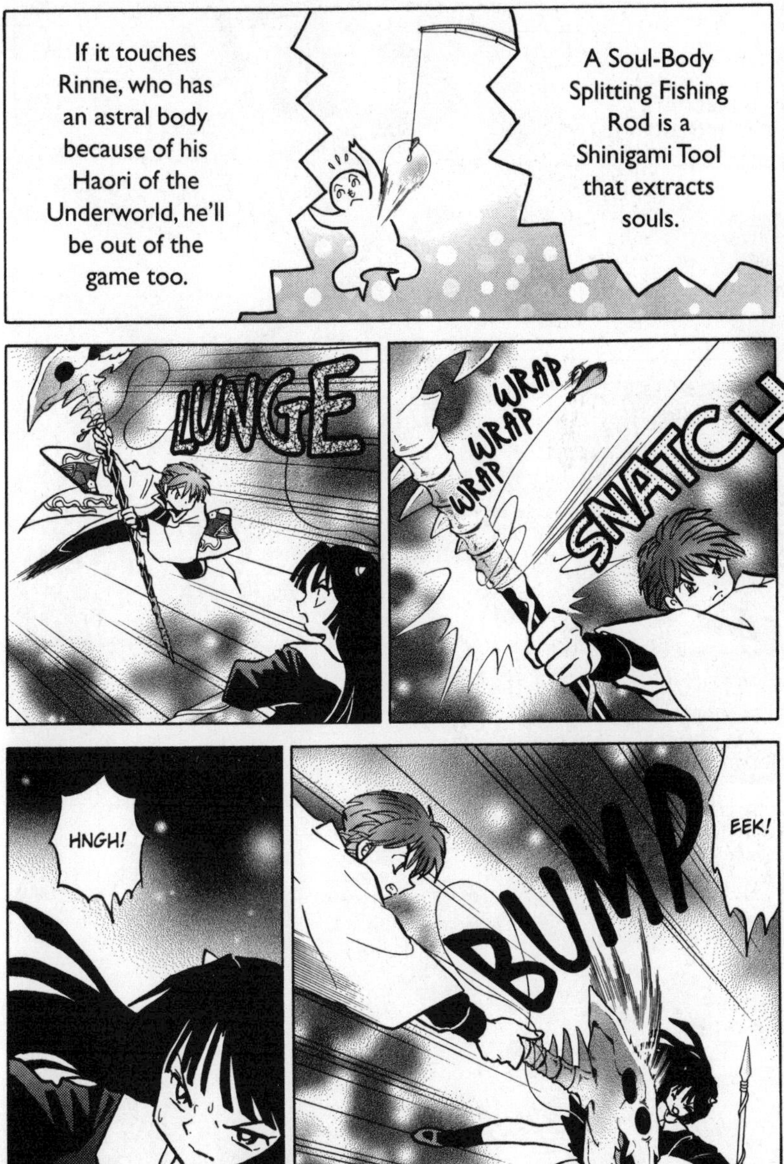
A Soul-Body Splitting Fishing Rod is a Shinigami Tool that extracts souls.
If it touches Rinne, who has an astral body because of his Haori of the Underworld, he'll be out of the game too.
SNATCH
WRAP WRAP WRAP WRAP
LUNGE
EEK!
BUMP
HNGH!

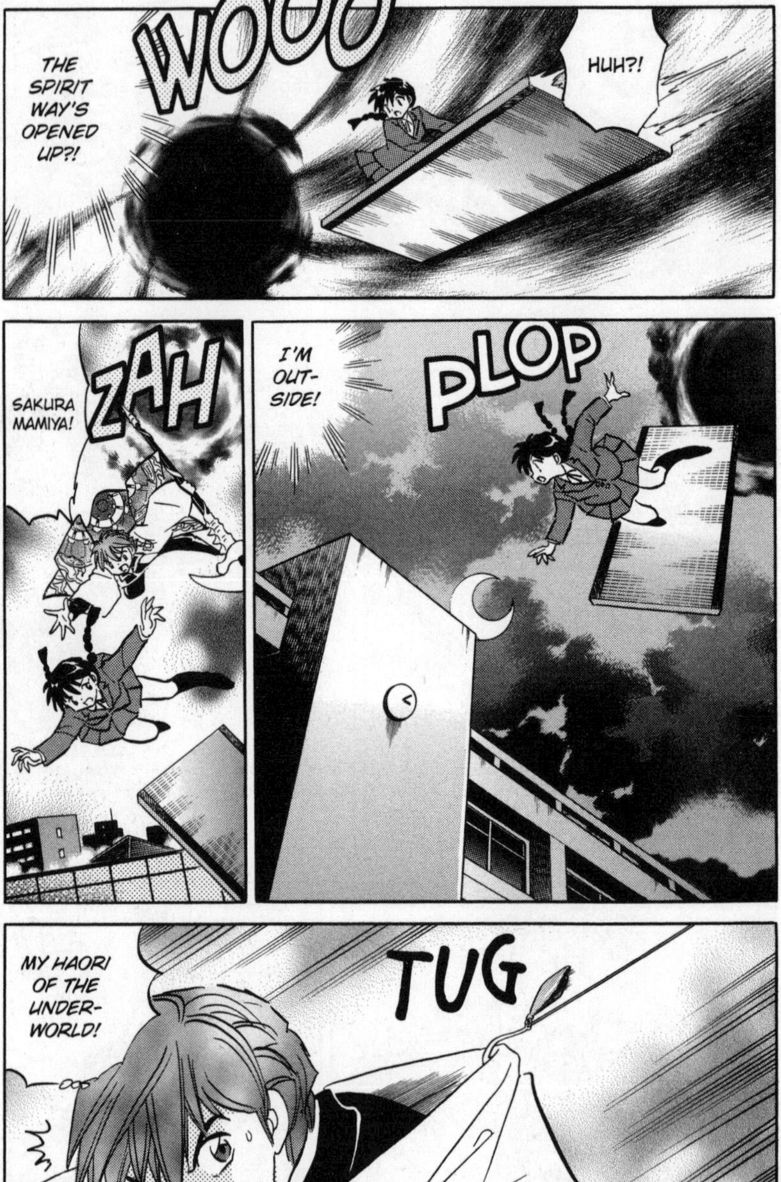
HUH?!
WOOO
THE SPIRIT WAY'S OPENED UP?!
PLOP
I'M OUT-SIDE!
ZAH
SAKURA MAMIYA!
TUG
MY HAORI OF THE UNDER-WORLD!

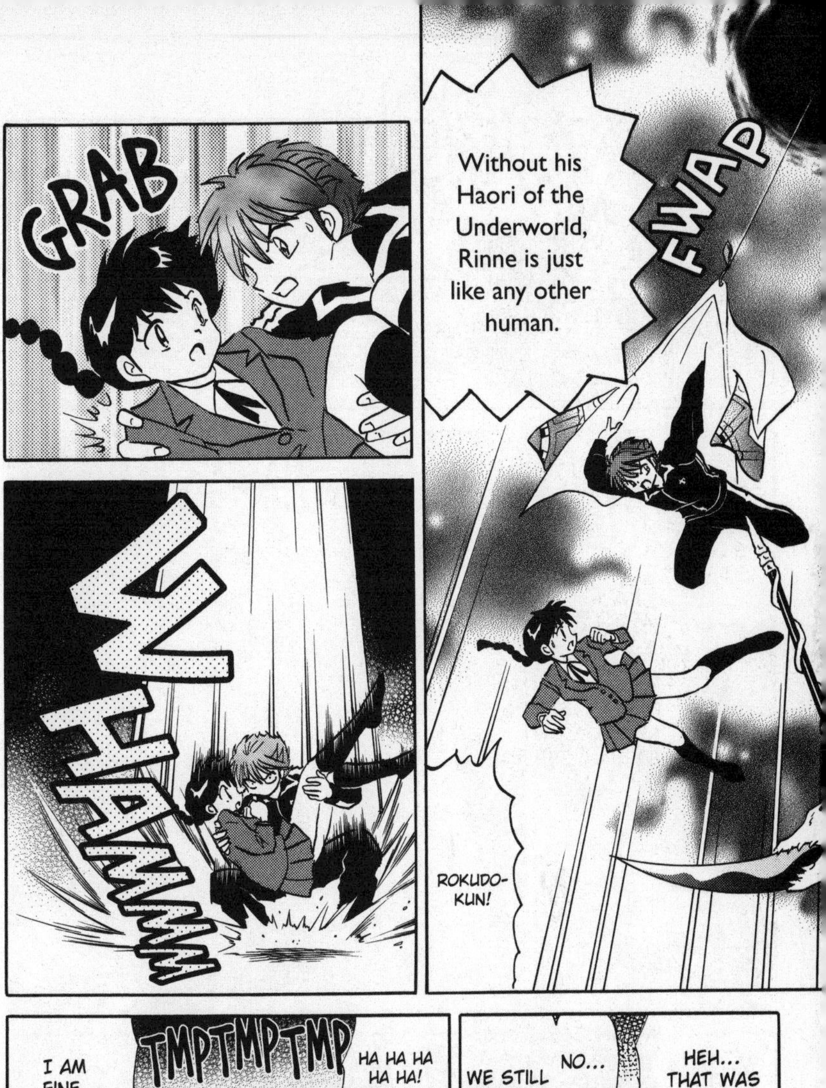
FWAP
Without his Haori of the Underworld, Rinne is just like any other human.
ROKUDO-KUN!
GRAB
WHAM
TMPTMPTMP
HA HA HA HA HA! WAIT FOR US!
I AM FINE.
SMOOSH
TSU-BASA-KUN?!
HEH... THAT WAS CLOSE...
NO...
WE STILL HIT THE GROUND.
CREAK
CREAK

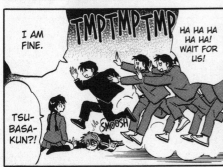

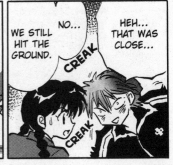

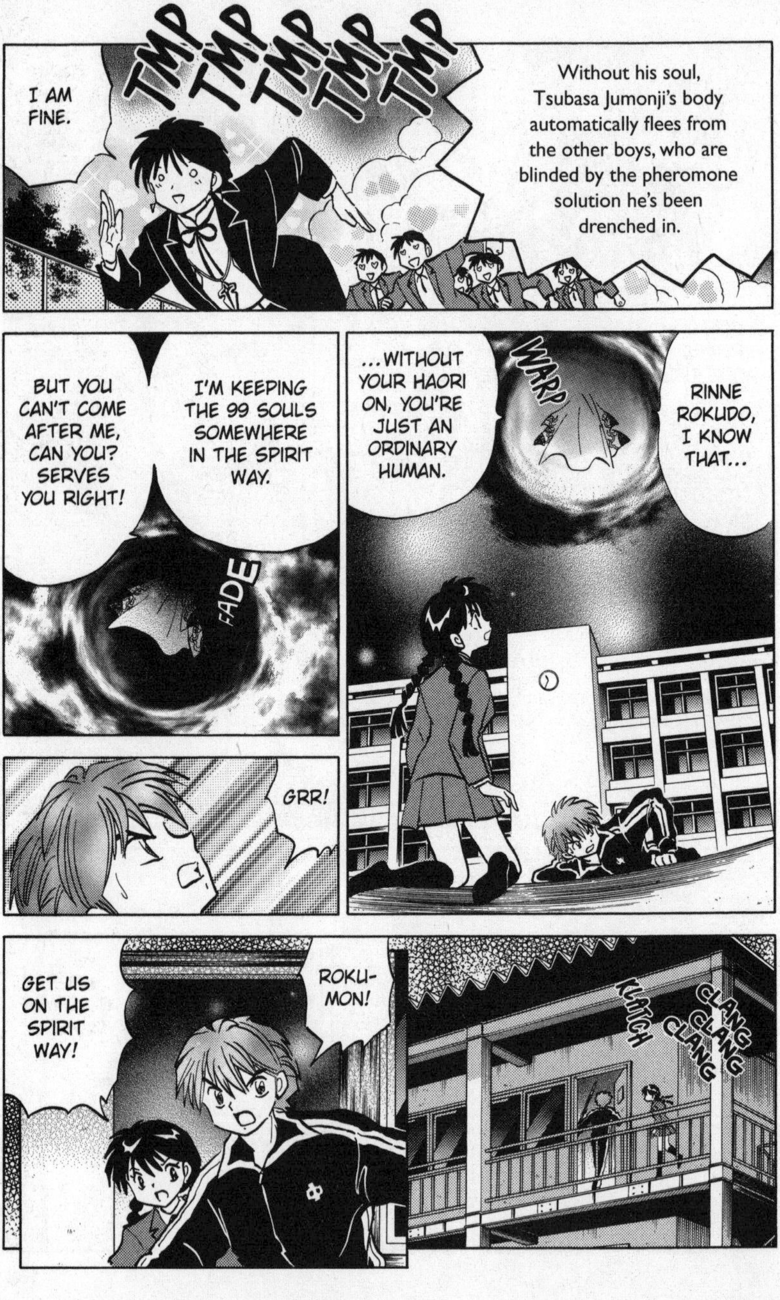
Without his soul, Tsubasa Jumonji's body automatically flees from the other boys, who are blinded by the pheromone solution he's been drenched in.
TMP TMP TMP TMP TMP
I AM FINE.
RINNE ROKUDO, I KNOW THAT...
WARP
...WITHOUT YOUR HAORI ON, YOU'RE JUST AN ORDINARY HUMAN.
I'M KEEPING THE 99 SOULS SOMEWHERE IN THE SPIRIT WAY.
BUT YOU CAN'T COME AFTER ME, CAN YOU? SERVES YOU RIGHT!
FADE
GRR!
CLANG CLANG CLANG
KLATCH
ROKU-MON!
GET US ON THE SPIRIT WAY!

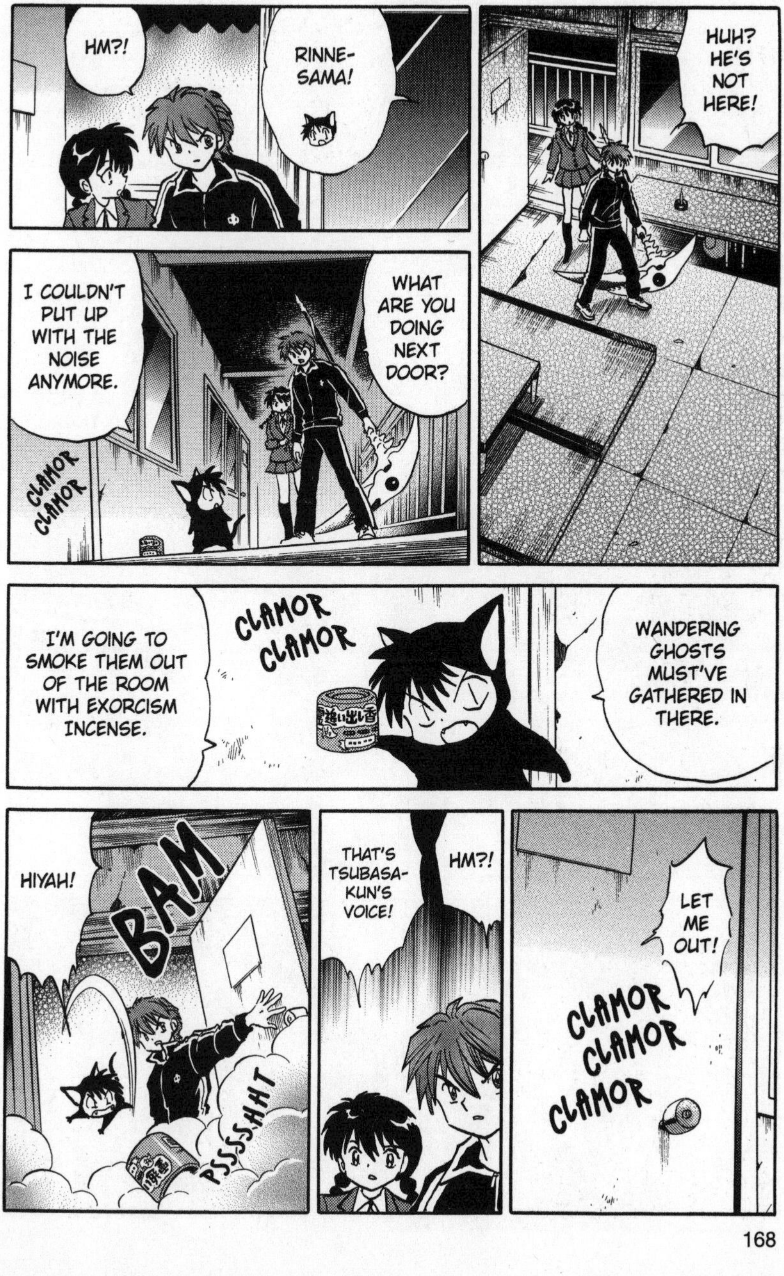
HUH? HE'S NOT HERE!
RINNE-SAMA!
HM?!
WHAT ARE YOU DOING NEXT DOOR?
I COULDN'T PUT UP WITH THE NOISE ANYMORE.
CLAMOR CLAMOR
WANDERING GHOSTS MUST'VE GATHERED IN THERE.
CLAMOR CLAMOR
I'M GOING TO SMOKE THEM OUT OF THE ROOM WITH EXORCISM INCENSE.
LET ME OUT!
CLAMOR CLAMOR CLAMOR
HM?!
THAT'S TSUBASA-KUN'S VOICE!
BAM
HIYAH!
PSSSSHHT

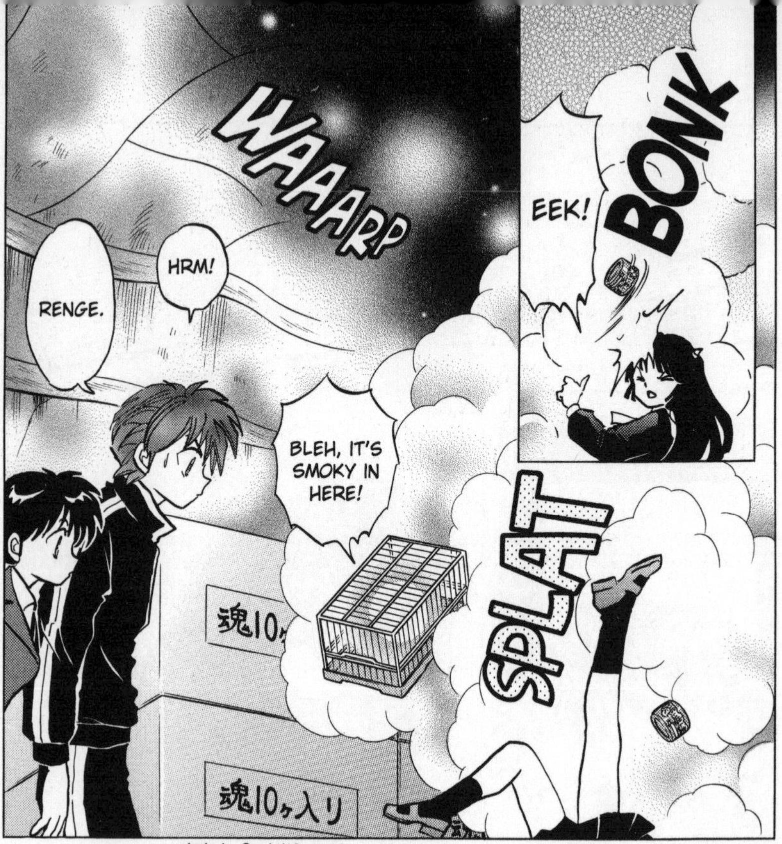
EEK!
BONK
WAAAARP
HRM!
RENGE.
BLEH, IT'S SMOKY IN HERE!
SPLAT
魂10ヶ
魂10ヶ入り
Labels: Souls/10-count

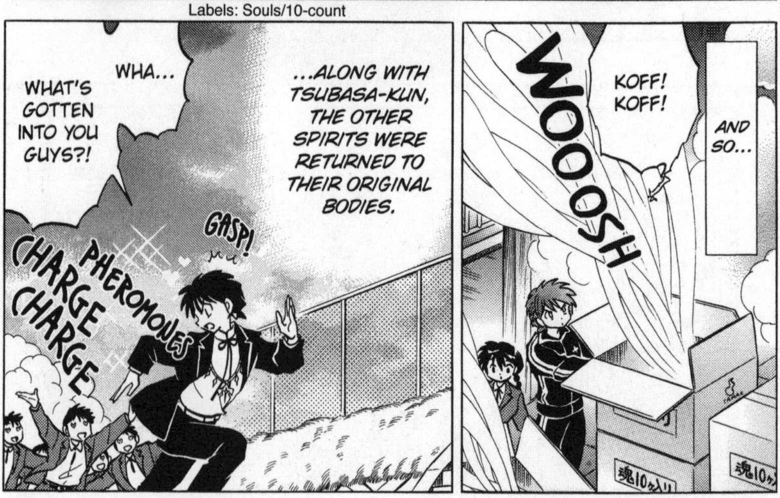
AND SO...
KOFF! KOFF!
WOOOOSH
...ALONG WITH TSUBASA-KUN, THE OTHER SPIRITS WERE RETURNED TO THEIR ORIGINAL BODIES.
WHA...
WHAT'S GOTTEN INTO YOU GUYS?!
GASP!
PHEROMONES
CHARGE
CHARGE
CHARGE
魂10ヶ入り
魂10ヶ

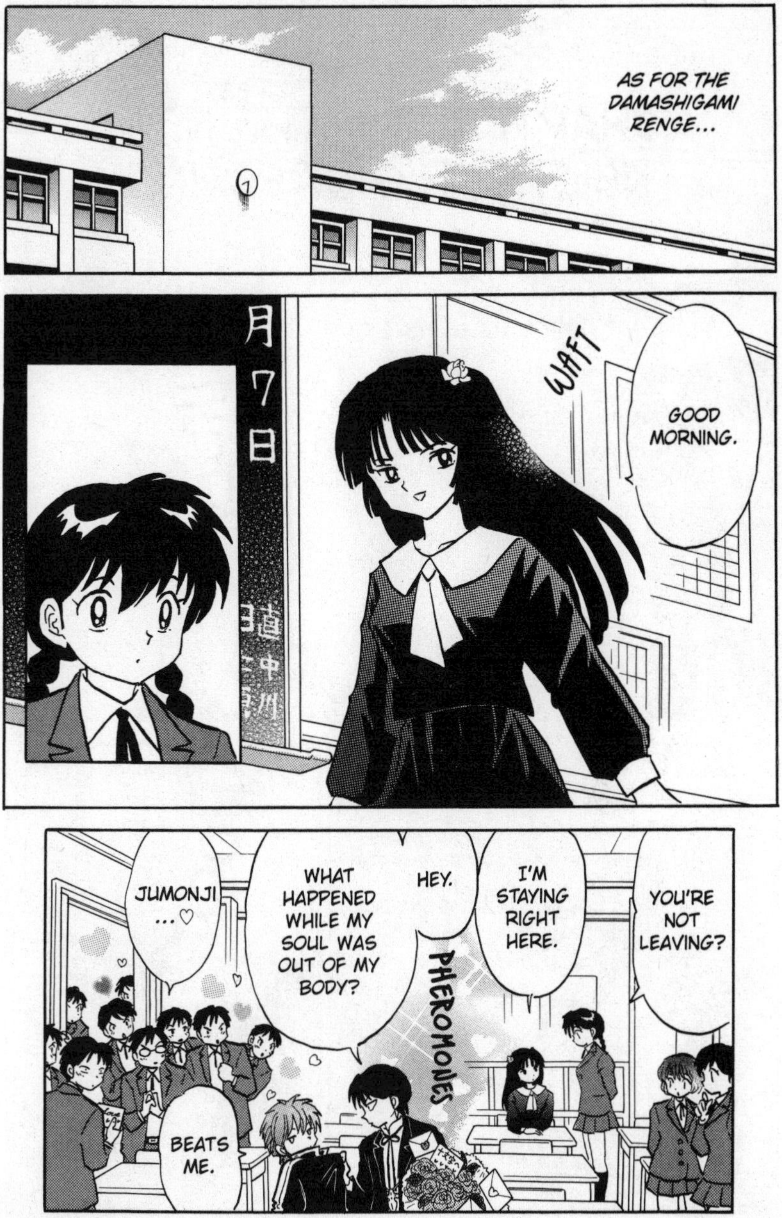
AS FOR THE DAMASHIGAMI RENGE...
GOOD MORNING.
WAFT
月7日
YOU'RE NOT LEAVING?
I'M STAYING RIGHT HERE.
HEY.
WHAT HAPPENED WHILE MY SOUL WAS OUT OF MY BODY?
PHEROMONES
JUMONJI ...♡
BEATS ME.

CHAPTER 138: THE NEW NEIGHBOR'S GREETING

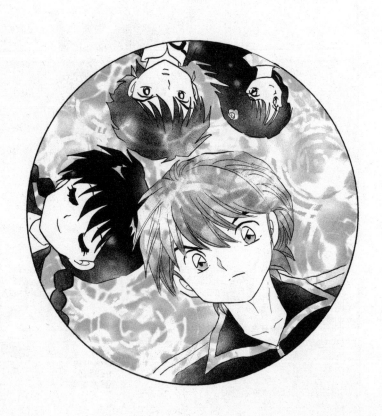

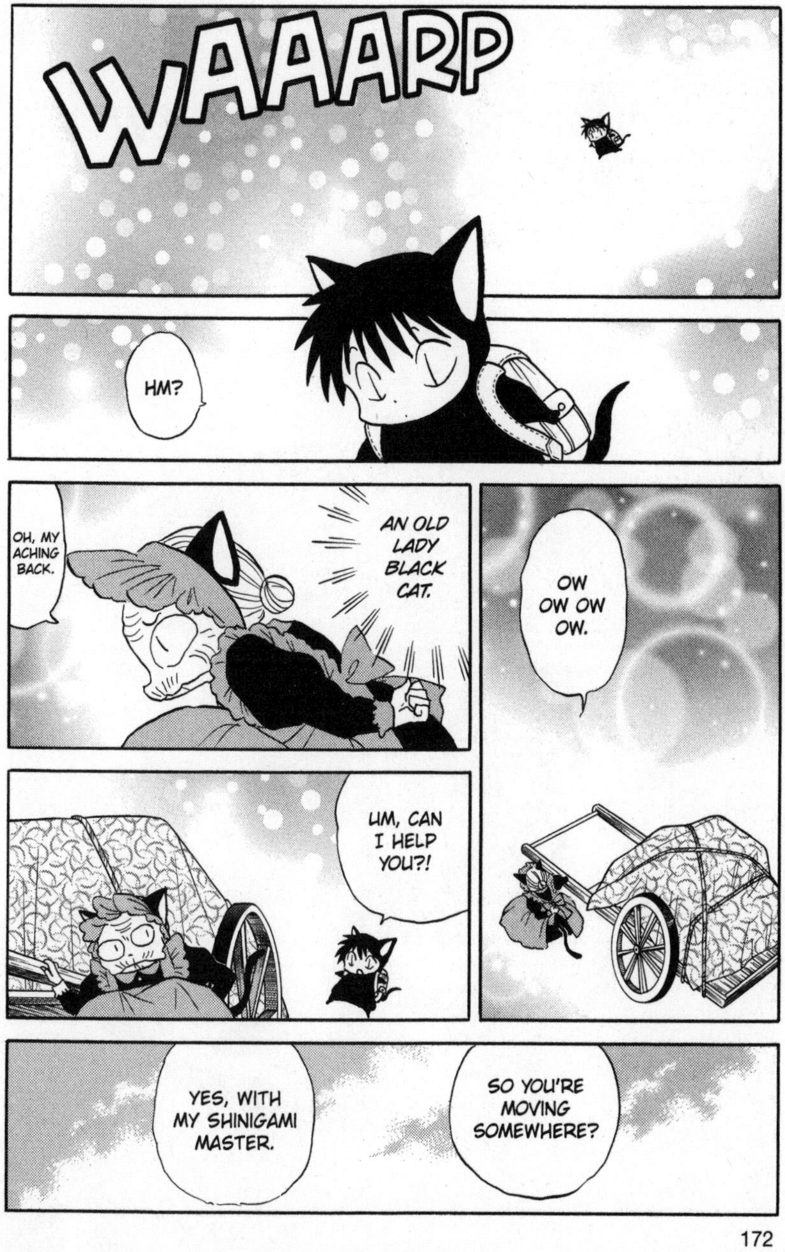
WAAARP
HM?
OW OW OW OW.
AN OLD LADY BLACK CAT.
OH, MY ACHING BACK.
UM, CAN I HELP YOU?!
SO YOU'RE MOVING SOMEWHERE?
YES, WITH MY SHINIGAMI MASTER.

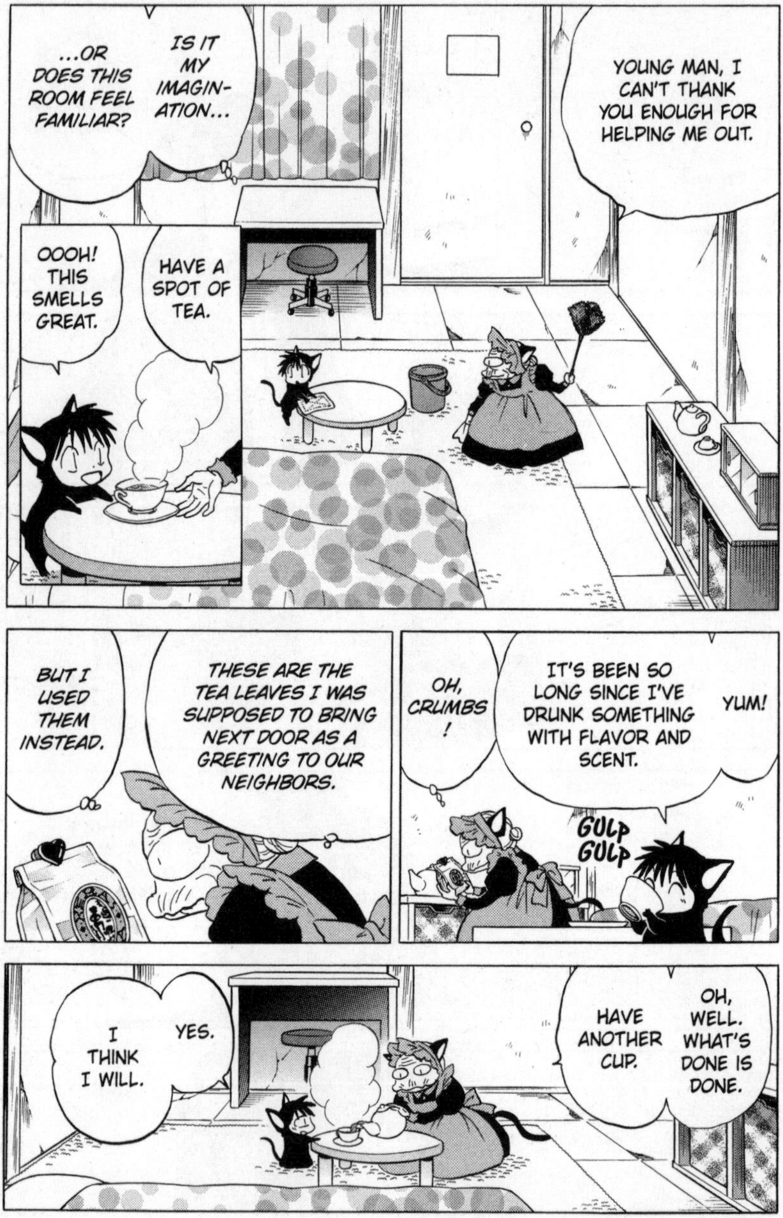
YOUNG MAN, I CAN'T THANK YOU ENOUGH FOR HELPING ME OUT.
IS IT MY IMAGINATION...
...OR DOES THIS ROOM FEEL FAMILIAR?
HAVE A SPOT OF TEA.
OOOH! THIS SMELLS GREAT.
YUM!
IT'S BEEN SO LONG SINCE I'VE DRUNK SOMETHING WITH FLAVOR AND SCENT.
GULP GULP
OH, CRUMBS!
THESE ARE THE TEA LEAVES I WAS SUPPOSED TO BRING NEXT DOOR AS A GREETING TO OUR NEIGHBORS.
BUT I USED THEM INSTEAD.
OH, WELL. WHAT'S DONE IS DONE.
HAVE ANOTHER CUP.
YES.
I THINK I WILL.

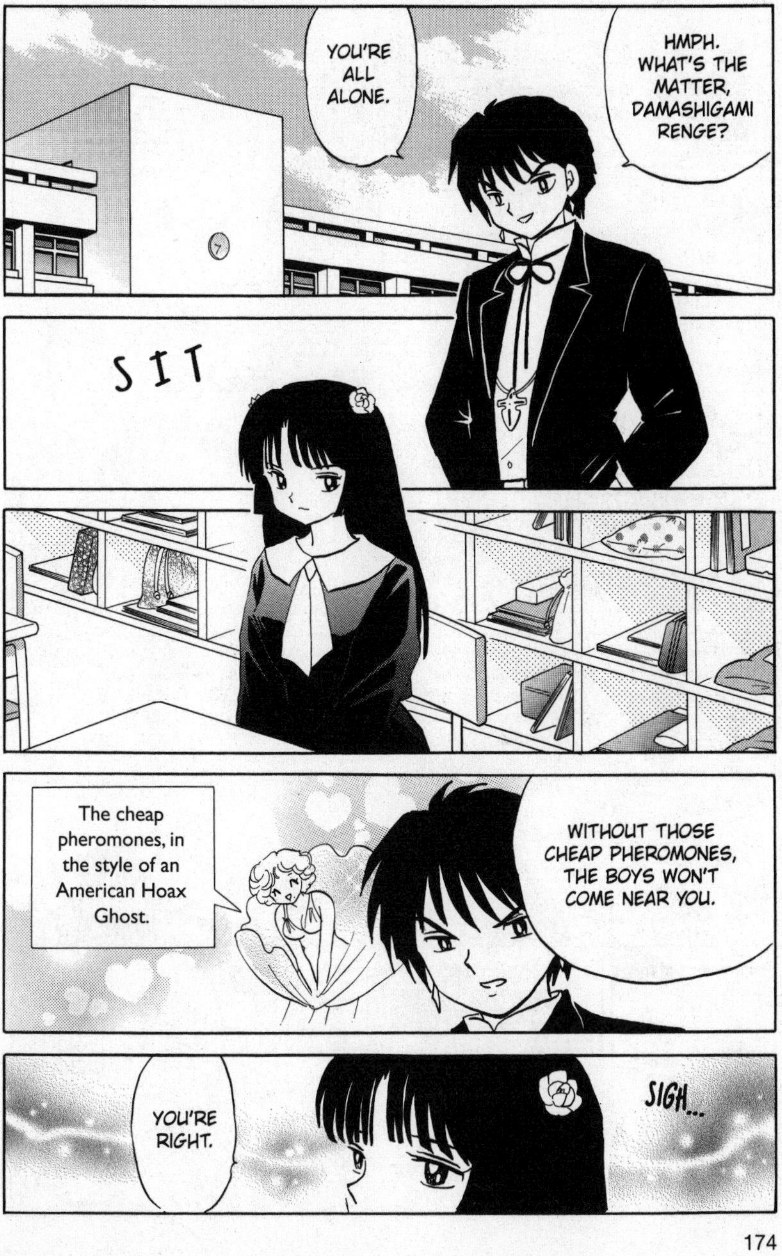
HMPH. WHAT'S THE MATTER, DAMASHIGAMI RENGE?
YOU'RE ALL ALONE.
SIT
WITHOUT THOSE CHEAP PHEROMONES, THE BOYS WON'T COME NEAR YOU.
The cheap pheromones, in the style of an American Hoax Ghost.
SIGH...
YOU'RE RIGHT.

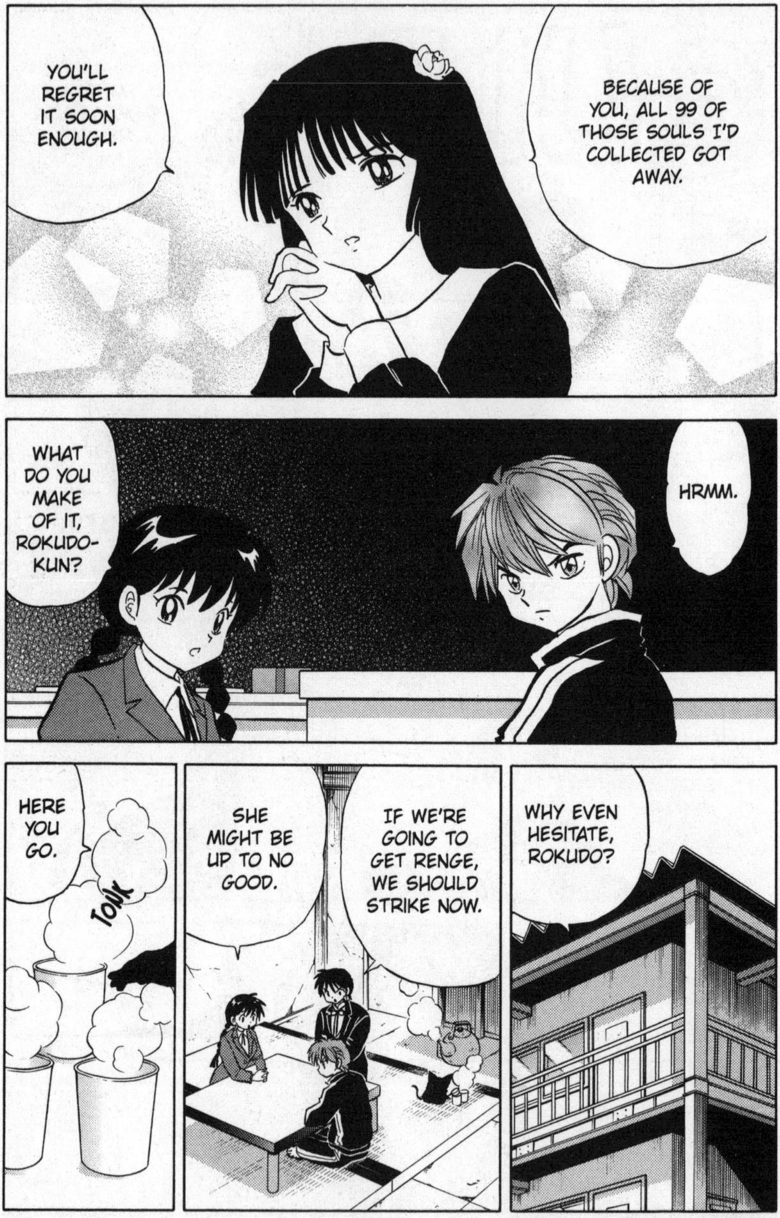
BECAUSE OF YOU, ALL 99 OF THOSE SOULS I'D COLLECTED GOT AWAY.
YOU'LL REGRET IT SOON ENOUGH.
HRMM.
WHAT DO YOU MAKE OF IT, ROKUDO-KUN?
WHY EVEN HESITATE, ROKUDO?
IF WE'RE GOING TO GET RENGE, WE SHOULD STRIKE NOW.
SHE MIGHT BE UP TO NO GOOD.
HERE YOU GO.
TOUK

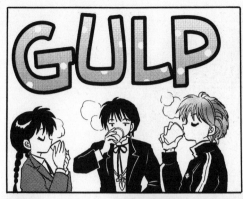

RIGHT.
THANKS, ROKUMON.
GULP
GASP!
TH-THIS IS...
ROKUMON, IS THIS ACTUAL TEA?!
HM?!
THAT'S A RARE SIGHT. I'VE ONLY EVER BEEN SERVED HOT OR COLD WATER IN YOUR HOME BEFORE.
HUH? I THINK I'VE SMELLED THIS SOMEWHERE BEFORE...
ROKUMON-CHAN, WHERE DID YOU GET THIS TEA?

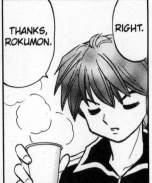

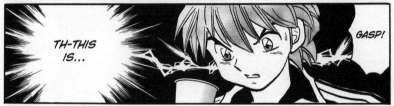

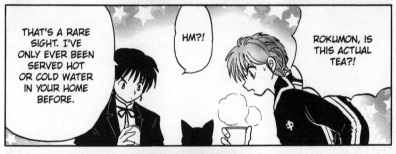

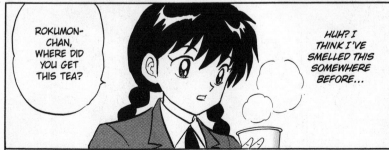

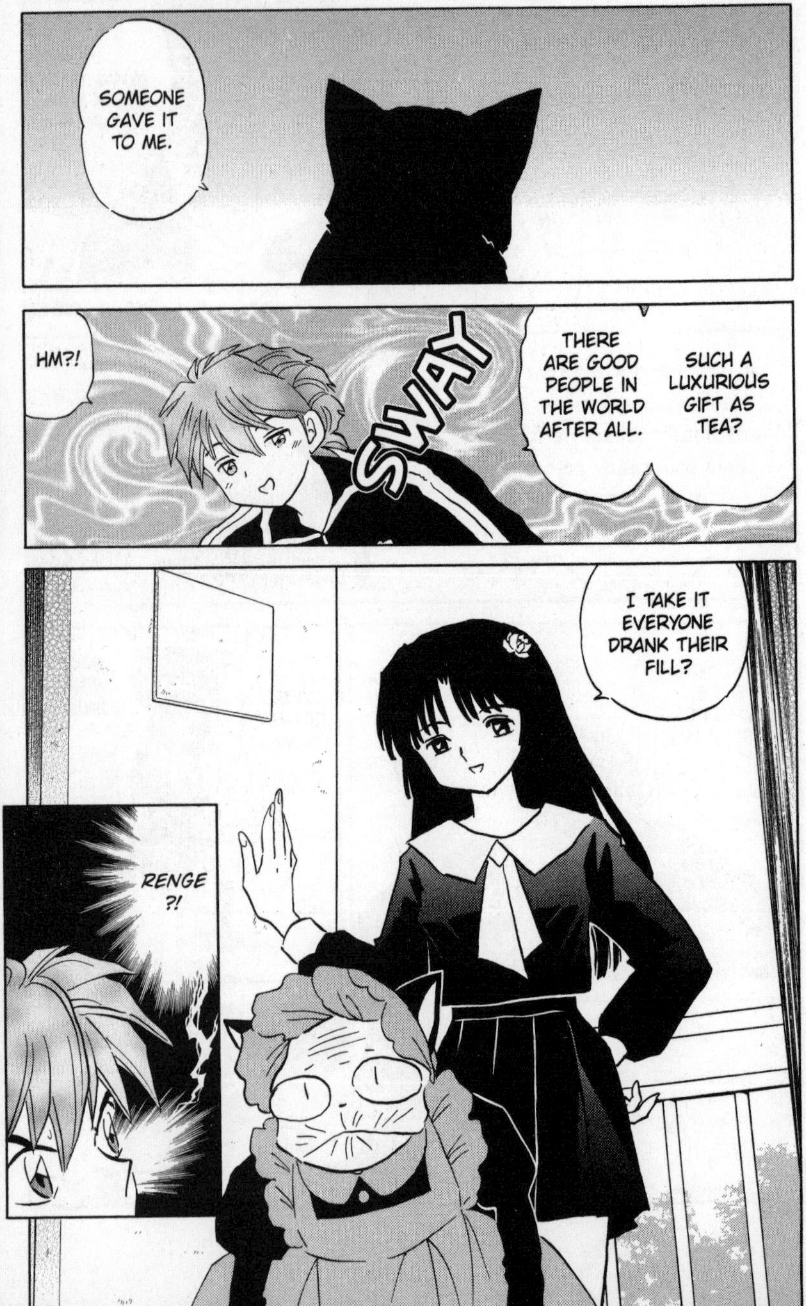
SOMEONE GAVE IT TO ME.
SUCH A LUXURIOUS GIFT AS TEA?
THERE ARE GOOD PEOPLE IN THE WORLD AFTER ALL.
SWAY
HM?!
I TAKE IT EVERYONE DRANK THEIR FILL?
RENGE ?!

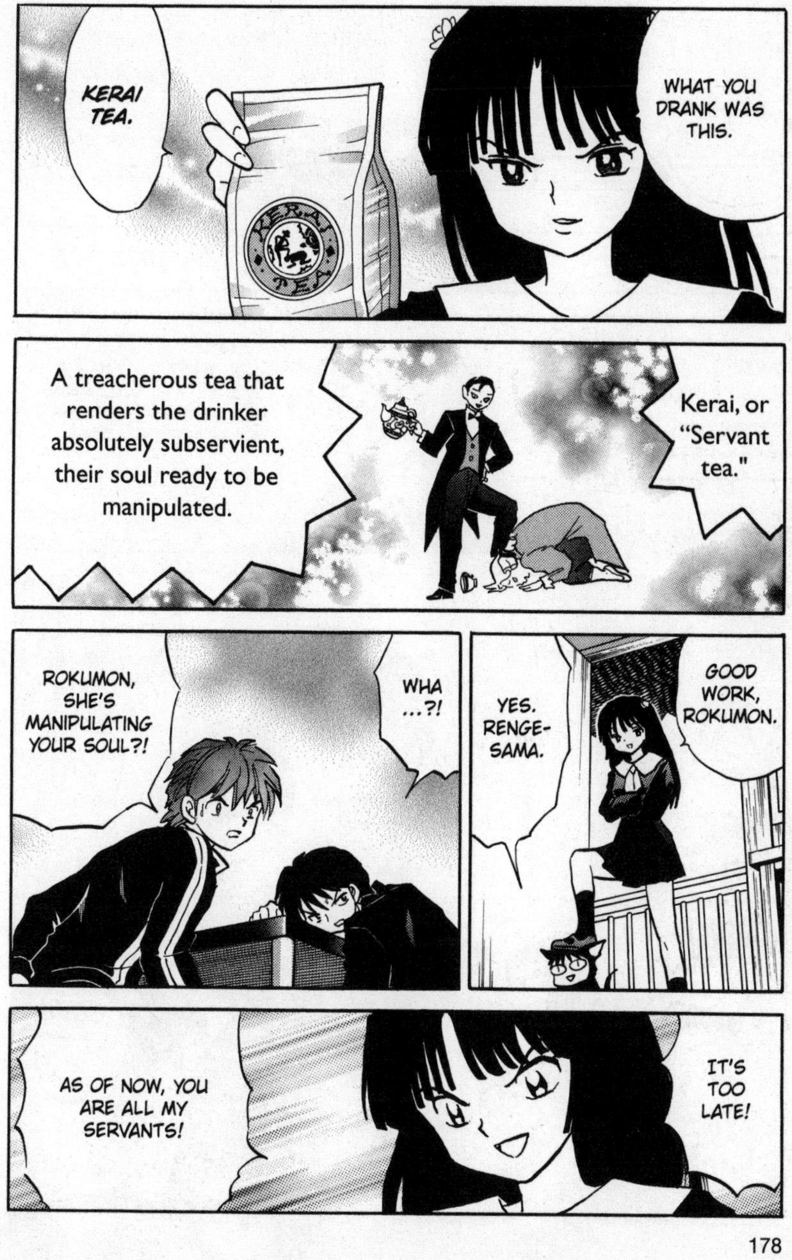
WHAT YOU DRANK WAS THIS.
KERAI TEA.
Kerai, or "Servant tea."
A treacherous tea that renders the drinker absolutely subservient, their soul ready to be manipulated.
GOOD WORK, ROKUMON.
YES. RENGE-SAMA.
WHA ...?!
ROKUMON, SHE'S MANIPULATING YOUR SOUL?!
IT'S TOO LATE!
AS OF NOW, YOU ARE ALL MY SERVANTS!

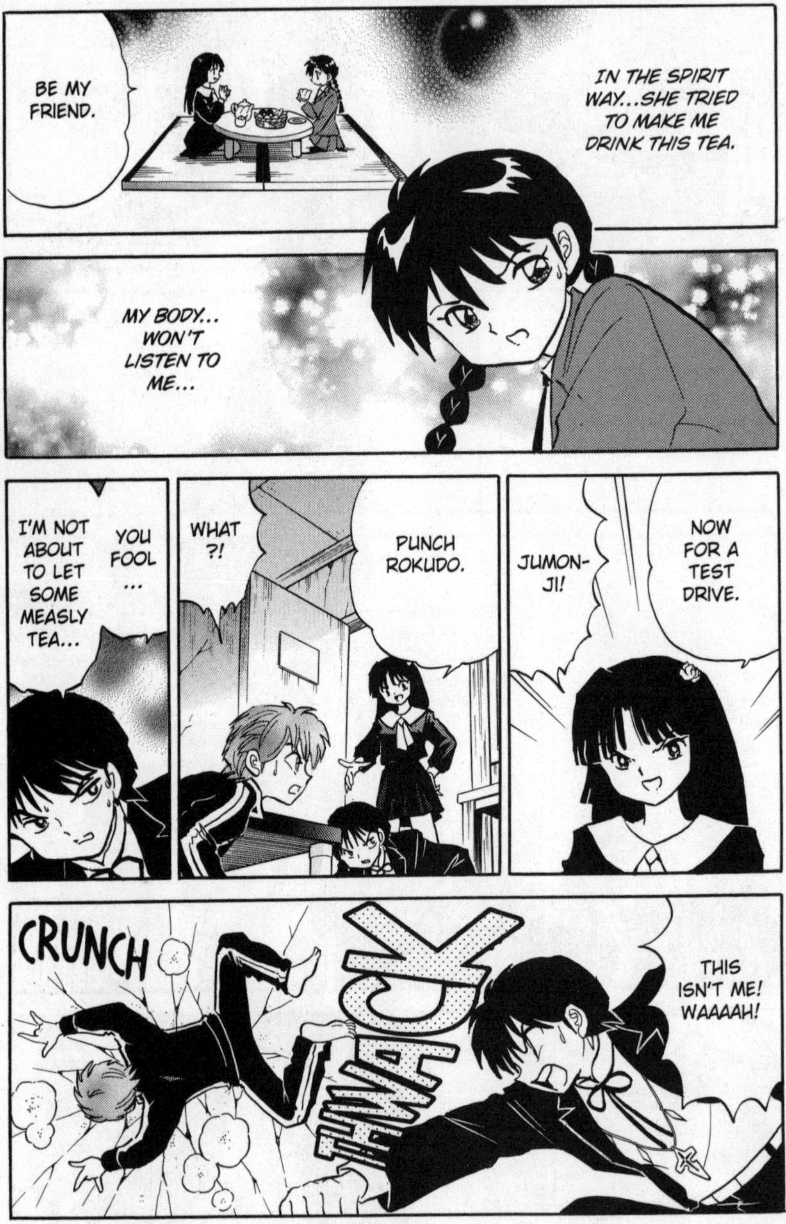

IN THE SPIRIT WAY...SHE TRIED TO MAKE ME DRINK THIS TEA.
BE MY FRIEND.
MY BODY... WON'T LISTEN TO ME...
NOW FOR A TEST DRIVE.
JUMON-JI!
PUNCH ROKUDO.
WHAT ?!
YOU FOOL ...
I'M NOT ABOUT TO LET SOME MEASLY TEA...
THIS ISN'T ME! WAAAAH!
THWACK
CRUNCH

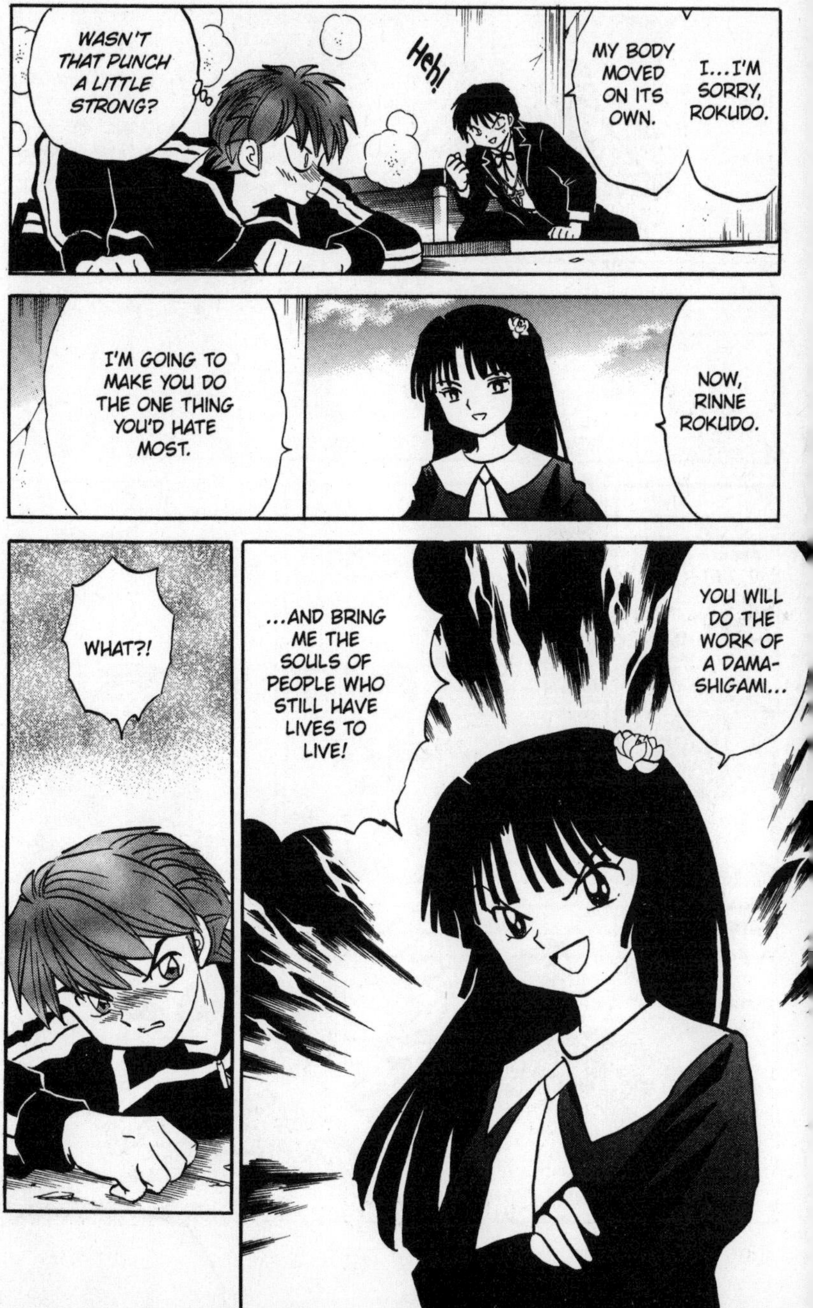
I...I'M SORRY, ROKUDO.
MY BODY MOVED ON ITS OWN.
Heh!
WASN'T THAT PUNCH A LITTLE STRONG?
NOW, RINNE ROKUDO.
I'M GOING TO MAKE YOU DO THE ONE THING YOU'D HATE MOST.
YOU WILL DO THE WORK OF A DAMA-SHIGAMI...
...AND BRING ME THE SOULS OF PEOPLE WHO STILL HAVE LIVES TO LIVE!
WHAT?!

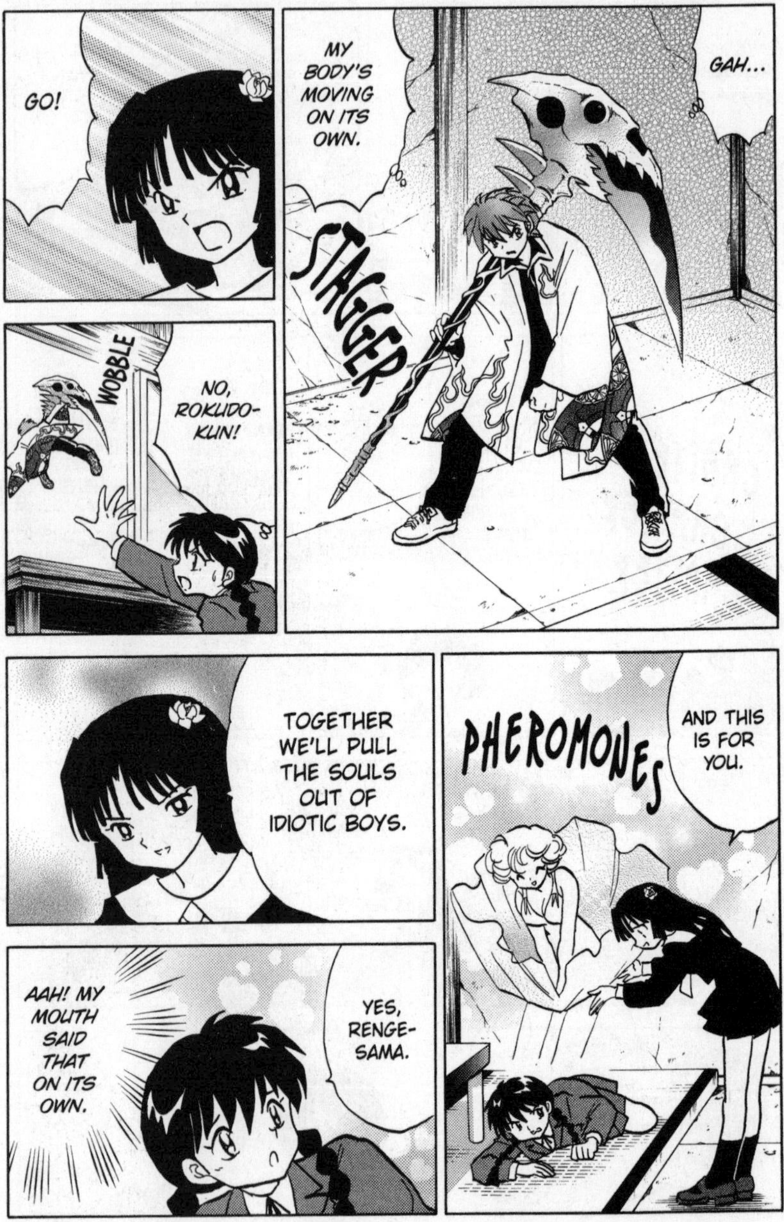
GAH...
MY BODY'S MOVING ON ITS OWN.
STAGGER
GO!
WOBBLE
NO, ROKUDO-KUN!
AND THIS IS FOR YOU.
PHEROMONES
TOGETHER WE'LL PULL THE SOULS OUT OF IDIOTIC BOYS.
YES, RENGE-SAMA.
AAH! MY MOUTH SAID THAT ON ITS OWN.

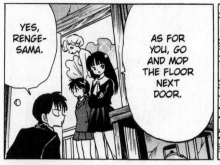

WAIT! I WON'T LET YOU...!
AS FOR YOU, GO AND MOP THE FLOOR NEXT DOOR.
YES, RENGE-SAMA.
SAKURA-CHAN'S NOT HERE.
HEY, RIKA-CHAN. DON'T YOU THINK IT'S STRANGE?
WHAT, MIHO-CHAN?
EVER SINCE THAT RENGE SHIMA GIRL TRANS-FERRED HERE...
HM?
CHATTER CHATTER CHATTER
PLACE YOUR PRESENTS HERE.
SAKURA MAMIYA'S SO CUTE.
HEY, WAIT YOUR TURN!
HUH?!
SAKURA-CHAN?
Neither of them can see the Pheromone Spirit.

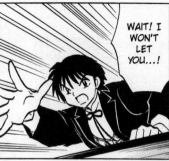

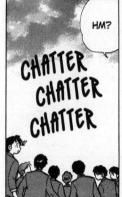

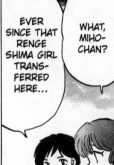

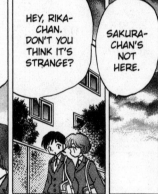

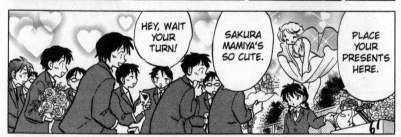

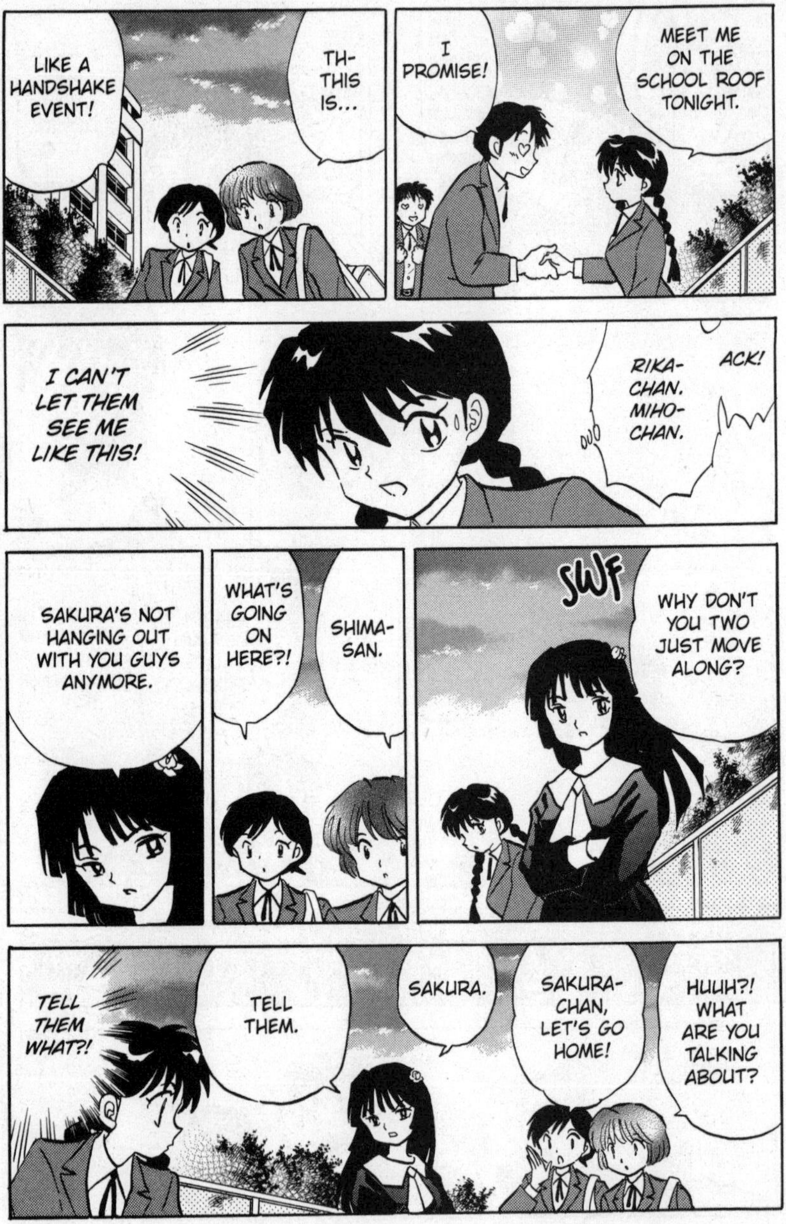
MEET ME ON THE SCHOOL ROOF TONIGHT.
I PROMISE!
TH- THIS IS...
LIKE A HANDSHAKE EVENT!
ACK!
RIKA-CHAN. MIHO-CHAN.
I CAN'T LET THEM SEE ME LIKE THIS!
SWF
WHY DON'T YOU TWO JUST MOVE ALONG?
SHIMA-SAN.
WHAT'S GOING ON HERE?!
SAKURA'S NOT HANGING OUT WITH YOU GUYS ANYMORE.
HUUH?! WHAT ARE YOU TALKING ABOUT?
SAKURA-CHAN, LET'S GO HOME!
SAKURA.
TELL THEM.
TELL THEM WHAT?!

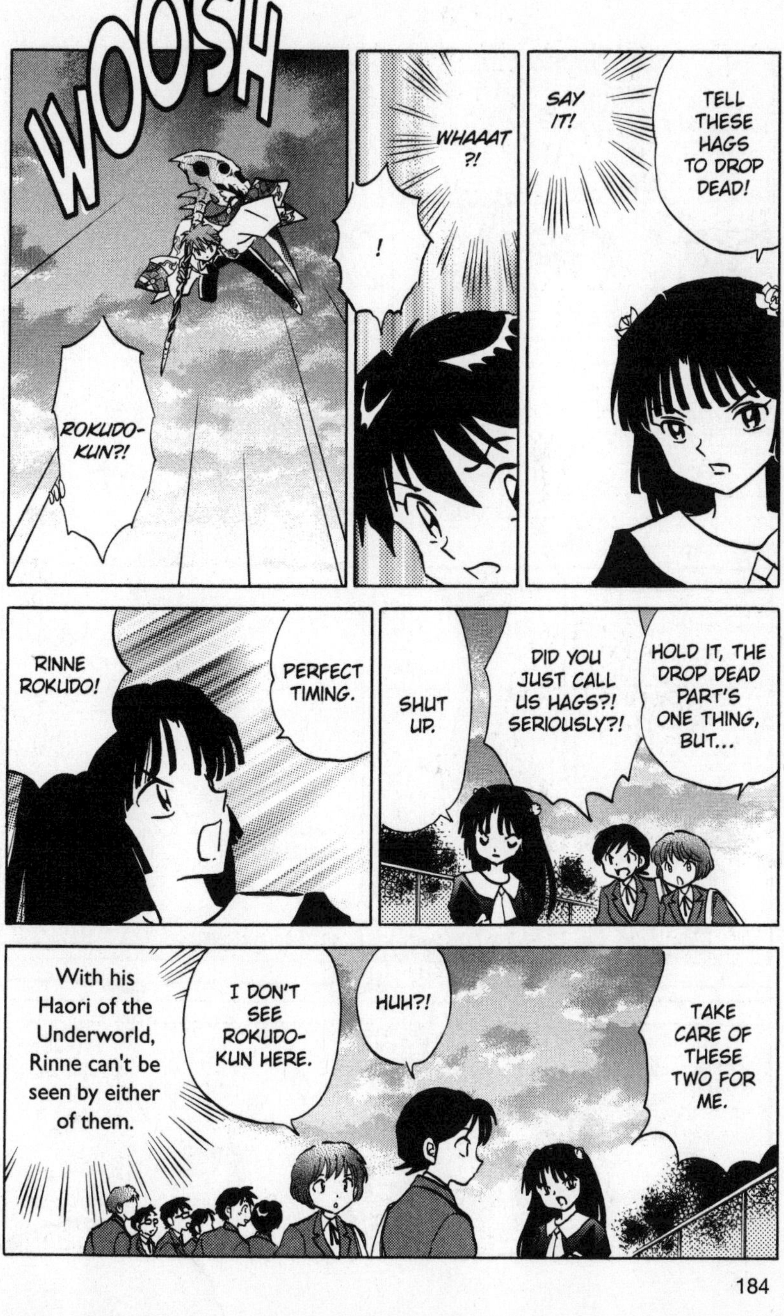
TELL THESE HAGS TO DROP DEAD!
SAY IT!
WHAAAT ?!
!
WOOSH
ROKUDO-KUN?!
HOLD IT, THE DROP DEAD PART'S ONE THING, BUT...
DID YOU JUST CALL US HAGS?! SERIOUSLY?!
SHUT UP.
PERFECT TIMING.
RINNE ROKUDO!
TAKE CARE OF THESE TWO FOR ME.
HUH?!
I DON'T SEE ROKUDO-KUN HERE.
With his Haori of the Underworld, Rinne can't be seen by either of them.

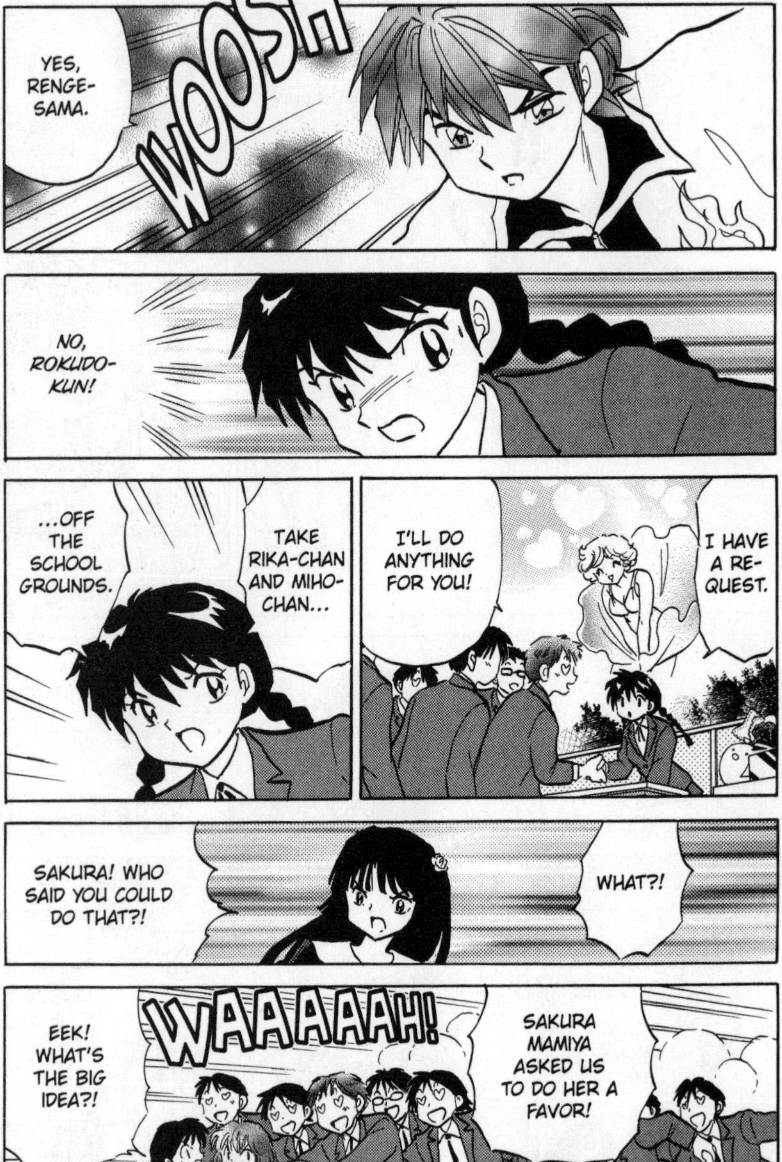
WOOSH
YES, RENGE-SAMA.
NO, ROKUDO-KUN!
I HAVE A REQUEST.
I'LL DO ANYTHING FOR YOU!
TAKE RIKA-CHAN AND MIHO-CHAN...
...OFF THE SCHOOL GROUNDS.
WHAT?!
SAKURA! WHO SAID YOU COULD DO THAT?!
SAKURA MAMIYA ASKED US TO DO HER A FAVOR!
WAAAAAH!
EEK! WHAT'S THE BIG IDEA?!

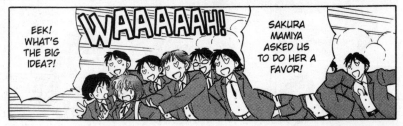

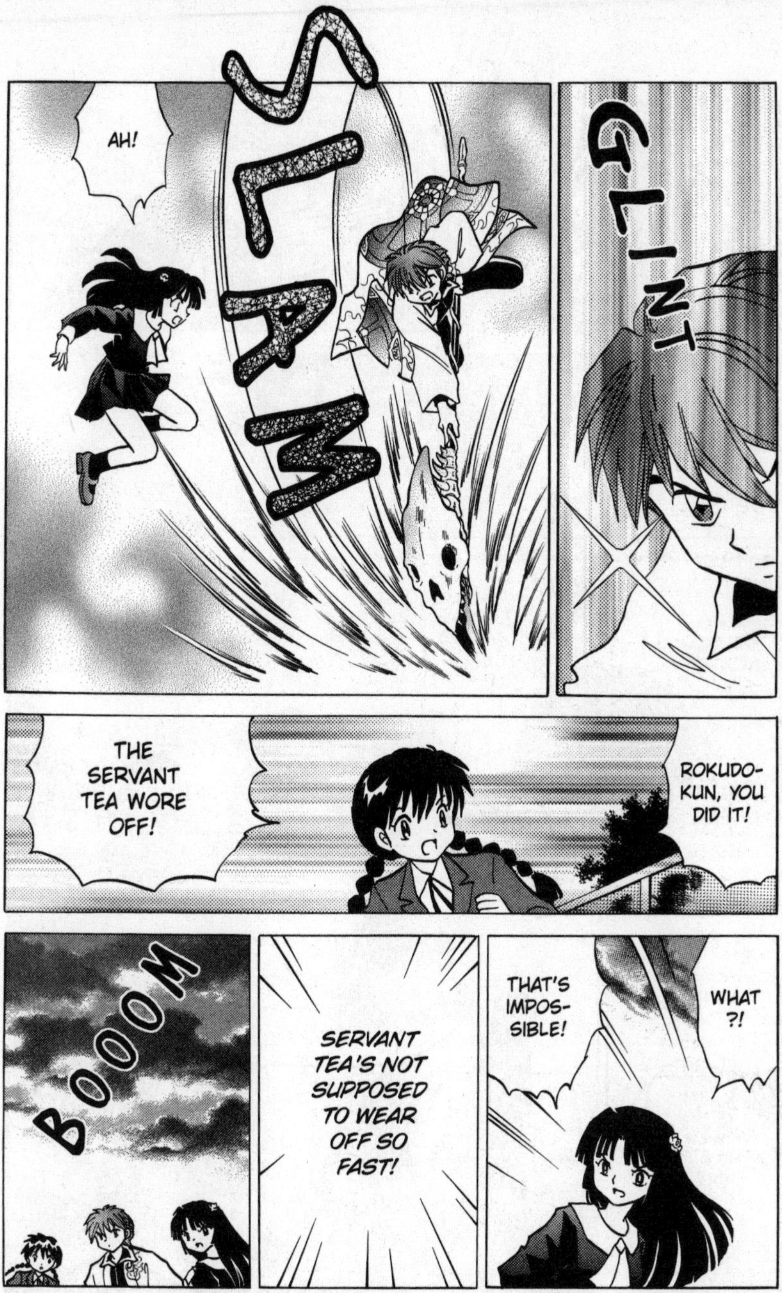
GLINT
SLAM
AH!
ROKUDO-KUN, YOU DID IT!
THE SERVANT TEA WORE OFF!
WHAT?!
THAT'S IMPOSSIBLE!
SERVANT TEA'S NOT SUPPOSED TO WEAR OFF SO FAST!
BOOOOM

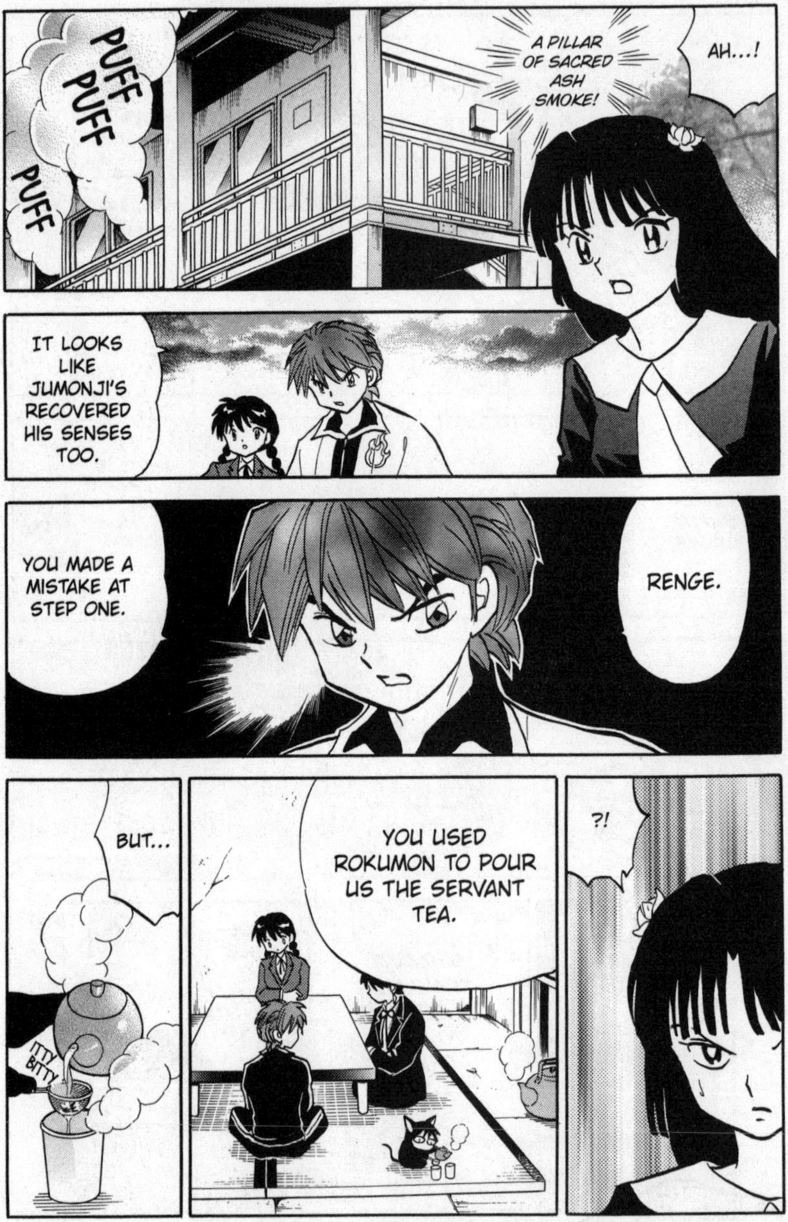
AH...!
A PILLAR OF SACRED ASH SMOKE!
PUFF PUFF
PUFF
IT LOOKS LIKE JUMONJI'S RECOVERED HIS SENSES TOO.
RENGE.
YOU MADE A MISTAKE AT STEP ONE.
?!
YOU USED ROKUMON TO POUR US THE SERVANT TEA.
BUT...
ITTY BITTY

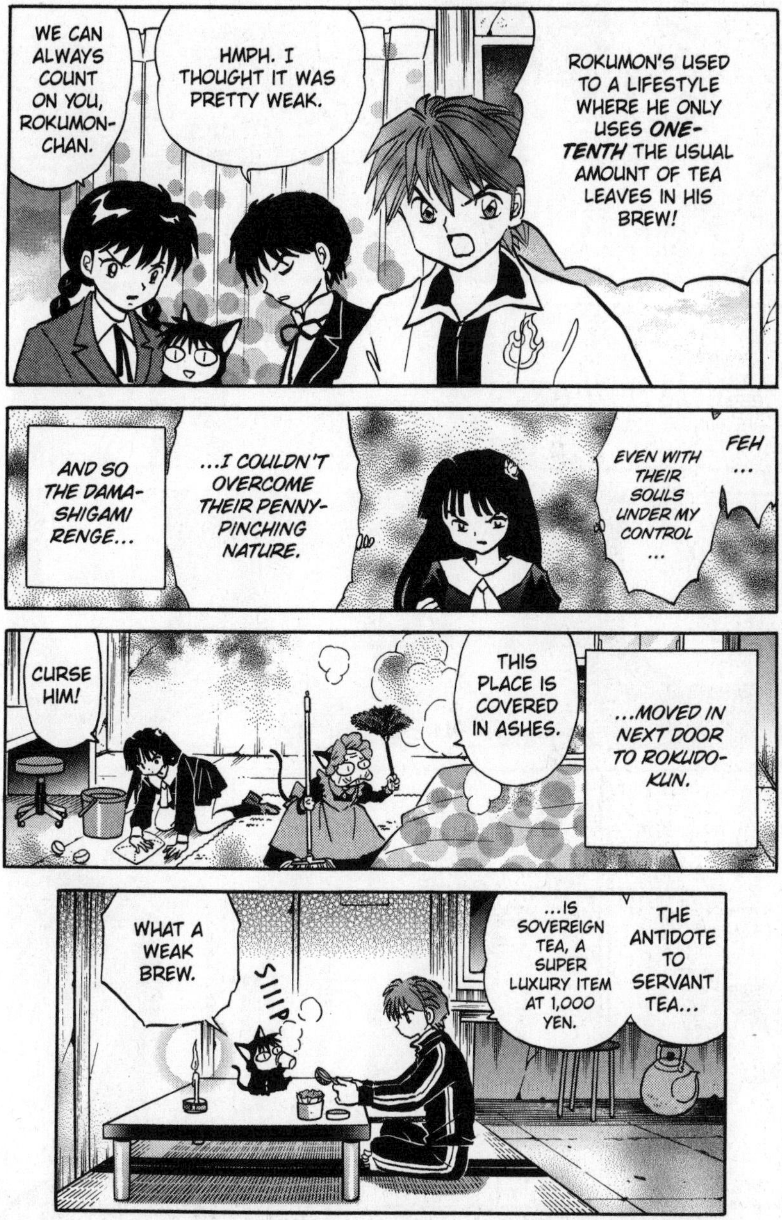
ROKUMON'S USED TO A LIFESTYLE WHERE HE ONLY USES ***ONE-TENTH*** THE USUAL AMOUNT OF TEA LEAVES IN HIS BREW!
HMPH. I THOUGHT IT WAS PRETTY WEAK.
WE CAN ALWAYS COUNT ON YOU, ROKUMON-CHAN.
FEH...
EVEN WITH THEIR SOULS UNDER MY CONTROL...
...I COULDN'T OVERCOME THEIR PENNY-PINCHING NATURE.
AND SO THE DAMA-SHIGAMI RENGE...
...MOVED IN NEXT DOOR TO ROKUDO-KUN.
THIS PLACE IS COVERED IN ASHES.
CURSE HIM!
THE ANTIDOTE TO SERVANT TEA...
...IS SOVEREIGN TEA, A SUPER LUXURY ITEM AT 1,000 YEN.
SIIIP
WHAT A WEAK BREW.

RIN-NE VOLUME 14 -END-

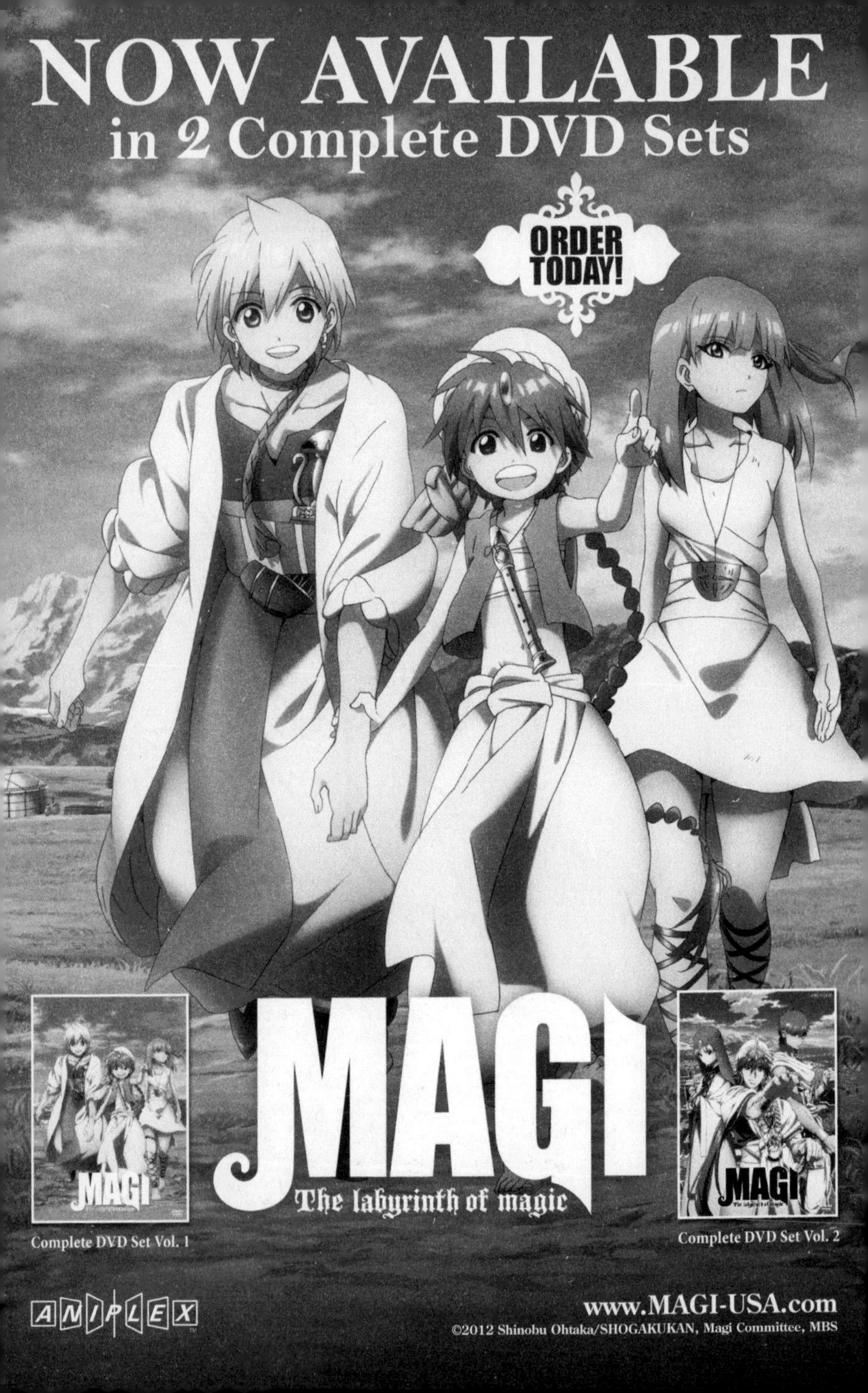
NOW AVAILABLE
in 2 Complete DVD Sets
ORDER TODAY!
MAGI
The labyrinth of magic
Complete DVD Set Vol. 1
Complete DVD Set Vol. 2
ANIPLEX
www.MAGI-USA.com
©2012 Shinobu Ohtaka/SHOGAKUKAN, Magi Committee, MBS

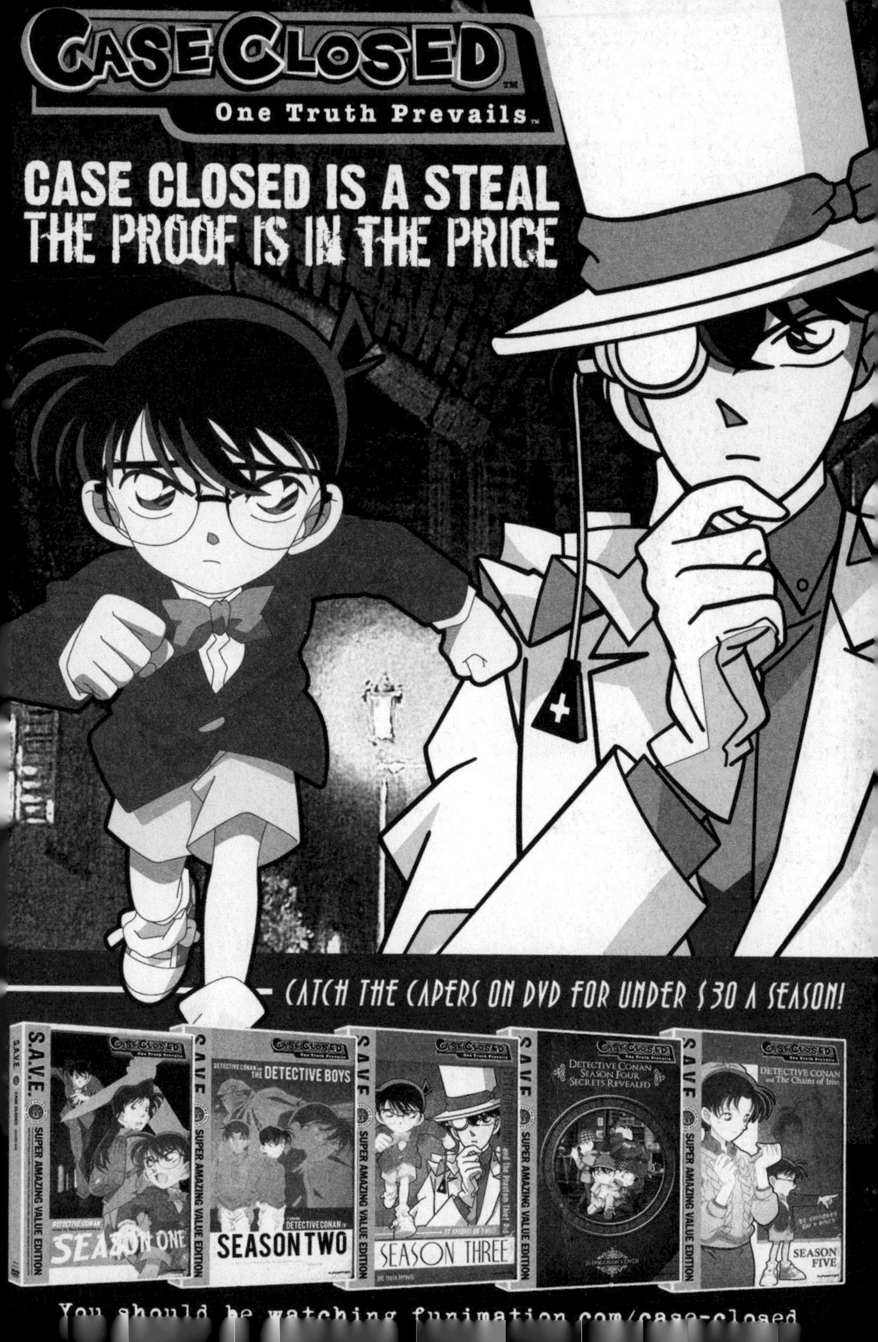
CASE CLOSED
One Truth Prevails
CASE CLOSED IS A STEAL
THE PROOF IS IN THE PRICE
CATCH THE CAPERS ON DVD FOR UNDER $30 A SEASON!
S.A.V.E.
SUPER AMAZING VALUE EDITION
SEASON ONE
DETECTIVE CONAN and THE DETECTIVE BOYS
SEASON TWO
SEASON THREE
DETECTIVE CONAN SEASON FOUR SECRETS REVEALED
DETECTIVE CONAN and The Chains of Iron
SEASON FIVE
You should be watching funimation.com/case-closed

DISCOVER ANIME
IN A WHOLE NEW WAY!

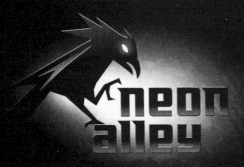

www.neonalley.com

What it is...

- Streaming anime delivered 24/7 straight to your TV via your connected video game console
- All English dubbed content
- Anime, martial arts movies, and more

Go to **neonalley.com** for news, updates and to see if Neon Alley is available in your area.

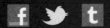

Hey! You'
the Wrong

This is the end of this graphic novel!

To properly enjoy this VIZ
graphic novel, please turn
it around and begin reading
from right to left. Unlike
English, Japanese is read
right to left, so Japanese
comics are read in reverse
order from the way English
comics are typically read.

This book has been printed
in the original Japanese
format in order to preserve
the orientation of the
original artwork. Have fun
with it!

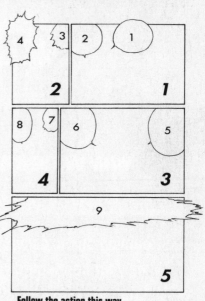

Follow the action this way

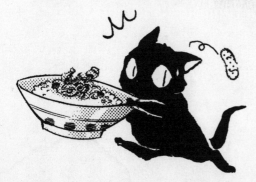